RESTful Web Services

Other resources from O'Reilly

Related titles

Ajax on Rails

Capistrano and the Rails
  Application Lifecycle

Learning Java™

Learning Python™

Rails Cookbook™

Ruby Cookbook™

Ruby on Rails: Up and
  Running

Web Services on Rails

oreilly.com

oreilly.com is more than a complete catalog of O'Reilly books. You'll also find links to news, events, articles, weblogs, sample chapters, and code examples.

oreillynet.com is the essential portal for developers interested in open and emerging technologies, including new platforms, programming languages, and operating systems.

Conferences

O'Reilly brings diverse innovators together to nurture the ideas that spark revolutionary industries. We specialize in documenting the latest tools and systems, translating the innovator's knowledge into useful skills for those in the trenches. Please visit *conferences.oreilly.com* for our upcoming events.

Safari Bookshelf (*safari.oreilly.com*) is the premier online reference library for programmers and IT professionals. Conduct searches across more than 1,000 books. Subscribers can zero in on answers to time-critical questions in a matter of seconds. Read the books on your Bookshelf from cover to cover or simply flip to the page you need. Try it today for free.

RESTful Web Services

Leonard Richardson and Sam Ruby

O'REILLY®

Beijing · Cambridge · Farnham · Köln · Paris · Sebastopol · Taipei · Tokyo

RESTful Web Services

by Leonard Richardson and Sam Ruby

Published by O'Reilly Media, Inc., 1005 Gravenstein Highway North, Sebastopol, CA 95472

O'Reilly books may be purchased for educational, business, or sales promotional use. Online editions are also available for most titles (*http://safari.oreilly.com*). For more information, contact our corporate/institutional sales department: (800) 998-9938 or *corporate@oreilly.com*.

Editor: Mike Loukides		**Indexer:** Joe Wizda	
Copy Editor: Peggy Wallace		**Cover Designer:** Karen Montgomery	
Production Editor: Laurel R.T. Ruma		**Interior Designer:** David Futato	
Proofreader: Laurel R.T. Ruma		**Illustrators:** Robert Romano and Jessamyn Read	

Printing History:

May 2007:   First Edition

RepKover.

This book uses RepKover™, a durable and flexible lay-flat binding.

ISBN-10: 0-596-52926-0
ISBN-13: 978-0-596-52926-0

[M]   [11/07]

For Woot, Moby, and Beet.
—Leonard

For Christopher, Catherine, and Carolyn.
—Sam

Table of Contents

Foreword xi

Preface xiii

1. The Programmable Web and Its Inhabitants 1
    Kinds of Things on the Programmable Web   4
    HTTP: Documents in Envelopes   5
    Method Information   8
    Scoping Information   11
    The Competing Architectures   13
    Technologies on the Programmable Web   18
    Leftover Terminology   20

2. Writing Web Service Clients 23
    Web Services Are Web Sites   23
    del.icio.us: The Sample Application   26
    Making the Request: HTTP Libraries   29
    Processing the Response: XML Parsers   38
    JSON Parsers: Handling Serialized Data   44
    Clients Made Easy with WADL   47

3. What Makes RESTful Services Different? 49
    Introducing the Simple Storage Service   49
    Object-Oriented Design of S3   50
    Resources   52
    HTTP Response Codes   54
    An S3 Client   55
    Request Signing and Access Control   64
    Using the S3 Client Library   70
    Clients Made Transparent with ActiveResource   71
    Parting Words   77

4. The Resource-Oriented Architecture 79

Resource-Oriented What Now?   79
What's a Resource?   81
URIs   81
Addressability   84
Statelessness   86
Representations   91
Links and Connectedness   94
The Uniform Interface   97
That's It!   105

5. Designing Read-Only Resource-Oriented Services 107

Resource Design   108
Turning Requirements Into Read-Only Resources   109
Figure Out the Data Set   110
Split the Data Set into Resources   112
Name the Resources   117
Design Your Representations   123
Link the Resources to Each Other   135
The HTTP Response   137
Conclusion   140

6. Designing Read/Write Resource-Oriented Services 143

User Accounts as Resources   144
Custom Places   157
A Look Back at the Map Service   165

7. A Service Implementation 167

A Social Bookmarking Web Service   167
Figuring Out the Data Set   168
Resource Design   171
Design the Representation(s) Accepted from the Client   183
Design the Representation(s) Served to the Client   184
Connect Resources to Each Other   185
What's Supposed to Happen?   186
What Might Go Wrong?   187
Controller Code   188
Model Code   205
What Does the Client Need to Know?   209

8. REST and ROA Best Practices 215

Resource-Oriented Basics   215

The Generic ROA Procedure 216
Addressability 216
State and Statelessness 217
Connectedness 218
The Uniform Interface 218
This Stuff Matters 221
Resource Design 227
URI Design 233
Outgoing Representations 234
Incoming Representations 234
Service Versioning 235
Permanent URIs Versus Readable URIs 236
Standard Features of HTTP 237
Faking PUT and DELETE 251
The Trouble with Cookies 252
Why Should a User Trust the HTTP Client? 253

9. **The Building Blocks of Services** **259**
Representation Formats 259
Prepackaged Control Flows 272
Hypermedia Technologies 284

10. **The Resource-Oriented Architecture Versus Big Web Services** **299**
What Problems Are Big Web Services Trying to Solve? 300
SOAP 300
WSDL 304
UDDI 309
Security 310
Reliable Messaging 311
Transactions 312
BPEL, ESB, and SOA 313
Conclusion 314

11. **Ajax Applications as REST Clients** **315**
From AJAX to Ajax 315
The Ajax Architecture 316
A del.icio.us Example 317
The Advantages of Ajax 320
The Disadvantages of Ajax 320
REST Goes Better 322
Making the Request 323
Handling the Response 324
JSON 325

Don't Bogart the Benefits of REST 326
Cross-Browser Issues and Ajax Libraries 327
Subverting the Browser Security Model 331

12. Frameworks for RESTful Services **339**
Ruby on Rails 339
Restlet 343
Django 354

A. Some Resources for REST and Some RESTful Resources **365**
Standards and Guides 365
Services You Can Use 367

B. The HTTP Response Code Top 42 .... **371**
Three to Seven Status Codes: The Bare Minimum 372
1xx: Meta 373
2xx: Success 374
3xx: Redirection 377
4xx: Client-Side Error 380
5xx: Server-Side Error 387

C. The HTTP Header Top Infinity **389**
Standard Headers 390
Nonstandard Headers 404

Index **409**

Foreword

The world of web services has been on a fast track to supernova ever since the architect astronauts spotted another meme to rocket out of pragmatism and into the universe of enterprises. But, thankfully, all is not lost. A renaissance of HTTP appreciation is building and, under the banner of REST, shows a credible alternative to what the merchants of complexity are trying to ram down everyone's throats; a simple set of principles that every day developers can use to connect applications in a style native to the Web.

RESTful Web Services shows you how to use those principles without the drama, the big words, and the miles of indirection that have scared a generation of web developers into thinking that web services are so hard that you have to rely on BigCo implementations to get anything done. Every developer working with the Web needs to read this book.

—David Heinemeier Hansson

Preface

A complex system that works is invariably found to have evolved from a simple system that worked.

—John Gall
Systemantics

We wrote this book to tell you about an amazing new technology. It's here, it's hot, and it promises to radically change the way we write distributed systems. We're talking about the World Wide Web.

Okay, it's not a new technology. It's not as hot as it used to be, and from a technical standpoint it's not incredibly amazing. But everything else is true. In 10 years the Web has changed the way we live, but it's got more change left to give. The Web is a simple, ubiquitous, yet overlooked platform for distributed programming. The goal of this book is to pull out that change and send it off into the world.

It may seem strange to claim that the Web's potential for distributed programming has been overlooked. After all, this book competes for shelf space with any number of other books about web services. The problem is, most of today's "web services" have nothing to do with the Web. In opposition to the Web's simplicity, they espouse a heavyweight architecture for distributed object access, similar to COM or CORBA. Today's "web service" architectures reinvent or ignore every feature that makes the Web successful.

It doesn't have to be that way. We know the technologies behind the Web can drive useful remote services, because those services exist and we use them every day. We know such services can scale to enormous size, because they already do. Consider the Google search engine. What is it but a remote service for querying a massive database and getting back a formatted response? We don't normally think of web sites as "services," because that's programming talk and a web site's ultimate client is a human, but services are what they are.

Every web application—every web site—is a service. You can harness this power for programmable applications if you work with the Web instead of against it, if you don't bury its unique power under layers of abstraction. It's time to put the "web" back into "web services."

The features that make a web site easy for a web surfer to use also make a web service API easy for a programmer to use. To find the principles underlying the design of these services, we can just translate the principles for human-readable web sites into terms that make sense when the surfers are computer programs.

That's what we do in this book. Our goal throughout is to show the power (and, where appropriate, the limitations) of the basic web technologies: the HTTP application protocol, the URI naming standard, and the XML markup language. Our topic is the set of principles underlying the Web: Representational State Transfer, or REST. For the first time, we set down best practices for "RESTful" web services. We cut through the confusion and guesswork, replacing folklore and implicit knowledge with concrete advice.

We introduce the Resource-Oriented Architecture (ROA), a commonsense set of rules for designing RESTful web services. We also show you the view from the client side: how you can write programs to consume RESTful services. Our examples include real-world RESTful services like Amazon's Simple Storage Service (S3), the various incarnations of the Atom Publishing Protocol, and Google Maps. We also take popular services that fall short of RESTfulness, like the del.icio.us social bookmarking API, and rehabilitate them.

The Web Is Simple

Why are we so obsessed with the Web that we think it can do everything? Perhaps we are delusional, the victims of hype. The web is certainly the most-hyped part of the Internet, despite the fact that HTTP is not the most popular Internet protocol. Depending on who's measuring, the bulk of the world's Internet traffic comes from email (thanks to spam) or BitTorrent (thanks to copyright infringement). If the Internet were to disappear tomorrow, email is the application people would miss the most. So why the Web? What makes HTTP, a protocol designed to schlep project notes around a physics lab, also suited for distributed Internet applications?

Actually, to say that HTTP was designed for *anything* is to pay it a pretty big compliment. HTTP and HTML have been called "the Whoopee Cushion and Joy Buzzer of Internet protocols, only comprehensible as elaborate practical jokes"—and that's by someone who *likes* them.[*] The first version of HTTP sure looked like a joke. Here's a sample interaction between client and server:

Client request	Server response
GET /hello.txt	Hello, world!

---

[*] Clay Shirky, "In Praise of Evolvable Systems" (*http://www.shirky.com/writings/evolve.html*)

That's it. You connected to the server, gave it the path to a document, and then the server sent you the contents of that document. You could do little else with HTTP 0.9. It looked like a featureless rip-off of more sophisticated file transfer protocols like FTP.

This is, surprisingly, a big part of the answer. With tongue only slightly in cheek we can say that HTTP is uniquely well suited to distributed Internet applications because it has no features to speak of. You tell it what you want, and it gives it to you. In a twist straight out of a kung-fu movie,† HTTP's weakness is its strength, its simplicity its power.

In that first version of HTTP, cleverly disguised as a lack of features, we can see *addressability* and *statelessness*: the two basic design decisions that made HTTP an improvement on its rivals, and that keep it scalable up to today's mega-sites. Many of the features lacking in HTTP 0.9 have since turned out to be unnecessary or counterproductive. Adding them back actually cripples the Web. Most of the rest were implemented in the 1.0 and 1.1 revisions of the protocol. The other two technologies essential to the success of the Web, URIs and HTML (and, later, XML), are also simple in important senses.

Obviously, these "simple" technologies are powerful enough to give us the Web and the applications we use on it. In this book we go further, and claim that the World Wide Web is a simple and flexible environment for distributed *programming*. We also claim to know the reason for this: that there is no essential difference between the human web designed for our own use, and the "programmable web" designed for consumption by software programs. We say: if the Web is good enough for humans, it's good enough for robots. We just need to make some allowances. Computer programs are good at building and parsing complex data structures, but they're not as flexible as humans when it comes to interpreting documents.

Big Web Services Are Not Simple

There are a number of protocols and standards, mostly built on top of HTTP, designed for building Web Services (note the capitalization). These standards are collectively called the WS-* stack. They include WS-Notification, WS-Security, WSDL, and SOAP. Throughout this book we give the name "Big Web Services" to this collection of technologies as a fairly gentle term of disparagement.

This book does not cover these standards in any great detail. We believe you can implement web services without implementing Big Web Services: that the Web should be all the service you need. We believe the Web's basic technologies are good enough to be considered the default platform for distributed services.

Some of the WS-* standards (such as SOAP) can be used in ways compatible with REST and our Resource-Oriented Architecture. In practice, though, they're used to

---

† *Legend of The Drunken Protocol* (1991)

implement Remote Procedure Call applications over HTTP. Sometimes an RPC style is appropriate, and sometimes other needs take precedence over the virtues of the Web. This is fine.

What we don't like is needless complexity. Too often a programmer or a company brings in Big Web Services for a job that plain old HTTP could handle just fine. The effect is that HTTP is reduced to a transport protocol for an enormous XML payload that explains what's "really" going on. The resulting service is far too complex, impossible to debug, and won't work unless your clients have the exact same setup as you do.

Big Web Services do have one advantage: modern tools can create a web service from your code with a single click, especially if you're developing in Java or C#. If you're using these tools to generate RPC-style web services with the WS-* stack, it probably doesn't matter to you that a RESTful web service would be much simpler. The tools hide all the complexity, so who cares? Bandwidth and CPU are cheap.

This attitude works when you're working in a homogeneous group, providing services behind a firewall for other groups like yours. If your group has enough political clout, you may be able to get people to play your way outside the firewall. But if you want your service to grow to Internet scale, you'll have to handle clients you never planned for, using custom-built software stacks to do things to your service you never imagined were possible. Your users will want to integrate your service with other services you've never heard of. Sound difficult? This already happens on the Web every day.

Abstractions are never perfect. Every new layer creates failure points, interoperability hassles, and scalability problems. New tools can hide complexity, but they can't justify it—and they always add it. Getting a service to work with the Web as a whole means paying attention to adaptability, scalability, and maintainability. Simplicity—that despised virtue of HTTP 0.9—is a prerequisite for all three. The more complex the system, the more difficult it is to fix when something goes wrong.

If you provide RESTful web services, you can spend your complexity on additional features, or on making multiple services interact. Success in providing services also means being part of the Web instead of just "on" the Web: making your information available under the same rules that govern well-designed web sites. The closer you are to the basic web protocols, the easier this is.

The Story of the REST

REST is simple, but it's well defined and not an excuse for implementing web services as half-assed web sites because "they're the same." Unfortunately, until now the main REST reference was chapter five of Roy Fielding's 2000 Ph.D. dissertation, which is a good read for a Ph.D. dissertation, but leaves most of the real-world questions unanswered. [‡] That's because it presents REST not as an architecture but as a way of judging architectures. The term "RESTful" is like the term "object-oriented." A language, a framework, or an application may be designed in an object-oriented way, but that doesn't make its architecture *the* object-oriented architecture.

Even in object-oriented languages like C++ and Ruby, it's possible to write programs that are not truly object-oriented. HTTP in the abstract does very well on the criteria of REST. (It ought to, since Fielding co-wrote the HTTP standard and wrote his dissertation to describe the architecture of the Web.) But real web sites, web applications, and web services often betray the principles of REST. How can you be sure you're correctly applying the principles to the problem of designing a specific web service?

Most other sources of information on REST are informal: mailing lists, wikis, and weblogs (I list some of the best in Appendix A). Up to now, REST's best practices have been a matter of folklore. What's needed is a concrete architecture based on the REST meta-architecture: a set of simple guidelines for implementing typical services that fulfill the potential of the Web. We present one such architecture in this book as the Resource-Oriented Architecture (see Chapter 4). It's certainly not the only possible high-level RESTful architecture, but we think it's a good one for designing web services that are easy for clients to use.

We wrote the ROA to bring the best practices of web service design out of the realm of folklore. What we've written is a suggested baseline. If you've tried to figure out REST in the past, we hope our architecture gives you confidence that what you're doing is "really" REST. We also hope the ROA will help the community as a whole make faster progress in coming up with and codifying best practices. We want to make it easy for programmers to create distributed web applications that are elegant, that do the job they're designed for, and that participate in the Web instead of merely living on top of it.

We know, however, that it's not enough to have all these technical facts at your disposal. We've both worked in organizations where major architectural decisions didn't go our way. You can't succeed with a RESTful architecture if you never get a chance to use it. In addition to the technical know-how, we must give you the vocabulary to argue for RESTful solutions. We've positioned the ROA as a simple alternative to the RPC-style architecture used by today's SOAP+WSDL services. The RPC architecture exposes internal *algorithms* through a complex programming-language-like interface that's different for every service. The ROA exposes internal *data* through a simple document-processing interface that's always the same. In Chapter 10, we compare the two architectures and show how to argue for the ROA.

---

‡ Fielding, Roy Thomas. *Architectural Styles and the Design of Network-Based Software Architectures*, Doctoral dissertation, University of California, Irvine, 2000 (*http://www.ics.uci.edu/~fielding/pubs/dissertation/top.htm*)

Reuniting the Webs

Programmers have been using web sites as web services for years—unofficially, of course.§ It's difficult for a computer to understand web pages designed for human consumption, but that's never stopped hackers from fetching pages with automated clients and screen-scraping the interesting bits. Over time, this drive was sublimated into programmer-friendly technologies for exposing a web site's functionality in officially sanctioned ways—RSS, XML-RPC, and SOAP. These technologies formed a programmable web, one that extended the human web for the convenience of software programs.

Our ultimate goal in this book is to reunite the programmable web with the human web. We envision a single interconnected network: a World Wide Web that runs on one set of servers, uses one set of protocols, and obeys one set of design principles. A network that you can use whether you're serving data to human beings or computer programs.

The Internet and the Web did not have to exist. They come to us courtesy of misallocated defense money, skunkworks engineering projects, worse-is-better engineering practices, big science, naive liberal idealism, cranky libertarian politics, technofetishism, and the sweat and capital of programmers and investors who thought they'd found an easy way to strike it rich.

The result is, amazingly, a simple, open (for now), almost universal platform for networked applications. This platform contains much of human knowledge and supports most fields of human endeavor. We think it's time to seriously start applying its rules to distributed programming, to open up that information and those processes to automatic clients. If you agree, this book will show you to do it.

What's in This Book?

In this book we focus on practical issues: how to design and implement RESTful web services, and clients for those services. Our secondary focus is on theory: what it means to be RESTful, and why web services should be more RESTful instead of less. We don't cover everything, but we try to hit today's big topics, and because this is the first book of its kind, we return to the core issue—how to design a RESTful service—over and over again.

The first three chapters introduce web services from the client's perspective and show what's special about RESTful services.

---

§ For an early example, see Jon Udell's 1996 *Byte* article "On-Line Componentware" (*http://www.byte.com/art/9611/sec9/art1.htm*). Note: "A powerful capability for ad hoc distributed computing arises naturally from the architecture of the Web." That's from 1996, folks.

Chapter 1, The Programmable Web and Its Inhabitants

In this chapter we introduce web services in general: programs that go over the Web and ask a foreign server to provide data or run an algorithm. We demonstrate the three common web service architectures: RESTful, RPC-style, and REST-RPC hybrid. It shows sample HTTP requests and responses for each architecture, along with typical client code.

Chapter 2, Writing Web Service Clients

In this chapter we show you how to write clients for existing web services, using an HTTP library and an XML parser. We introduce a popular REST-RPC service (the web service for the social bookmarking site del.icio.us) and demonstrate clients written in Ruby, Python, Java, C#, and PHP. We also give technology recommendations for several other languages, without actually showing code. JavaScript and Ajax are covered separately in Chapter 11.

Chapter 3, What Makes RESTful Services Different?

We take the lessons of Chapter 2 and apply them to a purely RESTful service: Amazon's Simple Storage Service (S3). While building an S3 client we illustrate some important principles of REST: resources, representations, and the uniform interface.

The next six chapters form the core of the book. They focus on designing and implementing your own RESTful services.

Chapter 4, The Resource-Oriented Architecture

A formal introduction to REST, not in its abstract form but in the context of a specific architecture for web services. Our architecture is based on four important REST concepts: resources, their names, their representations, and the links between them. Its services should be judged by four RESTful properties: addressability, statelessness, connectedness, and the uniform interface.

Chapter 5, Designing Read-Only Resource-Oriented Services

We present a procedure for turning an idea or a set of requirements into a set of RESTful resources. These resources are read-only: clients can get data from your service but they can't send any data of their own. We illustrate the procedure by designing a web service for serving navigable maps, inspired by the Google Maps web application.

Chapter 6, Designing Read/Write Resource-Oriented Services

We extend the procedure from the previous chapter so that clients can create, modify, and delete resources. We demonstrate by adding two new kinds of resource to the map service: user accounts and user-defined places.

Chapter 7, A Service Implementation

We remodel an RPC-style service (the del.icio.us REST-RPC hybrid we wrote clients for back in Chapter 2) as a purely RESTful service. Then we implement that service as a Ruby on Rails application. Fun for the whole family!

Chapter 8, REST and ROA Best Practices

In this chapter we collect our earlier suggestions for service design into one place, and add new suggestions. We show how standard features of HTTP can help you with common problems and optimizations. We also give resource-oriented designs for tough features like transactions, which you may have thought were impossible to do in RESTful web services.

Chapter 9, The Building Blocks of Services

Here we describe extra technologies that work on top of REST's big three of HTTP, URI, and XML. Some of these technologies are file formats for conveying state, like XHTML and its microformats. Some are hypermedia formats for showing clients the levers of state, like WADL. Some are sets of rules for building RESTful web services, like the Atom Publishing Protocol.

The last three chapters cover specialized topics, each of which could make for a book in its own right:

Chapter 10, The Resource-Oriented Architecture Versus Big Web Services

We compare our architecture, and REST in general, to another leading brand. We think that RESTful web services are simpler, more scalable, easier to use, better attuned to the philosophy of the Web, and better able to handle a wide variety of clients than are services based on SOAP, WSDL, and the WS-* stack.

Chapter 11, Ajax Applications as REST Clients

Here we explain the Ajax architecture for web applications in terms of web services: an Ajax application is just a web service client that runs inside your web browser. That makes this chapter an extension of Chapter 2. We show how to write clients for RESTful web services using XMLHttpRequest and the standard JavaScript library.

Chapter 12, Frameworks for RESTful Services

In the final chapter we cover three popular frameworks that make it easy to implement RESTful web services: Ruby on Rails, Restlet (for Java), and Django (for Python).

We also have three appendixes we hope you find useful:

Appendix A, Some Resources for REST and Some RESTful Resources

The first part lists interesting standards, tutorials, and communities related to RESTful web services. The second part lists some existing, public RESTful web services that you can use and learn from.

Appendix B, The HTTP Response Code Top 42

Describes every standard HTTP response code (plus one extension), and explains when you'd use each one in a RESTful web service.

Appendix C, The HTTP Header Top Infinity

Does the same thing for HTTP headers. It covers every standard HTTP header, and a few extension headers that are useful for web services.

Which Parts Should You Read?

We organized this book for the reader who's interested in web services in general: someone who learns by doing, but who doesn't have much experience with web services. If that describes you, the simplest path through this book is the best. You can start at the beginning, read through Chapter 9, and then read onward as you're interested.

If you have more experience, you might take a different path through the book. If you're only concerned with writing clients for existing services, you'll probably focus on Chapters 1, 2, 3, and 11—the sections on service design won't do you much good. If you want to create your own web service, or you're trying to figure out what REST really means, you might start reading from Chapter 3. If you want to compare REST to the WS-* technologies, you might start by reading Chapters 1, 3, 4, and 10.

Administrative Notes

This book has two authors (Leonard and Sam), but for the rest of the book we'll be merging our identities into a single authorial "I." In the final chapter (Chapter 12), the authorial "I" gets a little bit more crowded, as Django and Restlet developers join in to show how their frameworks let you build RESTful services.

We assume that you're a competent programmer, but not that you have any experience with web programming in particular. What we say in this book is not tied to any programming language, and we include sample code for RESTful clients and services in a variety of languages. But whenever we're not demonstrating a specific framework or language, we use Ruby (*http://www.ruby-lang.org/*) as our implementation language.

We chose Ruby because it's concise and easy to read, even for programmers who don't know the language. (And because it's nice and confusing in conjunction with Sam's last name.) Ruby's standard web framework, Ruby on Rails, is also one of the leading implementation platforms for RESTful web services. If you don't know Ruby, don't worry: we include lots of comments explaining Ruby-specific idioms.

The sample programs in this book are available for download from this book's official web site (*http://www.oreilly.com/catalog/9780596529260*). This includes the entire Rails application from Chapter 7, and the corresponding Restlet and Django applications from Chapter 12. It also includes Java implementations of many of the clients that only show up in the book as Ruby implementations. These client programs use the Restlet library, and were written by Restlet developers Jerome Louvel and Dave Pawson. If you're more familiar with Java than with Ruby, these implementations may help you grasp the concepts behind the code. Most notably, there's a full Java implementation of the Amazon S3 client from Chapter 3 in there.

Conventions Used in This Book

The following typographical conventions are used in this book:

Italic

> Indicates new terms, URLs, email addresses, filenames, and file extensions.

`Constant width`

> Used for program listings, as well as within paragraphs to refer to program elements such as variable or function names, databases, data types, environment variables, statements, and keywords.

`Constant width bold`

> Shows commands or other text that should be typed literally by the user.

`Constant width italic`

> Shows text that should be replaced with user-supplied values or by values determined by context.

 This icon signifies a tip, suggestion, or general note.

 This icon indicates a warning or caution.

Using Code Examples

This book is here to help you get your job done. In general, you may use the code in this book in your programs and documentation. You do not need to contact us for permission unless you're reproducing a significant portion of the code. For example, writing a program that uses several chunks of code from this book does not require permission. Selling or distributing a CD-ROM of examples from O'Reilly books does require permission. Answering a question by citing this book and quoting example code does not require permission. Incorporating a significant amount of example code from this book into your product's documentation does require permission.

We appreciate, but do not require, attribution. An attribution usually includes the title, author, publisher, and ISBN. For example: "*RESTful Web Services* by Leonard Richardson and Sam Ruby. Copyright 2007 O'Reilly Media, Inc., 978-0-596-52926-0."

If you feel your use of code examples falls outside fair use or the permission given above, feel free to contact us at *permissions@oreilly.com*.

Safari® Enabled

 When you see a Safari® Enabled icon on the cover of your favorite technology book, that means the book is available online through the O'Reilly Network Safari Bookshelf.

Safari offers a solution that's better than e-books. It's a virtual library that lets you easily search thousands of top tech books, cut and paste code samples, download chapters, and find quick answers when you need the most accurate, current information. Try it for free at *http://safari.oreilly.com*.

How to Contact Us

Please address comments and questions concerning this book to the publisher:

> O'Reilly Media, Inc.
> 1005 Gravenstein Highway North
> Sebastopol, CA 95472
> 800-998-9938 (in the United States or Canada)
> 707-829-0515 (international or local)
> 707 829-0104 (fax)

We have a web page for this book, where we list errata, examples, and any additional information. You can access this page at:

> *http://www.oreilly.com/catalog/9780596529260*

To comment or ask technical questions about this book, send email to:

> *bookquestions@oreilly.com*

For more information about our books, conferences, Resource Centers, and the O'Reilly Network, see our web site at:

> *http://www.oreilly.com*

Acknowledgments

We're ultimately indebted to the people whose work made us see that we could program directly with HTTP. For Sam, it was Rael Dornfest with his Blosxom blogging application. Leonard's experience stems from building screen-scraping applications in the mid-90s. His thanks go to those whose web design made their sites usable as web services: notably, the pseudonymous author of the online comic "Pokey the Penguin."

Once we had this insight, Roy Fielding was there to flesh it out. His thesis named and defined something that was for us only a feeling. Roy's theoretical foundation is what we've tried to build on.

In writing this book we had an enormous amount of help from the REST community. We're grateful for the feedback we got from Benjamin Carlyle, David Gourley, Joe Gregorio, Marc Hadley, Chuck Hinson, Pete Lacey, Larry Liberto, Benjamin Pollack, Aron Roberts, Richard Walker, and Yohei Yamamoto. Others helped us unknowingly, through their writings: Mark Baker, Tim Berners-Lee, Alex Bunardzic, Duncan Cragg, David Heinemeier Hansson, Ian Hickson, Mark Nottingham, Koranteng Ofosu-Amaah, Uche Ogbuji, Mark Pilgrim, Paul Prescod, Clay Shirky, Brian Totty, and Jon Udell. Of course, all opinions in this book, and any errors and omissions, are our own.

Our editor Michael Loukides was helpful and knowledgeable throughout the process of developing this book. We'd also like to thank Laurel Ruma and everyone else at O'Reilly for their production work.

Finally, Jerome Louvel, Dave Pawson, and Jacob Kaplan-Moss deserve special thanks. Their knowledge of Restlet and Django made Chapter 12 possible.

## CHAPTER 1

The Programmable Web and Its Inhabitants

When you write a computer program, you're not limited to the algorithms you can think up. Your language's standard library gives you some algorithms. You can get more from books, or in third-party libraries you find online. Only if you're on the very cutting edge should you have to come up with your own algorithms.

If you're lucky, the same is true for data. Some applications are driven entirely by the data the users type in. Sometimes data just comes to you naturally: if you're analyzing spam, you should have no problem getting all you need. You can download a few public data sets—word lists, geographical data, lists of prime numbers, public domain texts —as though they were third-party libraries. But if you need some other kind of data, it doesn't look good. Where's the data going to come from? More and more often, it's coming from the programmable web.

When you—a human being—want to find a book on a certain topic, you probably point your web browser to the URI of an online library or bookstore: say, *http:// www.amazon.com/*.

 The common term for the address of something on the Web is "URL." I say "URI" throughout this book because that's what the HTTP standard says. Every URI on the Web is also a URL, so you can substitute "URL" wherever I say "URI" with no loss of meaning.

You're served a web page, a document in HTML format that your browser renders graphically. You visually scan the page for a search form, type your topic (say, "web services") into a text box, and submit the form. At this point your web browser makes a second HTTP request, to a URI that incorporates your topic. To continue the Amazon example, the second URI your browser requests would be something like *http:// amazon.com/s?url=search-alias%3Dstripbooks&field-keywords=web+services*.

The web server at amazon.com responds by serving a second document in HTML format. This document contains a description of your search results, links to additional search options, and miscellaneous commercial enticements (see Example 1-1). Again, your browser renders the document in graphical form, and you look at it and decide what to do from there.

Example 1-1. Part of the HTML response from amazon.com

```
...
<a href="http://www.amazon.com/Restful-Web-Services-Leonard-Richardson/dp/...>
 <span class="srTitle">RESTful Web Services</span>
</a>

by Leonard Richardson and Sam Ruby

<span class="bindingBlock">
 (<span class="binding">Paperback</span> - May 1, 2007)
</span>
```

The Web you use is full of data: book information, opinions, prices, arrival times, messages, photographs, and miscellaneous junk. It's full of *services*: search engines, online stores, weblogs, wikis, calculators, and games. Rather than installing all this data and all these programs on your own computer, you install one program—a web browser—and access the data and services through it.

The programmable web is just the same. The main difference is that instead of arranging its data in attractive HTML pages with banner ads and cute pastel logos, the programmable web usually serves stark, brutal XML documents. The programmable web is not neccessarily for human consumption. Its data is intended as input to a software program that does something amazing.

Example 1-2 shows a Ruby script that uses the programmable web to do a traditional human web task: find the titles of books matching a keyword. It hides the web access under a programming language interface, using the Ruby/Amazon library (*http://www.caliban.org/ruby/ruby-amazon.shtml*).

Example 1-2. Searching for books with a Ruby script

```
#!/usr/bin/ruby -w
# amazon-book-search.rb
require 'amazon/search'

if ARGV.size != 2
  puts "Usage: #{$0} [Amazon Web Services AccessKey ID] [text to search for]"
  exit
end
access_key, search_request = ARGV
req = Amazon::Search::Request.new(access_key)
# For every book in the search results...
req.keyword_search(search_request, 'books', Amazon::Search::LIGHT) do |book|
  # Print the book's name and the list of authors.
```

```
    puts %{"#{book.product_name}" by #{book.authors.join(', ')}}}
  end
```

To run this program, you'll need to sign up for an Amazon Web Services account (*http://aws.amazon.com/*) and customize the Ruby code with your Access Key ID. Here's a sample run of the program:

```
$ ruby amazon-search.rb C1D4NQS41IMK2 "restful web services"
"RESTful Web Services" by Leonard Richardson, Sam Ruby
"Hacking with Ruby: Ruby and Rails for the Real World" by Mark Watson
```

At its best, the programmable web works the same way as the human web. When *amazon-book-search.rb* calls the method `Amazon::Search::Request#keyword_search`, the Ruby program starts acting like a web browser. It makes an HTTP request to a URI: in this case, something like *http://xml.amazon.com/onca/xml3?KeywordSearch=restful +web+services&mode=books&f=xml&type=lite&page=1*. The web server at `xml.amazon.com` responds with an XML document. This document, shown in Example 1-3, describes the search results, just like the HTML document you see in your web browser, but in a more structured form.

Example 1-3. Part of the XML response from xml.amazon.com

```
...
<ProductName>RESTful Web Services</ProductName>
<Catalog>Book</Catalog>
<Authors>
 <Author>Leonard Richardson</Author>
 <Author>Sam Ruby</Author>
</Authors>
<ReleaseDate>01 May, 2007</ReleaseDate>
...
```

Once a web browser has submitted its HTTP request, it has a fairly easy task. It needs to render the response in a way a human being can understand. It doesn't need to figure out what the HTTP response means: that's the human's job. A web service client doesn't have this luxury. It's programmed in advance, so it has to be both the web browser that fetches the data, and the "human" who decides what the data means. Web service clients must automatically extract meaning from HTTP responses and make decisions based on that meaning.

In Example 1-2, the web service client parses the XML document, extracts some interesting information (book titles and authors), and prints that information to standard output. The program *amazon-book-search.rb* is effectively a small, special-purpose web browser, relaying data to a human reader. It could easily do something else with the Amazon book data, something that didn't rely on human intervention at all: stick the book titles into a database, maybe, or use the author information to drive a recommendation engine.

And the data doesn't have to always flow toward the client. Just as you can bend parts of the human web to your will (by posting on your weblog or buying a book), you can write clients that modify the programmable web. You can use it as a storage space or as another source of algorithms you don't have to write yourself. It depends on what service you need, and whether you can find someone else to provide it.

Example 1-4 is an example of a web service client that modifies the programmable web: the s3sh command shell for Ruby (*http://amazon.rubyforge.org/*). It's one of many clients written against another of Amazon's web services: S3, or the Simple Storage Service (*http://aws.amazon.com/s3*). In Chapter 3 I cover S3's workings in detail, so if you're interested in using s3sh for yourself, you can read up on S3 there.

To understand this s3sh transcript, all you need to know is that Amazon S3 lets its clients store labelled pieces of data ("objects") in labelled containers ("buckets"). The s3sh program builds an interactive programming interface on top of S3. Other clients use S3 as a backup tool or a web host. It's a very flexible service.

Example 1-4. Manipulating the programmable web with s3sh and S3

```
$ s3sh
>> Service.buckets.collect { |b| b.name }
=> ["example.com"]

>> my_bucket = Bucket.find("example.com")

>> contents = open("disk_file.txt").read
=> "This text is the contents of the file disk_file.txt"

>> S3Object.store("mydir/mydocument.txt", contents, my_bucket.name)

>> my_bucket['directory/document.txt'].value
=> "This text is the contents of the file disk_file.txt"
```

In this chapter I survey the current state of the programmable web. What technologies are being used, what architectures are they used to implement, and what design styles are the most popular? I show some real code and some real HTTP conversations, but my main goal in this chapter is to get you thinking about the World Wide Web as a way of connecting computer programs to each other, on the same terms as it connects human beings to each other.

Kinds of Things on the Programmable Web

The programmable web is based on HTTP and XML. Some parts of it serve HTML, JavaScript Object Notation (JSON), plain text, or binary documents, but most parts use XML. And it's all based on HTTP: if you don't use HTTP, you're not on the web.* Beyond that small island of agreement there is little but controversy. The terminology isn't set, and different people use common terms (like "REST," the topic of this book) in ways that combine into a vague and confusing mess. What's missing is a coherent way of classifying the programmable web. With that in place, the meanings of individual terms will become clear.

Imagine the programmable web as an ecosystem, like the ocean, containing many kinds of strange creatures. Ancient scientists and sailors classified sea creatures by their superficial appearance: whales were lumped in with the fish. Modern scientists classify animals according to their position in the evolutionary tree of all life: whales are now grouped with the other mammals. There are two analogous ways of classifying the services that inhabit the programmable web: by the technologies they use (URIs, SOAP, XML-RPC, and so on), or by the underlying architectures and design philosophies.

Usually the two systems for classifying sea creatures get along. You don't need to do DNA tests to know that a tuna is more like a grouper than a sea anemone. But if you really want to understand why whales can't breathe underwater, you need to stop classifying them as fish (by superficial appearance) and start classifying them as mammals (by underlying architecture).[†]

When it comes to classifying the programmable web, most of today's terminology sorts services by their superficial appearances: the technologies they use. These classifications work in most cases, but they're conceptually lacking and they lead to whale-fish mistakes. I'm going to present a taxonomy based on architecture, which shows how technology choices follow from underlying design principles. I'm exposing divisions I'll come back to throughout the book, but my main purpose is to zoom in on the parts of the programmable web that can reasonably be associated with the term "REST."

HTTP: Documents in Envelopes

If I was classifying marine animals I'd start by talking about the things they have in common: DNA, cellular structure, the laws of embryonic development. Then I'd show how animals distinguish themselves from each other by specializing away from the common ground. To classify the programmable web, I'd like to start off with an overview of HTTP, the protocol that all web services have in common.

HTTP is a document-based protocol, in which the client puts a document in an envelope and sends it to the server. The server returns the favor by putting a response document in an envelope and sending it to the client. HTTP has strict standards for what the envelopes should look like, but it doesn't much care what goes inside. Example 1-5 shows a sample envelope: the HTTP request my web browser sends when I

---

[*] Thanks to Big Web Services' WS-Addressing standard, it's now possible to create a web service that's not on the Web: one that uses email or TCP as its transport protocol instead of HTTP. I don't think absolutely everything has to be on the Web, but it does seem like you should have to call this bizarre spectacle something other than a web service. This point isn't really important, since in practice nearly everyone uses HTTP. Thus the footnote. The only exceptions I know of are eBay's web services, which can send you SOAP documents over email as well as HTTP.

[†] Melville, in *Moby-Dick*, spends much of Chapter 22 ("Cetology") arguing that the whale is a fish. This sounds silly but he's not denying that whales have lungs and give milk; he's arguing for a definition of "fish" based on appearance, as opposed to Linnaeus's definition "from the law of nature" (*ex lege naturae*).

visit the homepage of `oreilly.com`. I've truncated two lines to make the text fit on the printed page.

Example 1-5. An HTTP GET request for http://www.oreilly.com/index.html

```
GET /index.html HTTP/1.1
Host: www.oreilly.com
User-Agent: Mozilla/5.0 (X11; U; Linux i686; en-US; rv:1.7.12)...
Accept: text/xml,application/xml,application/xhtml+xml,text/html;q=0.9,...
Accept-Language: us,en;q=0.5
Accept-Encoding: gzip,deflate
Accept-Charset: ISO-8859-15,utf-8;q=0.7,*;q=0.7
Keep-Alive: 300
Connection: keep-alive
```

In case you're not familiar with HTTP, now is a good time to point out the major parts of the HTTP request. I use these terms throughout the book.

The HTTP method

In this request, the method is "GET." In other discussions of REST you may see this called the "HTTP verb" or "HTTP action."

The name of the HTTP method is like a method name in a programming language: it indicates how the client expects the server to process this envelope. In this case, the client (my web browser) is trying to GET some information from the server (`www.oreilly.com`).

The path

This is the portion of the URI to the right of the hostname: here, *http://www.oreilly.com/index.html* becomes "/index.html." In terms of the envelope metaphor, the path is the address on the envelope. In this book I sometimes refer to the "URI" as shorthand for just the path.

The request headers

These are bits of metadata: key-value pairs that act like informational stickers slapped onto the envelope. This request has eight headers: `Host`, `User-Agent`, `Accept`, and so on. There's a standard list of HTTP headers (see Appendix C), and applications can define their own.

The entity-body, also called the document or representation

This is the document that inside the envelope. This particular request has no entity-body, which means the envelope is empty! This is typical for a GET request, where all the information needed to complete the request is in the path and the headers.

The HTTP response is also a document in a envelope. It's almost identical in form to the HTTP request. Example 1-6 shows a trimmed version of what the server at `oreilly.com` sends my web browser when I make the request in Example 1-5.

Example 1-6. The response to an HTTP GET request for http://www.oreilly.com/index.html

```
HTTP/1.1 200 OK
Date: Fri, 17 Nov 2006 15:36:32 GMT
```

```
Server: Apache
Last-Modified: Fri, 17 Nov 2006 09:05:32 GMT
Etag: "7359b7-a7fa-455d8264
Accept-Ranges: bytes
Content-Length: 43302
Content-Type: text/html
X-Cache: MISS from www.oreilly.com
Keep-Alive: timeout=15, max=1000
Connection: Keep-Alive

<!DOCTYPE html PUBLIC "-//W3C//DTD XHTML 1.0 Transitional//EN"
        "http://www.w3.org/TR/xhtml1/DTD/xhtml1-transitional.dtd">
<html xmlns="http://www.w3.org/1999/xhtml" xml:lang="en" lang="en">
<head>
...
<title>oreilly.com -- Welcome to O'Reilly Media, Inc.</title>
...
```

The response can be divided into three parts:

The HTTP response code

> This numeric code tells the client whether its request went well or poorly, and how the client should regard this envelope and its contents. In this case the GET operation must have succeeded, since the response code is 200 ("OK"). I describe the HTTP response codes in Appendix B.

The response headers

> Just as with the request headers, these are informational stickers slapped onto the envelope. This response has 11 headers: Date, Server, and so on.

The entity-body or representation

> Again, this is the document inside the envelope, and this time there actually is one! The entity-body is the fulfillment of my GET request. The rest of the response is just an envelope with stickers on it, telling the web browser how to deal with the document.

> The most important of these stickers is worth mentioning separately. The response header Content-Type gives the *media type* of the entity-body. In this case, the media type is text/html. This lets my web browser know it can render the entity-body as an HTML document: a web page.

> There's a standard list of media types (*http://www.iana.org/assignments/media-types/*). The most common media types designate textual documents (text/html), structured data documents (application/xml), and images (image/jpeg). In other discussions of REST or HTTP, you may see the media type called the "MIME type," "content type," or "data type."

Method Information

HTTP is the one thing that all "animals" on the programmable web have in common. Now I'll show you how web services distinguish themselves from each other. There are two big questions that today's web services answer differently. If you know how a web service answers these questions, you'll have a good idea of how well it works with the Web.

The first question is how the client can convey its intentions to the server. How does the server know a certain request is a request to retrieve some data, instead of a request to delete that same data or to overwrite it with different data? Why should the server do *this* instead of doing *that*?

I call the information about what to do with the data the *method information*. One way to convey method information in a web service is to put it in the HTTP method. Since this is how RESTful web services do it, I'll have a lot more to say about this later. For now, note that the five most common HTTP methods are GET, HEAD, PUT, DELETE, and POST. This is enough to distinguish between "retrieve some data" (GET), "delete that same data" (DELETE), and "overwrite it with different data" (PUT).

The great advantage of HTTP method names is that they're standardized. Of course, the space of HTTP method names is much more limited than the space of method names in a programming language. Some web services prefer to look for application-specific method names elsewhere in the HTTP request: usually in the URI path or the request document.

Example 1-7 is a client for a web service that keeps its method information in the path: the web service for Flickr, Yahoo!'s online photo-sharing application. This sample application searches Flickr for photos. To run this program, you'll need to create a Flickr account and apply for an API key (*http://www.flickr.com/services/api/keys/apply/*).

Example 1-7. Searching Flickr for pictures

```
#!/usr/bin/ruby -w
# flickr-photo-search.rb
require 'open-uri'
require 'rexml/document'

# Returns the URI to a small version of a Flickr photo.
def small_photo_uri(photo)
  server = photo.attribute('server')
  id = photo.attribute('id')
  secret = photo.attribute('secret')
  return "http://static.flickr.com/#{server}/#{id}_#{secret}_m.jpg"
end

# Searches Flickr for photos matching a certain tag, and prints a URI
# for each search result.
def print_each_photo(api_key, tag)
  # Build the URI
  uri = "http://www.flickr.com/services/rest?method=flickr.photos.search" +
```

```
    "&api_key=#{api_key}&tags=#{tag}"

  # Make the HTTP request and get the entity-body.
  response = open(uri).read

  # Parse the entity-body as an XML document.
  doc = REXML::Document.new(response)

  # For each photo found...
  REXML::XPath.each(doc, '//photo') do |photo|
    # ...generate and print its URI
    puts small_photo_uri(photo) if photo
  end
end

# Main program
#
if ARGV.size < 2
  puts "Usage: #{$0} [Flickr API key] [search term]"
  exit
end

api_key, tag = ARGV
print_each_photo(api_key, tag)
```

XPath: The Bluffer's Guide

XPath is a domain-specific language for slicing up XML documents without writing a lot of code. It has many intimidating features, but you can get by with just a little bit of knowledge. The key is to think of an XPath expression as a rule for extracting tags or other elements from an XML document. There aren't many XPath expressions in this book, but I'll explain every one I use.

To turn an XPath expression into English, read it from right to left. The expression //photo means:

Find every photo tag   photo
no matter where it is in the document.   //

The Ruby code REXML::XPath.each(doc, '//photo') is a cheap way to iterate over every photo tag without having to traverse the XML tree.

This program makes HTTP requests to URIs like *http://www.flickr.com/services/rest? method=flickr.photos.search&api_key=xxx&tag=penguins*. How does the server know what the client is trying to do? Well, the method name is pretty clearly flickr.photos.search. Except: the HTTP method is GET, and I am *getting* information, so it might be that the method thing is a red herring. Maybe the method information really goes in the HTTP action.

This hypothesis doesn't last for very long, because the Flickr API supports many methods, not just "get"-type methods such as `flickr.photos.search` and `flickr.people.findByEmail`, but also methods like `flickr.photos.addTags`, `flickr.photos.comments.deleteComment`, and so on. All of them are invoked with an HTTP GET request, regardless of whether or not they "get" any data. It's pretty clear that Flickr is sticking the method information in the `method` query variable, and expecting the client to ignore what the HTTP method says.

By contrast, a typical SOAP service keeps its method information in the entity-body and in a HTTP header. Example 1-8 is a Ruby script that searches the Web using Google's SOAP-based API.

Example 1-8. Searching the Web with Google's search service

```
#!/usr/bin/ruby -w
# google-search.rb
require 'soap/wsdlDriver'

# Do a Google search and print out the title of each search result
def print_page_titles(license_key, query)
  wsdl_uri = 'http://api.google.com/GoogleSearch.wsdl'
  driver = SOAP::WSDLDriverFactory.new(wsdl_uri).create_rpc_driver
  result_set = driver.doGoogleSearch(license_key, query, 0, 10, true, ' ',
                                     false, ' ', ' ', ' ')
  result_set.resultElements.each { |result| puts result.title }
end

# Main program.
if ARGV.size < 2
  puts "Usage: #{$0} [Google license key] [query]"
  exit
end

license_key, query = ARGV
print_page_titles(license_key, query)
```

 While I was writing this book, Google announced that it was deprecating its SOAP search service in favor of a RESTful, resource-oriented service (which, unfortunately, is encumbered by legal restrictions on use in a way the SOAP service isn't). I haven't changed the example because Google's SOAP service still makes the best example I know of, and because I don't expect you to actually run this program. I just want you to look at the code, and the SOAP and WSDL documents the code relies on.

OK, that probably wasn't very informative, because the WSDL library hides most of the details. Here's what happens. When you call the `doGoogleSearch` method, the WSDL library makes a POST request to the "endpoint" of the Google SOAP service, located at the URI *http://api.google.com/search/beta2*. This single URI is the destination for every API call, and only POST requests are ever made to it. All of these details are in the WSDL file found at *http://api.google.com/GoogleSearch.wsdl*, which contains details like the definition of **doGoogleSearch** (Example 1-9).

Example 1-9. Part of the WSDL description for Google's search service

```
<operation name="doGoogleSearch">
 <input message="typens:doGoogleSearch"/>
 <output message="typens:doGoogleSearchResponse"/>
</operation>
```

Since the URI and the HTTP method never vary, the method information—that "do-GoogleSearch"—can't go in either place. Instead, it goes into the entity-body of the POST request. Example 1-10 shows what HTTP request you might make to do a search for REST.

Example 1-10. A sample SOAP RPC call

```
POST search/beta2 HTTP/1.1
Host: api.google.com
Content-Type: application/soap+xml
SOAPAction: urn:GoogleSearchAction

<?xml version="1.0" encoding="UTF-8"?>
<soap:Envelope xmlns:soap="http://schemas.xmlsoap.org/soap/envelope/">
 <soap:Body>
  <gs:doGoogleSearch xmlns:gs="urn:GoogleSearch">
   <q>REST</q>
   ...
  </gs:doGoogleSearch>
 </soap:Body>
</soap:Envelope>
```

The method information is "doGoogleSearch." That's the name of the XML tag inside the SOAP **Envelope**, it's the name of the **operation** in the WSDL file, and it's the name of the Ruby method in Example 1-8. It's also found in the value of the **SOAPAction** HTTP request header: some SOAP implementations look for it there instead of inside the entity-body.

Let's bring things full circle by considering not the Google SOAP search API, but the Google search engine itself. To use your web browser to search Google's data set for REST, you'd send a GET request to *http://www.google.com/search?q=REST* and get an HTML response back. The method information is kept in the HTTP method: you're GETting a list of search results.

Scoping Information

The other big question web services answer differently is how the client tells the server which part of the data set to operate on. Given that the server understands that the client wants to (say) delete some data, how can it know which data the client wants to delete? Why should the server operate on *this* data instead of *that* data?

I call this information the *scoping information*. One obvious place to put it is in the URI path. That's what most web sites do. Think once again about a search engine URI like *http://www.google.com/search?q=REST*. There, the method information is "GET," and the scoping information is "/search?q=REST." The client is trying to GET a list of search results about REST, as opposed to trying to GET something else: say, a list of search results about jellyfish (the scoping information for that would be "/search?q=jellyfish"), or the Google home page (that would be "/").

Many web services put scoping information in the path. Flickr's is one: most of the query variables in a Flickr API URI are scoping information. `tags=penguin` scopes the `flickr.photos.search` method so it only searches for photos tagged with "penguin." In a service where the method information defines a method in the programming language sense, the scoping information can be seen as a set of arguments to that method. You could reasonably expect to see `flickr.photos.search(tags=penguin)` as a line of code in some programming language.

The alternative is to put the scoping information into the entity-body. A typical SOAP web service does it this way. Example 1-10 contains a `q` tag whose contents are the string "REST." That's the scoping information, nestled conveniently inside the `doGoogleSearch` tag that provides the method information.

The service design determines what information is method information and what's scoping information. This is most obvious in cases like Flickr and Google, where the web site and the web service do the same thing but have different designs. These two URIs contain the same information:

- *http://flickr.com/photos/tags/penguin*
- *http://api.flickr.com/services/rest/?method=flickr.photos.search&tags=penguin*

In the first URI, the method information is "GET" and the scoping information is "photos tagged 'penguin.'" In the second URI, the method information is "do a photo search" and the scoping information is "penguin." From a technical standpoint, there's no difference between the two: both of them use HTTP GET. The differences only become apparent at the level of architecture, when you take a step back and notice values for `methodname` like `flickr.photos.delete`, which take HTTP's GET method into places it wasn't meant to go.

Another example: in the Google SOAP API, the fact that you're doing a search is method information (`doGoogleSearch`). The search query is scoping information (`q`). On the Google web site, both "search" and the value for "q" are scoping information. The method information is HTTP's standard GET. (If the Google SOAP API offered a method called `doGoogleSearchForREST`, it would be defining the method information so expansively that you'd need no scoping information to do a search for REST.)

The Competing Architectures

Now that I've identified the two main questions that web services answer differently, I can group web services by their answers to the questions. In my studies I've identified three common web service architectures: RESTful resource-oriented, RPC-style, and REST-RPC hybrid. I'll cover each in turn.

RESTful, Resource-Oriented Architectures

The main topic of this book is the web service architectures which can be considered RESTful: those which get a good score when judged on the criteria set forth in Roy Fielding's dissertation. Now, lots of architectures are technically RESTful,‡ but I want to focus on the architectures that are best for web services. So when I talk about RESTful web services, I mean services that look like the Web. I'm calling this kind of service *resource-oriented*. In Chapter 3 I'll introduce the basic concepts of resource-oriented REST, in the context of a real web service: Amazon's Simple Storage Service. Starting in Chapter 5, I'll talk you through the defining characteristics of REST, and define a good architecture for RESTful web services: the Resource-Oriented Architecture.

In RESTful architectures, the method information goes into the HTTP method. In Resource-Oriented Architectures, the scoping information goes into the URI. The combination is powerful. Given the first line of an HTTP request to a resource-oriented RESTful web service ("GET /reports/open-bugs HTTP/1.1"), you should understand basically what the client wants to do. The rest of the request is just details; indeed, you can make many requests using only one line of HTTP. If the HTTP method doesn't match the method information, the service isn't RESTful. If the scoping information isn't in the URI, the service isn't resource-oriented. These aren't the *only* requirements, but they're good rules of thumb.

A few well-known examples of RESTful, resource-oriented web services include:

- Services that expose the Atom Publishing Protocol (*http://www.ietf.org/html.char ters/atompub-charter.html*) and its variants such as GData (*http://code.google.com/ apis/gdata/*)
- Amazon's Simple Storage Service (S3) (*http://aws.amazon.com/s3*)
- Most of Yahoo!'s web services (*http://developer.yahoo.com/*)
- Most other read-only web services that don't use SOAP
- Static web sites
- Many web applications, especially read-only ones like search engines

---

‡ More than you'd think. The Google SOAP API for web search technically has a RESTful architecture. So do many other read-only SOAP and XML-RPC services. But these are bad architectures for web services, because they look nothing like the Web.

Whenever I cover unRESTful architectures, as well as architectures that aren't resource-oriented, I do it with some ulterior motive. In this chapter, I want to put RESTful web services into perspective, against the larger backdrop of the programmable web. In Chapter 2, I'm widening the book's coverage of real web services, and showing that you can use the same client tools whether or not a service exactly fits my preferred architecture. In Chapter 10, I'm making an argument in a long-running debate about what the programmable web *should* look like.

RPC-Style Architectures

An RPC-style web service accepts an envelope full of data from its client, and sends a similar envelope back. The method and the scoping information are kept inside the envelope, or on stickers applied to the envelope. What *kind* of envelope is not important to my classification, but HTTP is a popular envelope format, since any web service worthy of the name must use HTTP anyway. SOAP is another popular envelope format (transmitting a SOAP document over HTTP puts the SOAP envelope inside an HTTP envelope). Every RPC-style service defines a brand new vocabulary. Computer programs work this way as well: every time you write a program, you define functions with different names. By contrast, all RESTful web services share a standard vocabulary of HTTP methods. Every object in a RESTful service responds to the same basic interface.

The XML-RPC protocol for web services is the most obvious example of the RPC architecture. XML-RPC is mostly a legacy protocol these days, but I'm going to start off with it because it's relatively simple and easy to explain. Example 1-11 shows a Ruby client for an XML-RPC service that lets you look up anything with a Universal Product Code.

Example 1-11. An XML-RPC example: looking up a product by UPC

```ruby
#!/usr/bin/ruby -w
# xmlrpc-upc.rb

require 'xmlrpc/client'
def find_product(upc)
  server = XMLRPC::Client.new2('http://www.upcdatabase.com/rpc')
  begin
    response = server.call('lookupUPC', upc)
  rescue XMLRPC::FaultException => e
    puts "Error: "
    puts e.faultCode
    puts e.faultString
  end
end

puts find_product("001441000055")['description']
# "Trader Joe's Thai Rice Noodles"
```

An XML-RPC service models a programming language like C. You call a function (lookupUPC) with some arguments ("001441000055") and get a return value back. The method data (the function name) and the scoping data (the arguments) are put inside an XML document. Example 1-12 gives a sample document.

Example 1-12. An XML document describing an XML-RPC request

```
<?xml version="1.0" ?>
 <methodCall>
  <methodName>lookupUPC</methodName>
  <params>
   <param><value><string>001441000055</string></value></param>
  </params>
 </methodCall>
```

This XML document is put into an envelope for transfer to the server. The envelope is an HTTP request with a method, URI, and headers (see Example 1-13). The XML document becomes the entity-body inside the HTTP envelope.

Example 1-13. An HTTP envelope that contains an XML document which describes an XML-RPC request

```
POST /rpc HTTP/1.1
Host: www.upcdatabase.com
User-Agent: XMLRPC::Client (Ruby 1.8.4)
Content-Type: text/xml; charset=utf-8
Content-Length: 158
Connection: keep-alive

<?xml version="1.0" ?>
<methodCall>
 <methodName>lookupUPC</methodName>
 ...
</methodCall>
```

The XML document changes depending on which method you're calling, but the HTTP envelope is always the same. No matter what you do with the UPC database service, the URI is always *http://www.upcdatabase.com/rpc* and the HTTP method is always POST. Simply put, an XML-RPC service ignores most features of HTTP. It exposes only one URI (the "endpoint"), and supports only one method on that URI (POST).

Where a RESTful service would expose different URIs for different values of the scoping information, an RPC-style service typically exposes a URI for each "document processor": something that can open the envelopes and transform them into software commands. For purposes of comparison, Example 1-14 shows what that code might look like if the UPC database were a RESTful web service.

Example 1-14. A hypothetical code sample: a RESTful UPC lookup service

```
require 'open-uri'
upc_data = open('http://www.upcdatabase.com/upc/00598491').read()
...
```

Here, the method information is contained in the HTTP method. The default HTTP method is GET, which is equivalent in this scenario to `lookupUPC`. The scoping information is contained in the URI. The hypothetical service exposes an enormous number of URIs: one for every possible UPC. By contrast, the HTTP envelope is empty: an HTTP GET request contains no entity-body at all.

For another example of a client for an RPC-style service, look back at Example 1-8. Google's SOAP search API is an RPC-style service that uses SOAP as its envelope format.

A service that uses HTTP POST heavily or exclusively is probably an RPC-style service. Again, this isn't a sure sign, but it's a tip-off that the service isn't very interested in putting its method information in the HTTP method. An otherwise RESTful service that uses HTTP POST a lot tends to move toward a REST-RPC hybrid architecture.

A few well-known examples of RPC-style web services:

- All services that use XML-RPC
- Just about every SOAP service (see the "Technologies on the Programmable Web" section later in this chapter for a defense of this controversial statement)
- A few web applications (generally poorly designed ones)

REST-RPC Hybrid Architectures

This is a term I made up for describing web services that fit somewhere in between the RESTful web services and the purely RPC-style services. These services are often created by programmers who know a lot about real-world web applications, but not much about the theory of REST.

Take another look at this URI used by the Flickr web service: *http://www.flickr.com/services/rest?api_key=xxx&method=flickr.photos.search&tags=penguin*. Despite the "rest" in the URI, this was clearly designed as an RPC-style service, one that uses HTTP as its envelope format. It's got the scoping information ("photos tagged 'penguin'") in the URI, just like a RESTful resource-oriented service. But the method information ("search for photos") also goes in the URI. In a RESTful service, the method information would go into the HTTP method (GET), and whatever was leftover would become scoping information. As it is, this service is simply using HTTP as an envelope format, sticking the method and scoping information wherever it pleases. This is an RPC-style service. Case closed.

Except...look at Example 1-15.

Example 1-15. A sample HTTP request to the Flickr web service
```
GET services/rest?api_key=xxx&method=flickr.photos.search&tags=penguin HTTP/1.1
Host: www.flickr.com
```

That's the HTTP request a client makes when remotely calling this procedure. Now it looks like the method information is in the HTTP method. I'm sending a GET request to get something. What am I getting? A list of search results for photos tagged "penguin." What used to look like method information ("photoSearch()") now looks like scoping information ("photos/tag/penguin"). Now the web service looks RESTful.

This optical illusion happens when an RPC-style service uses plain old HTTP as its envelope format, and when both the method and the scoping information happen to live into the URI portion of the HTTP request. If the HTTP method is GET, and the point of the web service request is to "get" information, it's hard to tell whether the method information is in the HTTP method or in the URI. Look at the HTTP requests that go across the wire and you see the requests you'd see for a RESTful web service. They may contain elements like "method=flickr.photos.search" but that could be interpreted as scoping information, the way "photos/" and "search/" are scoping information. These RPC-style services have elements of RESTful web services, more or less by accident. They're only using HTTP as a convenient envelope format, but they're using it in a way that overlaps with what a RESTful service might do.

Many read-only web services qualify as entirely RESTful and resource-oriented, even though they were designed in the RPC style! But if the service allows clients to write to the data set, there will be times when the client uses an HTTP method that doesn't match up with the true method information. This keeps the service from being as RESTful as it could be. Services like these are the ones I consider to be REST-RPC hybrids.

Here's one example. The Flickr web API asks clients to use HTTP GET even when they want to modify the data set. To delete a photo you make a GET request to a URI that includes `method=flickr.photos.delete`. That's just not what GET is for, as I'll show in "Split the Data Set into Resources [115]. The Flickr web API is a REST-RPC hybrid: RESTful when the client is retrieving data through GET, RPC-style when the client is modifying the data set.

A few well-known examples of REST-RPC hybrid services include:

- The del.icio.us API
- The "REST" Flickr web API
- Many other allegedly RESTful web services
- Most web applications

From a design standpoint, I don't think anybody sets out to to design a service as a REST-RPC hybrid. Because of the way HTTP works, any RPC-style service that uses plain HTTP and exposes multiple URIs tends to end up either RESTful or hybrid. Many programmers design web services exactly as they'd design web applications, and end up with hybrid services.

The existence of hybrid architectures has caused a lot of confusion. The style comes naturally to people who've designed web applications, and it's often claimed that hybrid architectures are RESTful: after all, they work "the same way" as the human web. A lot of time has been spent trying to distinguish RESTful web services from these mysterious others. My classification of the "others" as REST-RPC hybrids is just the latest in a long line of neologisms. I think this particular neologism is the most accurate and useful way to look at these common but baffling services. If you've encountered other ways of describing them ("HTTP+POX" is the most popular at the time of writing), you might want read on, where I explain those other phrases in terms of what I'm saying in this book.

The Human Web Is on the Programmable Web

In the previous sections I claimed that all static web sites are RESTful. I claimed that web applications fall into one of the three categories, the majority being REST-RPC hybrids. Since the human web is made entirely of static web sites and web applications, this means that the entire human web is also on the programmable web! By now this should not be surprising to you. A web browser is a software program that makes HTTP requests and processes the responses somehow (by showing them to a human). That's exactly what a web service client is. *If it's on the Web, it's a web service.*

My goal in this book is not to make the programmable web bigger. That's almost impossible: the programmable web already encompasses nearly everything with an HTTP interface. My goal is to help make the programmable web *better*: more uniform, better-structured, and using the features of HTTP to greatest advantage.

Technologies on the Programmable Web

I've classified web services by their underlying architectures, distinguishing the fish from the whales. Now I can examine the technologies they use, without confusing technology and architecture.

HTTP

All web services use HTTP, but they use it in different ways. A request to a RESTful web services puts the method information in the HTTP method and the scoping information in the URI. RPC-style web services tend to ignore the HTTP method, looking for method and scoping information in the URI, HTTP headers, or entity-body. Some RPC-style web services use HTTP as an envelope containing a document, and others only use it as an unlabelled envelope containing another envelope.

URI

Again, all web services use URIs, but in different ways. What I'm about to say is a generalization, but a fairly accurate one. A RESTful, resource-oriented service exposes a URI for every piece of data the client might want to operate on. A REST-RPC hybrid exposes a URI for every operation the client might perform: one URI to fetch a piece of data, a different URI to delete that same data. An RPC-style service exposes one URI

---

for every processes capable of handling Remote Procedure Calls (RPC). There's usually only one such URI: the service "endpoint."

XML-RPC

A few, mostly legacy, web services use XML-RPC on top of HTTP. XML-RPC is a data structure format for representing function calls and their return values. As the name implies, it's explicitly designed to use an RPC style.

SOAP

Lots of web services use SOAP on top of HTTP. SOAP is an envelope format, like HTTP, but it's an XML-based envelope format.

Now I'm going to say something controversial. *To a first approximation, every current web service that uses SOAP also has an RPC architecture.* This is controversial because many SOAP programmers think the RPC architecture is déclassé and prefer to call their services "message-oriented" or "document-oriented" services.

Well, all web services are message-oriented, because HTTP itself is message-oriented. An HTTP request is just a message: an envelope with a document inside. The question is what that document says. SOAP-based services ask the client to stick a second envelope (a SOAP document) inside the HTTP envelope. Again, the real question is what it says inside the envelope. A SOAP envelope can contain any XML data, just as an HTTP envelope can contain any data in its entity-body. But in every *existing* SOAP service, the SOAP envelope contains a description of an RPC call in a format similar to that of XML-RPC.

There are various ways of shuffling this RPC description around and giving it different labels—"document/literal" or "wrapped/literal"—but any way you slice it, you have a service with a large vocabulary of method information, a service that looks for scoping information inside the document rather than on the envelope. These are defining features of the RPC architecture.

I emphasize that this is not a fact about SOAP, just a fact about how it's currently used. SOAP, like HTTP, is just a way of putting data in an envelope. Right now, though, the only data that ever gets put in that envelope is XML-RPC-esque data about how to call a remote function, or what's the return value from such a function. I argue this point in more detail in Chapter 10.

WS-*

These standards define special XML "stickers" for the SOAP envelope. The stickers are analogous to HTTP headers.

WSDL

The Web Service Description Language (WSDL) is an XML vocabulary used to describe SOAP-based web services. A client can load a WSDL file and know exactly which RPC-style methods it can call, what arguments those methods expect, and which data types they return. Nearly every SOAP service in existence exposes a WSDL file, and most SOAP services would be very difficult to use without their WSDL files serving as guides. As I discuss in Chapter 10, WSDL bears more responsiblity than any other technology for maintaining SOAP's association with the RPC style.

WADL

The Web Application Description Language (WADL) is an XML vocabulary used to describe RESTful web services. As with WSDL, a generic client can load a WADL file and be immediately equipped to access the full functionality of the corresponding web service. I discuss WADL in Chapter 9.

Since RESTful services have simpler interfaces, WADL is not nearly as neccessary to these services as WSDL is to RPC-style SOAP services. This is a good thing, since as of the time of writing there are few real web services providing official WADL files. Yahoo!'s web search service is one that does.

Leftover Terminology

Believe it not, there are some common terms used in discussions of REST that I haven't mentioned yet. I haven't mentioned them because I think they're inaccurate or entirely outside the scope of this book. But I owe you explanations of *why* I think this, so you can decide whether or not you agree. Feel free to skip this section if you haven't heard these terms.

Service-Oriented Architecture
> This is a big industry buzzword. I'm not going to dwell on it for two reasons. First, the term is not very well defined. Second, to the extent that it is defined, it means something like: "a software architecture based on the production and consumption of web services." In this book I talk about the design of individual services. A book on service-oriented architecture should work on a slightly higher level, showing how to use services as software components, how to integrate them into a coherent whole. I don't cover that sort of thing in this book.

SOAP as a competitor to REST
> If you get involved with web service debates you'll hear this one a lot. You won't hear it here because it gives the wrong impression. The primary competitors to RESTful architectures are RPC architectures, not specific technologies like SOAP. It is true that basically every SOAP service that now exists has an RPC architecture, but SOAP is just a way of putting a document in an envelope with stickers on it,

like HTTP. SOAP is tied to the RPC architecture mainly by historical contingency and the current generation of automated tools.

There is a real tension here, but it's not one I'll cover much in this book. Roughly speaking, it's the tension between services that put their documents in a SOAP envelope and then an HTTP envelope; and services that only use the HTTP envelope.

HTTP+POX

Stands for HTTP plus Plain Old XML. This term covers roughly those services I call REST-RPC hybrid services. They overlap with RESTful designs, especially when it comes to retrieving data, but their basic architecture is RPC-oriented.

I don't like this term because Plain Old XML is inaccurate. The interesting thing about these services is not that they produce plain old XML documents (as opposed to XML documents wrapped in SOAP envelopes). Some of these services don't serve XML at all: they serve JSON, plain text, or binary files. No, the interesting thing about these services is their RPC architecture. *That's* what puts them in opposition to REST.

STREST

Means Service-Trampled REST. This is another term for REST-RPC hybrid architectures. It's more accurate than HTTP+POX since it conveys the notion of a RESTful architecture taken over by something else: in this case, the RPC style.

This is a cute acronym but I don't like it, because it buys into a myth that the only true web services are RPC-style services. After all, the service that trampled your REST was an RPC service. If you think that REST services are real services, it doesn't make sense to cry "Help! I had some REST but then this *Service* got into it!" RPC-Trampled REST would be more accurate, but that's a lousy acronym.

High and low REST

Yet another way of distinguishing between truly RESTful services and the ones I call REST-RPC hybrids. High REST services are just those that adhere closely to the Fielding dissertation. Among other things, they put method information in the HTTP method and scoping information in the URI. Low REST services are presumed to have deviated. Since low REST services tend to deviate from orthodoxy in a particular direction (toward the RPC style), I prefer a more specific terminology.

## CHAPTER 2

Writing Web Service Clients

Web Services Are Web Sites

In Chapter 1 I showed some quick examples of clients for existing, public web services. Some of the services had resource-oriented RESTful architectures, some had RPC-style architectures, and some were hybrids. Most of the time, I accessed these services through wrapper libraries instead of making the HTTP requests myself.

You can't always rely on the existence of a convenient wrapper library for your favorite web service, especially if you wrote the web service yourself. Fortunately, it's easy to write programs that work directly with HTTP requests and responses. In this chapter I show how to write clients for RESTful and hybrid architecture services, in a variety of programming languages.

Example 2-1 is a bare HTTP client for a RESTful web service: Yahoo!'s web search. You might compare it to Example 1-8, the client from the previous chapter that runs against the RPC-style SOAP interface to Google's web search.

Example 2-1. Searching the Web with Yahoo!'s web service

```ruby
#!/usr/bin/ruby
# yahoo-web-search.rb
require 'open-uri'
require 'rexml/document'
require 'cgi'

BASE_URI = 'http://api.search.yahoo.com/WebSearchService/V1/webSearch'

def print_page_titles(term)
  # Fetch a resource: an XML document full of search results.
  term = CGI::escape(term)
  xml = open(BASE_URI + "?appid=restbook&query=#{term}").read

  # Parse the XML document into a data structure.
  document = REXML::Document.new(xml)

  # Use XPath to find the interesting parts of the data structure.
  REXML::XPath.each(document, '/ResultSet/Result/Title/[]') do |title|
```

```
    puts title
  end
end

(puts "Usage: #{$0} [search term]"; exit) if ARGV.empty?
print_page_titles(ARGV.join(' '))
```

This "web service" code looks just like generic HTTP client code. It uses Ruby's standard open-uri library to make an HTTP request and Ruby's standard REXML library to parse the output. I'd use the same tools to fetch and process a web page. These two URIs:

- *http://api.search.yahoo.com/WebSearchService/V1/webSearch?
  appid=restbook&query=jellyfish*
- *http://search.yahoo.com/search?p=jellyfish*

point to different forms of the same thing: "a list of search results for the query 'jellyfish.'" One URI serves HTML and is intended for use by web browsers; the other serves XML and is intended for use by automated clients.

XPath Exposition

Reading from right to left, the expression /ResultSet/Result/Title/[] means:

Find the direct children	[]
of every Title tag	Title/
that's the direct child of a Result tag	Result/
that's the direct child of the ResultSet tag	ResultSet/
at the root of the document.	/

If you look at the XML files served by the Yahoo! search service, you'll see a Result Set tag that contains Result tags, each of which contains a Title tag. The contents of those tags are what I'm after in Example 2-1.

There is no magic dust that makes an HTTP request a web service request. You can make requests to a RESTful or hybrid web service using nothing but your programming language's HTTP client library. You can process the results with a standard XML parser. Every web service request involves the same three steps:

1. Come up with the data that will go into the HTTP request: the HTTP method, the URI, any HTTP headers, and (for requests using the PUT or POST method) any document that needs to go in the request's entity-body.

2. Format the data as an HTTP request, and send it to the appropriate HTTP server.

---

3. Parse the response data—the response code, any headers, and any entity-body—into the data structures the rest of your program needs.

In this chapter I show how different programming languages and libraries implement this three-step process.

Wrappers, WADL, and ActiveResource

Although a web service request is just an HTTP request, any given web service has a logic and a structure that is missing from the World Wide Web as a whole. If you follow the three-step algorithm every time you make a web service request, your code will be a mess and you'll never take advantage of that underlying structure.

Instead, as a smart programmer you'll quickly notice the patterns underlying your requests to a given service, and write wrapper methods that abstract away the details of HTTP access. The `print_page_titles` method defined in Example 2-1 is a primitive wrapper. As a web service gets popular, its users release polished wrapper libraries in various languages. Some service providers offer official wrappers: Amazon gives away clients in five different languages for its RESTful S3 service. That hasn't stopped outside programmers from writing their own S3 client libraries, like jbucket and s3sh.

Wrappers make service programming easy, because the API of a wrapper library is tailored to one particular service. You don't have to think about HTTP at all. The downside is that each wrapper is slightly different: learning one wrapper doesn't prepare you for the next one.

This is a little disappointing. After all, these services are just variations on the three-step algorithm for making HTTP requests. Shouldn't there be some way of abstracting out the differences between services, some library that can act as a wrapper for the entire space of RESTful and hybrid services?

This is the problem of service description. We need a language with a vocabulary that can describe the variety of RESTful and hybrid services. A document written in this language could script a generic web service client, making it act like a custom-written wrapper. The SOAP RPC community has united around WSDL as its service description language. The REST community has yet to unite around a description language, so in this book I do my bit to promote WADL as a resource-oriented alternative to WSDL. I think it's the simplest and most elegant solution that solves the whole problem. I show a simple WADL client in this chapter and it is covered in detail in the "WADL" section.

There's also a generic client called ActiveResource, still in development. ActiveResource makes it easy to write clients for many kinds of web services written with the Ruby on Rails framework. I cover ActiveResource at the end of Chapter 3.

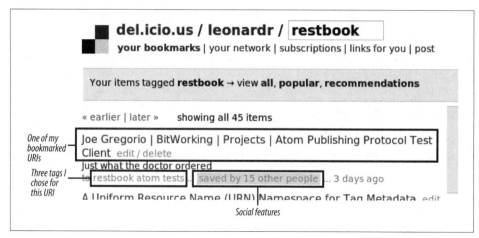

Figure 2-1. del.icio.us screenshot

del.icio.us: The Sample Application

In this chapter I walk through the life cycle of a web service request from the client's point of view. Though most of this book's code examples are written in Ruby, in this chapter I show code written in a variety of programming languages. My example throughout this chapter is the web service provided by the social bookmarking web site del.icio.us (*http://del.icio.us/*). You can read a prose description of this web service at *http://del.icio.us/help/api/*.

> If you're not familiar with del.icio.us, here's a brief digressionary introduction. del.icio.us is a web site that works like your web browser's bookmark feature, but it's public and better-organized (see Figure 2-1). When you save a link to del.icio.us, it's associated with your account so you can find it later. You can also share your bookmarks with others.
>
> You can associate short strings, called *tags*, with a URI. Tags are versatile little suckers. They make it easy for you to find a URI later, they make it possible to group URIs together, and when multiple people tag the same URI, they create a machine-readable vocabulary for that URI.

The del.icio.us web service gives you programmatic access to your bookmarks. You can write programs that bookmark URIs, convert your browser bookmarks to del.icio.us bookmarks, or fetch the URIs you've bookmarked in the past. The best way to visualize the del.icio.us web service is to use the human-oriented web site for a while. There's no fundamental difference between the del.icio.us web site and the del.icio.us web service, but there are variations:

- The web site is rooted at *http://del.icio.us/* and the web service is rooted at *https://api.del.icio.us/v1/*. The web site communicates with clients through HTTP, the web service uses secure HTTPS.

- The web site and the web service expose different URI structures. To get your recent bookmarks from the web site, you fetch `https://del.icio.us/{your-username}`. To get your recent bookmarks from the web service, you fetch *https://api.del.icio.us/v1/posts/recent*.

- The web site serves HTML documents, and the web service serves XML documents. The formats are different, but they contain the same data.

- The web site lets you see a lot of information without logging in or even having an account. The web service makes you authenticate for every request.

- Both offer features for personal bookmark management, but the web site also has social features. On the web site, you can see lists of URIs other people have bookmarked, lists of people who have bookmarked a particular URI, lists of URIs tagged with a certain tag, and lists of popular bookmarks. The web service only lets you see your own bookmarks.

These variations are important but they don't make the web service a different kind of thing from the web site. The web service is a stripped-down web site that uses HTTPS and serves funny-looking documents. (You can flip this around and look at the web site as a more functional web service, though the del.icio.us administrators discourage this viewpoint.) This is a theme I'm coming back to again and again: web services should work under same rules as web sites.

Aside from its similarity to a web site, the del.icio.us web service does not have a very RESTful design. The programmers have laid out the service URIs in a way that suggests an RPC-style rather than a resource-oriented design. All requests to the del.icio.us web service use the HTTP GET method: the real method information goes into the URI and might conflict with "GET". A couple sample URIs should illustrate this point: consider *https://api.del.icio.us/v1/posts/add* and *https://api.del.icio.us/v1/tags/rename*. Though there's no explicit `methodName` variable, the del.icio.us API is just like the Flickr API I covered in Chapter 1. The method information ("add" and "rename") is kept in the URIs, not in the HTTP method.

So why have I chosen del.icio.us for the sample clients in this chapter? Three reasons. First, del.icio.us is an easy application to understand, and its web service is popular and easy to use.

Second, I want to make it clear that what I say in the coming chapters is prescriptive, not descriptive. When you implement a web service, following the constraints of REST will give your clients a nice, usable web service that acts like the web. But when you implement a web service *client*, you have to work with the service as it is. The only alternatives are to lobby for a change or boycott the service. If a web service designer has never heard of REST, or thinks that hybrid services are "RESTful," there's little you can do about it. Most existing services are hybrids or full-blown RPC services. A snooty client that can feed only on the purest of REST services isn't very useful, and won't be for the forseeable future. Servers should be idealistic; clients must be pragmatic. This is a variant of Postel's Law: "Be conservative in what you do; be liberal in which you accept from others."

Third, in Chapter 7 I present a bookmark-tracking web service that's similar to del.icio.us but designed on RESTful principles. I want to introduce the social book-marking domain to you now, so you'll be thinking about it as I introduce the principles of REST and my Resource-Oriented Architecture. In Chapter 7, when I design and implement a RESTful interface to del.icio.us-like functionality, you'll see the difference.

What the Sample Clients Do

In the sections that follow, I show you simple del.icio.us clients in a variety of programming languages. All of these clients do exactly the same thing, and it's worth spelling out what that is. First, they open up a TCP/IP socket connection to port 443 (the standard HTTPS port) on the server at `api.del.icio.us`. Then they send something like the HTTP request in Example 2-2. The del.icio.us web service sends back something like the HTTP response in Example 2-3, then closes the socket connection. Like all HTTP responses, this one has three parts: a status code, a set of headers, and an entity-body. In this case, the entity-body is an XML document.

Example 2-2. A possible request to the del.icio.us web service

```
GET /v1/posts/recent HTTP/1.1
Host: api.del.icio.us
Authorization: Basic dXNlcm5hbWU6cGFzc3dvcmQ=
```

Example 2-3. A possible response from the del.icio.us web service

```
200 OK
Content-Type: text/xml
Date: Sun, 29 Oct 2006 15:09:36 GMT
Connection: close

<?xml version='1.0' standalone='yes'?>
<posts tag="" user="username">
  <post href="http://www.foo.com/" description="foo" extended=""
    hash="14d59bdc067e3c1f8f792f51010ae5ac" tag="foo"
    time="2006-10-29T02:56:12Z" />
  <post href="http://amphibians.com/" description="Amphibian Mania"
    extended="" hash="688b7b2f2241bc54a0b267b69f438805" tag="frogs toads"
    time="2006-10-28T02:55:53Z" />
</posts>
```

The clients I write are only interested in the entity-body part. Specifically, they're only interested in the `href` and `description` attributes of the `post` tags. They'll parse the XML document into a data structure and use the XPath expression `/posts/post` to iterate over the `post` tags. They'll print to standard output the `href` and `description` attribute of every del.icio.us bookmark:

```
foo: http://www.foo.com/
Amphibian Mania: http://amphibians.com/
```

XPath Exposition

Reading from right to left, the XPath expression **/posts/post** means:

Find every post tag	post
that's the direct child of the posts tag	posts/
at the root of the document.	/

Making the Request: HTTP Libraries

Every modern programming language has one or more libraries for making HTTP requests. Not all of these libraries are equally useful, though. To build a fully general web service client you need an HTTP library with these features:

- It must support HTTPS and SSL certificate validation. Web services, like web sites, use HTTPS to secure communication with their clients. Many web services (del.icio.us is one example) won't accept plain HTTP requests at all. A library's HTTPS support often depends on the presense of an external SSL library written in C.

- It must support at least the five main HTTP methods: GET, HEAD, POST, PUT, and DELETE. Some libraries support only GET and POST. Others are designed for simplicity and support only GET.

  You can get pretty far with a client that only supports GET and POST: HTML forms support only those two methods, so the entire human web is open to you. You can even do all right with just GET, because many web services (among them del.icio.us and Flickr) use GET even where they shouldn't. But if you're choosing a library for all your web service clients, or writing a general client like a WADL client, you need a library that supports all five methods. Additional methods like OPTIONS and TRACE, and WebDAV extensions like MOVE, are a bonus.

- It must allow the programmer to customize the data sent as the entity-body of a PUT or POST request.

- It must allow the programmer to customize a request's HTTP headers.

- It must give the programmer access to the response code and headers of an HTTP response; not just access to the entity-body.

- It must be able to communicate through an HTTP proxy. The average programmer may not think about this, but many HTTP clients in corporate environments can

---

only work through a proxy. Intermediaries like HTTP proxies are also a standard part of the REST meta-architecture, though not one I'll be covering in much detail.

Optional Features

There are also some features of an HTTP library that make life easier as you write clients for RESTful and hybrid services. These features mostly boil down to knowledge about HTTP headers, so they're technically optional. You can implement them yourself so long as your library gives you access to request and response HTTP headers. The advantage of library support is that you don't have to worry about the details.

- An HTTP library should automatically request data in compressed form to save bandwidth, and transparently decompress the data it receives. The HTTP request header here is `Accept-Encoding`, and the response header is `Encoding`. I discuss these in more detail in Chapter 8.

- It should automatically cache the responses to your requests. The second time you request a URI, it should return an item from the cache if the object on the server hasn't changed. The HTTP headers here are `ETag` and `If-Modified-Since` for the request, and `Etag` and `Last-Modified` for the response. These, too, I discuss in Chapter 8.

- It should transparently support the most common forms of HTTP authentication: Basic, Digest, and WSSE. It's useful to support custom, company-specific authentication methods such as Amazon's, or to have plug-ins that support them.

  The request header is `Authorization` and the response header (the one that demands authentication) is `WWW-Authenticate`. I cover the standard HTTP authentication methods, plus WSSE, in Chapter 8. I cover Amazon's custom authentication method in Chapter 3.

- It should be able to transparently follow HTTP redirects, while avoiding infinite redirects and redirect loops. This should be an optional convenience for the user, rather than something that happens on every single redirect. A web service may reasonably send a status code of 303 ("See Other") without implying that the client should *go fetch that other URI right now!*

- It should be able to parse and create HTTP cookie strings, rather than forcing the programmer to manually set the `Cookie` header. This is not very important for RESTful services, which shun cookies, but it's very important if you want to use the human web.

When you're writing code against a specific service, you may be able to do without some or all of these features. Ruby's standard `open-uri` library only supports GET requests. If you're writing a client for del.icio.us, there's no problem, since that web service expects only GET requests. But try to use `open-uri` with Amazon S3 (which uses GET, HEAD, PUT, and DELETE), and you'll quickly run into a wall. In the next sections I recommend good HTTP client libraries for some popular programming languages.

Ruby: rest-open-uri and net/http

Ruby comes with two HTTP client libraries, open-uri and the lower-level net/http. Either can make HTTPS requests if you've got the net/https extension installed. Windows installations of Ruby should be able to make HTTPS requests out of the box. If you're not on Windows, you may have to install net/https separately.[*]

The open-uri library has a simple and elegant interface that lets you treat URIs as filenames. To read a web page, you simply open its URI and read data from the "filehandle." You can pass in a hash to open containing custom HTTP headers and open-specific keyword arguments. This lets you set up a proxy, or specify authentication information.

Unfortunately, right now open-uri only supports one HTTP method: GET. That's why I've made some minor modifications to open-uri and made the result available as the rest-open-uri Ruby gem.[†] I've added two keyword arguments to open::method, which lets you customize the HTTP method, and :body, which lets you send data in the entity-body.

Example 2-4 is an implementation of the standard del.icio.us example using the open-uri library (rest-open-uri works the same way). This code parses the response document using the REXML::Document parser, which you've seen before.

Example 2-4. A Ruby client using open-uri

```ruby
#!/usr/bin/ruby -w
# delicious-open-uri.rb

require 'rubygems'
require 'open-uri'
require 'rexml/document'

# Fetches a del.icio.us user's recent bookmarks, and prints each one.
def print_my_recent_bookmarks(username, password)
  # Make the HTTPS request.
  response = open('https://api.del.icio.us/v1/posts/recent',
                  :http_basic_authentication => [username, password])

  # Read the response entity-body as an XML document.
  xml = response.read
```

---

[*] On Debian GNU/Linux and Debian-derived systems like Ubuntu, the package name is libopenssl-ruby. If your packaging system doesn't include net/https, you'll have to download it from *http://www.nongnu.org/rubypki/* and install it by hand.

[†] For more information on Ruby gems, see *http://rubygems.org/*. Once you have the gem program installed, you can install rest-open-uri with the command gem install rest-open-uri. Hopefully my modifications to open-uri will one day make it into the core Ruby code, and the rest-open-uri gem will become redundant.

```
  # Turn the document into a data structure.
  document = REXML::Document.new(xml)

  # For each bookmark...
  REXML::XPath.each(document, "/posts/post") do |e|
    # Print the bookmark's description and URI
    puts "#{e.attributes['description']}: #{e.attributes['href']}"
  end
end

# Main program
username, password = ARGV
unless username and password
  puts "Usage: #{$0} [username] [password]"
  exit
end
print_my_recent_bookmarks(username, password)
```

I mentioned earlier that Ruby's stock open-uri can only make HTTP GET requests. For many purposes, GET is enough, but if you want to write a Ruby client for a fully RESTful service like Amazon's S3, you'll either need to use rest-open-uri, or turn to Ruby's low-level HTTP library: net/http.

This built-in library provides the Net::HTTP class, which has several methods for making HTTP requests (see Table 2-1). You can build a complete HTTP client out of this class, using nothing more than the Ruby standard library. In fact, open-uri and rest-open-uri are based on Net::HTTP. Those libraries only exist because Net::HTTP provides no simple, easy-to-use interface that supports all the features a REST client needs (proxies, HTTPS, headers, and so on). That's why I recommend you use rest-open-uri.

Table 2-1. HTTP feature matrix for Ruby HTTP client libraries

	open-uri	rest-open-uri	Net:HTTP
HTTPS	Yes (assuming the net/https library is installed)	"	"
HTTP verbs	GET	All	All
Custom data	No	Yes	Yes
Custom headers	Yes	"	"
Proxies	Yes	"	"
Compression	No	"	"
Caching	No	"	"
Auth methods	Basic	"	"
Cookies	No	"	"
Redirects	Yes	Yes	No

Python: httplib2

The Python standard library comes with two HTTP clients: `urllib2`, which has a file-like interface like Ruby's `open-uri`; and `httplib`, which works more like Ruby's `Net::HTTP`. Both offer transparent support for HTTPS, assuming your copy of Python was compiled with SSL support. There's also an excellent third-party library, Joe Gregorio's `httplib2` (*http://bitworking.org/projects/httplib2/*), which is the one I recommend in general. `httplib2` is an excellent piece of software, supporting nearly every feature on my wish list—most notably, transparent caching. Table 2-2 lists the features available in each library.

Table 2-2. HTTP feature matrix for Python HTTP client libraries

	urllib2	httplib	httplib2
HTTPS	Yes (assuming Python was compiled with SSL support)	"	"
HTTP verbs	GET, POST	All	All
Custom data	Yes	"	"
Custom headers	Yes	"	"
Proxies	Yes	No	No
Compression	No	No	Yes
Caching	No	No	Yes
Auth methods	Basic, Digest	None	Basic, Digest, WSSE, Google
Cookies	Yes (Use `urllib2.build_opener(HTTPCookiePro cessor)`)	No	No
Redirects	Yes	No	Yes

Example 2-5 is a del.icio.us client that uses `httplib2`. It uses the ElementTree library to parse the del.icio.us XML.

Example 2-5. A del.icio.us client in Python

```
#!/usr/bin/python2.5
# delicious-httplib2.py
import sys
from xml.etree import ElementTree
import httplib2

# Fetches a del.icio.us user's recent bookmarks, and prints each one.
def print_my_recent_bookmarks(username, password):
    client = httplib2.Http(".cache")
    client.add_credentials(username, password)

    # Make the HTTP request, and fetch the response and the entity-body.
    response, xml = client.request('https://api.del.icio.us/v1/posts/recent')

    # Turn the XML entity-body into a data structure.
    doc = ElementTree.fromstring(xml)
```

```
    # Print information about every bookmark.
    for post in doc.findall('post'):
        print "%s: %s" % (post.attrib['description'], post.attrib['href'])

# Main program
if len(sys.argv) != 3:
    print "Usage: %s [username] [password]" % sys.argv[0]
    sys.exit()

username, password = sys.argv[1:]
print_my_recent_bookmarks(username, password)
```

Java: HttpClient

The Java standard library comes with an HTTP client, `java.net.HttpURLConnection`. You can get an instance by calling `open` on a `java.net.URL` object. Though it supports most of the basic features of HTTP, programming to its API is very difficult. The Apache Jakarta project has a competing client called HttpClient (*http://jakarta.apache.org/commons/httpclient/*), which has a better design. There's also Restlet (*http://www.restlet.org/*). I cover Restlet as a server library in Chapter 12, but it's also an HTTP client library. The class `org.restlet.Client` makes it easy to make simple HTTP requests, and the class `org.restlet.data.Request` hides the `HttpURLConnection` programming neccessary to make more complex requests. Table 2-3 lists the features available in each library.

Table 2-3. HTTP feature matrix for Java HTTP client libraries.

	HttpURLConnection	HttpClient	Restlet
HTTPS	Yes	"	"
HTTP verbs	All	"	"
Custom data	Yes	"	"
Custom headers	Yes	"	"
Proxies	Yes	"	"
Compression	No	No	Yes
Caching	Yes	No	Yes
Auth methods	Basic, Digest, NTLM	"	Basic, Amazon
Cookies	Yes	"	"
Redirects	Yes	"	"

Example 2-6 is a Java client for del.icio.us that uses HttpClient. It works in Java 1.5 and up, and it'll work in previous versions if you install the Xerces parser (see "Java: javax.xml, Xerces, or XMLPull" later in this chapter).

Example 2-6. A del.icio.us client in Java

```java
// DeliciousApp.java
import java.io.*;

import org.apache.commons.httpclient.*;
import org.apache.commons.httpclient.auth.AuthScope;
import org.apache.commons.httpclient.methods.GetMethod;

import org.w3c.dom.*;
import org.xml.sax.SAXException;
import javax.xml.parsers.*;
import javax.xml.xpath.*;

/**
 * A command-line application that fetches bookmarks from del.icio.us
 * and prints them to strandard output.
 */
public class DeliciousApp
{
  public static void main(String[] args)
    throws HttpException, IOException, ParserConfigurationException,
           SAXException, XPathExpressionException
  {
    if (args.length != 2)
    {
      System.out.println("Usage: java -classpath [CLASSPATH] "
                           + "DeliciousApp [USERNAME] [PASSWORD]");
      System.out.println("[CLASSPATH] - Must contain commons-codec, " +
                           "commons-logging, and commons-httpclient");
      System.out.println("[USERNAME]  - Your del.icio.us username");
      System.out.println("[PASSWORD]  - Your del.icio.us password");
      System.out.println();

      System.exit(-1);
    }

    // Set the authentication credentials.
    Credentials creds = new UsernamePasswordCredentials(args[0], args[1]);
    HttpClient client = new HttpClient();
    client.getState().setCredentials(AuthScope.ANY, creds);

    // Make the HTTP request.
    String url = "https://api.del.icio.us/v1/posts/recent";
    GetMethod method = new GetMethod(url);
    client.executeMethod(method);
    InputStream responseBody = method.getResponseBodyAsStream();

    // Turn the response entity-body into an XML document.
    DocumentBuilderFactory docBuilderFactory =
      DocumentBuilderFactory.newInstance();
    DocumentBuilder docBuilder =
      docBuilderFactory.newDocumentBuilder();
    Document doc = docBuilder.parse(responseBody);
    method.releaseConnection();
```

```
// Hit the XML document with an XPath expression to get the list
// of bookmarks.
XPath xpath = XPathFactory.newInstance().newXPath();
NodeList bookmarks = (NodeList)xpath.evaluate("/posts/post", doc,
                                       XPathConstants.NODESET);

// Iterate over the bookmarks and print out each one.
for (int i = 0; i < bookmarks.getLength(); i++)
{
    NamedNodeMap bookmark = bookmarks.item(i).getAttributes();
    String description = bookmark.getNamedItem("description")
        .getNodeValue();
    String uri = bookmark.getNamedItem("href").getNodeValue();
    System.out.println(description + ": " + uri);
}

System.exit(0);
  }
}
```

C#: System.Web.HTTPWebRequest

The .NET Common Language Runtime (CLR) defines HTTPWebRequest for making HTTP requests, and NetworkCredential for authenticating the client to the server. The HTTPWebRequest constructor takes a URI. The NetworkCredential constructor takes a username and password (see Example 2-7).

Example 2-7. A del.icio.us client in C#

```
using System;
using System.IO;
using System.Net;
using System.Xml.XPath;

public class DeliciousApp {
    static string user = "username";
    static string password = "password";
    static Uri uri = new Uri("https://api.del.icio.us/v1/posts/recent");

    static void Main(string[] args) {
        HttpWebRequest request = (HttpWebRequest) WebRequest.Create(uri);
        request.Credentials = new NetworkCredential(user, password);
        HttpWebResponse response = (HttpWebResponse) request.GetResponse();

        XPathDocument xml = new
        XPathDocument(response.GetResponseStream());
        XPathNavigator navigator = xml.CreateNavigator();
        foreach (XPathNavigator node in navigator.Select("/posts/post")) {
          string description = node.GetAttribute("description","");
          string href = node.GetAttribute("href","");
          Console.WriteLine(description + ": " + href);
        }
    }
}
```

PHP: libcurl

PHP comes with a binding to the C library `libcurl`, which can do pretty much anything you might want to do with a URI (see Example 2-8).

Example 2-8. A del.icio.us client in PHP

```php
<?php
  $user = "username";
  $password = "password";

  $request = curl_init();
  curl_setopt($request, CURLOPT_URL,
              'https://api.del.icio.us/v1/posts/recent');
  curl_setopt($request, CURLOPT_USERPWD, "$user:$password");
  curl_setopt($request, CURLOPT_RETURNTRANSFER, true);

  $response = curl_exec($request);
  $xml = simplexml_load_string($response);
  curl_close($request);

  foreach ($xml->post as $post) {
    print "$post[description]: $post[href]\n";
  }
?>
```

JavaScript: XMLHttpRequest

If you're writing a web service client in JavaScript, you probably intend it to run inside a web browser as part of an Ajax application. All modern web browsers implement a HTTP client library for JavaScript called `XMLHttpRequest`.

Because Ajax clients are developed differently from standalone clients, I've devoted an entire chapter to them: Chapter 11. The first example in that chapter is a del.icio.us client, so you can skip there right now without losing the flow of the examples.

The Command Line: curl

This example is a bit different: it doesn't use a programming language at all. A program called curl (*http://curl.haxx.se/*) is a capable HTTP client that runs from the Unix or Windows command line. It supports most HTTP methods, custom headers, several authentication mechanisms, proxies, compression, and many other features. You can use curl to do quick one-off HTTP requests, or use it in conjunction with shell scripts. Here's curl in action, grabbing a user's del.icio.us bookmarks:

```
$ curl https://username:password@api.del.icio.us/v1/posts/recent
<?xml version='1.0' standalone='yes'?>
<posts tag="" user="username">
 ...
</posts>
```

Other Languages

I don't have the space or the expertise to cover every popular programming language in depth with a del.icio.us client example. I can, however, give brief pointers to HTTP client libraries for some of the many languages I haven't covered yet.

ActionScript

Flash applications, like JavaScript applications, generally run inside a web browser. This means that when you write an ActionScript web service client you'll probably use the Ajax architecture described in Chapter 11, rather than the standalone architecture shown in this chapter.

ActionScript's `XML` class gives functionality similar to JavaScript's `XmlHttpRequest`. The `XML.load` method fetches a URI and parses the response document into an XML data structure. ActionScript also provides a class called `LoadVars`, which works on form-encoded key-value pairs instead of on XML documents.

C

The libwww library for C was the very first HTTP client library, but most C programmers today use libcurl (*http://curl.haxx.se/libcurl/*), the basis for the curl command-line tool. Earlier I mentioned PHP's bindings to libcurl, but there are also bindings for more than 30 other languages. If you don't like my recommendations, or I don't mention your favorite programming language in this chapter, you might look at using the libcurl bindings.

C++

Use libcurl, either directly or through an object-oriented wrapper called cURLpp (*http://rrette.com/curlpp.html*).

Common Lisp

simple-http (*http://www.enterpriselisp.com/software/simple-http/*) is easy to use, but doesn't support anything but basic HTTP, GET, and POST. The AllegroServe web server library (*http://opensource.franz.com/aserve/*) includes a complete HTTP client library.

Perl

The standard HTTP library for Perl is libwww-perl (also known as LWP), available from CPAN or most Unix packaging systems. libwww-perl has a long history and is one of the best-regarded Perl libraries. To get HTTPS support, you should also install the `Crypt:SSLeay` module (available from CPAN).

Processing the Response: XML Parsers

The entity-body is usually the most important part of an HTTP response. Where web services are concerned, the entity-body is usually an XML document, and the client gets most of the information it needs by running this document through an XML parser.

Now, there are many HTTP client libraries, but they all have exactly the same task. Given a URI, a set of headers, and a body document, the client's job is to construct an HTTP request and send it to a certain server. Some libraries have more features than others: cookies, authentication, caching, and the other ones I mentioned. But all these extra features are implemented within the HTTP request, usually as extra headers. A library might offer an object-oriented interface (like `Net::HTTP`) or a file-like interface (like `open-uri`), but both interfaces do the same thing. There's only one kind of HTTP client library.

But there are *three* kinds of XML parsers. It's not just that some XML parsers have features that others lack, or that one interface is more natural than another. There are two basic XML parsing strategies: the document-based strategy of DOM and other tree-style parsers, and the event-based strategy of SAX and "pull" parsers. You can get a tree-style or a SAX parser for any programming language, and a pull parser for almost any language.

The document-based, tree-style strategy is the simplest of the three models. A tree-style parser models an XML document as a nested data structure. Once you've got this data structure, you can search and process it with XPath queries, CSS selectors, or custom navigation functions: whatever your parser supports. A DOM parser is a tree-style parser that implements a specific interface defined by the W3C.

The tree-style strategy is easy to use, and it's the one I use the most. With a tree-style parser, the document is just an object like the other objects in your program. The big shortcoming is that you have to deal with the document as a whole. You can't start working on the document until you've processed the whole thing into a tree, and you can't avoid loading the whole document into memory. For documents that are simple but very large, this is inefficient. It would be a lot better to handle tags as they're parsed.

Instead of a data structure, a SAX-style or pull parser turns a document into a stream of events. Starting and closing tags, XML comments, and entity declarations are all events.

A pull parser is useful when you need to handle almost every event. A pull parser lets you handle one event at a time, "pulling" the next one from the stream as needed. You can take action in response to individual events as they come in, or build up a data structure for later use—presumably a smaller data structure than the one a tree-style parser would build. You can stop parsing the document at any time and come back to it later by pulling the next event from the stream.

A SAX parser is more complex, but useful when you only care about a few of the many events that will be streaming in. You drive a SAX parser by registering callback methods with it. Once you're done defining callbacks, you set the parser loose on a document. The parser turns the document into a series of events, and processes every event in the document without stopping. When an event comes along that matches one of your callbacks, the parser triggers that callback, and your custom code runs. Once the callback completes, the SAX parser goes back to processing events without stopping.

The advantage of the document-based approach is that it gives you random access to the document's contents. With event-based parsers, once the events have fired, they're gone. If you want to trigger them again you need to re-parse the document. What's more, an event-based parser won't notice that a malformed XML document is malformed until it tries to parse the bad spot, and crashes. Before passing a document into an event-based parser, you'll need to make sure the document is well formed, or else accept that your callback methods can be triggered for a document that turns out not to be good.

Some programming languages come with a standard set of XML parsers. Others have a canonical third-party parser library. For the sake of performance, some languages also have bindings to fast parsers written in C. I'd like to go through the list of languages again now, and make recommendations for document- and event-based XML parsers. I'll rate commonly available parsers on speed, the quality of their interface, how well they support XPath (for tree-style parsers), how strict they are, and whether or not they support schema-based validation. Depending on the application, a strict parser may be a good thing (because an XML document will be parsed the correct way or not at all) or a bad thing (because you want to use a service that generates bad XML).

In the sample del.icio.us clients given above, I showed not only how to use my favorite HTTP client library for a language, but how to use my favorite tree-style parser for that language. To show you how event-based parsers work, I'll give two more examples of del.icio.us clients using Ruby's built-in SAX and pull parsers.

Ruby: REXML, I Guess

Ruby comes with a standard XML parser library, REXML, that supports both DOM and SAX interfaces, and has good XPath support. Unfortunately, REXML's internals put it in a strange middle ground: it's too strict to be used to parse bad XML, but not strict enough to reject *all* bad XML.

I use REXML throughout this book because it's the default choice, and because I only deal with well-formed XML. If you want to *guarantee* that you only deal with well-formed XML, you'll need to install the Ruby bindings to the GNOME project's libxml2 library (described in "Other Languages" later in this chapter).

If you want to be able to handle bad markup, the best choice is hpricot (*http://code.whytheluckystiff.net/hpricot/*), available as the hpricot gem. It's fast (it uses a C extension), and it has an intuitive interface including support for common XPath expressions.

Example 2-9 is an implementation of the del.icio.us client using REXML's SAX interface.

Example 2-9. A Ruby client using a SAX parser

```
#!/usr/bin/ruby -w
# delicious-sax.rb
```

```
require 'open-uri'
require 'rexml/parsers/sax2parser'

def print_my_recent_bookmarks(username, password)
  # Make an HTTPS request and read the entity-body as an XML document.
  xml = open('https://api.del.icio.us/v1/posts/recent',
             :http_basic_authentication => [username, password])

  # Create a SAX parser whose destiny is to parse the XML entity-body.
  parser = REXML::Parsers::SAX2Parser.new(xml)

  # When the SAX parser encounters a 'post' tag...
  parser.listen(:start_element, ["post"]) do |uri, tag, fqtag, attributes|
    # ...it should print out information about the tag.
    puts "#{attributes['description']}: #{attributes['href']}"
  end

  # Make the parser fulfil its destiny to parse the XML entity-body.
  parser.parse
end

# Main program.
username, password = ARGV
unless username and password
  puts "Usage: #{$0} [USERNAME] [PASSWORD]"
  exit
end
print_my_recent_bookmarks(username, password)
```

In this program, the data isn't parsed (or even read from the HTTP connection) until the call to SAXParser#parse. Up to that point I'm free to call listen and set up pieces of code to run in response to parser events. In this case, the only event I'm interested in is the start of a post tag. My code block gets called every time the parser finds a post tag. This is the same as parsing the XML document with a tree-style parser, and running the XPath expression "//post" against the object tree. What does my code block do? The same thing my other example programs do when they find a post tag: print out the values of the description and href attributes.

This implementation is faster and much more memory-efficient than the equivalent tree-style implementation. However, complex SAX-based programs are much more difficult to write than equivalent tree-style programs. Pull parsers are a good compromise. Example 2-10 shows a client implementation that uses REXML's pull parser interface.

Example 2-10. A del.icio.us client using REXML's pull parser

```
#!/usr/bin/ruby -w
# delicious-pull.rb
require 'open-uri'
require 'rexml/parsers/pullparser'

def print_my_recent_bookmarks(username, password)
  # Make an HTTPS request and read the entity-body as an XML document.
```

```ruby
  xml = open('https://api.del.icio.us/v1/posts/recent',
             :http_basic_authentication => [username, password])

  # Feed the XML entity-body into a pull parser
  parser = REXML::Parsers::PullParser.new(xml)

  # Until there are no more events to pull...
  while parser.has_next?
    # ...pull the next event.
    tag = parser.pull
    # If it's a 'post' tag...
    if tag.start_element?
      if tag[0] == 'post'
        # Print information about the bookmark.
        attrs = tag[1]
        puts "#{attrs['description']}: #{attrs['href']}"
      end
    end
  end
end

# Main program.
username, password = ARGV
unless username and password
  puts "Usage: #{$0} [USERNAME] [PASSWORD]"
  exit
end
print_my_recent_bookmarks(username, password)
```

Python: ElementTree

The world is full of XML parsers for Python. There are *seven* different XML interfaces in the Python 2.5 standard library alone. For full details, see the Python library reference (*http://docs.python.org/lib/markup.html*).

For tree-style parsing, the best library is ElementTree (*http://effbot.org/zone/element-index.htm*). It's fast, it has a sensible interface, and as of Python 2.5 you don't have to install anything because it's in the standard library. On the downside, its support for XPath is limited to simple expressions—of course, nothing else in the standard library supports XPath at all. If you need full XPath support, try 4Suite (*http://4suite.org/*).

Beautiful Soup (*http://www.crummy.com/software/BeautifulSoup/*) is a slower tree-style parser that is very forgiving of invalid XML, and offers a programmatic interface to a document. It also handles most character set conversions automatically, letting you work with Unicode data.

For SAX-style parsing, the best choice is the `xml.sax` module in the standard library. The PyXML (*http://pyxml.sourceforge.net/*) suite includes a pull parser.

Java: javax.xml, Xerces, or XMLPull

Java 1.5 includes the XML parser written by the Apache Xerces project. The core classes are found in the packages `javax.xml.*`, (for instance, `javax.xml.xpath`). The DOM interface lives in `org.w3c.dom.*`, and the SAX interface lives in `org.xml.sax.*`. If you're using a previous version of Java, you can install Xerces yourself and take advantage of the same interface found in Java 1.5 (*http://xerces.apache.org/xerces2-j/*).

There are a variety of pull parsers for Java. Sun's Web Services Developer Pack includes a pull parser in the `javax.xml.stream` package.

For parsing bad XML, you might try TagSoup (*http://home.ccil.org/~cowan/XML/tagsoup/*).

C#: System.Xml.XmlReader

The .NET Common Language Runtime comes with a pull parser interface, in contrast to the more typical (and more complex) SAX-style interface. You can also create a full W3C DOM tree using `XmlDocument`. The `XPathDocument` class lets you iterate over nodes in the tree that match an XPath expression.

If you need to handle broken XML documents, check out Chris Lovett's `SgmlReader` at *http://www.gotdotnet.com/Community/UserSamples/*.

PHP

You can create a SAX-style parser with the function `xml_parser_create`, and a pull parser with the `XMLReader` extension. The `DOM` PHP extension (included in PHP 5) provides a tree-style interface to the GNOME project's libxml2 C library. You might have an easier time using SimpleXML, a tree-style parser that's not an official DOM implementation. That's what I used in Example 2-8.

There's also a pure PHP DOM parser called DOMIT! (*http://sourceforge.net/projects/domit-xmlparser*).

JavaScript: responseXML

If you're using `XMLHttpRequest` to write an Ajax client, you don't have to worry about the XML parser at all. If you make a request and the response entity-body is in XML format, the web browser parses it with its own tree-style parser, and makes it available through the `responseXML` property of the `XMLHttpRequest` object. You manipulate this document with JavaScript DOM methods: the same ones you use to manipulate HTML documents displayed in the browser. Chapter 11 has more information on how to use `responseXML`—and how to handle non-XML documents with the `responseData` member.

There's a third-party XML parser, XML for <SCRIPT> (*http://xmljs.sourceforge.net/*), which works independently of the parser built into the client's web browser. "XML for <SCRIPT>" offers DOM and SAX interfaces, and supports XPath queries.

Other Languages

ActionScript

When you load a URI with `XML.load`, it's automatically parsed into an `XML` object, which exposes a tree-style interface.

C

Expat (*http://expat.sourceforge.net/*) is the most popular SAX-style parser. The GNOME project's libxml2 (*http://xmlsoft.org/*) contains DOM, pull, and SAX parsers.

C++

You can use either of the C parsers, or the object-oriented Xerces-C++ parser (*http://xml.apache.org/xerces-c/*). Like the Java version of Xerces, Xerces-C++ exposes both DOM and SAX interfaces.

Common Lisp

Use SXML (*http://common-lisp.net/project/s-xml/*). It exposes a SAX-like interface, and can also turn an XML document into tree-like S-expressions or Lisp data structures.

Perl

As with Python, there are a variety of XML parsers for Perl. They're all available on CPAN. `XML::XPath` has XPath support, and `XML::Simple` turns an XML document into standard Perl data structures. For SAX-style parsing, use `XML::SAX::PurePerl`. For pull parsing, use `XML::LibXML::Reader`. The Perl XML FAQ (*http://perl-xml.sourceforge.net/faq/*) has an overview of the most popular Perl XML libraries.

JSON Parsers: Handling Serialized Data

Most web services return XML documents, but a growing number return simple data structures (numbers, arrays, hashes, and so on), serialized as JSON-formatted strings. JSON is usually produced by services that expect to be consumed by the client half of an Ajax application. The idea is that it's a lot easier for a browser to get a JavaScript data structure from a JSON data structure than from an XML document. Every web browser offers a slightly different JavaScript interface to its XML parser, but a JSON string is nothing but a tightly constrained JavaScript program, so it works the same way in every browser.

Of course, JSON is not *tied* to JavaScript, any more than JavaScript is to Java. JSON makes a lightweight alternative to XML-based approaches to data serialization, like XML Schema. The JSON web site (*http://www.json.org/*) links to implementations in many languages, and I refer you to that site rather than mentioning a JSON library for every language.

JSON is a simple and language-independent way of formatting programming language data structures (numbers, arrays, hashes, and so on) as strings. Example 2-11 is a JSON representation of a simple data structure: a mixed-type array.

Example 2-11. A mixed-type array in JSON format

```
[3, "three"]
```

By comparison, Example 2-12 is one possible XML representation of the same data.

Example 2-12. A mixed-type array in XML-RPC format

```
<value>
 <array>
  <data>
   <value><i4>3</i4></value>
   <value><string>three</string></value>
  </data>
 </array>
</value>
```

Since a JSON string is nothing but a tightly constrained JavaScript program, you can "parse" JSON simply by calling **eval** on the string. This is very fast, but you shouldn't do it unless you control the web service that served your JSON. An untested or untrusted web service can send the client buggy or malicious JavaScript programs instead of real JSON structures. For the JavaScript examples in Chapter 11, I use a JSON parser written in JavaScript and available from *json.org* (see Example 2-13).

Example 2-13. A JSON demo in JavaScript

```
<!-- json-demo.html -->
<!-- In a real application, you would save json.js locally
     instead of fetching it from json.org every time. -->
<script type="text/javascript" src="http://www.json.org/json.js">
</script>

<script type="text/javascript">
 array = [3, "three"]
 alert("Converted array into JSON string: '" + array.toJSONString() + "'")
  json = "[4, \"four\"]"
 alert("Converted JSON '" + json + "' into array:")
 array2 = json.parseJSON()
 for (i=0; i < array2.length; i++)
 {
   alert("Element #" + i + " is " + array2[i])
 }
</script>
```

The Dojo JavaScript framework has a JSON library in the **dojo.json** package, so if you're using Dojo you don't have to install anything extra. A future version of the

ECMAScript standard may define JSON serialization and deserialization methods as part of the JavaScript language, making third-party libraries obsolete.

In this book's Ruby examples, I'll use the JSON parser that comes from the `json` Ruby gem. The two most important methods are `Object#to_json` and `JSON.parse`. Try running the Ruby code in Example 2-14 through the `irb` interpreter.

Example 2-14. A JSON demo in Ruby

```ruby
# json-demo.rb
require 'rubygems'
require 'json'

[3, "three"].to_json            # => "[3,\"three\"]"
JSON.parse('[4, "four"]')       # => [4, "four"]
```

Right now, Yahoo! Web Services are the most popular public web services to serve JSON (*http://developer.yahoo.com/common/json.html*). Example 2-15 shows a command-line program, written in Ruby, that uses the Yahoo! News web service to get a JSON representation of current news stories.

Example 2-15. Searching the Web with Yahoo!'s web service (JSON edition)

```ruby
#!/usr/bin/ruby
# yahoo-web-search-json.rb
require 'rubygems'
require 'json'
require 'open-uri'
$KCODE = 'UTF8'

# Search the web for a term, and print the titles of matching web pages.
def search(term)
  base_uri = 'http://api.search.yahoo.com/NewsSearchService/V1/newsSearch'

  # Make the HTTP request and read the response entity-body as a JSON
  # document.
  json = open(base_uri + "?appid=restbook&output=json&query=#{term}").read

  # Parse the JSON document into a Ruby data structure.
  json = JSON.parse(json)

  # Iterate over the data structure...
  json['ResultSet']['Result'].each do
    # ...and print the title of each web page.
    |r| puts r['Title']
  end
end

# Main program.
unless ARGV[0]
  puts "Usage: #{$0} [search term]"
  exit
end
search(ARGV[0])
```

Compare this to the program *yahoo-web-search.rb* in Example 2-1. That program has the same basic structure, but it works differently. It asks for search results formatted as XML, parses the XML, and uses an XPath query to extract the result titles. This program parses a JSON data structure into a native-language data structure (a hash), and traverses it with native-language operators instead of XPath.

If JSON is so simple, why not use it for everything? You could do that, but I don't recommend it. JSON is good for representing data structures in general, and the Web mainly serves *documents*: irregular, self-describing data structures that link to each other. XML and HTML are specialized for representing documents. A JSON representation of a web page would be hard to read, just like the XML representation of an array in Example 2-12 was hard to read. JSON is useful when you need to describe a data structure that doesn't fit easily into the document paradigm: a simple list, for instance, or a hash.

Clients Made Easy with WADL

So far I've presented code in a variety of languages, but it always follows the same three-step pattern. To call a web service I build up the elements of an HTTP request (method, URI, headers, and entity-body). I use an HTTP library to turn that data into a real HTTP request, and the library sends the request to the appropriate server. Then I use an XML parser to parse the response into a data structure or a series of events. Once I make the request, I'm free to use the response data however I like. In this regard all RESTful web services, and most hybrid services, are the same. What's more, as I'll show in the chapters to come, all RESTful web services use HTTP the same way: HTTP has what's called a uniform interface.

Can I take advantage of this similarity? Abstract this pattern out into a generic "REST library" that can access any web service that supports the uniform interface? There's precedent for this. The Web Service Description Language (WSDL) describes the differences between RPC-style web services in enough detail that a generic library can access any RPC-style SOAP service, given an appropriate WSDL file.

For RESTful and hybrid services, I recommend using the Web *Application* Description Language. A WADL file describes the HTTP requests you can legitimately make of a service: which URIs you can visit, what data those URIs expect you to send, and what data they serve in return. A WADL library can parse this file and model the space of possible service requests as a native language API.

I describe WADL in more detail in Chapter 9, but here's a taste. The del.icio.us client shown in Example 2-16 is equivalent to the Ruby client in Example 2-4, but it uses Ruby's WADL library and a bootleg WADL file I created for del.icio.us. (I'll show you the WADL file in Chapter 8.)

Example 2-16. A Ruby/WADL client for del.icious

```ruby
#!/usr/bin/ruby
# delicious-wadl-ruby.rb
require 'wadl'

if ARGV.size != 2
  puts "Usage: #{$0} [username] [password]"
  exit
end
username, password = ARGV

# Load an application from the WADL file
delicious = WADL::Application.from_wadl(open("delicious.wadl"))

# Give authentication information to the application
service = delicious.v1.with_basic_auth(username, password)

begin
  # Find the "recent posts" functionality
  recent_posts = service.posts.recent

  # For every recent post...
  recent_posts.get.representation.each_by_param('post') do |post|
    # Print its description and URI.
    puts "#{post.attributes['description']}: #{post.attributes['href']}"
  end
rescue WADL::Faults::AuthorizationRequired
  puts "Invalid authentication information!"
end
```

Behind the scenes, this code makes exactly the same HTTP request as the other del.icio.us clients seen in this chapter. The details are hidden in the WADL file *delicious.wadl*, which is interpreted by the WADL client library inside `WADL::Application.from_WADL`. This code is not immediately recognizable as a web service client. That's a good thing: it means the library is doing its job. And yet, when we come back to this code in Chapter 9, you'll see that it follows the principles of REST as much as the examples that made their own HTTP requests. WADL abstracts away the details of HTTP, but not the underlying RESTful interface.

As of the time of writing, WADL adoption is very poor. If you want to use a WADL client for a service, instead of writing a language-specific client, you'll probably have to write the WADL file yourself. It's not difficult to write a bootleg WADL file for someone else's service: I've done it for del.icio.us and a few other services. You can even write a WADL file that lets you use a web application—designed for human use —as a web service. WADL is designed to describe RESTful web services, but it can describe almost anything that goes on the Web.

A Ruby library called ActiveResource takes a different strategy. It only works with certain kinds of web services, but it hides the details of RESTful HTTP access behind a simple object-oriented interface. I cover ActiveResource in the next chapter, after introducing some REST terminology.

## CHAPTER 3

What Makes RESTful Services Different?

I pulled a kind of bait-and-switch on you earlier, and it's time to make things right. Though this is a book about RESTful web services, most of the real services I've shown you are REST-RPC hybrids like the del.icio.us API: services that don't quite work like the rest of the Web. This is because right now, there just aren't many well-known RESTful services that work like the Web. In previous chapters I wanted to show you clients for real services you might have heard of, so I had to take what I could get.

The del.icio.us and Flickr APIs are good examples of hybrid services. They work like the Web when you're fetching data, but they're RPC-style services when it comes time to modify the data. The various Yahoo! search services are very RESTful, but they're so simple that they don't make good examples. The Amazon E-Commerce Service (seen in Example 1-2) is also quite simple, and defects the RPC style on a few obscure but important points.

These services are all useful. I think the RPC style is the wrong one for web services, but that never prevents me from writing an RPC-style client if there's interesting data on the other side. I can't use Flickr or the del.icio.us API as examples of how to *design* RESTful web services, though. That's why I covered them early in the book, when the only thing I was trying to show was what's on the programmable web and how to write HTTP clients. Now that we're approaching a heavy design chapter, I need to show you what a service looks like when it's RESTful and resource-oriented.

Introducing the Simple Storage Service

Two popular web services can answer this call: the Atom Publishing Protocol (APP), and Amazon's Simple Storage Service (S3). (Appendix A lists some publicly deployed RESTful web services, many of which you may not have heard of.) The APP is less an actual service than a set of instructions for building a service, so I'm going to start with S3, which actually exists at a specific place on the Web. In Chapter 9 I discuss the APP,

Atom, and related topics like Google's GData. For much of the rest of this chapter, I'll explore S3.

S3 is a way of storing any data you like, structured however you like. You can keep your data private, or make it accessible by anyone with a web browser or BitTorrent client. Amazon hosts the storage and the bandwidth, and charges you by the gigabyte for both. To use the example S3 code in this chapter, you'll need to sign up for the S3 service by going to *http://aws.amazon.com/s3*. The S3 technical documentation is at *http://docs.amazonwebservices.com/AmazonS3/2006-03-01/*.

There are two main uses for S3, as a:

Backup server
> You store your data through S3 and don't give anyone else access to it. Rather than buying your own backup disks, you're renting disk space from Amazon.

Data host
> You store your data on S3 and give others access to it. Amazon serves your data through HTTP or BitTorrent. Rather than paying an ISP for bandwidth, you're paying Amazon. Depending on your existing bandwidth costs this can save you a lot of money. Many of today's web startups use S3 to serve data files.

Unlike the services I've shown so far, S3 is not inspired by any existing web site. The del.icio.us API is based on the del.icio.us web site, and the Yahoo! search services are based on corresponding web sites, but there's no web page on *amazon.com* where you fill out HTML forms to upload your files to S3. S3 is intended only for programmatic use. (Of course, if you use S3 as a data host, people will use it through their web browsers, without even knowing they're making a web service call. It'll act like a normal web site.)

Amazon provides sample libraries for Ruby, Python, Java, C#, and Perl (see *http://developer.amazonwebservices.com/connect/kbcategory.jspa?categoryID=47*). There are also third-party libraries, like Ruby's AWS::S3 (*http://amazon.rubyforge.org/*), which includes the s3sh shell I demonstrated back in Example 1-4.

Object-Oriented Design of S3

S3 is based on two concepts: S3 "buckets" and S3 "objects." An object is a named piece of data with some accompanying metadata. A bucket is a named container for objects. A bucket is analogous to the filesystem on your hard drive, and an object to one of the files on that filesystem. It's tempting to compare a bucket to a *directory* on a filesystem, but filesystem directories can be nested and buckets can't. If you want a directory structure inside your bucket, you need to simulate one by giving your objects names like "directory/subdirectory/file-object."

A Few Words About Buckets

A bucket has one piece of information associated with it: the name. A bucket name can only contain the characters A through Z, a through z, 0 through 9, underscore, period, and dash. I recommend staying away from uppercase letters in bucket names.

As I mentioned above, buckets cannot contain other buckets: only objects. Each S3 user is limited to 100 buckets, and your bucket name cannot conflict with anyone else's. I recommend you either keep everything in one bucket, or name each bucket after one of your projects or domain names.

A Few Words About Objects

An object has four parts to it:

- A reference to the parent bucket.
- The data stored in that object (S3 calls this the "value").
- A name (S3 calls it the "key").
- A set of metadata key-value pairs associated with the object. This is mostly custom metadata, but it may also include values for the standard HTTP headers `Content-Type` and `Content-Disposition`.

If I wanted to host the O'Reilly web site on S3, I'd create a bucket called "oreilly.com," and fill it with objects whose keys were "" (the empty string), "catalog," "catalog/9780596529260," and so on. These objects correspond to the URIs *http://oreilly.com/*, *http://oreilly.com/catalog*, and so on. The object's values would be the HTML contents of O'Reilly's web pages. These S3 objects would have their `Content-Type` metadata value set to `text/html`, so that people browsing the site would be served these objects as HTML documents, as opposed to XML or plain text.

What If S3 Was a Standalone Library?

If S3 was implemented as an object-oriented code library instead of a web service, you'd have two classes `S3Bucket` and `S3Object`. They'd have getter and setter methods for their data members: `S3Bucket#name`, `Object.value=`, `S3Bucket#addObject`, and the like. The `S3Bucket` class would have an instance method `S3Bucket#getObjects` that returned a list of `S3Object` instances, and a class method `S3Bucket.getBuckets` that returned all of your buckets. Example 3-1 shows what the Ruby code for this class might look like.

Example 3-1. S3 implemented as a hypothetical Ruby library

```ruby
class S3Bucket
  # A class method to fetch all of your buckets.
  def self.getBuckets
  end

  # An instance method to fetch the objects in a bucket.
```

```
    def getObjects
    end
    ...
  end

  class S3Object
    # Fetch the data associated with this object.
    def data
    end

    # Set the data associated with this object.
    def data=(new_value)
    end
    ...
  end
```

Resources

Amazon exposes S3 as two different web services: a RESTful service based on plain HTTP envelopes, and an RPC-style service based on SOAP envelopes. The RPC-style service exposes functions much like the methods in Example 3-1's hypothetical Ruby library: ListAllMyBuckets, CreateBucket, and so on. Indeed, many RPC-style web services are automatically generated from their implementation methods, and expose the same interfaces as the programming-language code they call behind the scenes. This works because most modern programming (including object-oriented programming) is procedural.

The RESTful S3 service exposes all the functionality of the RPC-style service, but instead of doing it with custom-named functions, it exposes standard HTTP objects called *resources*. Instead of responding to custom method names like getObjects, a resource responds to one or more of the six standard HTTP methods: GET, HEAD, POST, PUT, DELETE, and OPTIONS.

The RESTful S3 service provides three types of resources. Here they are, with sample URIs for each:

- The list of your buckets (https://s3.amazonaws.com/). There's only one resource of this type.

- A particular bucket (https://s3.amazonaws.com/{*name-of-bucket*}/). There can be up to 100 resources of this type.

- A particular S3 object inside a bucket (https://s3.amazonaws.com/{*name-of-bucket*}/{*name-of-object*}). There can be infinitely many resources of this type.

Each method from my hypothetical object-oriented S3 library corresponds to one of the six standard methods on one of these three types of resources. The getter method S3Object#name corresponds to a GET request on an "S3 object" resource, and the setter method S3Object#value= corresponds to a PUT request on the same resource. Factory methods like `S3Bucket.getBuckets` and relational methods like `S3Bucket#getObjects` correspond to GET methods on the "bucket list" and "bucket" resources.

Every resource exposes the same interface and works the same way. To get an object's value you send a GET request to that object's URI. To get only the metadata for an object you send a HEAD request to the same URI. To create a bucket, you send a PUT request to a URI that incorporates the name of the bucket. To add an object to a bucket, you send PUT to a URI that incorporates the bucket name and object name. To delete a bucket or an object, you send a DELETE request to its URI.

The S3 designers didn't just make this up. According to the HTTP standard this is what GET, HEAD, PUT, and DELETE are *for*. These four methods (plus POST and OP-TIONS, which S3 doesn't use) suffice to describe *all* interaction with resources on the Web. To expose your programs as web services, you don't need to invent new vocabularies or smuggle method names into URIs, or do anything except think carefully about your resource design. Every REST web service, no matter how complex, supports the same basic operations. All the complexity lives in the resources.

Table 3-1 shows what happens when you send an HTTP request to the URI of an S3 resource.

Table 3-1. S3 resources and their methods

	GET	HEAD	PUT	DELETE
The bucket list (/)	List your buckets	-	-	-
A bucket (/{bucket})	List the bucket's objects	-	Create the bucket	Delete the bucket
An object (/{bucket}/{object})	Get the object's value and metadata	Get the object's metadata	Set the object's value and metadata	Delete the object

That table looks kind of ridiculous. Why did I take up valuable space by printing it? Everything just does what it says. And *that* is why I printed it. In a well-designed REST-ful service, *everything does what it says*.

You may well be skeptical of this claim, given the evidence so far. S3 is a pretty generic service. If all you're doing is sticking data into named slots, then of course you can implement the service using only generic verbs like GET and PUT. In Chapter 5 and Chapter 6 I'll show you strategies for mapping *any* kind of action to the uniform interface. For a sample preconvincing, note that I was able to get rid of `S3Bucket.getBuckets` by defining a new resource as "the list of buckets," which responds only to GET. Also note that `S3Bucket#addObject` simply disappeared as a natural consequence of the resource design, which requires that every object be associated with some bucket.

Compare this to S3's RPC-style SOAP interface. To get the bucket list through SOAP, the method name is `ListAllMyBuckets`. To get the contents of a bucket, the method name is `ListBucket`. With the RESTful interface, it's always GET. In a RESTful service, the URI designates an object (in the object-oriented sense) and the method names are standardized. The same few methods work the same way across resources and services.

HTTP Response Codes

Another defining feature of a RESTful architecture is its use of HTTP response codes. If you send a request to S3, and S3 handles it with no problem, you'll probably get back an HTTP response code of 200 ("OK"), just like when you successfully fetch a web page in your browser. If something goes wrong, the response code will be in the 3xx, 4xx, or 5xx range: for instance, 500 ("Internal Server Error"). An error response code is a signal to the client that the metadata and entity-body should not be interpreted as a response to the request. It's not what the client asked for: it's the server's attempt to tell the client about a problem. Since the response code isn't part of the document or the metadata, the client can see whether or not an error occurred just by looking at the first three bytes of the response.

Example 3-2 shows a sample error response. I made an HTTP request for an object that didn't exist (`https://s3.amazonaws.com/crummy.com/nonexistent/object`). The response code is 404 ("Not Found").

Example 3-2. A sample error response from S3

```
404 Not Found
Content-Type: application/xml
Date: Fri, 10 Nov 2006 20:04:45 GMT
Server: AmazonS3
Transfer-Encoding: chunked
X-amz-id-2: /sBIPQxHJCsyRXJwGWNzxuL5P+K96/Wvx4FhvVACbjRfNbhbDyBH5RC511sIzOwO
X-amz-request-id: ED2168503ABB7BF4

<?xml version="1.0" encoding="UTF-8"?>
<Error>
 <Code>NoSuchKey</Code>
 <Message>The specified key does not exist.</Message>
 <Key>nonexistent/object</Key>
 <RequestId>ED2168503ABB7BF4</RequestId>
 <HostId>/sBIPQxHJCsyRXJwGWNzxuL5P+K96/Wvx4FhvVACbjRfNbhbDyBH5RC511sIzOwO</HostId>
</Error>
```

HTTP response codes are underused on the human web. Your browser doesn't show you the HTTP response code when you request a page, because who wants to look at a numeric code when you can just look at the document to see whether something went wrong? When an error occurs in a web application, most web applications send 200 ("OK") along with a human-readable document that talks about the error. There's very little chance a human will mistake the error document for the document they requested.

On the programmable web, it's just the opposite. Computer programs are good at taking different paths based on the value of a numeric variable, and very bad at figuring out what a document "means." In the absence of prearranged rules, there's no way for a program to tell whether an XML document contains data or describes an error. HTTP response codes are the rules: rough conventions about how the client should approach an HTTP response. Because they're not part of the entity-body or metadata, a client can understand what happened even if it has no clue how to read the response.

S3 uses a variety of response codes in addition to 200 ("OK") and 404 ("Not Found"). The most common is probably 403 ("Forbidden"), used when the client makes a request without providing the right credentials. S3 also uses a few others, including 400 ("Bad Request"), which indicates that the server couldn't understand the data the client sent; and 409 ("Conflict"), sent when the client tries to delete a bucket that's not empty. For a full list, see the S3 technical documentation under "The REST Error Response." I describe *every* HTTP response code in Appendix B, with a focus on their application to web services. There are 39 official HTTP response codes, but only about 10 are important in everyday use.

An S3 Client

The Amazon sample libraries, and the third-party contributions like AWS::S3, eliminate much of the need for custom S3 client libraries. But I'm not telling you about S3 just so you'll know about a useful web service. I want to use it to illustrate the theory behind REST. So I'm going to write a Ruby S3 client of my own, and dissect it for you as I go along.

Just to show it can be done, my library will implement an object-oriented interface, like the one from Example 3-1, on top of the S3 service. The result will look like ActiveRecord or some other object-relational mapper. Instead of making SQL calls under the covers to store data in a database, though, it'll make HTTP requests under the covers to store data on the S3 service. Rather than give my methods resource-specific names like getBuckets and getObjects, I'll try to use names that reflect the underlying RESTful interface: get, put, and so on.

The first thing I need is an interface to Amazon's rather unusual web service authorization mechanism. But that's not as interesting as seeing the web service in action, so I'm going to skip it for now. I'm going to create a very small Ruby module called S3::Authorized, just so my other S3 classes can include it. I'll come back to it at the end, and fill in the details.

Example 3-3 shows a bit of throat-clearing code.

Example 3-3. S3 Ruby client: Initial code

```
#!/usr/bin/ruby -w
# S3lib.rb

# Libraries neccessary for making HTTP requests and parsing responses.
require 'rubygems'
require 'rest-open-uri'
```

```
require 'rexml/document'

# Libraries neccessary for request signing
require 'openssl'
require 'digest/sha1'
require 'base64'
require 'uri'

module S3 # This is the beginning of a big, all-encompassing module.

module Authorized
  # Enter your public key (Amazon calls it an "Access Key ID") and
  # your private key (Amazon calls it a "Secret Access Key"). This is
  # so you can sign your S3 requests and Amazon will know who to
  # charge.
  @@public_key = ''
  @@private_key = ''

  if @@public_key.empty? or @@private_key.empty?
    raise "You need to set your S3 keys."
  end

  # You shouldn't need to change this unless you're using an S3 clone like
  # Park Place.
  HOST = 'https://s3.amazonaws.com/'
end
```

The only interesting aspect of this bare-bones S3::Authorized is that it's where you should plug in the two cryptographic keys associated with your Amazon Web Services account. Every S3 request you make includes your public key (Amazon calls it an "Access Key ID") so that Amazon can identify you. Every request you make must be cryptographically signed with your private key (Amazon calls it a "Secret Access Key") so that Amazon knows it's really you. I'm using the standard cryptographic terms, even though your "private key" is not totally private—Amazon knows it too. It is private in the sense that you should never reveal it to anyone else. If you do, the person you reveal it to will be able to make S3 requests and have Amazon charge you for it.

The Bucket List

Example 3-4 shows an object-oriented class for my first resource, the list of buckets. I'll call the class for this resource S3::BucketList.

Example 3-4. S3 Ruby client: the S3::BucketList class

```
# The bucket list.
class BucketList
  include Authorized

  # Fetch all the buckets this user has defined.
  def get
    buckets = []
```

```
# GET the bucket list URI and read an XML document from it.
doc = REXML::Document.new(open(HOST).read)

# For every bucket...
REXML::XPath.each(doc, "//Bucket/Name") do |e|
  # ...create a new Bucket object and add it to the list.
  buckets << Bucket.new(e.text) if e.text
end
return buckets
  end
end
```

XPath Exposition

Reading from right to left, the XPath expression //Bucket/Name means:

Find every Name tag	Name
that's the direct child of a Bucket tag	Bucket/
anywhere in the document.	//

Now my file is a real web service client. If I call S3::BucketList#get I make a secure HTTP GET request to *https://s3.amazonaws.com/*, which happens to be the URI of the resource "a list of your buckets." The S3 service sends back an XML document that looks something like Example 3-5. This is a *representation* (as I'll start calling it in the next chapter) of the resource "a list of your buckets." It's just some information about the current state of that list. The Owner tag makes it clear whose bucket list it is (my AWS account name is evidently "leonardr28"), and the Buckets tag contains a number of Bucket tags describing my buckets (in this case, there's one Bucket tag and one bucket).

Example 3-5. A sample "list of your buckets"
```
<?xml version='1.0' encoding='UTF-8'?>
<ListAllMyBucketsResult xmlns='http://s3.amazonaws.com/doc/2006-03-01/'>
 <Owner>
  <ID>c0363f7260f2f5fcf38d48039f4fb5cab21b060577817310be5170e7774aad70</ID>
  <DisplayName>leonardr28</DisplayName>
 </Owner>
 <Buckets>
  <Bucket>
   <Name>crummy.com</Name>
   <CreationDate>2006-10-26T18:46:45.000Z</CreationDate>
  </Bucket>
 </Buckets>
</ListAllMyBucketsResult>
```

For purposes of this small client application, the Name is the only aspect of a bucket I'm interested in. The XPath expression //Bucket/Name gives me the name of every bucket, which is all I need to create Bucket objects.

As we'll see, one thing that's missing from this XML document is *links*. The document gives the name of every bucket, but says nothing about where the buckets can be found on the Web. In terms of the REST design criteria, this is the major shortcoming of Amazon S3. Fortunately, it's not too difficult to program a client to calculate a URI from the bucket name. I just follow the rule I gave earlier: `https://s3.amazonaws.com/{name-of-bucket}`.

The Bucket

Now, as shown in Example 3-6, let's write the `S3::Bucket` class, so that `S3::BucketList.get` will have something to instantiate.

Example 3-6. S3 Ruby client: the S3::Bucket class

```
# A bucket that you've stored (or will store) on the S3 application.
class Bucket
  include Authorized
  attr_accessor :name

  def initialize(name)
    @name = name
  end

  # The URI to a bucket is the service root plus the bucket name.
  def uri
    HOST + URI.escape(name)
  end

  # Stores this bucket on S3. Analagous to ActiveRecord::Base#save,
  # which stores an object in the database. See below in the
  # book text for a discussion of acl_policy.
  def put(acl_policy=nil)
    # Set the HTTP method as an argument to open(). Also set the S3
    # access policy for this bucket, if one was provided.
    args = {:method => :put}
    args["x-amz-acl"] = acl_policy if acl_policy

    # Send a PUT request to this bucket's URI.
    open(uri, args)
    return self
  end

  # Deletes this bucket. This will fail with HTTP status code 409
  # ("Conflict") unless the bucket is empty.
  def delete
    # Send a DELETE request to this bucket's URI.
    open(uri, :method => :delete)
  end
```

Here are two more web service methods: `S3::Bucket#put` and `S3::Bucket#delete`. Since the URI to a bucket uniquely identifies the bucket, deletion is simple: you send a DELETE request to the bucket URI, and it's gone. Since a bucket's name goes into its URI, and a bucket has no other settable properties, it's also easy to create a bucket: just send a PUT request to its URI. As I'll show when I write `S3::Object`, a PUT request is more complicated when not all the data can be stored in the URI.

Earlier I compared my `S3::` classes to ActiveRecord classes, but `S3::Bucket#put` works a little differently from an ActiveRecord implementation of **save**. A row in an Active-Record-controlled database table has a numeric unique ID. If you take an ActiveRecord object with ID 23 and change its name, your change is reflected as a change to the database record with ID 23:

```
SET name="newname" WHERE id=23
```

The permanent ID of an S3 bucket is its URI, and the URI includes the name. If you change the name of a bucket and call **put**, the client doesn't rename the old bucket on S3: it creates a new, empty bucket at a new URI with the new name. This is a result of design decisions made by the S3 programmers. It doesn't have to be this way. The Ruby on Rails framework has a different design: when it exposes database rows through a RESTful web service, the URI to a row incorporates its numeric database IDs. If S3 was a Rails service you'd see buckets at URIs like **/buckets/23**. Renaming the bucket wouldn't change the URI.

Now comes the last method of `S3::Bucket`, which I've called **get**. Like `S3::BucketList.get`, this method makes a GET request to the URI of a resource (in this case, a "bucket" resource), fetches an XML document, and parses it into new instances of a Ruby class (see Example 3-7). This method supports a variety of ways to filter the contents of S3 buckets. For instance, you can use **:Prefix** to retrieve only objects whose keys start with a certain string. I won't cover these filtering options in detail. If you're interested in them, see the S3 technical documentation on "Listing Keys."

Example 3-7. S3 Ruby client: the S3::Bucket class (concluded)

```
# Get the objects in this bucket: all of them, or some subset.
#
# If S3 decides not to return the whole bucket/subset, the second
# return value will be set to true. To get the rest of the objects,
# you'll need to manipulate the subset options (not covered in the
# book text).
#
# The subset options are :Prefix, :Marker, :Delimiter, :MaxKeys.
# For details, see the S3 docs on "Listing Keys".
def get(options={})
  # Get the base URI to this bucket, and append any subset options
  # onto the query string.
  uri = uri()
  suffix = '?'

  # For every option the user provided...
  options.each do |param, value|
    # ...if it's one of the S3 subset options...
    if [:Prefix, :Marker, :Delimiter, :MaxKeys].member? :param
      # ...add it to the URI.
      uri << suffix << param.to_s << '=' << URI.escape(value)
```

```
      suffix = '&'
    end
  end

  # Now we've built up our URI. Make a GET request to that URI and
  # read an XML document that lists objects in the bucket.
  doc = REXML::Document.new(open(uri).read)
  there_are_more = REXML::XPath.first(doc, "//IsTruncated").text == "true"

  # Build a list of S3::Object objects.
  objects = []
  # For every object in the bucket...
  REXML::XPath.each(doc, "//Contents/Key") do |e|
    # ...build an S3::Object object and append it to the list.
    objects << Object.new(self, e.text) if e.text
  end
  return objects, there_are_more
  end
end
```

XPath Exposition

Reading from right to left, the XPath expression //IsTruncated means:

Find every IsTruncated tag	IsTruncated
anywhere in the document.	//

Make a GET request of the application's root URI, and you get a representation of the resource "a list of your buckets." Make a GET request to the URI of a "bucket" resource, and you get a representation of the bucket: an XML document like the one in Example 3-8, containing a Contents tag for every element of the bucket.

Example 3-8. A sample bucket representation

```
<?xml version='1.0' encoding='UTF-8'?>
<ListBucketResult xmlns="http://s3.amazonaws.com/doc/2006-03-01/">
 <Name>crummy.com</Name>
 <Prefix></Prefix>
 <Marker></Marker>
 <MaxKeys>1000</MaxKeys>
 <IsTruncated>false</IsTruncated>
 <Contents>
  <Key>mydocument</Key>
  <LastModified>2006-10-27T16:01:19.000Z</LastModified>
  <ETag>"93bede57fd3818f93eedce0def329cc7"</ETag>
  <Size>22</Size>
  <Owner>
   <ID>
    c0363f7260f2f5fcf38d48039f4fb5cab21b060577817310be5170e7774aad70</ID>
    <DisplayName>leonardr28</DisplayName>
  </Owner>
```

```
<StorageClass>STANDARD</StorageClass>
  </Contents>
</ListBucketResult>
```

In this case, the portion of the document I find interesting is the list of a bucket's objects. An object is identified by its key, and I use the XPath expression "//Contents/Key" to fetch that information. I'm also interested in a certain Boolean variable ("//IsTruncated"): whether this document contains keys for every object in the bucket, or whether S3 decided there were too many to send in one document and truncated the list.

Again, the main thing missing from this representation is links. The document lists lots of information about the objects, but not their URIs. The client is expected to know how to turn an object name into that object's URI. Fortunately, it's not too hard to build an object's URI, using the rule I already gave: `https://s3.amazonaws.com/{name-of-bucket}/{name-of-object}`.

The S3 Object

Now we're ready to implement an interface to the core of the S3 service: the object. Remember that an S3 object is just a data string that's been given a name (a key) and a set of metadata key-value pairs (such as `Content-Type="text/html"`). When you send a GET request to the bucket list, or to a bucket, S3 serves an XML document that you have to parse. When you send a GET request to an object, S3 serves whatever data string you PUT there earlier—byte for byte.

Example 3-9 shows the beginning of `S3::Object`, which should be nothing new by now.

Example 3-9. S3 Ruby client: the S3::Object class

```
# An S3 object, associated with a bucket, containing a value and metadata.
class Object
  include Authorized

  # The client can see which Bucket this Object is in.
  attr_reader :bucket

  # The client can read and write the name of this Object.
  attr_accessor :name

  # The client can write this Object's metadata and value.
  # I'll define the corresponding "read" methods later.
  attr_writer :metadata, :value

  def initialize(bucket, name, value=nil, metadata=nil)
    @bucket, @name, @value, @metadata = bucket, name, value, metadata
  end

  # The URI to an Object is the URI to its Bucket, and then its name.
  def uri
    @bucket.uri + '/' + URI.escape(name)
  end
```

What comes next is my first implementation of an HTTP HEAD request. I use it to fetch an object's metadata key-value pairs and populate the *metadata* hash with it (the actual implementation of store_metadata comes at the end of this class). Since I'm using rest-open-uri, the code to make the HEAD request looks the same as the code to make any other HTTP request (see Example 3-10).

Example 3-10. S3 Ruby client: the S3::Object#metadata method

```ruby
# Retrieves the metadata hash for this Object, possibly fetching
# it from S3.
def metadata
  # If there's no metadata yet...
  unless @metadata
    # Make a HEAD request to this Object's URI, and read the metadata
    # from the HTTP headers in the response.
    begin
      store_metadata(open(uri, :method => :head).meta)
    rescue OpenURI::HTTPError => e
      if e.io.status == ["404", "Not Found"]
        # If the Object doesn't exist, there's no metadata and this is not
        # an error.
        @metadata = {}
      else
        # Otherwise, this is an error.
        raise e
      end
    end

  end
  return @metadata
end
```

The goal here is to fetch an object's metadata without fetching the object itself. This is the difference between downloading a movie review and downloading the movie, and when you're paying for the bandwidth it's a big difference. This distinction between metadata and representation is not unique to S3, and the solution is general to all resource-oriented web services. The HEAD method gives *any* client a way of fetching the metadata for *any* resource, without also fetching its (possibly enormous) representation.

Of course, sometimes you do want to download the movie, and for that you need a GET request. I've put the GET request in the accessor method S3::Object#value, in Example 3-11. Its structure mirrors that of S3::Object#metadata.

Example 3-11. S3 Ruby client: the S3::Object#value method

```ruby
# Retrieves the value of this Object, possibly fetching it
# (along with the metadata) from S3.
def value
  # If there's no value yet...
  unless @value
    # Make a GET request to this Object's URI.
    response = open(uri)
```

```
    # Read the metadata from the HTTP headers in the response.
    store_metadata(response.meta) unless @metadata
    # Read the value from the entity-body
    @value = response.read
  end
  return @value
end
```

The client stores objects on the S3 service the same way it stores buckets: by sending a PUT request to a certain URI. The bucket PUT is trivial because a bucket has no distinguishing features other than its name, which goes into the URI of the PUT request. An object PUT is more complex. This is where the HTTP client specifies an object's metadata (such as Content-Type) and value. This information will be made available on future HEAD and GET requests.

Fortunately, setting up the PUT request is not terribly complicated, because an object's value is whatever the client says it is. I don't have to wrap the object's value in an XML document or anything. I just send the data as is, and set HTTP headers that correspond to the items of metadata in my metadata hash (see Example 3-12).

Example 3-12. S3 Ruby client: the S3::Object#put method

```
# Store this Object on S3.
def put(acl_policy=nil)

  # Start from a copy of the original metadata, or an empty hash if
  # there is no metadata yet.
  args = @metadata ? @metadata.clone : {}

  # Set the HTTP method, the entity-body, and some additional HTTP
  # headers.
  args[:method] = :put
  args["x-amz-acl"] = acl_policy if acl_policy
  if @value
    args["Content-Length"] = @value.size.to_s
    args[:body] = @value
  end

  # Make a PUT request to this Object's URI.
  open(uri, args)
  return self
end
```

The S3::Object#delete implementation (see Example 3-13) is identical to S3::Bucket#delete.

Example 3-13. S3 Ruby client: the S3::Object#delete method

```
# Deletes this Object.
def delete
  # Make a DELETE request to this Object's URI.
  open(uri, :method => :delete)
end
```

And Example 3-14 shows the method for turning HTTP response headers into S3 object metadata. Except for `Content-Type`, you should prefix all the metadata headers you set with the string "x-amz-meta-". Otherwise they won't make the round trip to the S3 server and back to a web service client. S3 will think they're quirks of your client software and discard them.

Example 3-14. S3 Ruby client: the S3::Object#store_metadata method

```
private

# Given a hash of headers from a HTTP response, picks out the
# headers that are relevant to an S3 Object, and stores them in the
# instance variable @metadata.
def store_metadata(new_metadata)
  @metadata = {}
  new_metadata.each do |h,v|
    if RELEVANT_HEADERS.member?(h) || h.index('x-amz-meta') == 0
      @metadata[h] = v
    end
  end
end
RELEVANT_HEADERS = ['content-type', 'content-disposition', 'content-range',
                    'x-amz-missing-meta']
end
```

Request Signing and Access Control

I've put it off as long as I can, and now it's time to deal with S3 authentication. If your main interest is in RESTful services in general, feel free to skip ahead to the section on using the S3 library in clients. But if the inner workings of S3 have piqued your interest, read on.

The code I've shown you so far makes HTTP requests all right, but S3 rejects them, because they don't contain the all-important `Authorization` header. S3 has no proof that you're the owner of your own buckets. Remember, Amazon charges you for the data stored on their servers and the bandwidth used in transferring that data. If S3 accepted requests to your buckets with no authorization, anyone could store data in your buckets and you'd get charged for it.

Most web services that require authentication use a standard HTTP mechanism to make sure you are who you claim to be. But S3's needs are more complicated. With most web services you never want anyone else using your data. But one of the uses of S3 is as a hosting service. You might want to host a big movie file on S3, let anyone download it with their BitTorrent client, and have Amazon send you the bill.

Or you might be *selling* access to movie files stored on S3. Your e-commerce site takes payment from a customer and gives them an S3 URI they can use to download the movie. You're delegating to someone else the right to make a particular web service call (a GET request) as you, and have it charged to your account.

The standard mechanisms for HTTP authentication can't provide security for that kind of application. Normally, the person who's sending the HTTP request needs to know the actual password. You can prevent someone from spying on your password, but you can't say to someone else: "here's my password, but you must promise only to use it to request this one URI."

This is a job for public-key cryptography. Every time you make an S3 request, you use your "private" key (remember, not truly private: Amazon knows it too) to sign the important parts of the request. That'd be the URI, the HTTP method you're using, and a few of the HTTP headers. Only someone with the "private" key can create these signatures for your requests, which is how Amazon knows it's okay to charge you for the request. But once you've signed a request, you can send the signature to a third party without revealing your "private" key. The third party is then free to send an identical HTTP request to the one you signed, and have Amazon charge you for it. In short: someone else can make a specific request as you, for a limited time, without having to know your "private" key.

There is a simpler way to give anonymous access to your S3 objects, and I discuss it below. But there's no way around signing your own requests, so even a simple library like this one must support request signing if it's going to work. I'm reopening the `S3::Authorized` Ruby module now. I'm going to give it the ability to intercept calls to the `open` method, and sign HTTP requests before they're made. Since `S3::BucketList`, `S3::Bucket`, and `S3::Object` have all `included` this module, they'll inherit this ability as soon as I define it. Without the code I'm about to write, all those `open` calls I defined in the classes above will send unsigned HTTP requests that just bounce off S3 with response code 403 ("Forbidden"). With this code, you'll be able to generate signed HTTP requests that pass through S3's security measures (and cost you money). The code in Example 3-15 and the other examples that follow is heavily based on Amazon's own example S3 library.

Example 3-15. S3 Ruby client: the S3::Authorized module

```ruby
module Authorized
  # These are the standard HTTP headers that S3 considers interesting
  # for purposes of request signing.
  INTERESTING_HEADERS = ['content-type', 'content-md5', 'date']

  # This is the prefix for custom metadata headers. All such headers
  # are considered interesting for purposes of request signing.
  AMAZON_HEADER_PREFIX = 'x-amz-'

  # An S3-specific wrapper for rest-open-uri's implementation of
  # open(). This implementation sets some HTTP headers before making
  # the request. Most important of these is the Authorization header,
  # which contains the information Amazon will use to decide who to
  # charge for this request.
  def open(uri, headers_and_options={}, *args, &block)
    headers_and_options = headers_and_options.dup
    headers_and_options['Date'] ||= Time.now.httpdate
    headers_and_options['Content-Type'] ||= ''
```

```
      signed = signature(uri, headers_and_options[:method] || :get,
                          headers_and_options)
      headers_and_options['Authorization'] = "AWS #{@@public_key}:#{signed}"
      Kernel::open(uri, headers_and_options, *args, &block)
    end
```

The tough work here is in the signature method, not yet defined. This method needs to construct an encrypted string to go into a request's Authorization header: a string that convinces the S3 service that it's really you sending the request—or that you've authorized someone else to make the request at your expense (see Example 3-16).

Example 3-16. S3 Ruby client: the Authorized#signature module

```
    # Builds the cryptographic signature for an HTTP request. This is
    # the signature (signed with your private key) of a "canonical
    # string" containing all interesting information about the request.
    def signature(uri, method=:get, headers={}, expires=nil)
      # Accept the URI either as a string, or as a Ruby URI object.
      if uri.respond_to? :path
        path = uri.path
      else
        uri = URI.parse(uri)
        path = uri.path + (uri.query ? "?" + query : "")
      end

      # Build the canonical string, then sign it.
      signed_string = sign(canonical_string(method, path, headers, expires))
    end
```

Well, this method passes the buck again, by calling sign on the result of canonical_string. Let's look at those two methods, starting with canonical_string. It turns an HTTP request into a string that looks something like Example 3-17. That string contains everything interesting (from S3's point of view) about an HTTP request, in a specific format. The interesting data is the HTTP method (PUT), the Content-type ("text/plain"), a date, a few other HTTP headers ("x-amz-metadata"), and the path portion of the URI ("/crummy.com/myobject"). This is the string that sign will sign. Anyone can create this string, but only the S3 account holder and Amazon know how to produce the correct signature.

Example 3-17. The canonical string for a sample request

```
    PUT

    text/plain
    Fri, 27 Oct 2006 21:22:41 GMT
    x-amz-metadata:Here's some metadata for the myobject object.
    /crummy.com/myobject
```

When Amazon's server receives your HTTP request, it generates the canonical string, signs it (again, Amazon has a copy of your "private" key), and sees whether the two signatures match. That's how S3 authentication works. If the signatures match, your request goes through. Otherwise, you get a response code of 403 ("Forbidden").

Example 3-18 shows the code to generate the canonical string.

Example 3-18. S3 Ruby client: the Authorized#canonical_string method

```ruby
# Turns the elements of an HTTP request into a string that can be
# signed to prove a request comes from your web service account.
def canonical_string(method, path, headers, expires=nil)

  # Start out with default values for all the interesting headers.
  sign_headers = {}
  INTERESTING_HEADERS.each { |header| sign_headers[header] = '' }

  # Copy in any actual values, including values for custom S3
  # headers.
  headers.each do |header, value|
    if header.respond_to? :to_str
      header = header.downcase
      # If it's a custom header, or one Amazon thinks is interesting...
      if INTERESTING_HEADERS.member?(header) ||
          header.index(AMAZON_HEADER_PREFIX) == 0
        # Add it to the header has.
        sign_headers[header] = value.to_s.strip
      end
    end
  end

  # This library eliminates the need for the x-amz-date header that
  # Amazon defines, but someone might set it anyway. If they do,
  # we'll do without HTTP's standard Date header.
  sign_headers['date'] = '' if sign_headers.has_key? 'x-amz-date'

  # If an expiration time was provided, it overrides any Date
  # header. This signature will be valid until the expiration time,
  # not only during the single second designated by the Date header.
  sign_headers['date'] = expires.to_s if expires

  # Now we start building the canonical string for this request. We
  # start with the HTTP method.
  canonical = method.to_s.upcase + "\n"

  # Sort the headers by name, and append them (or just their values)
  # to the string to be signed.
  sign_headers.sort_by { |h| h[0] }.each do |header, value|
    canonical << header << ":" if header.index(AMAZON_HEADER_PREFIX) == 0
    canonical << value << "\n"
  end

  # The final part of the string to be signed is the URI path. We
  # strip off the query string, and (if neccessary) tack one of the
  # special S3 query parameters back on: 'acl', 'torrent', or
  # 'logging'.
  canonical << path.gsub(/\?.*$/, '')

  for param in ['acl', 'torrent', 'logging']
    if path =~ Regexp.new("[&?]#{param}($|&|=)")
      canonical << "?" << param
```

```
        break
      end
    end
    return canonical
  end
```

The implementation of **sign** is just a bit of plumbing around Ruby's standard crypto-graphic and encoding interfaces (see Example 3-19).

Example 3-19. S3 Ruby client: the Authorized#sign method

```
# Signs a string with the client's secret access key, and encodes the
# resulting binary string into plain ASCII with base64.
def sign(str)
  digest_generator = OpenSSL::Digest::Digest.new('sha1')
  digest = OpenSSL::HMAC.digest(digest_generator, @@private_key, str)
  return Base64.encode64(digest).strip
end
```

Signing a URI

My S3 library has one feature still to be implemented. I've mentioned a few times that S3 lets you sign an HTTP request and give the URI to someone else, letting them make that request as you. Here's the method that lets you do this: **signed_uri** (see Example 3-20). Instead of making an HTTP request with **open**, you pass the **open** arguments into this method, and it gives you a signed URI that anyone can use as you. To limit abuse, a signed URI works only for a limited time. You can customize that time by passing a **Time** object in as the keyword argument **:expires**.

Example 3-20. S3 Ruby client: the Authorized#signed_uri method

```
# Given information about an HTTP request, returns a URI you can
# give to anyone else, to let them them make that particular HTTP
# request as you. The URI will be valid for 15 minutes, or until the
# Time passed in as the :expires option.
def signed_uri(headers_and_options={})
  expires = headers_and_options[:expires] || (Time.now.to_i + (15 * 60))
  expires = expires.to_i if expires.respond_to? :to_i
  headers_and_options.delete(:expires)
  signature = URI.escape(signature(uri, headers_and_options[:method],
                                   headers_and_options, nil))
  q = (uri.index("?")) ? "&" : "?"
  "#{uri}#{q}Signature=#{signature}&Expires=#{expires}&AWSAccessKeyId=#{@@public_key}"
  end
end

end # Remember the all-encompassing S3 module? This is the end.
```

Here's how it works. Suppose I want to give a customer access to my hosted file at *https://s3.amazonaws.com/BobProductions/KomodoDragon.avi*. I can run the code in Example 3-21 to generate a URI for my customer.

Example 3-21. Generating a signed URI

```
#!/usr/bin/ruby1.9
# s3-signed-uri.rb
require 'S3lib'

bucket = S3::Bucket.new("BobProductions")
object = S3::Object.new(bucket, "KomodoDragon.avi")
puts object.signed_uri
# "https://s3.amazonaws.com/BobProductions/KomodoDragon.avi
# ?Signature=J%2Fu6kxT3jOzHaFXjsLbowgpzExQ%3D
# &Expires=1162156499&AWSAccessKeyId=OF9DBXKB5274JKTJ8DG2"
```

That URI will be valid for 15 minutes, the default for my `signed_uri` implementation. It incorporates my public key (`AWSAccessKeyId`), the expiration time (`Expires`), and the cryptographic `Signature`. My customer can visit this URI and download the movie file *KomodoDragon.avi*. Amazon will charge me for my customer's use of their bandwidth. If my customer modifies any part of the URI (maybe they to try to download a second movie too), the S3 service will reject their request. An untrustworthy customer can send the URI to all of their friends, but it will stop working in 15 minutes.

You may have noticed a problem here. The canonical string usually includes the value of the `Date` header. When my customer visits the URI you signed, their web browser will surely send a different value for the `Date` header. That's why, when you're generating a canonical string to give to someone else, you set an *expiration* date instead of a request date. Look back to Example 3-18 and the implementation of `canonical_string`, where the expiration date (if provided) overwrites any value for the `Date` header.

Setting Access Policy

What if I want to make an object publicly accessible? I want to serve my files to the world and let Amazon deal with the headaches of server management. Well, I could set an expiration date very far in the future, and give out the enormous signed URI to everyone. But there's an easier way to get the same results: allow anonymous access. You can do this by setting the *access policy* for a bucket or object, telling S3 to respond to unsigned requests for it. You do this by sending the `x-amz-acl` header along with the PUT request that creates the bucket or object.

That's what the `acl_policy` argument to `Bucket#put` and `Object#put` does. If you want to make a bucket or object publicly readable or writable, you pass an appropriate value in for `acl_policy`. My client sends that value as part of the custom HTTP request header `X-amz-acl`. Amazon S3 reads this request header and sets the rules for bucket or object access appropriately.

The client in Example 3-22 creates an S3 object that anyone can read by visiting its URI at `https://s3.amazonaws.com/BobProductions/KomodoDragon-Trailer.avi`. In this scenario, I'm not selling my movies: just using Amazon as a hosting service so I don't have to serve movies from my own web site.

Example 3-22. Creating a publicly-readable object

```
#!/usr/bin/ruby -w
# s3-public-object.rb
require 'S3lib'

bucket = S3::Bucket.new("BobProductions")
object = S3::Object.new(bucket, "KomodoDragon-Trailer.avi")
object.put("public-read")
```

S3 understands four access policies:

private

> The default. Only requests signed by your "private" key are accepted.

public-read

> Unsigned GET requests are accepted: anyone can download an object or list a bucket.

public-write

> Unsigned GET and PUT requests are accepted. Anyone can modify an object, or add objects to a bucket.

authenticated-read

> Unsigned requests are rejected, but read requests can be signed by the "private" key of *any* S3 user, not just your own. Basically, anyone with an S3 account can download your object or list your bucket.

There are also fine-grained ways of granting access to a bucket or object, which I won't cover. If you're interested, see the section "Setting Access Policy with REST" in the S3 technical documentation. That section reveals a parallel universe of extra resources. Every bucket /{name-of-bucket} has a shadow resource /{name-of-bucket}?acl corresponding to that bucket's access control rules, and every object /{name-of-bucket}/{name-of-object} has a shadow ACL resource /{name-of-bucket}/{name-of-object}?acl. By sending PUT requests to these URIs, and including XML representations of access control lists in the request entity-bodies, you can set specific permissions and limit access to particular S3 users.

Using the S3 Client Library

I've now shown you a Ruby client library that can access just about the full capabilities of Amazon's S3 service. Of course, a library is useless without clients that use it. In the previous section I showed you a couple of small clients to demonstrate points about security, but now I'd like to show something a little more substantial.

Example 3-23 is a simple command-line S3 client that can create a bucket and an object, then list the contents of the bucket. This client should give you a high-level picture of how S3's resources work together. I've annotated the lines of code that trigger HTTP requests, by describing the HTTP requests in comments off to the right.

Example 3-23. A sample S3 client

```ruby
#!/usr/bin/ruby -w
# s3-sample-client.rb
require 'S3lib'

# Gather command-line arguments
bucket_name, object_name, object_value = ARGV
unless bucket_name
  puts "Usage: #{$0} [bucket name] [object name] [object value]"
  exit
end

# Find or create the bucket.
buckets = S3::BucketList.new.get                 # GET /
bucket = buckets.detect { |b| b.name == bucket_name }
if bucket
  puts "Found bucket #{bucket_name}."
else
  puts "Could not find bucket #{bucket_name}, creating it."
  bucket = S3::Bucket.new(bucket_name)
  bucket.put                                     # PUT /{bucket}
end

# Create the object.
object = S3::Object.new(bucket, object_name)
object.metadata['content-type'] = 'text/plain'
object.value = object_value
object.put                                       # PUT /{bucket}/{object}

# For each object in the bucket...
bucket.get[0].each do |o|                         # GET /{bucket}
  # ...print out information about the object.
  puts "Name: #{o.name}"
  puts "Value: #{o.value}"                        # GET /{bucket}/{object}
  puts "Metadata hash: #{o.metadata.inspect}"
  puts
end
```

Clients Made Transparent with ActiveResource

Since all RESTful web services expose basically the same simple interface, it's not a big chore to write a custom client for every web service. It is a little wasteful, though, and there are two alternatives. You can describe a service with a WADL file (introduced in the previous chapter, and covered in more detail in Chapter 9), and then access it with a generic WADL client. There's also a Ruby library called ActiveResource that makes it trivial to write clients for certain kinds of web services.

ActiveResource is designed to run against web services that expose the rows and tables of a relational database. WADL can describe almost any kind of web service, but ActiveResource only works as a client for web services that follow certain conventions. Right now, Ruby on Rails is the only framework that follows the conventions. But any web service can answer requests from an ActiveResource client: it just has to expose its database through the same RESTful interface as Rails.

As of the time of writing, there are few publicly available web services that can be used with an ActiveResource client (I list a couple in Appendix A). To show you an example I'm going create a small Rails web service of my own. I'll be able to drive my service with an ActiveResource client, without writing any HTTP client or XML parsing code.

Creating a Simple Service

My web service will be a simple notebook: a way of keeping timestamped notes to myself. I've got Rails 1.2 installed on my computer, so I can create the notebook service like this:

```
$ rails notebook
$ cd notebook
```

I create a database on my system called `notebook_development`, and edit the Rails file *notebook/config/database.yml* to give Rails the information it needs to connect to my database. Any general guide to Rails will have more detail on these initial steps.

Now I've created a Rails application, but it doesn't do anything. I'm going to generate code for a simple, RESTful web service with the `scaffold_resource` generator. I want my notes to contain a timestamp and a body of text, so I run the following command:

```
$ ruby script/generate scaffold_resource note date:date body:text
create  app/views/notes
create  app/views/notes/index.rhtml
create  app/views/notes/show.rhtml
create  app/views/notes/new.rhtml
create  app/views/notes/edit.rhtml
create  app/views/layouts/notes.rhtml
create  public/stylesheets/scaffold.css
create  app/models/note.rb
create  app/controllers/notes_controller.rb
create  test/functional/notes_controller_test.rb
create  app/helpers/notes_helper.rb
create  test/unit/note_test.rb
create  test/fixtures/notes.yml
create  db/migrate
create  db/migrate/001_create_notes.rb
route   map.resources :notes
```

Rails has generated a complete set of web service code—model, view, and controller —for my "note" object. There's code in `db/migrate/001_create_notes.rb` that creates a database table called `notes` with three fields: a unique ID, a date (`date`), and a piece of text (`body`).

The model code in `app/models/note.rb` provides an ActiveResource interface to the database table. The controller code in `app/controllers/notes_controller.rb` exposes that interface to the world through HTTP, and the views in *app/views/notes* define the

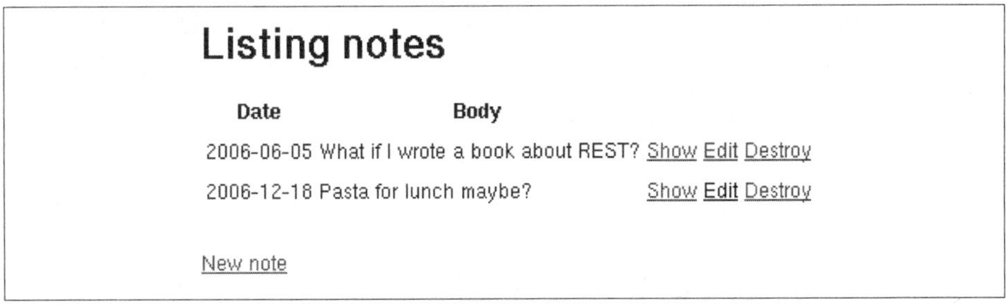

Listing notes

Date	Body			
2006-06-05	What if I wrote a book about REST?	Show	Edit	Destroy
2006-12-18	Pasta for lunch maybe?	Show	Edit	Destroy

New note

Figure 3-1. The notebook web application with a few entered notes

user interface. It adds up to a RESTful web service—not a very fancy one, but one that's good enough for a demo or to use as a starting point.

Before starting the service I need to initialize the database:

```
$ rake db:migrate
== CreateNotes: migrating ========================================================
-- create_table(:notes)
   -> 0.0119s
== CreateNotes: migrated (0.0142s) ========================================================
```

Now I can start the notebook application and start using my service:

```
$ script/server
=> Booting WEBrick...
=> Rails application started on http://0.0.0.0:3000
=> Ctrl-C to shutdown server; call with --help for options
```

An ActiveResource Client

The application I just generated is not much use except as a demo, but it demos some pretty impressive features. First, it's both a web service and a web application. I can visit *http://localhost:3000/notes* in my web browser and create notes through the web interface. After a while the view of *http://localhost:3000/notes* might look like Figure 3-1.

If you've ever written a Rails application or seen a Rails demo, this should look familiar. But in Rails 1.2, the generated model and controller can also act as a RESTful web service. A programmed client can access it as easily as a web browser can.

Unfortunately, the ActiveResource client itself was not released along with Rails 1.2. As of the time of writing, it's still being developed on the tip of the Rails development tree. To get the code I need to check it out from the Subversion version control repository:

```
$ svn co http://dev.rubyonrails.org/svn/rails/trunk activeresource_client
$ cd activeresource_client
```

Now I'm ready to write ActiveResource clients for the notebook's web service. Example 3-24 is a client that creates a note, modifies it, lists the existing notes, and then deletes the note it just created.

Example 3-24. An ActiveResource client for the notebook service

```ruby
#!/usr/bin/ruby -w
# activeresource-notebook-manipulation.rb

require 'activesupport/lib/active_support'
require 'activeresource/lib/active_resource'

# Define a model for the objects exposed by the site
class Note < ActiveResource::Base
  self.site = 'http://localhost:3000/'
end

def show_notes
  notes = Note.find :all              # GET /notes.xml
  puts "I see #{notes.size} note(s):"
  notes.each do |note|
    puts " #{note.date}: #{note.body}"
  end
end

new_note = Note.new(:date => Time.now, :body => "A test note")
new_note.save                          # POST /notes.xml

new_note.body = "This note has been modified."
new_note.save                          # PUT /notes/{id}.xml

show_notes

new_note.destroy                       # DELETE /notes/{id}.xml

puts
show_notes
```

Example 3-25 shows the output when I run that program:

Example 3-25. A run of activeresource-notebook-manipulation.rb

```
I see 3 note(s):
 2006-06-05: What if I wrote a book about REST?
 2006-12-18: Pasta for lunch maybe?
 2006-12-18: This note has been modified.

I see 2 note(s):
 2006-06-05: What if I wrote a book about REST?
 2006-12-18: Pasta for lunch maybe?
```

If you're familiar with ActiveRecord, the object-relational mapper that connects Rails to a database, you'll notice that the ActiveResource interface looks almost exactly the same. Both libraries provide an object-oriented interface to a wide variety of objects, each of which exposes a uniform interface. With ActiveRecord, the objects live in a database and are exposed through SQL, with its SELECT, INSERT, UPDATE, and DELETE. With ActiveResource, they live in a Rails application and are exposed through HTTP, with its GET, POST, PUT, and DELETE.

Example 3-26 is an excerpt from the Rails server logs at the time I ran my ActiveResource client. The GET, POST, PUT, and DELETE requests correspond to the commented lines of code back in Example 3-24.

Example 3-26. The HTTP requests made by activeresource-notebook-manipulation.rb

```
"POST /notes.xml HTTP/1.1" 201
"PUT /notes/5.xml HTTP/1.1" 200
"GET /notes.xml HTTP/1.1" 200
"DELETE /notes/5.xml HTTP/1.1" 200
"GET /notes.xml HTTP/1.1" 200
```

What's going on in these requests? The same thing that's going on in requests to S3: resource access through HTTP's uniform interface. My notebook service exposes two kinds of resources:

- The list of notes (/notes.xml). Compare to an S3 bucket, which is a list of objects.
- A note (/notes/{id}.xml). Compare to an S3 object.

These resources expose GET, PUT, and DELETE, just like the S3 resources do. The list of notes also supports POST to create a new note. That's a little different from S3, where objects are created with PUT, but it's just as RESTful.

When the client runs, XML documents are transferred invisibly between client and server. They look like the documents in Example 3-27 or 3-28: simple depictions of the underlying database rows.

Example 3-27. The response entity-body from a GET request to /notes.xml

```
<?xml version="1.0" encoding="UTF-8"?>
<notes>
 <note>
  <body>What if I wrote a book about REST?</body>
  <date type="date">2006-06-05</date>
  <id type="integer">2</id>
 </note>
 <note>
  <body>Pasta for lunch maybe?</body>
  <date type="date">2006-12-18</date>
  <id type="integer">3</id>
 </note>
</notes>
```

Example 3-28. A request entity-body sent as part of a PUT request to /notes/5.xml

```
<?xml version="1.0" encoding="UTF-8"?>
<note>
 <body>This note has been modified.</body>
</note>
```

A Python Client for the Simple Service

Right now the only ActiveResource client library is the Ruby library, and Rails is the only framework that exposes ActiveResource-compatible services. But nothing's happening here except HTTP requests that pass XML documents into certain URIs and get XML documents back. There's no reason why a client in some other language couldn't send those XML documents, or why some other framework couldn't expose the same URIs.

Example 3-29 is a Python implementation of the client program from Example 3-24. It's longer than the Ruby program, because it can't rely on ActiveResource. It has to build its own XML documents and make its own HTTP requests, but its structure is almost exactly the same.

Example 3-29. A Python client for an ActiveResource service

```python
#!/usr/bin/python
# activeresource-notebook-manipulation.py

from elementtree.ElementTree import Element, SubElement, tostring
from elementtree import ElementTree
import httplib2
import time

BASE = "http://localhost:3000/"
client = httplib2.Http(".cache")

def showNotes():
    headers, xml = client.request(BASE + "notes.xml")
    doc = ElementTree.fromstring(xml)
    for note in doc.findall('note'):
        print "%s: %s" % (note.find('date').text, note.find('body').text)

newNote = Element("note")
date = SubElement(newNote, "date")
date.attrib['type'] = "date"
date.text = time.strftime("%Y-%m-%d", time.localtime())
body = SubElement(newNote, "body")
body.text = "A test note"

headers, ignore = client.request(BASE + "notes.xml", "POST",
                                 body= tostring(newNote),
                                 headers={'content-type' : 'application/xml'})
newURI = headers['location']

modifiedBody = Element("note")
body = SubElement(modifiedBody, "body")
body.text = "This note has been modified"

client.request(newURI, "PUT",
               body=tostring(modifiedBody),
               headers={'content-type' : 'application/xml'})

showNotes()
```

```
client.request(newURI, "DELETE")

print
showNotes()
```

Parting Words

Because RESTful web services have simple and well-defined interfaces, it's not difficult to clone them or swap out one implementation for another. Park Place (*http://code.whytheluckystiff.net/parkplace*) is a Ruby application that exposes the same HTTP interface as S3. You can use Park Place to host your own version of S3. S3 libraries and client programs will work against your Park Place server just as they now do against *https://s3.amazonaws.com/*.

It's also possible to clone ActiveResource. No one has done this yet, but it shouldn't be difficult to write a general ActiveResource client for Python or any other dynamic language. In the meantime, writing a one-off client for an ActiveResource-compatible service is no more difficult than writing a client for any other RESTful service.

By now you should feel comfortable with the prospect of writing a client for any RESTful or REST-RPC hybrid service, whether it serves XML, HTML, JSON, or some mixture. It's all just HTTP requests and document parsing.

You should also be getting a feel for what differentiates RESTful web services like S3 and Yahoo!'s search services from RPC-style and hybrid services like the Flickr and del.icio.us APIs. This is not a judgement about the service's content, only about its architecture. In woodworking it's important to work with the grain of the wood. The Web, too, has a grain, and a RESTful web service is one that works with it.

In the coming chapters I'll show how you can create web services that are more like S3 and less like the del.icio.us API. This culminates in Chapter 7, which reinvents del.icio.us as a RESTful web service.

## CHAPTER 4

The Resource-Oriented Architecture

I've shown you the power of REST, but I haven't shown you in any systematic way how that power is structured or how to expose it. In this chapter I outline a concrete RESTful architecture: the Resource-Oriented Architecture (ROA). The ROA is a way of turning a problem into a RESTful web service: an arrangement of URIs, HTTP, and XML that works like the rest of the Web, and that programmers will enjoy using.

In Chapter 1 I classified RESTful web services by their answers to two questions. These answers correspond to two of the four defining features of REST:

- The scoping information ("why should the server send this data instead of that data?") is kept in the URI. This is the principle of *addressability*.
- The method information ("why should the server send this data instead of deleting it?") is kept in the HTTP method. There are only a few HTTP methods, and everyone knows ahead of time what they do. This is the principle of the *uniform interface*.

In this chapter I introduce the moving parts of the Resource-Oriented Architecture: resources (of course), their names, their representations, and the links between them. I explain and promote the properties of the ROA: addressability, statelessness, connectedness, and the uniform interface. I show how the web technologies (HTTP, URIs, and XML) implement the moving parts to make the properties possible.

In the previous chapters I illustrated concepts by pointing to existing web services, like S3. I continue that tradition in this chapter, but I'll also illustrate concepts by pointing to existing web sites. Hopefully I've convinced you by now that web sites are web services, and that many web applications (such as search engines) are RESTful web services. When I talk about abstract concepts like addressability, it's useful to show you real URIs, which you can type into your web browser to see the concepts in action.

Resource-Oriented What Now?

Why come up with a new term, Resource-Oriented Architecture? Why not just say REST? Well, I do say REST, on the cover of this book, and I hold that everything in the

Resource-Oriented Architecture is also RESTful. But REST is not an architecture: it's a set of design criteria. You can say that one architecture meets those criteria better than another, but there is no one "REST architecture."

Up to now, people have tended to mint one-off architectures as they design their services, according to their own understandings of REST. The most obvious outcome of this is the wide variety of REST-RPC hybrid web services that their creators claim are RESTful. I'm trying to put a stop to that by presenting a set of concrete rules for building web services that really will be RESTful. In the next two chapters I'll even show simple procedures you can follow to turn requirements into resources. If you don't like my rules, you'll at least have an idea of what you can change and stay RESTful.

As a set of design criteria, REST is very general. In particular, it's not tied to the Web. Nothing about REST depends on the mechanics of HTTP or the structure of URIs. But I'm talking about *web* services, so I explicitly tie the Resource-Oriented Architecture to the technologies of the Web. I want to talk about how to do REST with HTTP and URIs, in specific programming languages. If the future produces RESTful architectures that don't run on top of the Web, their best practices will probably look similar to the ROA, but the details will be different. We'll cross that bridge when we come to it.

The traditional definition of REST leaves a lot of open space, which practitioners have seeded with folklore. I deliberately go further than Roy Fielding in his dissertation, or the W3C in their standards: I want to clear some of that open space so that the folklore has room to grow into a well-defined set of best practices. Even if REST were an architecture, it wouldn't be fair to call my architecture by the same name. I'd be tying my empirical observations and suggestions to the more general thoughts of those who built the Web.

My final reason for coming up with a new term is that "REST" is a term used in religious nerd wars. When it's used, the implication is usually that there is one true RESTful architecture and it's the one the speaker prefers. People who prefer another RESTful architecture disagree. The REST community fragments, despite a general agreement on basic things like the value of URIs and HTTP.

Ideally there would be no religious wars, but I've seen enough to know that wishing won't end them. So I'm giving a distinctive name to my philosophy of how RESTful applications should be designed. When these ideas are, inevitably, used as fodder in wars, people who disagree with me can address aspects of the Resource-Oriented Architecture separate from other RESTful architectures, and from REST in general. Clarity is the first step toward understanding.

The phrases "resource-oriented" and "resource-oriented architecture" have been used to describe RESTful architectures in general.[*] I don't claim that "Resource-Oriented Architecture" is a completely original term, but I think that my usage meshes well with preexisting uses, and that it's better to use this term than claim to speak for REST as a whole.

What's a Resource?

A resource is anything that's important enough to be referenced as a thing in itself. If your users might "want to create a hypertext link to it, make or refute assertions about it, retrieve or cache a representation of it, include all or part of it by reference into another representation, annotate it, or perform other operations on it", then you should make it a resource.[†]

Usually, a resource is something that can be stored on a computer and represented as a stream of bits: a document, a row in a database, or the result of running an algorithm. A resource may be a physical object like an apple, or an abstract concept like courage, but (as we'll see later) the representations of such resources are bound to be disappointing.

Here are some possible resources:

- Version 1.0.3 of the software release
- The latest version of the software release
- The first weblog entry for October 24, 2006
- A road map of Little Rock, Arkansas
- Some information about jellyfish
- A directory of resources pertaining to jellyfish
- The next prime number after 1024
- The next five prime numbers after 1024
- The sales numbers for Q42004
- The relationship between two acquaintances, Alice and Bob
- A list of the open bugs in the bug database

URIs

What makes a resource a resource? *It has to have at least one URI.* The URI is the name and address of a resource. If a piece of information doesn't have a URI, it's not a resource and it's not really on the Web, except as a bit of data describing some other resource.

---

[*] The earliest instance of "resource-oriented" I've found is a 2004 IBM developerWorks article by James Snell: "Resource-oriented vs. activity-oriented Web services" (*http://www-128.ibm.com/developerworks/xml/library/ws-restvsoap/*). Alex Bunardzic used "Resource-Oriented Architecture" in August 2006, before this book was announced: *http://jooto.com/blog/index.php/2006/08/08/replacing-service-oriented-architecture-with-resource-oriented-architecture/*. I don't agree with everything in those articles, but I do acknowledge their priority in terminology.

[†] "The Architecture of the World Wide Web" (*http://www.w3.org/TR/2004/REC-webarch-20041215/#p39*), which is full of good quotes, incidentally: "Software developers should expect that sharing URIs across applications will be useful, even if that utility is not initially evident." This could be the battle cry of the ROA.

Remember the sample session in Preface, when I was making fun of HTTP 0.9? Let's say this is a HTTP 0.9 request for `http://www.example.com/hello.txt`:

Client request	Server response
GET /hello.txt	Hello, world!

An HTTP client manipulates a resource by connecting to the server that hosts it (in this case, `www.example.com`), and sending the server a method ("GET") and a path to the resource ("/hello.txt"). Today's HTTP 1.1 is a little more complex than 0.9, but it works the same way. Both the server and the path come from the resource's URI.

Client request	Server response
GET /hello.txt HTTP/1.1	200 OK
Host: www.example.com	Content-Type: text/plain
	Hello, world!

The principles behind URIs are well described by Tim Berners-Lee in Universal Resource Identifiers—Axioms of Web Architecture (*http://www.w3.org/DesignIssues/Axioms*). In this section I expound the principles behind constructing URIs and assigning them to resources.

The URI is the fundamental technology of the Web. There were hypertext systems before HTML, and Internet protocols before HTTP, but they didn't talk to each other. The URI interconnected all these Internet protocols into a Web, the way TCP/IP interconnected networks like Usenet, Bitnet, and CompuServe into a single Internet. Then the Web co-opted those other protocols and killed them off, just like the Internet did with private networks.

Today we surf the Web (not Gopher), download files from the Web (not FTP sites), search publications from the Web (not WAIS), and have conversations on the Web (not Usenet newsgroups). Version control systems like Subversion and arch work over the Web, as opposed to the custom CVS protocol. Even email is slowly moving onto the Web.

The web kills off other protocols because it has something most protocols lack: a simple way of labeling every available item. Every resource on the Web has at least one URI. You can stick a URI on a billboard. People can see that billboard, type that URI into their web browsers, and go right to the resource you wanted to show them. It may seem strange, but this everyday interaction was impossible before URIs were invented.

URIs Should Be Descriptive

Here's the first point where the ROA builds upon the sparse recommendations of the REST thesis and the W3C recommendations. I propose that a resource and its URI ought to have an intuitive correspondence. Here are some good URIs for the resources I listed above:

- http://www.example.com/software/releases/1.0.3.tar.gz
- http://www.example.com/software/releases/latest.tar.gz
- http://www.example.com/weblog/2006/10/24/0
- http://www.example.com/map/roads/USA/AR/Little_Rock
- http://www.example.com/wiki/Jellyfish
- http://www.example.com/search/Jellyfish
- http://www.example.com/nextprime/1024
- http://www.example.com/next-5-primes/1024
- http://www.example.com/sales/2004/Q4
- http://www.example.com/relationships/Alice;Bob
- http://www.example.com/bugs/by-state/open

URIs should have a structure. They should vary in predictable ways: you should not go to /search/Jellyfish for jellyfish and /i-want-to-know-about/Mice for mice. If a client knows the structure of the service's URIs, it can create its own entry points into the service. This makes it easy for clients to use your service in ways you didn't think of.

This is not an absolute rule of REST, as we'll see in the "Name the Resources" section. URIs do not technically have to have any structure or predictability, but I think they should. This is one of the rules of good web design, and it shows up in RESTful and REST-RPC hybrid services alike.

The Relationship Between URIs and Resources

Let's consider some edge cases. Can two resources be the same? Can two URIs designate the same resource? Can a single URI designate two resources?

By definition, no two resources can be the same. If they were the same, you'd only have one resource. However, at some moment in time two different resources may point to the same data. If the current software release is 1.0.3, then *http://www.example.com/software/releases/1.0.3.tar.gz* and *http://www.example.com/software/releases/latest.tar.gz* will refer to the same file for a while. But the ideas behind those two URIs are different: one of them always points to a particular version, and the other points to whatever version is newest at the time the client accesses it. That's two concepts and two resources. You wouldn't link to latest when reporting a bug in version 1.0.3.

A resource may have one URI or many. The sales numbers available at *http://www.example.com/sales/2004/Q4* might also be available at *http://www.example.com/sales/Q42004*. If a resource has multiple URIs, it's easier for clients to refer to the resource. The downside is that each additional URI dilutes the value of all the others. Some clients use one URI, some use another, and there's no automatic way to verify that all the URIs refer to the same resource.

 One way to get around this is to expose multiple URIs for the same resource, but have one of them be the "canonical" URI for that resource. When a client requests the canonical URI, the server sends the appropriate data along with response code of 200 ("OK"). When a client requests one of the other URIs, the server sends a response code 303 ("See Also") along with the canonical URI. The client can't see whether two URIs point to the same resource, but it can make two HEAD requests and see if one URI redirects to the other or if they both redirect to a third URI.

Another way is to serve all the URIs as though they were the same, but give the "canonical" URI in the Content-Location response header whenever someone requests a non-canonical URI.

Fetching sales/2004/Q4 might get you the same bytestream as fetching sales/Q42004, because they're different URIs for the same resource: "sales for the last quarter of 2004." Fetching releases/1.0.3.tar.gz might give you the exact same bytestream as fetching releases/latest.tar.gz, but they're different resources because they represent different things: "version 1.0.3" and "the latest version."

Every URI designates exactly one resource. If it designated more than one, it wouldn't be a *Universal* Resource Identifier. However, when you fetch a URI the server may send you information about multiple resources: the one you requested and other, related ones. When you fetch a web page, it usually conveys some information of its own, but it also has links to other web pages. When you retrieve an S3 bucket with an Amazon S3 client, you get a document that contains information about the bucket, and information about related resources: the objects in the bucket.

Addressability

Now that I've introduced resources and their URIs, I can go in depth into two of the features of the ROA: addressability and statelessness.

An application is addressable if it exposes the interesting aspects of its data set as resources. Since resources are exposed through URIs, an addressable application exposes a URI for every piece of information it might conceivably serve. This is usually an infinite number of URIs.

From the end-user perspective, addressability is the most important aspect of any web site or application. Users are clever, and they'll overlook or work around almost any deficiency if the data is interesting enough, but it's very difficult to work around a lack of addressability.

Consider a real URI that names a resource in the genre "directory of resources about jellyfish": *http://www.google.com/search?q=jellyfish*. That jellyfish search is just as much a real URI as *http://www.google.com*. If HTTP wasn't addressable, or if the Google search engine wasn't an addressable web application, I wouldn't be able to publish that URI in a book. I'd have to tell you: "Open a web connection to `google.com`, type 'jellyfish' in the search box, and click the 'Google Search' button."

 This isn't an academic worry. Until the mid-1990s, when `ftp://` URIs became popular for describing files on FTP sites, people had to write things like: "Start an anonymous FTP session on `ftp.example.com`. Then change to directory `pub/files/` and download file *file.txt*." URIs made FTP as addressable as HTTP. Now people just write: "Download *ftp:// ftp.example.com/pub/files/file.txt*." The steps are the same, but now they can be carried out by machine.

But HTTP and Google are both addressable, so I can print that URI in a book. You can read it and type it in. When you do, you end up where I was when I went through the Google web application.

You can then bookmark that page and come back to it later. You can link to it on a web page of your own. You can email the URI to someone else. If HTTP wasn't addressable, you'd have to download the whole page and send the HTML file as an attachment.

To save bandwidth, you can set up an HTTP proxy cache on your local network. The first time someone requests *http://www.google.com/search?q=jellyfish*, the cache will save a local copy of the document. The next time someone hits that URI, the cache might serve the saved copy instead of downloading it again. These things are possible only if every page has a unique identifying string: an address.

It's even possible to chain URIs: to use one URI as input to another one. You can use an external web service to validate a page's HTML, or to translate its text into another language. These web services expect a URI as input. If HTTP wasn't addressable, you'd have no way of telling them which resource you wanted them to operate on.

Amazon's S3 service is addressable because every bucket and every object has its own URI, as does the bucket list. Buckets and objects that don't exist yet aren't yet resources, but they too have their own URIs: you can create a resource by sending a PUT request to its URI.

The filesystem on your home computer is another addressable system. Command-line applications can take a path to a file and do strange things to it. The cells in a spreadsheet are also addressable; you can plug the name of a cell into a formula, and the formula will use whatever value is currently in that cell. URIs are the file paths and cell addresses of the Web.

Addressability is one of the best things about web applications. It makes it easy for clients to use web sites in ways the original designers never imagined. Following this one rule gives you and your users many of the benefits of REST. This is why REST-RPC services are so common: they combine addressability with the procedure-call programming model. It's why I gave resources top billing in the name of the Resource-Oriented Architecture: because resources are the kind of thing that's addressable.

This seems natural, the way the Web should work. Unfortunately, many web applications *don't* work this way. This is especially true of Ajax applications. As I show in Chapter 11, most Ajax applications are just clients for RESTful or hybrid web services. But when you use these clients as though they are web sites, you notice that they don't *feel* like web sites.

No need to pick on the little guys; let's continue our tour of the Google properties by considering the Gmail online email service. From the end-user perspective, there is only one Gmail URI: *https://mail.google.com/*. Whatever you do, whatever pieces of information you retrieve from or upload to Gmail, you'll never see a different URI. The resource "email messages about jellyfish" isn't addressable, the way Google's "web pages about jellyfish" is.[‡] Yet behind the scenes, as I show in Chapter 11, is a web site that is addressable. The list of email messages about jellyfish *does* have a URI: it's *https://mail.google.com/mail/?q=jellyfish&search=query&view=tl*. The problem is, you're not the consumer of that web site. The web site is really a web service, and the real consumer is a JavaScript program running inside your web browser.[§] The Gmail web service is addressable, but the Gmail web application that uses it is not.

Statelessness

Addressability is one of the four main features of the ROA. The second is statelessness. I'll give you two definitions of statelessness: a somewhat general definition and a more practical definition geared toward the ROA.

Statelessness means that every HTTP request happens in complete isolation. When the client makes an HTTP request, it includes all information neccessary for the server to fulfill that request. The server never relies on information from previous requests. If that information was important, the client would have sent it again in this request.

[‡] Compare the Ajax interface against the more addressable version of Gmail you get by starting off at the URI *https://mail.google.com/mail/?ui=html*. If you use this plain HTML interface, the resource "email messages about jellyfish" *is* addressable.

[§] Other consumers of this web service include the libgmail library for Python (*http://libgmail.sourceforge.net/*).

More practically, consider statelessness in terms of addressability. Addressability says that every interesting piece of information the server can provide should be exposed as a resource, and given its own URI. Statelessness says that the *possible states* of the server are also resources, and should be given their own URIs. The client should not have to coax the server into a certain state to make it receptive to a certain request.

On the human web, you often run into situations where your browser's back button doesn't work correctly, and you can't go back and forth in your browser history. Sometimes this is because you performed an irrevocable action, like posting a weblog entry or buying a book, but often it's because you're at a web site that violates the principle of statelessness. Such a site expects you to make requests in a certain order: A, B, then C. It gets confused when you make request B a second time instead of moving on to request C.

Let's take the search example again. A search engine is a web service with an infinite number of possible states: at least one for every string you might search for. Each state has its own URI. You can ask the service for a directory of resources about mice: *http://www.google.com/search?q=mice*. You can ask for a directory of resources about jellyfish: *http://www.google.com/search?q=jellyfish*. If you're not comfortable creating a URI from scratch, you can ask the service for a form to fill out: *http://www.google.com/*.

When you ask for a directory of resources about mice or jellyfish, you don't get the whole directory. You get a single *page* of the directory: a list of the 10 or so items the search engine considers the best matches for your query. To get more of the directory you must make more HTTP requests. The second and subsequent pages are distinct states of the application, and they need to have their own URIs: something like *http://www.google.com/search?q=jellyfish&start=10*. As with any addressable resource, you can transmit that state of the application to someone else, cache it, or bookmark it and come back to it later.

Figure 4-1 is a simple state diagram showing how an HTTP client might interact with four states of a search engine.

This is a stateless application because every time the client makes a request, it ends up back where it started. Each request is totally disconnected from the others. The client can make requests for these resources any number of times, in any order. It can request page 2 of "mice" before requesting page 1 (or not request page 1 at all), and the server won't care.

By way of contrast, Figure 4-2 shows the same states arranged statefully, with states leading sensibly into each other. Most desktop applications are designed this way.

That's a lot better organized, and if HTTP were designed to allow stateful interaction, HTTP requests could be a lot simpler. When the client started a session with the search engine it could be automatically fed the search form. It wouldn't have to send any request data at all, because the first response would be predetermined. If the client was looking at the first 10 entries in the mice directory and wanted to see entries 11–20, it

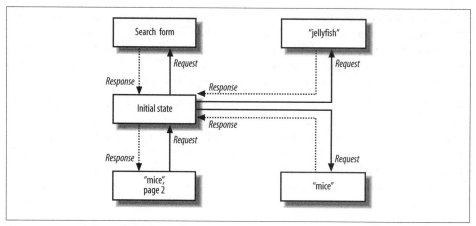

Figure 4-1. A stateless search engine

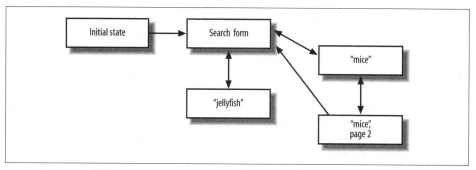

Figure 4-2. A stateful search engine

could just send a request that said "start=10". It wouldn't have to send /search?
q=mice&start=10, repeating the intitial assertions: "I'm searching, and searching for
mice in particular."

FTP works this way: it has a notion of a "working directory" that stays constant over
the course of a session unless you change it. You might log in to an FTP server, cd to a
certain directory, and get a file from that directory. You can get another file from the
same directory, without having to issue a second cd command. Why doesn't HTTP
support this?

State would make individual HTTP requests simpler, but it would make the HTTP
protocol much more complicated. An FTP client is much more complicated than an
HTTP client, precisely because the session state must be kept in sync between client
and server. This is a complex task even over a reliable network, which the Internet is
not.

To eliminate state from a protocol is to eliminate a lot of failure conditions. The server
never has to worry about the client timing out, because no interaction lasts longer than

a single request. The server never loses track of "where" each client is in the application, because the client sends all neccessary information with each request. The client never ends up performing an action in the wrong "working directory" due to the server keeping some state around without telling the client.

Statelessness also brings new features. It's easier to distribute a stateless application across load-balanced servers. Since no two requests depend on each other, they can be handled by two different servers that never coordinate with each other. Scaling up is as simple as plugging more servers into the load balancer. A stateless application is also easy to cache: a piece of software can decide whether or not to cache the result of an HTTP request just by looking at that one request. There's no nagging uncertainty that state from a previous request might affect the cacheability of this one.

The client benefits from statelessness as well. A client can process the "mice" directory up to page 50, bookmark /search?q=mice&start=50, and come back a week later without having to grind through dozens of predecessor states. A URI that works when you're hours deep into an HTTP session will work the same way as the first URI sent in a new session.

To make your service addressabile you have to put in some work, dissect your application's data into sets of resources. HTTP is an intrinsically stateless protocol, so when you write web services, you get statelessness by default. You have to do something to break it.

The most common way to break statelessness is to use your framework's version of HTTP sessions. The first time a user visits your site, he gets a unique string that identifies his session with the site. The string may be kept in a cookie, or the site may propagate a unique string through all the URIs it serves a particular client. Here's an session cookie being set by a Rails application:

```
Set-Cookie: _session_id=c1c934bbe6168dcb904d21a7f5644a2d; path=/
```

This URI propagates the session ID in a PHP application: http://www.example.com/forums?PHPSESSID=27314962133.

The important thing is, that nonsensical hex or decimal number is not the state. It's a key into a data structure on the server, and the data structure contains the state. There's nothing unRESTful about stateful URIs: that's how the server communicates possible next states to the client. However, there *is* something unRESTful about cookies, as I discuss in "The Trouble with Cookies." To use a web browser analogy, cookies break a web service client's back button.

Think of the query variable start=10 in a URI, embedded in an HTML page served by the Google search engine. That's the server sending a possible next state to the client.

But those URIs need to *contain* the state, not just provide a key to state stored on the server. start=10 means something on its own, and PHPSESSID=27314962133 doesn't. RESTfulness requires that the state stay on the client side, and be transmitted to the server for every request that needs it. The server can nudge the client toward new states, by sending stateful links for the client to follow, but it can't keep any state of its own.

Application State Versus Resource State

When we talk about "statelessness," what counts as "state"? What's the difference between persistent data, the useful server-side data that makes us want to use web services in the first place, and this state we're trying to keep off the server? The Flickr web service lets you upload pictures to your account, and those pictures are stored on the server. It would be crazy to make the client send every one of its pictures along with every request to flickr.com, just to keep the server from having to store any state. That would defeat the whole point of the service. But what's the difference between this scenario, and state about the client's session, which I claim should be kept off the server?

The problem is one of terminology. Statelessness implies there's only one kind of state and that the server should go without it. Actually, there are two kinds of state. From this point on in the book I'm going to distinguish between *application state*, which ought to live on the client, and *resource state*, which ought to live on the server.

When you use a search engine, your current query and your current page are bits of client state. This state is different for every client. You might be on page 3 of the search results for "jellyfish," and I might be on page 1 of the search results for "mice." The page number and the query are different because we took different paths through the application. Our respective clients store different bits of application state.

A web service only needs to care about your application state when you're actually making a request. The rest of the time, it doesn't even know you exist. This means that whenever a client makes a request, it must include all the application states the server will need to process it. The server might send back a page with links, telling the client about other requests it might want to make in the future, but then it can forget all about the client until the next request. That's what I mean when I say a web service should be "stateless." The client should be in charge of managing its own path through the application.

Resource state is the same for every client, and its proper place is on the server. When you upload a picture to Flickr, you create a new resource: the new picture has its own URI and can be the target of future requests. You can fetch, modify, and delete the "picture" resource through HTTP. It's there for everybody: I can fetch it too. The picture is a bit of resource state, and it stays on the server until a client deletes it.

Client state can show up when you don't expect it. Lots of web services make you sign up for a unique string they call an API key or application key. You send in this key with every request, and the server restricts uses it to restrict you to a certain number of requests a day. For instance, an API key for Google's deprecated SOAP search API is good for 1,000 requests a day. That's client state: it's different for every client. Once you exceed the limit, the behavior of the service changes dramatically: on request 1,000 you get your data, and on request 1,001 you get an error. Meanwhile, I'm on request 402 and the service still works fine for me.

Of course, clients can't be trusted to self-report this bit of application state: the temptation to cheat is too great. So servers keep this kind of application state on the server, violating statelessness. The API key is like the Rails `_session_id` cookie, a key into a server-side client session that lasts one day. This is fine as far as it goes, but there's a scalability price to be paid. If the service is to be distributed across multiple machines, every machine in the cluster needs to know that you're on request 1,001 and I'm on request 402 (technical term: *session replication*), so that every machine knows to deny you access and let me through. Alternatively, the load balancer needs to make sure that every one of your requests goes to the same machine in the cluster (technical term: *session affinity*). Statelessness removes this requirement. As a service designer, you only need to start thinking about data replication when your *resource* state needs to be split across multiple machines.

Representations

When you split your application into resources, you increase its surface area. Your users can construct an appropriate URI and enter your application right where they need to be. But the resources aren't the data; they're just the service designer's idea of how to split up the data into "a list of open bugs" or "information about jellyfish." A web server can't send an idea; it has to send a series of bytes, in a specific file format, in a specific language. This is a *representation* of the resource.

A resource is a source of representations, and a representation is just some data about the current state of a resource. Most resources are themselves items of data (like a list of bugs), so an obvious representation of a resource is the data itself. The server might present a list of open bugs as an XML document, a web page, or as comma-separated text. The sales numbers for the last quarter of 2004 might be represented numerically or as a graphical chart. Lots of news sites make their articles available in an ad-laden format, and in a stripped-down "printer-friendly" format. These are all different representations of the same resources.

But some resources represent physical objects, or other things that can't be reduced to information. What's a good representation for such things? You don't need to worry about perfect fidelity: a representation is *any useful information* about the state of a resource.

Consider a physical object, a soda machine, hooked up to a web service.‖ The goal is to let the machine's customers avoid unneccessary trips to the machine. With the service, customers know when the soda is cold, and when their favorite brand is sold out.

‖ This idea is based on the CMU Coke machine (*http://www.cs.cmu.edu/%7Ecoke/*), which for many years was observed by instruments and whose current state was accessible through the Finger protocol. The machine is still around, though at the time of writing its state was not accessible online.

Nobody expects the physical cans of soda to be made available through the web service, because physical objects aren't data. But they do have data *about* them: metadata. Each slot in the soda machine can be instrumented with a device that knows about the flavor, price, and temperature of the next available can of soda. Each slot can be exposed as a resource, and so can the soda machine as a whole. The metadata from the instruments can be used in representations of the resources.

Even when one of an object's representations contains the actual data, it may also have representations that contain metadata. An online bookstore may serve two representations of a book:

1. One containing only metadata, like a cover image and reviews, used to advertise the book.
2. An electronic copy of the data in the book, sent to you via HTTP when you pay for it.

Representations can flow the other way, too. You can send a representation of a new resource to the server and have the server create the resource. This is what happens when you upload a picture to Flickr. Or you can give the server a new representation of an existing resource, and have the server modify the resource to bring it in line with the new representation.

Deciding Between Representations

If a server provides multiple representations of a resource, how does it figure out which one the client is asking for? For instance, a press release might be put out in both English and Spanish. Which one does a given client want?

There are a number of ways to figure this out within the constraints of REST. The simplest, and the one I recommend for the Resource-Oriented Architecture, is to give a distinct URI to each representation of a resource. *http://www.example.com/releases/104.en* could designate the English representation of the press release, and *http://www.example.com/releases/104.es* could designate the Spanish representation.

I recommend this technique for ROA applications because it means the URI contains all information neccessary for the server to fulfill the request. The disadvantage, as whenever you expose multiple URIs for the same resource, is dilution: people who talk about the press release in different languages appear to be talking about different things. You can mitigate this problem somewhat by exposing the URI *http://www.example.com/releases/104* to mean the release as a Platonic form, independent of any language.

The alternative way is called *content negotiation*. In this scenario the only exposed URI is the Platonic form URI, *http://www.example.com/releases/104*. When a client makes a request for that URI, it provides special HTTP request headers that signal what kind of representations the client is willing to accept.

Your web browser has a setting for language preferences: which languages you'd prefer to get web pages in. The browser submits this information with every HTTP request, in the `Accept-Language` header. The server usually ignores this information because most web pages are available in only one language. But it fits with what we're trying to do here: expose different-language representations of the same resource. When a client requests *http://www.example.com/releases/104*, the server can decide whether to serve the English or the Spanish representation based on the client's `Accept-Language` header.

The Google search engine is a good place to try this out. You can get your search results in almost any language by changing your browser language settings, or by manipulating the `hl` query variable in the URI (for instance, `hl=tr` for Turkish). The search engine supports both content negotiation and different URIs for different representations.

A client can also set the `Accept` header to specify which file format it prefers for representations. A client can say it prefers XHTML to HTML, or SVG to any other graphics format.

The server is allowed to use any of this request metadata when deciding which representation to send. Other types of request metadata include payment information, authentication credentials, the time of the request, caching directives, and even the IP address of the client. All of these might make a difference in the server's decision of what data to include in the representation, which language and which format to use, and even whether to send a representation at all or to deny access.

It's RESTful to keep this information in the HTTP headers, and it's RESTful to put it in the URI. I recommend keeping as much of this information as possible in the URI, and as little as possible in request metadata. I think URIs are more useful than metadata. URIs get passed around from person to person, and from program to program. The request metadata almost always gets lost in transition.

Here's a simple example of this dilemma: the W3C HTML validator, a web service available at *http://validator.w3.org/*. Here's a URI to a resource on the W3C's site, a validation report on the English version of my hypothetical press release: `http://validator.w3.org/check?uri=http%3A%2F%2Fwww.example.com%2Freleases%2F104.en`.

Here's another resource: a validation report on the Spanish version of the press release: `http://validator.w3.org/check?uri=http%3A%2F%2Fwww.example.com%2Freleases%2F104.es`.

Every URI in your web space becomes a resource in the W3C's web application, whether or not it designates a distinct resource on your site. If your press release has a separate URI for each representation, you can get two resources from the W3C: validation reports for the English and the Spanish versions of the press release.

But if you only expose the Platonic form URI, and serve both representations from that URI, you can only get one resource from the W3C. That would be a validation report

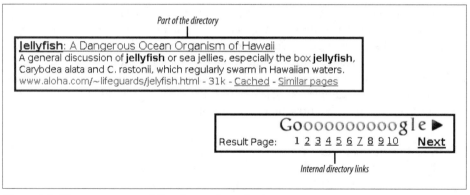

Figure 4-3. Closeup on a page of Google search results

for the *default* version of the press release (probably the English one). You've got no way of knowing whether or not the Spanish representation contains HTML formatting errors. If the server doesn't expose the Spanish press release as its own URI, there's no corresponding resource available on the W3C site. This doesn't mean you can't expose that Platonic form URI: just that it shouldn't be the only URI you use.

Unlike humans, computer programs are very bad at dealing with representations they didn't expect. I think an automated web client should be as explicit as possible about the representation it wants. This almost always means specifying a representation in the URL.

Links and Connectedness

Sometimes representations are little more than serialized data structures. They're intended to be sucked of their data and discarded. But in the most RESTful services, representations are hypermedia: documents that contain not just data, but links to other resources.

Let's take the search example again. If you go to Google's directory of documents about jellyfish (*http://www.google.com/search?q=jellyfish*), you see some search results, and a set of internal links to other pages of the directory. Figure 4-3 shows a representative sample of the page.

There's data here, and links. The data says that somewhere on the Web, someone said such-and-such about jellyfish, with emphasis on two species of Hawaiian jellyfish. The links give you access to other resources: some within the Google search "web service," and some elsewhere on the Web:

- The external web page that talks about jellyfish: `http://www.aloha.com/~life guards/jelyfish.html`. The main point of this web service, of course, is to present links of this sort.

- A link to a Google-provided cache of the extrenal page (the "Cached" link). These links always have long URIs that point to Google-owned IP addresses, like `http://209.85.165.104/search?q=cache:FQrLzPUOtKQJ...`

- A link to a directory of pages Google thinks are related to the external page (*http://www.google.com/search?q=related:www.aloha.com/~lifeguards/jelyfish.html*, linked as "Similar pages"). This is another case of a web service taking a URI as input.

- A set of navigation links that take you to different pages of the "jellyfish" directory: *http://www.google.com/search?q=jellyfish&start=10*, *http://www.google.com/search?q=jellyfish&start=20*, and so on.

Earlier in this chapter, I showed what might happen if HTTP was a stateful protocol like FTP. Figure 4-2 shows the paths a stateful HTTP client might take during a "session" with `www.google.com`. HTTP doesn't really work that way, but that figure does a good job of showing how we use the human web. To use a search engine we start at the home page, fill out a form to do a search, and then click links to go to subsequent pages of results. We don't usually type in one URI after another: we follow links and fill out forms.

If you've read about REST before, you might have encountered an axiom from the Fielding dissertation: "Hypermedia as the engine of application state." This is what that axiom means: the current state of an HTTP "session" is not stored on the server as a resource state, but tracked by the client as an application state, and created by the path the client takes through the Web. The server guides the client's path by serving "hypermedia": links and forms inside hypertext representations.

The server sends the client guidelines about which states are near the current one. The "next" link on *http://www.google.com/search?q=jellyfish* is a *lever of state*: it shows you how to get from the current state to a related one. This is very powerful. A document that contains a URI points to another possible state of the application: "page two," or "related to this URI," or "a cached version of this URI." Or it may be pointing to a possible state of a totally different application.

I'm calling the quality of having links *connectedness*. A web service is connected to the extent that you can put the service in different states just by following links and filling out forms. I'm calling this "connectedness" because "hypermedia as the engine of application state" makes the concept sound more difficult than it is. All I'm saying is that resources should link to each other in their representations.

The human web is easy to use because it's well connected. Any experienced user knows how to type URIs into the browser's address bar, and how to jump around a site by modifying the URI, but many users do all their web surfing from a single starting point: the browser home page set by their ISP. This is possible because the Web is well connected. Pages link to each other, even across sites.

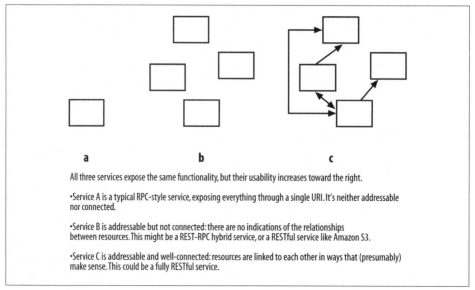

a   b   c

All three services expose the same functionality, but their usability increases toward the right.

•Service A is a typical RPC-style service, exposing everything through a single URI. It's neither addressable nor connected.

•Service B is addressable but not connected: there are no indications of the relationships between resources. This might be a REST-RPC hybrid service, or a RESTful service like Amazon S3.

•Service C is addressable and well-connected: resources are linked to each other in ways that (presumably) make sense. This could be a fully RESTful service.

Figure 4-4. One service three ways

But most web services are not internally connected, let alone connected to each other. Amazon S3 is a RESTful web service that's addressible and stateless, but not connected. S3 representations never include URIs. To GET an S3 bucket, you have to know the rules for constructing the bucket's URI. You can't just GET the bucket list and follow a link to the bucket you want.

Example 4-1 shows an S3 bucket list that I've changed (I added a `URI` tag) so that it's connected. Compare to Example 3-5, which has no `URI` tag. This is just one way of introducing URIs into an XML representation. As resources become better-connected, the relationships between them becomes more obvious (see Figure 4-4).

Example 4-1. A connected "list of your buckets"

```
<?xml version='1.0' encoding='UTF-8'?>
<ListAllMyBucketsResult xmlns='http://s3.amazonaws.com/doc/2006-03-01/'>
 <Owner>
  <ID>c0363f7260f2f5fcf38d48039f4fb5cab21b060577817310be5170e7774aad70</ID>
  <DisplayName>leonardr28</DisplayName>
 </Owner>
 <Buckets>
  <Bucket>
   <Name>crummy.com</Name>
   <URI>https://s3.amazonaws.com/crummy.com</URI>
   <CreationDate>2006-10-26T18:46:45.000Z</CreationDate>
  </Bucket>
 </Buckets>
</ListAllMyBucketsResult>
```

The Uniform Interface

All across the Web, there are only a few basic things you can do to a resource. HTTP provides four basic methods for the four most common operations:

- Retrieve a representation of a resource: *HTTP GET*
- Create a new resource: *HTTP PUT* to a new URI, or *HTTP POST* to an existing URI (see the "POST" section below)
- Modify an existing resource: *HTTP PUT* to an existing URI
- Delete an existing resource: *HTTP DELETE*

I'll explain how these four are used to represent just about any operation you can think of. I'll also cover two HTTP methods for two less common operations: HEAD and OPTIONS.

GET, PUT, and DELETE

These three should be familiar to you from the S3 example in Chapter 3. To fetch or delete a resource, the client just sends a GET or DELETE request to its URI. In the case of a GET request, the server sends back a representation in the response entity-body. For a DELETE request, the response entity-body may contain a status message, or nothing at all.

To create or modify a resource, the client sends a PUT request that usually includes an entity-body. The entity-body contains the client's proposed new representation of the resource. What data this is, and what format it's in, depends on the service. Whatever it looks like, this is the point at which application state moves onto the server and becomes resource state.

Again, think of the S3 service, where there are two kinds of resources you can create: buckets and objects. To create an object, you send a PUT request to its URI and include the object's content in the entity-body of your request. You do the same thing to modify an object: the new content overwrites any old content.

Creating a bucket is a little different because you don't have to specify an entity-body in the PUT request. A bucket has no resource state except for its name, and the name is part of the URI. (This is not quite true. The objects in a bucket are also elements of that bucket's resource state: after all, they're listed when you GET a bucket's representation. But every S3 object is a resource of its own, so there's no need to *manipulate* an object through its bucket. Every object exposes the uniform interface and you can manipulate it separately.) Specify the bucket's URI and you've specified its representation. PUT requests for most resources do include an entity-body containing a representation, but as you can see it's not a requirement.

HEAD and OPTIONS

There are three other HTTP methods I consider part of the uniform interface. Two of them are simple utility methods, so I'll cover them first.

- Retrieve a metadata-only representation: *HTTP HEAD*
- Check which HTTP methods a particular resource supports: *HTTP OPTIONS*

saw the HEAD method exposed by the S3 services's resources in Chapter 3. An S3 client uses HEAD to fetch metadata about a resource without downloading the possibly enormous entity-body. That's what HEAD is for. A client can use HEAD to check whether a resource exists, or find out other information about the resource, without fetching its entire representation. HEAD gives you exactly what a GET request would give you, but without the entity-body.

 There are two standard HTTP methods I don't cover in this book: TRACE and CONNECT. TRACE is used to debug proxies, and CONNECT is used to forward some other protocol through an HTTP proxy.

The OPTIONS method lets the client discover what it's allowed to do to a resource. The response to an OPTIONS request contains the HTTP `Allow` header, which lays out the subset of the uniform interface this resource supports. Here's a sample `Allow` header:

    Allow: GET, HEAD

That particular header means the client can expect the server to act reasonably to a GET or HEAD request for this resource, but that the resource doesn't support any other HTTP methods. Effectively, this resource is read-only.

The headers the client sends in the request may affect the `Allow` header the server sends in response. For instance, if you send a proper `Authorization` header along with an OPTIONS request, you may find that you're allowed to make GET, HEAD, PUT, and DELETE requests against a particular URI. If you send the same OPTIONS request but omit the `Authorization` header, you may find that you're only allowed to make GET and HEAD requests. The OPTIONS method lets the client do simple access control checks.

In theory, the server can send additional information in response to an OPTIONS request, and the client can send OPTIONS requests that ask very specific questions about the server's capabilities. Very nice, except there are no accepted standards for what a client might ask in an OPTIONS request. Apart from the `Allow` header there are no accepted standards for what a server might send in response. Most web servers and frameworks feature very poor support for OPTIONS. So far, OPTIONS is a promising idea that nobody uses.

POST

Now we come to that most misunderstood of HTTP methods: POST. This method essentially has two purposes: one that fits in with the constraints of REST, and one that goes outside REST and introduces an element of the RPC style. In complex cases like this it's best to go back to the original text. Here's what RFC 2616, the HTTP standard, says about POST (this is from section 9.5):

> POST is designed to allow a uniform method to cover the following functions:
>
> - Annotation of existing resources;
> - Posting a message to a bulletin board, newsgroup, mailing list, or similar group of articles;
> - Providing a block of data, such as the result of submitting a form, to a data-handling process;
> - Extending a database through an append operation.
>
> The actual function performed by the POST method is determined by the server and is usually dependent on the Request-URI. The posted entity is subordinate to that URI in the same way that a file is subordinate to a directory containing it, a news article is subordinate to a newsgroup to which it is posted, or a record is subordinate to a database.

What does this mean in the context of REST and the ROA?

Creating subordinate resources

In a RESTful design, POST is commonly used to create subordinate resources: resources that exist in relation to some other "parent" resource. A weblog program may expose each weblog as a resource (/weblogs/myweblog), and the individual weblog entries as subordinate resources (/weblogs/myweblog/entries/1). A web-enabled database may expose a table as a resource, and the individual database rows as its subordinate resources. To create a weblog entry or a database record, you POST to the parent: the weblog or the database table. What data you post, and what format it's in, depends on the service, but as with PUT, this is the point where application state becomes resource state. You may see this use of POST called *POST(a)*, for "append". When I say "POST" in this book, I almost always mean POST(a).

Why can't you just use PUT to create subordinate resources? Well, sometimes you can. An S3 object is a subordinate resource: every S3 object is contained in some S3 bucket. But we don't create an S3 object by sending a POST request to the bucket. We send a PUT request directly to the URI of the object. The difference between PUT and POST is this: the client uses PUT when it's in charge of deciding which URI the new resource should have. The client uses POST when the *server* is in charge of deciding which URI the new resource should have.

The S3 service expects clients to create S3 objects with PUT, because an S3 object's URI is completely determined by its name and the name of the bucket. If the client knows enough to create the object, it knows what its URI will be. The obvious URI to use as the target of the PUT request is the one the bucket will live at once it exists.

But consider an application in which the server has more control over the URIs: say, a weblog program. The client can gather all the information neccessary to create a weblog entry, and still not know what URI the entry will have once created. Maybe the server bases the URIs on ordering or an internal database ID: will the final URI be `/weblogs/myweblog/entries/1` or `/weblogs/myweblog/entries/1000`? Maybe the final URI is based on the posting time: what time does the server think it is? The client shouldn't have to know these things.

The POST method is a way of creating a new resource without the client having to know its exact URI. In most cases the client only needs to know the URI of a "parent" or "factory" resource. The server takes the representation from the entity-body and use it to create a new resource "underneath" the "parent" resource (the meaning of "underneath" depends on context).

The response to this sort of POST request usually has an HTTP status code of 201 ("Created"). Its `Location` header contains the URI of the newly created subordinate resource. Now that the resource actually exists and the client knows its URI, future requests can use the PUT method to modify that resource, GET to fetch a representation of it, and DELETE to delete it.

Table 4-1 shows how a PUT request to a URI might create or modify the underlying resource; and how a POST request to the same URI might create a new, subordinate resource.

Table 4-1. PUT actions

	PUT to a new resource	PUT to an existing resource	POST
`/weblogs`	N/A (resource already exists)	No effect	Create a new weblog
`/weblogs/myweblog`	Create this weblog	Modify this weblog's settings	Create a new weblog entry
`/weblogs/myweblog/entries/1`	N/A (how would you get this URI?)	Edit this weblog entry	Post a comment to this weblog entry

Appending to the resource state

The information conveyed in a POST to a resource doesn't have to result in a whole new subordinate resource. Sometimes when you POST data to a resource, it appends the information you POSTed to its own state, instead of putting it in a new resource.

Consider an event logging service that exposes a single resource: the log. Say its URI is `/log`. To get the log you send a GET request to `/log`.

Now, how should a client append to the log? The client might send a PUT request to `/log`, but the PUT method has the implication of creating a new resource, or overwriting old settings with new ones. The client isn't doing either: it's just appending information to the end of the log.

The POST method works here, just as it would if each log entry was exposed as a separate resource. The semantics of POST are the same in both cases: the client adds subordinate information to an existing resource. The only difference is that in the case of the weblog and weblog entries, the subordinate information showed up as a new resource. Here, the subordinate information shows up as new data in the parent's representation.

Overloaded POST: The not-so-uniform interface

That way of looking at things explains most of what the HTTP standard says about POST. You can use it to create resources underneath a parent resource, and you can use it to append extra data onto the current state of a resource. The one use of POST I haven't explained is the one you're probably most familiar with, because it's the one that drives almost all web applications: providing a block of data, such as the result of submitting a form, to a data-handling process.

What's a "data-handling process"? That sounds pretty vague. And, indeed, just about anything can be a data-handling process. Using POST this way turns a resource into a tiny message processor that acts like an XML-RPC server. The resource accepts POST requests, examines the request, and decides to do... something. Then it decides to serve to the client... some data.

I call this use of POST *overloaded POST*, by analogy to operator overloading in a programming language. It's overloaded because a single HTTP method is being used to signify any number of non-HTTP methods. It's confusing for the same reason operator overloading can be confusing: you thought you knew what HTTP POST did, but now it's being used to achieve some unknown purpose. You might see overloaded POST called *POST(p)*, for "process."

When your service exposes overloaded POST, you reopen the question: "why should the server do this instead of that?" Every HTTP request has to contain method information, and when you use overloaded POST it can't go into the HTTP method. The POST method is just a directive to the server, saying: "Look inside the HTTP request for the real method information." The real information may be in the URI, the HTTP headers, or the entity-body. However it happens, an element of the RPC style has crept into the service.

When the method information isn't found in the HTTP method, the interface stops being uniform. The real method information might be anything. As a REST partisan I don't like this very much, but occasionally it's unavoidable. By Chapter 9 you'll have seen how just about any scenario you can think of can be exposed through HTTP's uniform interface, but sometimes the RPC style is the easiest way to express complex operations that span multiple resources.

You may need to expose overloaded POST even if you're only using POST to create subordinate resources or to append to a resource's representation. What if a single resource supports both kinds of POST? How does the server know whether a client is POSTing to create a subordinate resource, or to append to the existing resource's representation? You may need to put some additional method information elsewhere in the HTTP request.

Overloaded POST should not be used to cover up poor resource design. Remember, a resource can be anything. It's usually possible to shuffle your resource design so that the uniform interface applies, rather than introduce the RPC style into your service.

Safety and Idempotence

If you expose HTTP's uniform interface as it was designed, you get two useful properties for free. When correctly used, GET and HEAD requests are *safe*. GET, HEAD, PUT and DELETE requests are *idempotent*.

Safety

A GET or HEAD request is a request to read some data, not a request to change any server state. The client can make a GET or HEAD request 10 times and it's the same as making it once, or never making it at all. When you GET *http://www.google.com/search?q=jellyfish*, you aren't changing anything about the directory of jellyfish resources. You're just retrieving a representation of it. A client should be able to send a GET or HEAD request to an unknown URI and feel safe that nothing disastrous will happen.

This is not to say that GET and HEAD requests can't have side effects. Some resources are hit counters that increment every time a client GETs them. Most web servers log every incoming request to a log file. These are side effects: the server state, and even the resource state, is changing in response to a GET request. But the client didn't ask for the side effects, and it's not responsible for them. A client should never make a GET or HEAD request just for the side effects, and the side effects should never be so big that the client might wish it hadn't made the request.

Idempotence

Idempotence is a slightly tricker notion. The idea comes from math, and if you're not familiar with idempotence, a math example might help. An idempotent operation in math is one that has the same effect whether you apply it once, or more than once. Multiplying a number by zero is idempotent: $4 \times 0 \times 0 \times 0$ is the same as 4×0.[#] By analogy, an operation on a resource is idempotent if making one request is the same as

---

[#] Multiplying a number by one is both safe and idempotent: $4 \times 1 \times 1 \times 1$ is the same as 4×1, which is the same as 4. Multiplication by zero is not safe, because 4×0 is not the same as 4. Multiplying by any other number is neither safe nor idempotent.

making a series of identical requests. The second and subsequent requests leave the resource state in exactly the same state as the first request did.

PUT and DELETE operations are idempotent. If you DELETE a resource, it's gone. If you DELETE it again, it's still gone. If you create a new resource with PUT, and then resend the PUT request, the resource is still there and it has the same properties you gave it when you created it. If you use PUT to change the state of a resource, you can resend the PUT request and the resource state won't change again.

The practical upshot of this is that you shouldn't allow your clients to PUT representations that change a resource's state in relative terms. If a resource keeps a numeric value as part of its resource state, a client might use PUT to set that value to 4, or 0, or 50, but not to increment that value by 1. If the initial value is 0, sending two PUT requests that say "set the value to 4" leaves the value at 4. If the initial value is 0, sending two PUT requests that say "increment the value by 1" leaves the value not at 1, but at 2. That's not idempotent.

Why safety and idempotence matter

Safety and idempotence let a client make reliable HTTP requests over an unreliable network. If you make a GET request and never get a response, just make another one. It's safe: even if your earlier request went through, it didn't have any real effect on the server. If you make a PUT request and never get a response, just make another one. If your earlier request got through, your second request will have no additional effect.

POST is neither safe nor idempotent. Making two identical POST requests to a "factory" resource will probably result in two subordinate resources containing the same information. With overloaded POST, all bets are off.

The most common misuse of the uniform interface is to expose unsafe operations through GET. The del.icio.us and Flickr APIs both do this. When you GET *https://api.del.icio.us/posts/delete*, you're not fetching a representation: you're modifying the del.icio.us data set.

Why is this bad? Well, here's a story. In 2005 Google released a client-side caching tool called Web Accelerator. It runs in conjunction with your web browser and "pre-fetches" the pages linked to from whatever page you're viewing. If you happen to click one of those links, the page on the other side will load faster, because your computer has already fetched it.

Web Accelerator was a disaster. Not because of any problem in the software itself, but because the Web is full of applications that misuse GET. Web Accelerator assumed that GET operations were safe, that clients could make them ahead of time just in case a human being wanted to see the corresponding representations. But when it made those GET requests to real URIs, it changed the data sets. People lost data.

There's plenty of blame to go around: programmers shouldn't expose unsafe actions through GET, and Google shouldn't have released a real-world tool that didn't work with the real-world web. The current version of Web Accelerator ignores all URIs that contain query variables. This solves part of the problem, but it also prevents many resources that are safe to use through GET (such as Google web searches) from being pre-fetched.

Multiply the examples if you like. Many web services and web applications use URIs as input, and the first thing they do is send a GET request to fetch a representation of a resource. These services don't mean to trigger catastrophic side effects, but it's not up to them. It's up to the service to handle a GET request in a way that complies with the HTTP standard.

Why the Uniform Interface Matters

The important thing about REST is not that you use the specific uniform interface that HTTP defines. REST specifies a uniform interface, but it doesn't say *which* uniform interface. GET, PUT, and the rest are not a perfect interface for all time. What's important is the uniformity: that every service use HTTP's interface the same way.

The point is not that GET is the best name for a read operation, but that GET means "read" across the Web, no matter which resource you're using it on. Given a URI of a resource, there's no question of how you get a representation: you send an HTTP GET request to that URI. The uniform interface makes any two services as similar as any two web sites. Without the uniform interface, you'd have to learn how each service expected to receive and send information. The rules might even be different for different resources within a single service.

You can program a computer to understand what GET means, and that understanding will apply to every RESTful web service. There's not much to understand. The service-specific code can live in the handling of the representation. Without the uniform interface, you get a multiplicity of methods taking the place of GET: doSearch and getPage and nextPrime. Every service speaks a different language. This is also the reason I don't like overloaded POST very much: it turns the simple Esperanto of the uniform interface into a Babel of one-off sublanguages.

Some applications extend HTTP's uniform interface. The most obvious case is Web-DAV, which adds eight new HTTP methods including MOVE, COPY, and SEARCH. Using these methods in a web service would not violate any precept of REST, because REST doesn't say what the uniform interface should look like. Using them would violate my Resource-Oriented Architecture (I've explicitly tied the ROA to the standard HTTP methods), but your service could still be resource-oriented in a general sense.

The real reason not to use the WebDAV methods is that doing so makes your service incompatible with other RESTful services. Your service would use a different uniform interface than most other services. There are web services like Subversion that use the WebDAV methods, so your service wouldn't be all alone. But it would be part of a much smaller web. This is why making up your own HTTP methods is a very, very bad idea: your custom vocabulary puts you in a community of one. You might as well be using XML-RPC.

Another uniform interface consists solely of HTTP GET and overloaded POST. To fetch a representation of a resource, you send GET to its URI. To create, modify, or delete a resource, you send POST. This interface is perfectly RESTful, but, again, it doesn't conform to my Resource-Oriented Architecture. This interface is just rich enough to distinguish between safe and unsafe operations. A resource-oriented web application would use this interface, because today's HTML forms only support GET and POST.

That's It!

That's the Resource-Oriented Architecture. It's just four concepts:

1. Resources
2. Their names (URIs)
3. Their representations
4. The links between them

and four properties:

1. Addressability
2. Statelessness
3. Connectedness
4. A uniform interface

Of course, there are still a lot of open questions. How should a real data set be split into resources, and how should the resources be laid out? What should go into the actual HTTP requests and responses? I'm going to spend much of the rest of the book exploring issues like these.

## CHAPTER 5

Designing Read-Only Resource-Oriented Services

We've got some information we want to expose to people elsewhere on the network. We want to reach the widest possible combination of clients. Every programming language has an HTTP library, so the natural choice is to expose the data over HTTP. Every programming language has an XML parsing library, so we can format the data with XML and always be understood. Whee!

Sometimes that's as far as the train of thought goes. The solution is obvious, so the programmers set to work. Despite its vagueness, this technique gives surprisingly good results. Most people are intuitively familiar with what makes a good web site, and a good web service works much the same way.

Unfortunately, this gut-feeling approach combines everyone's gut feelings into a stew of web services that are usually not RESTful (they're REST-RPC hybrids), and which work alike only in superficial ways. If you understand *why* REST works, you can make your services safer, easier to use, and accessible through standard tools.

Some "web services" were never intended to be used as such, and have RESTful qualities seemingly by accident. Into this category fall the many well-designed web sites that have been screen-scraped over the years. So do many providers of images: for instance, the static map tiles served up to the Google Maps application, where you change the URI to address a different part of the Earth. An amusing example is Amazon product images, which can be manipulated in funny ways by putting extra strings in the URI.[*]

It is no accident that so many web sites are RESTful. A well-designed web site presents uncluttered representations of sensibly named resources, accessible through HTTP GET. Uncluttered representations are easy to parse or screen-scrape, and sensibly named resources are easy to address programmatically. Using GET to fetch a

---

[*] This trick is detailed in Nat Gertler's enjoyable article, "Abusing Amazon Images" (*http://www.aaugh.com/imageabuse.html*).

representation respects HTTP's uniform interface. Design a web site by these rules, and it will fit well with my Resource-Oriented Architecture.

Now that I've introduced the principles of REST, within the ROA, I'll show how to use the ROA to design programmatic services that serve data across the network. These simple services provide client access to a data set. They may even let clients filter or search the data. But they don't let clients modify the data or add to it. In Chapter 6 I talk about web services that let you store and modify information on the server. For now I'm focused on letting clients retrieve and search a data set.

I've split the discussion because many excellent web services do nothing more than send useful information out to the people that need it. These are not toy services. Any web-based database search falls into this category: web searches, book searches, even the stereotypical stock quote web service (okay, that one's probably just a toy). It's more manageable to cover the simpler cases—which do happen in real life—than to try to cover everything in one huge chapter. The lessons in the next chapter build directly on what I say in this one. After all, a web service that lets clients modify information must also let them retrieve it.

In this chapter I design a web service that serves information about maps. It's inspired by web applications like Google Maps, but those sites (and the third-party sites build atop them) are designed for ad hoc use by humans. As with any well-designed web site, you can consume Google Maps image tiles as a web service, but only somewhat illicitly and with difficulty. The fantasy service I design here is a programmer-friendly way to retrieve map data for any purpose, *including* a browser-based map navigation application like the Google Maps Ajax application.

I won't actually implement this service. An implementation would be too complex to fit in this book, and I don't own the necessary data anyway. (Note, though, that in Chapter 7 I use the lessons of this chapter to implement a social bookmarking service similar to del.icio.us). This chapter and the next aim to teach you how to see a problem from a resource-oriented point of view. Along the way I hope to demonstrate that the ROA's simple rules and uniform interface can represent an extremely powerful and fairly complex distributed service.

Resource Design

The standard design technique for object-oriented programs is to break a system down into its moving parts: its nouns. An object *is* something. Each noun ("Reader," "Column," "Story," "Comment") gets its own class, and behavior for interacting with the other nouns. By contrast, a good design technique for an RPC-style architecture is to break the system into its motions: its verbs. A procedure *does* something ("Subscribe to," "Read," "Comment on").

A resource *is* something, so I take an object-oriented approach to designing resources. In fact, the resource-oriented design strategy could be called "extreme object-oriented."

A class in a programming language can expose any number of methods and give them any names, but an HTTP resource exposes a uniform interface of at most six HTTP methods. These methods allow only the most basic operations: create (PUT or POST), modify (PUT), read (GET), and delete (DELETE). If necessary, you can extend this interface by overloading POST, turning a resource into a small RPC-style message processor, but you shouldn't need to do that very often.

A service can expose a Story resource, and a Story can exist in either draft or published form, but a client can't publish a draft Story to the live site. Not in so many words, anyway: "publish" isn't one of the six actions. A client *can* PUT a new representation for the Story which depicts it as published. The resource may then be available at a new URI, and may no longer require authentication to read. This is a subtle distinction, but one that keeps you from making dangerous design mistakes like exposing a special RPC-style "publish this article" URI through GET.

The uniform interface means that a resource-oriented design must treat as objects what an object-oriented design might consider verbs. In the ROA, a Reader can't subscribe to a regularly appearing Column, because "subscribe to" is not part of the uniform interface. There must be a third object, Subscription, representing that relationship between a Reader and a Column. This relationship object is subject to the uniform interface: it can be created, fetched (perhaps as a syndication feed), and deleted. "Subscription" might not show up as a first-class object in an object-oriented analysis, but it probably would appear as a table in an underlying database model. In a resource-oriented analysis, all object manipulation happens through resources that respect the uniform interface. Whenever I'm tempted to add a new method to one of my resource "classes," I'll resolve the problem by defining a new kind of resource.

Turning Requirements Into Read-Only Resources

I've come up with a procedure to follow once you have an idea of what you want your program to do.[†] It produces a set of resources that respond to a read-only subset of HTTP's uniform interface: GET and possibly HEAD. Once you get to the end of this procedure, you should be ready to implement your resources in whatever language and framework you like. If you want to expose a larger subset of the uniform interface, I present a slightly extended procedure in Chapter 6.

1. Figure out the data set
2. Split the data set into resources

   For each kind of resource:

3. Name the resources with URIs
4. Expose a subset of the uniform interface

[†] This procedure has a lot in common with Joe Gregorio's "How to create a REST Protocol" (*http://www.xml.com/pub/a/2004/12/01/restful-web.html*).

5. Design the representation(s) accepted from the client
6. Design the representation(s) served to the client
7. Integrate this resource into existing resources, using hypermedia links and forms
8. Consider the typical course of events: what's supposed to happen?
9. Consider error conditions: what might go wrong?

In the sections to come, I'll show, step by step, how following this procedure results in a RESTful web service that works like the Web. The only difference between what I do and what this procedure says is that I'm going to design all my resources at once, rather than take you through the same steps over and over again for each kind of resource.

Figure Out the Data Set

A web service starts with a data set, or at least an idea for one. This is the data set you'll be exposing and/or getting your users to build. Earlier I said my data set would be maps, but which maps? This is a fantasy, so I'll spread the net wide. My imaginary web service will serve maps in all projections and at all scales. Maps of the past, the present, and the supposed future. Maps of other planets and of individual cities. Political maps, road maps (which are just very detailed political maps), physical maps, geological maps, and topographic maps.

This is not every kind of map. I'll only serve maps that use a standard 2-D coordinate system: a way of identifying any given point on the map. The map need not be accurate, but it must be *addressable* (there's that word again) using latitude and longitude. This means I won't serve most maps of fictional places, maps that arbitrarily distort geography (the way subway maps do), or maps created before longitude could be measured accurately.

Maps are made out of points: in this case, points of latitude and longitude. Every map contains an infinite number of points, but I can have a map without keeping every one of those points in my data set. I just need some image data and a couple basic pieces of information about the map: what are the latitude and longitude of the map's corners? Or, if the map covers an entire planet, where on the map is the prime meridian?‡ Given that information, I can use standard geographical algorithms to locate and move between the infinitely many points on a map.§

A map is a map *of* some planet. (I say "planet" for simplicity's sake, but my system will serve maps of moons, asteroids, and any other body that has latitude and longitude.) A map is an interesting part of my data set, but so is the actual planet it represents. It's

---

‡ Fun fact: prime meridians for planetary bodies are usually chosen by reference to some arbitrary feature like a crater. For bodies like Jupiter and Io, whose features are always changing, the prime meridian is defined according to which way the body was facing at an arbitrary time.

§ A good reference for these algorithms is Ed Williams's "Aviation Formulary" (*http://williams.best.vwh.net/ avform.htm*).

---

convenient to refer to points on a planet, independent of any particular map, even though a planet doesn't have physical lines of latitude and longitude running around it. One obvious use: I want to be able to see what maps there are for a particular point on Earth. There are probably more maps covering a point in New York City than a point in the middle of the Pacific Ocean.

So my data set includes not only the maps and the points on the maps, but the very planets themselves, and every point on the planets. It may seem hubristic to treat the entire planet Earth as a resource, but remember that I'm not obliged to give a complete account of the state of any resource. If my representation of "Earth" is just a list of my maps of Earth, that's fine. The important thing is that the client can say "tell me about Earth," as opposed to "tell me about the political map of Earth," and I can give an answer.

Speaking of New York City and the Pacific Ocean, some points on a planet are more interesting than others. Most points have nothing much underneath them. Some points correspond to a cornfield or flat lunar plain, and others correspond to a city or a meteor crater. Some points on a planet are *places*. My users will be disproportionately interested in these points on the planets, and the corresponding points on my maps. They won't want to specify these places as latitude-longitude pairs. Indeed, many of my users will be trying to figure out where something is: they'll be trying to turn a known place into a point on a planet.

Fortunately, most places have agreed-upon names, like "San Francisco," "Eratosthenes," and "Mount Whitney." To make it easy for my users to identify places, my data set will include a mapping of place names to the corresponding points on the planets.‖ Note that a single planet may have multiple places with the same name. There might be one "Joe's Diner" on the Moon and a hundred on Earth, all distinct. If my user wants to find a particular Joe's Diner on Earth, they'll have to specify its location more precisely than just "Earth."

What about places that aren't points, like cities, countries, and rivers? For simplicity's sake, I'll make a well-chosen point stand for an area on a planet. For instance, I'll have a point on Earth near the geographic center of the U.S. that stands for the place called "the United States of America." (This is obviously a vast oversimplification. Many real GIS mapping programs represent such areas as *lists* of points, which form lines or polygons.)

Every place is of a certain type. Some places are cities, some mountains, some hot springs, some the current locations of ships, some areas of high pollution, and so on. I'll keep track of the type of each place. Two places of different types may correspond

---

‖ You may have a private name for a seemingly boring point on the map, like "the cornfield where I kissed Betty." This will come into play in Chapter 6 when I expand my web service so that clients can create their own place names. For now, I've got a preset database of names for each planet.

to the same point on a planet: some unfortunate's house may be built on top of a toxic waste dump.

My service can find a place on a planet, given its name, type, or description. It can show the place on any appropriate maps, and it can find places nearby. Given a street address, my service can locate the corresponding point on the planet Earth, and show it on a road map. Given the name of a country, it can locate the corresponding place on the planet (as a representative point), and show it on a political map.

If the client tries to find a place whose name is ambiguous (for instance, "Springfield") my service can list all appropriate points within the given scope. The client will also be able to search for places of a certain type, without requiring the user give specific names. So a user can search for "pollution sites near Reno, Nevada."

General Lessons

This is a standard first step in any analysis. Sometimes you get to choose your data set, and sometimes you're trying to expose data you've already got. You may come back to this step as you see how best to expose your data set as resources. I went through the design process two or three times before I figured out that points on a planet needed to be considered distinct from points on any particular map. Even now, the data set is chaotic, just a bundle of ideas. I'll give it shape when I divide it into resources.

I presented the results of a search operation ("places on Earth called Springfield") as part of the data set. An RPC-oriented analysis would treat these as actions that the client invokes—remember doGoogleSearch from the Google SOAP service. Compare this to how the Google web site works: in a resource-oriented analysis, ways of looking at the data are themselves pieces of data. If you consider an algorithm's output to be a resource, running the algorithm can be as simple as sending a GET to that resource.

So far I've said nothing about how a web service client can access this data set through HTTP. Right now I'm just gathering everything together in one place. I'm also ignoring any consideration of how these features should be implemented. If I actually planned to provide this service, the features I've announced so far would have a profound effect on the structure of my database, and I could start designing that part of the application as well. As it is, I'm going to wave away details of the backend implementation, and press on with the design of the web service.

Split the Data Set into Resources

Once you have a data set in mind, the next step is to decide how to expose the data as HTTP resources. Remember that a resource is *anything interesting enough to be the target of a hypertext link*. Anything that might be refereed to by name ought to have a name. Web services commonly expose three kinds of resources:

Predefined one-off resources for especially important aspects of the application.
This includes top-level directories of other available resources. Most services expose few or no one-off resources.

Example: A web site's homepage. It's a one-of-a-kind resource, at a well-known URI, which acts as a portal to other resources.

The root URI of Amazon's S3 service (*https://s3.amazonaws.com/*) serves a list of your S3 buckets. There's only one resource of this type on S3. You can GET this resource, but you can't DELETE it, and you can't modify it directly: it's modified only by operating on its buckets. It's a predefined resource that acts as a directory of child resources (the buckets).

A resource for every object exposed through the service.
One service may expose many kinds of objects, each with its own resource set. Most services expose a large or infinite number of these resources.

Example: Every S3 bucket you create is exposed as a resource. You can create up to 100 buckets, and they can have just about any names you want (it's just that your names can't conflict with anyone else's). You can GET and DELETE these resources, but once you've created them you can't modify them directly: they're modified only by operating on the objects they contain.

Every S3 object you create is also exposed as a resource. A bucket has room for any number of objects. You can GET, PUT, and DELETE these resources as you see fit.

Resources representing the results of algorithms applied to the data set.
This includes collection resources, which are usually the results of queries. Most services either expose an infinite number of algorithmic resources, or they don't expose any.

Example: A search engine exposes an infinite number of algorithmic resources. There's one for every search request you might possibly make. The Google search engine exposes one resource at *http://google.com/search?q=jellyfish* (that'd be "a directory of resources about jellyfish") and another at *http://google.com/search?q=chocolate* ("a directory of resources about chocolate"). Neither of these resources were explicitly defined ahead of time: Google translates *any* URI of the form *http://google.com/search?q={query}* into an algorithmic resource "a directory of resources about *{query}*."

I didn't cover this in much detail back in Chapter 3, but S3 also exposes an infinite number of algorithmic resources. If you're interested, look back to Example 3-7 and the implementation of `S3::Bucket#getObjects`. Some of S3's algorithmic resources work like a search engine for the objects in a bucket. If you're only interested in objects whose names start with the string "movies/", there's a resource for that: it's exposed through the URI *https://s3.amazonaws.com/MyBucket?Prefix=movies/*. You can GET this resource, but you can't manipulate it directly: it's just a view of the underlying data set.

Let's apply these categories to my fantasy map service. I need one special resource that lists the planets, just as S3 has a top-level resource that lists the buckets. It's reasonable to link to "the list of planets." Every planet is a resource: it's reasonable to link to "Venus." Every map of a planet is also a resource: it's reasonable to link to "the radar map of Venus." The list of planets is a resource of the first type, since there's only one of them. The planets and maps are also one-off resources: my service will serve a small number of maps for a small number of planets.

Here are some of the resources so far:

- The list of planets
- Mars
- Earth
- The satellite map of Mars
- The radar map of Venus
- The topographic map of Earth
- The political map of Earth

But I can't just serve entire maps and let our clients figure out the rest. Then I'd just be running a hosting service for huge static map files: a RESTful service to be sure, but not a very interesting one. I must also serve *parts* of maps, oriented on specific points and places.

Every point on a planet is potentially interesting, and so should be a resource. A point might represent a house, a mountain, or the current location of a ship. These are resources of the second type, because there are an infinite number of points on any planet. For every point on a planet there's a corresponding point on one or more maps. This is why I limited myself to addressable maps. When the map can be addressed by latitude and longitude, it's easy to turn a point on the planet into a point on a map.

Here are some more of the resources so far:

- 24.9195N 17.821E on Earth
- 24.9195N 17.821E on the political map of Earth
- 24.9195N 17.821E on Mars
- 44N 0W on the geologic map of Earth

I'll also serve *places*: points on a planet identified by name rather than by coordinates. My fantasy database contains a large but finite number of places. Each place has a type, a latitude and longitude, and each might also have additional associated data. For instance, an area of high pollution should "know" what pollutant is there and what the concentration is. As with points identified by latitude and longitude, the client should be able to move from a place on the planet to the corresponding point on any map.

Are Places Really Resources?

Are places really resources of their own or are they just alternate names for the "point on a planet" resources I just defined? After all, every place is just a geographic point. Maybe I've got a situation where a single resource has two names: one based on latitude and longitude, and one based on a human-readable name.

Well, consider a place representing the current location of a ship. It coincides with a specific point on the map, and it might be considered just an alternate name for that point. But in an hour, it'll coincide with a different point on the map. A business, too, might move over time from one point on the map to another. A place in this service is not a location: it's something that has location. A place has an independent life from the point on the map it occupies.

This is analogous to the discussion in Chapter 4 about whether "version 1.0.3" and "the latest version" point to the same resource. It may happen that they point to the same data right now, but there are two different things there, and each might be the target of a hypertext link. I might link to one and say "Version 1.0.3 has a bug." I might link to the other and say "download the latest version." Similarly, I might link to a point on Earth and say "The treasure is buried here." Or I might link to a place called "USS *Mutiny*" at the same coordinates and say "Our ship is currently here." Places are their own resources, and they're resources of the second type: each one corresponds to an object exposed through the service.

I said earlier that place names are ambiguous. There are about 6,000 (an approximation) cities and towns in the United States called Springfield. If a place name is unusual you can just say what planet it's on, and it's as good as specifying latitude and longitude. If a place name is common, you might have to specify more scoping information: giving a continent, country, or city along with the name of your place. Here are a few more sample resources:

- The Cleopatra crater on Venus
- The Ubehebe crater on Earth
- 1005 Gravenstein Highway North, Sebastopol, CA
- The headquarters of O'Reilly Media, Inc.
- The place called Springfield in Massachusetts, in the United States of America, on Earth

So far, this is pretty general stuff. Users want to know which maps we have, so we expose a one-off resource that lists the planets. Each planet is also a one-off resource that links to the available maps. A geographic point on a planet is addressable by latitude and longitude, so it makes sense to expose each point as an addressable resource. Every point on a planet corresponds to a point on one or more maps. Certain points are interesting and have names, so places on a planet are also accessible by name: a client can find them on the planet and then see that point on a map.

All I've done so far is describe the interactions between parts of a predefined data set. I haven't yet exposed any algorithmically-generated resources, but it's easy enough to add some. The most common kind of algorithmic resource is the list of search results. I'll allow my clients to search for places on a planet that have certain names, or that match place-specific criteria. Here are some sample algorithmic resources:

- Places on Earth called Springfield
- Container ships on Earth
- Craters on Mars more than 1 km in diameter
- Places on the moon named before 1900

Search results can be restricted to a particular area, not just a planet. Some more sample resources:

- Places in the United States named Springfield
- Sites of hot springs in Colorado
- Oil tankers or container ships near Indonesia
- Pizza restaurants in Worcester, MA
- Diners near Mount Rushmore
- Areas of high arsenic near 24.9195N 17.821E
- Towns in France with population less than 1,000

These are all algorithmically-generated resources, because they rely on the client providing an arbitrary search string ("Springfield") or combining unrelated elements ("Mount Rushmore" + diners, or "France" + towns + "population < 1000").

I could come up with new kinds of resources all day (in fact, that's what I did while writing this). But all the resources I've thought up so far fit into five basic types, just enough to make the fantasy interesting. Example 5-1 gives the master list of resource types.

Example 5-1. The five types of resources

1. The list of planets
2. A place on a planet—possibly the entire planet—identified by name
3. A geographic point on a planet, identified by latitude and longitude
4. A list of places on a planet that match some search criteria
5. A map of a planet, centered around a particular point

A real-life web service might define additional resources. Real web sites like Google Maps expose one obvious bit of functionality I haven't mentioned: driving directions. If I wanted to enhance my service I might expose a new algorithmically-generated resource which treats a set of driving directions as a relationship between two places. The representation of this resource might be a list of textual instructions, with references to points on a road map.

General Lessons

A RESTful web service exposes both its data and its algorithms through resources. There's usually a hierarchy that starts out small and branches out into infinitely many leaf nodes. The list of planets contains the planets, which contain points and places, which contain maps. The S3 bucket list contains the individual buckets, which contain the objects.

It takes a while to get the hang of exposing an algorithm as a set of resources. Instead of thinking in terms of actions ("do a search for places on the map"), you need to think in terms of the results of that action ("the list of places on the map matching a search criteria"). You may find yourself coming back to this step if you find that your design doesn't fit HTTP's uniform interface.

Name the Resources

I've decided on five types of resources (see Example 5-1). Now they need names. Resources are named with URIs, so let's pick some. Remember, in a resource-oriented service the URI contains all the scoping information. Our URIs need to answer questions like: "Why should the server operate on this map instead of that map?" and "Why should the server operate on this place instead of that place?"

I'll root my web service at *http://maps.example.com/*. For brevity's sake I sometimes use relative URIs in this chapter and the next; understand that they're relative to *http://maps.example.com/*. If I say /Earth/political, what I mean is *http://maps.example.com/Earth/political*.

Now let's consider the resources. The most basic resource is the list of planets. It makes sense to put this at the root URI, *http://maps.example.com/*. Since the list of planets encompasses the entire service, there's no scoping information at all for this resource (unless you count the service version as scoping information).

For the other resources I'd like to pick URIs that organize the scoping information in a natural way. There are three basic rules for URI design, born of collective experience:

1. Use path variables to encode hierarchy: /parent/child

2. Put punctuation characters in path variables to avoid implying hierarchy where none exists: /parent/child1;child2

3. Use query variables to imply inputs into an algorithm, for example: /search?q=jellyfish&start=20

Encode Hierarchy into Path Variables

Let's make URIs for the second class of resource: planets and places on planets. There's one piece of scoping information here: what planet are we looking at? (Earth? Venus? Ganymede?) This scoping information fits naturally into a hierarchy: the list of planets is at the top, and underneath it is every particular planet. Here are the URIs to some of my planets. I show hierarchy by using the slash character to separate pieces of scoping information.

- *http://maps.example.com/Venus*
- *http://maps.example.com/Earth*
- *http://maps.example.com/Mars*

To identify geographical places by name I'll just extend the hierarchy to the right. You'll know you've got a good URI design when it's easy to extend hierarchies by tacking on additional path variables. Here are some URIs to various places on planets:

- *http://maps.example.com/Venus*
- *http://maps.example.com/Venus/Cleopatra*
- *http://maps.example.com/Earth/France/Paris*
- *http://maps.example.com/Earth/Paris,%20France*
- *http://maps.example.com/Earth/Little%20Rock,AR*
- *http://maps.example.com/Earth/USA/Mount%20Rushmore*
- *http://maps.example.com/Earth/1005%20Gravenstein%20Highway%20North,%20Sebastopol,%20CA%2095472*

We're now deep into web service territory. Sending a GET to one of these URIs invokes a remote operation that takes a variable number of arguments, and can locate a place on a planet to any desired degree of precision. But the URIs themselves look like normal web site URIs you can bookmark, cache, put on billboards, and pass to other services as input—because that's what they are. Path variables are the best way to organize scoping information that can be arranged hierarchically. The same structure you see in a filesystem, or on a static web site, can correspond to an arbitrarily long list of path variables.

No Hierarchy? Use Commas or Semicolons

The next resources I need to name are geographic points on the globe, represented by latitude and longitude. Latitude and longitude are tied together, so a hierarchy isn't appropriate. A URI like */Earth/24.9195/17.821* doesn't make sense. The slash makes it look like longitude is a subordinate concept to latitude, the way `/Earth/Chicago` signals that Chicago is part of Earth.

Instead of using the slash to put two pieces of scoping information into a hierarchy, I recommend combining them on the same level of a hierarchy with a punctuation character: usually the semicolon or the comma. I'm going to use a comma to separate latitude and longitude. This yields URIs like the following:

- *http://maps.example.com/Earth/24.9195,17.821*
- *http://maps.example.com/Venus/3,-80*

Latitude and longitude can also be used as scoping information to uniquely identify a named place. A human would probably identify Mount Rushmore as `/Earth/USA/Mount %20Rushmore` or as `/v1/Earth/USA/SD/Mount%20Rushmore`, but `/v1/Earth/43.9;-103.46/ Mount%20Rushmore` would be more precise.

From a URI design perspective, the interesting thing here is that I'm stuffing two pieces of scoping information into one path variable. The first path variable denotes a planet, and the second one denotes both latitude and longitude. This kind of URI may look a little strange, because not many web sites or services use them right now, but they're catching on.

I recommend using commas when the order of the scoping information is important, and semicolons when the order doesn't matter. In this case the order matters: if you switch latitude and longitude, you get a different point on the planet. So I used commas to separate the two numbers. It doesn't hurt that people already use commas in written language to separate latitude and longitude: URIs should use our existing conventions when possible.

In another case the order might not matter. Consider a web service that lets you mix colors of paint to get the shade you want. If you're mixing red and blue paint, it doesn't matter whether you pour the red into the blue or the blue into the red: you get purple either way. So the URI `/color-blends/red;blue` identifies the same resource as `/color-blends/blue;red`. I think the semicolon is better than the comma here, because the order doesn't matter. This is just a typographical convention, but it helps a human being make sense of your web service URIs. The use of the semicolon feeds into an obscure idea called matrix URIs (*http://www.w3.org/DesignIssues/MatrixURIs.html*), a way of defining key-value pairs in URIs without using query variables. Some newer standards, like WADL, offer support for matrix URIs. They're especially useful if you ever need to put key-value pairs in the *middle* of a hierarchy.

URIs can become very long, especially when there's no limit to how deep you can nest the path variables. My web service might let clients name a place using a lot of explicit scoping information: `/Earth/North%20Amer ica/USA/California/Northern%20California/San%20Francisco%20Bay% 20Area/Sebastopol/...`

The HTTP standard doesn't impose any restrictions on URI length, but real web servers and clients do. For instance, Microsoft Internet Explorer can't handle URIs longer than 2,083 characters, and Apache won't respond to requests for URIs longer than 8 KBs. If some of your resources are only addressable given a great deal of scoping information, you may have to accept some of it in HTTP headers, or use overloaded POST and put scoping information in the entity-body.

Map URIs

Now that I've designed the URI to a geographic point on a planet, what about the corresponding point on a road map or satellite map? After all, the main point of this service is to serve maps.

Earlier I said I'd expose a resource for every point on a map. For simplicity's sake, I'm not exposing maps of named places, only points of latitude and longitude. In addition to a set of coordinates or the name of a place, I need the name of the planet and the type of map (satellite map, road map, or whatever). Here are some URIs to maps of planets, places, and points:

- *http://maps.example.com/radar/Venus*
- *http://maps.example.com/radar/Venus/65.9,7.00*
- *http://maps.example.com/geologic/Earth/43.9,-103.46*

Scale

A URI like `/satellite/Earth/41,-112` says nothing about how detailed the map should be. I'm going to extend the first path variable so that it doesn't just specify the type of map: it can also specify the scale. I'll expose a very small-scale map at `/satellite.10/ Earth`, a very large-scale map at `/satellite.1/Earth`, and maps of other scales in between. I'll choose a sensible default scale: probably a large scale like 2. Here are some possible URIs for the same map at different scales:

- `/satellite.10/Earth/41,-112`: 1:24,000; 2,000 feet to the inch. A map for hiking or prospecting. Centered on 41°N 112°W on Earth, this map would show the banks of Utah's Great Salt Lake.
- `/satellite.5/Earth/41,-112`: 1:250,000; 4 miles to the inch. The scale of a highway map. Centered on 41°N 112°W, this map would show the northern suburbs of Salt Lake City.

- `/satellite.1/Earth/41,-112`: 1:51,969,000; 820 miles to an inch. (That's 820 miles/inch *at the equator*. At this scale, the curvature of the earth distorts the scale of a 2D map.) The scale of a world map. Centered on 41°N 112°W, this map would show much of Utah and surrounding states.

The scale affects not only the natural size of the map in pixels, but which features are shown. A small town would be represented in fair detail on a map at scale 10, but would only be a point at scale 5 if it showed up at all.

How did I decide that scale 1 would be a large-scale map, and scale 10 would be a small-scale map? Why not the reverse? I used a common technique for URI design. I exaggerated the decision I was making, figured out how the generalized situation should work, and then scaled my decision back down.

Maps can always get more detailed, but there's a limit how small they can get.[#] If I decide to acquire some new data for my map service, I'd never buy a map that shows the world in less detail than the world map at scale 1. There'd be no point. However, it's quite possible that I'll find maps that are more detailed than the one at scale 10. When I find those maps, I can make them available through my service and assign them scales of 11, 12, and so on. If I'd assigned the most detailed map a scale of 1, I'd have to assign scales of 0, −1, and so on to any new maps. The URIs would look strange. This means larger numbers make good URIs for more detailed maps. I may never actually get those more detailed maps, but thinking about them revealed a truth about my URI design.

Algorithmic Resource? Use Query Variables

Most web applications don't store much state in path variables: they use query variables instead. You may have seen URIs like this:

- *http://www.example.com/colorpair?color1=red&color2=blue*
- *http://www.example.com/articles?start=20061201&end=20071201*
- *http://www.example.com/weblog?post=My-Opinion-About-Taxes*

Those URIs would look better without the query variables:

- *http://www.example.com/colorpair/red;blue*
- *http://www.example.com/articles/20061201-20071201*
- *http://www.example.com/weblog/My-Opinion-About-Taxes*

Sometimes, though, query variables are appropriate. Here's a Google search URI: *http://www.google.com/search?q=jellyfish*. If the Google web application used path variables, its URIs would look more like directories and less like the result of running an algorithm: *http://www.google.com/search/jellyfish*.

[#] Up to a point, anyway. See *On Exactitude in Science* by Jorge Luis Borges.

Both of those URIs would be legitimate resource-oriented names for the resource "a directory of web pages about jellyfish." The second one doesn't look quite right, though, because of how we're socialized to look at URIs. Path variables look like you're traversing a hierarchy, and query variables look like you're passing arguments into an algorithm. "Search" sounds like an algorithm. For example, `http://www.google.com/directory/jellyfish"` might work better than `/search/jellyfish`.

This perception of query variables is reinforced whenever we use the Web. When you fill out an HTML form in a web browser, the data you input is turned into query variables. There's no way to type "jellyfish" into a form and then be sent to *http://www.google.com/search/jellyfish*. The destination of an HTML form is hard-coded to *http://www.google.com/search/*, and when you fill out that form you end up at *http://www.google.com/search?q=jellyfish*. Your browser knows how to tack query variables onto a base URI. It doesn't know how to substitute variables into a generic URI like *http://www.google.com/search/{q}*.

Because of this precedent, a lot of REST-RPC hybrid services use query variables when it would be more idiomatic to use path variables. Even when a hybrid service happens to expose resources RESTfully, the resources have URIs that make them look like function calls: URIs such as *http://api.flickr.com/services/rest/?method=flickr.photos.search&tags=penguin*. Compare that URI to the corresponding URI on the human-usable Flickr site: *http://flickr.com/photos/tags/penguin*.

I've managed to avoid query variables so far: every planet, every point on a planet, and every corresponding map is addressable without them. I don't really like the way query variables look in a URI, and including them in a URI is a good way to make sure that URI gets ignored by tools like proxies, caches, and web crawlers. Think back to the Google Web Accelerator I mentioned in "Why safety and idempotence matter" in "Split the Data Set into Resources. It never pre-fetches a URI that includes a query variable, because that's the kind of URI exposed by poorly-designed web applications that abuse HTTP GET. My service won't abuse GET, of course, but outside applications have no way of knowing that.

But I've got one more type of resource to represent—lists of search results—and I'm out of tricks. It doesn't make sense to keep going down the hierarchy of place, and I can't keep piling on punctuation just to avoid the impression that my service is running an algorithm. Besides, this last type of resource *is* the result of running an algorithm. My search algorithm finds places that match map-specific criteria, just as a search engine finds web sites that match the client's keywords. Query variables are perfectly appropriate for naming algorithmic resources.

The search interface for places can get as complex as I need it to be. I could expose a `name` query variable for place names and `pollutant` for sites of high pollution and `cuisine` for restaurants and all sorts of other query variables. But let's imagine I've got the technology to make it simple. The only query variable I'll add is `show`, which lets the client specify in natural language what feature(s) they're searching for. The server will parse the client's values for show and figure out what places should be in the list of search results.

In "Split the Data Set into Resources" earlier in this chapter, I gave a whole lot of sample search resources: "places on Earth called Springfield," and so on. Here's how a client might use show to construct URIs for some of those resources.

- *http://maps.example.com/Earth?show=Springfield*
- *http://maps.example.com/Mars?show=craters+bigger+than+1km*
- *http://maps.example.com/Earth/Indonesia?show=oil+tankers&show=container +ships*
- *http://maps.example.com/Earth/USA/Mount%20Rushmore?show=diners*
- *http://maps.example.com/Earth/24.9195;17.821?show=arsenic*

Note that all of these URIs are searching the planet, not any particular map.

URI Recap

That's a lot of details. After all, this is the first place where my fantasy resources come into contact with the real world of HTTP. Even so, my service only supports three basic kinds of URI. To recap, here they are:

- The list of planets: /.
- A planet or a place on a planet: /{planet}/[{scoping-information}/][{place-name}]: The value of the optional variable {scoping-information} will be a hierarchy of place names like /USA/New%20England/Maine/ or it will be a latitude/longitude pair. The value of the optional variable {name} will be the name of the place.

  This type of URI can have values for show tacked onto its query string, to search for places near the given place.
- A map of a planet, or a point on a map: /{map-type}{scale}/{planet}/[{scoping-information}]. The value of the optional variable {scoping-information} will always be a latitude/longitude pair. The value of the optional variable {scale} will be a dot and a number.

Design Your Representations

I've decided which resources I'm exposing, and what their URIs will look like. Now I need to decide what data to send when a client requests a resource, and what data format to use. This is just a warmup, since much of Chapter 9 is devoted to a catalog of useful representation formats. Here, I have a specific service in mind, and I need to decide on a format (or a set of formats) that can meet the goals of any RESTful representation: to convey the current state of the resource, and to link to possible new application and resource states.

The Representation Talks About the State of the Resource

The main purpose of any representation is to convey the state of the resource. Remember that "resource state" is just any information about the underlying resource. In this case, the state is going to answer questions like: what does this part of the world look like, graphically? Where exactly is that meteor crater, in latitude and longitude? Where are the nearby restaurants and what are their names? Where are the container ships right now? Representations of different resources will represent different items of state.

The Representation Links to Other States

The other job of the representation is to provide levers of state. A resource's representation ought to link to nearby resources (whatever "nearby" means in context): possible new *application states*. The goal here is *connectedness*: the ability to get from one resource to another by following links.

This is how web sites work. You don't surf the Web by typing in URIs one after the other. You might type in one URI to get to a site's home page, but then you surf by following links and filling out forms. One web page (a "state" of the web site) contains links to other, related web pages (nearby "states").

Of course, a computer program can't look at a document and decide which links it wants to follow. It only has the wants the programmer gives it. If a web service includes links in its representations, the representations must also contain machine-readable signals as to where each link leads. A programmer can write his or her client to pick up on those signals and decide which link matches up with the goals of the moment.

These links are the levers of application state. If a resource can be modified with PUT, or it can spawn new resources in response to POST, its representation ought to also expose the levers of *resource state*. The representation ought to provide any necessary information about what the POST or PUT request should look like. I'm getting a little ahead of myself here, since all the resources in this chapter are read-only. For now, I'll be creating representations that expose the levers of application state.

Representing the List of Planets

The "home page" of my map service is a good place to start, and a good place to introduce the issues behind choosing a representation format. Basically, I want to display a list of links to the planets for which I have maps. What's a good format for a representation of a list?

There's always plain text. This representation in Example 5-2 shows one planet per line: the URI and then the name.

Example 5-2. A plain-text representation of the planet list

```
http://maps.example.com/Earth Earth
http://maps.example.com/Venus Venus
...
```

This is simple but it requires a custom parser. I generally think a structured data format is better than plain text, especially as representations get more complex. (Of course, if plain text is what you're serving, there's no need to dress it up as something else.) JSON keeps the simplicity of plain text but adds a little bit of structure (see Example 5-3).

Example 5-3. A JSON representation of the planet list

```
[{url="http://maps.example.com/Earth, description="Earth"},
 {url="http://maps.example.com/Venus, description="Venus"},
 ...]
```

The downside is that neither JSON nor plain text are generally considered "hypermedia" formats. Another popular option is a custom XML vocabulary, either with or without a schema definition (see Example 5-4).

Example 5-4. An XML representation of the planet list

```
<?xml version="1.0" standalone='yes'?>
<planets>
 <planet href="http://maps.example.com/Earth" name="Earth" />
 <planet href="http://maps.example.com/Venus" name="Venus" />
 ...
</maps>
```

These days, a custom XML vocabulary seems to be the default choice for web service representations. XML is excellent for representing documents, but I think it's actually pretty rare that you would have to come up with a custom vocabulary. The basic problems have already been solved, and most of the time you can reuse an existing XML vocabulary. As it happens, there's already an XML vocabulary for communicating lists of links called Atom.

I cover Atom in detail in Chapter 9. Atom will work to represent the list of planets, but it's not a very good fit. Atom is designed for lists of published texts, and most of its elements don't make sense in this context—what does it mean to know the "author" of a planet, or the date it was last modified? Fortunately, there's another good XML language for displaying lists of links: XHTML. Example 5-5 shows one more representation of the planet list, and this is the one I'm actually going to use.

Example 5-5. An XHTML representation of the planet list

```
<!DOCTYPE html PUBLIC "-//W3C//DTD XHTML 1.1//EN"
    "http://www.w3.org/TR/xhtml11/DTD/xhtml11.dtd">
<html xmlns="http://www.w3.org/1999/xhtml" xml:lang="en">

<head>
 <title>Planet List</title>
</head>
```

```
<body>

<ul class="planets">
 <li><a href="/Earth">Earth</a></li>
 <li><a href="/Venus">Venus</a></li>
 ...
</ul>

</body>
</html>
```

It might seem a little odd to use XHTML, a technology associated with the human web, as a representation format for a web service. I chose it for this example because HTML solves many general markup problems and you're probably already familiar with it. I'd probably choose it for a real web service, for exactly the same reasons. Though it's human-readable and easy to render attractively, nothing prevents well-formed HTML from being processed automatically like XML. XHTML is also extensible. I turned a generic XHTML list into a list of "planets" using XHTML's `class` attribute. This is a simple example of an XHTML *microformat*: a way of adding semantic meaning to XHTML's markup tags. I cover some standard microformats in Chapter 9.

Representing Maps and Points on Maps

What about the maps themselves? What do I serve if someone asks for a satellite map of the Moon? The obvious thing to send is an image, either in a traditional graphics format like PNG or as a SVG scalar graphic. Except for the largest-scale maps, these images will be huge. Is this OK? It depends on the audience for my web service.

If I'm serving clients with ultra-high bandwidth who expect to process huge chunks of map data, then huge files are exactly what they want. But it's more likely my clients will be like the users of existing map applications like Google and Yahoo! Maps: clients who want smaller-sized maps for human browsing.

If the client asks for a medium-scale hiking map centered around 43N 71W, it's surely a waste of bandwidth to send a map of the whole world centered around that point. Instead I should send a little bit of a hiking map, centered around that point, along with navigation links that let the client change the focus of the map. Even if the client asks for a detailed map of the whole world, I don't need to send the entire map: I can send part of the map and let the client fetch the rest as needed.

This is more or less how the online map sites work. If you visit *http://maps.google.com/*, you get a political map centered on the continental United States: that's its representation of "a map of Earth." If you visit *http://maps.google.com/maps?q=New+Hampshire*, you get a road map centered on Concord, the capital city. In either case, the map is divided into square "tile" images 256 pixels on a side. The client (your web browser) fetches tiles as needed and stitches them together to form a navigable map.

Google Maps splits the globe into a grid of 256-pixel square tiles, pretty much ignoring issues of latitude and longitude, and generates static images for each tile. It does this 10 times, once for every zoom level. This is efficient (though it does use a lot of storage space), but for pedagogical purposes I've chosen a conceptually simpler system. I'm assuming my map service can dynamically generate and serve a 256 ×256 image at any scale, centered on any point of latitude and longitude on any map.

 Google Maps's static tile system is more complex because it adds another coordinate system to the map. Besides latitude and longitude, you can also refer to a place by which tile it's on. This makes the navigation representation simpler, at the expense of complicating the design.

When the client requests a point on a map, I'll serve a hypermedia file that includes a link to a tiny map image (a single, dynamically-generated tile) centered on that point. When the client requests a map of an entire planet, I'll pick a point on that planet somewhat arbitrarily and serve a hypermedia file that links to an image centered on that point. These hypermedia files will include links to adjacent points on the map, which will include more links to adjacent points, and so on. The client can follow the navigation links to stitch many tiles together into a map of any desired size.

So Example 5-6 is one possible representation of *http://maps.example.com/road/ Earth*. Like my representation of the list of planets, it uses XHTML to convey resource state and to link to "nearby" resources. The resource state here is information about a certain point on the map. The "nearby" resources are nearby in a literal sense: they're nearby points.

Example 5-6. An XHTML representation of the road map of Earth

```
<!DOCTYPE html PUBLIC "-//W3C//DTD XHTML 1.1//EN"
    "http://www.w3.org/TR/xhtml11/DTD/xhtml11.dtd">
<html xmlns="http://www.w3.org/1999/xhtml" xml:lang="en">

<head>
 <title>Road Map of Earth</title>
</head>
<body>
...
<img class="map" src="/road.2/Earth/images/37.0,-95.png" alt="Map tile"/>
...
<a class="map_nav" href="46.0518,-95.8">North</a>
<a class="map_nav" href="41.3776,-89.7698">Northeast</a>
<a class="map_nav" href="36.4642,-84.5187">East</a>
<a class="map_nav" href="32.3513,-90.4459">Southeast</a>
...
<a class="zoom_in" href="/road.1/Earth/37.0;-95.8">Zoom out</a>
<a class="zoom_out" href="/road.3/Earth/37.0;-95.8">Zoom in</a>
...
</body>
</html>
```

Figure 5-1. A representation for /road/Earth.3/images/37.0,-95.png

Now when a client requests the resource "a road map of Earth" at the URI /road/ Earth, the representation they get is not an enormous, insanely detailed image that they can't deal with. It's a small XHTML document, one that includes links to several other resources.

A human being can just look at this document and know what it means. A computer program doesn't have that ability; it has to be programmed in advance by someone who can think about a whole class of these documents and write code to find which bits have the meaning. A web service works by making promises that it will serve representations of resources with a certain structure. That's why my representation is full of semantic cues like "zoom_in" and "Northeast". Programmers can write clients that pick up on the semantic cues.

Representing the Map Tiles

The representation of a road map of Earth, given in Example 5-6, has a lot of links in it. Most of these are links to XHTML documents that look a lot like "a road map of Earth" does: they're representations of points on the map at various zoom levels. The most important link, though, is the one in the IMG tag. That tag's src attribute references the URI *http://maps.example.com/road/Earth.8/images/37.0;-95.png*.

This is a new kind of resource, and I haven't really considered it before, but it's not hard to figure out what it is. This resource is "an image centered around 37°N 95.8°W on the road map of Earth." In my service, the representation of *that* resource will be a 256×256 image showing the geographic center of the continental U.S. (see Figure 5-1).

The image in Figure 5-1 is 256 pixels square, and represents an area of the Earth about 625 miles square. This image is distinct from the representation of "39°N 95.8°W on the road map of Earth." that would be an XHTML file like the one in Example 5-6. The

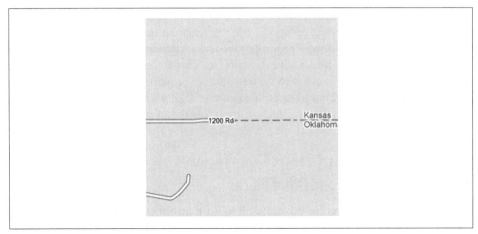

Figure 5-2. A representation for /road.8/Earth/images/37.0,-95.png

XHTML file would include this image by reference, and also link to a lot of nearby points on the map.

Here's another example: if the client requests `/road.8/Earth/32.37,-86.30`, my service will send an XHTML representation whose `IMG` tag references `/road.8/Earth/images/32.37,-86.30.png` (see Figure 5-2). This is a very detailed road map centered on 37.37° N, 86.30°W on Earth.

That image too is 256 pixels square, but it represents an area of the Earth only a half-mile square. Scale makes the difference.

The important thing here is not the exact setup of the tile system or the precise format of the URIs to the tile resources. What's important is what I'm putting into my representations. The URI `/road/Earth` refers to a resource: "a road map of Earth". You'd expect a pretty big image as the representation of that resource. You'd at least expect one that showed all of Earth. But my service sends an XHTML document that references a 256×256 tile image that doesn't even cover four U.S. states. How can that document be a good representation for "a road map of Earth"?

A representation conveys the state of its resource, but it doesn't have to convey the *entire* state of the resource. It just has to convey *some* state. The representation of "Earth" (coming up in a bit) isn't the actual planet Earth, and the representation of "a road map of the Earth" can reference just a simple image tile. But this representation does more than that: the XHTML file links this arbitrarily chosen point on the map to other nearby points on the part of the map directly to the north of this tile, directly to the east, and so on. The client can follow these links to other resources and piece together a larger picture. The map is made of a bunch of connected resources, and you can get as many graphical tiles as you need by following the links. So in a sense, this representation does convey all the state there is about the road map of Earth. You can get as much of that state as you want by following its links to other resources.

It's worth repeating here that if my clients actually need detailed multigigabyte maps, there's no point in me chopping up the state of the map into these tiny tiles. It'd be more efficient to have the representation of /road/Earth?zoom=1 convey the entire state of the map with one huge image. I've designed for clients that only really want part of a map, and wouldn't know what to do with one huge map of the earth if I gave it to them. The clients I have in mind can consume the XHTML files, load the appropriate images, and automatically follow links to stitch together a map that's as big as necessary. You could write an Ajax client for my web service that worked like the Google Maps application.

Representing Planets and Other Places

I've shown representations for the planet list, for maps of the planets, and for points on the maps. But how are you supposed to get from the planet list to, say, the road map of Earth? Presumably you click "Earth" in the planet list, sending a GET request to /Earth, and get back a representation of Earth. This representation includes a bunch of links to maps of Earth. At this point you follow a second link to the road map of Earth. Well, I just described the representation of Earth. My representation of a planet contains whatever useful information I have about the planet, as well as a set of links to other resources: maps of the planet (see Example 5-7).

Example 5-7. An XHTML representation of a place: the planet Earth

```
<!DOCTYPE html PUBLIC "-//W3C//DTD XHTML 1.1//EN"
    "http://www.w3.org/TR/xhtml11/DTD/xhtml11.dtd">
<html xmlns="http://www.w3.org/1999/xhtml" xml:lang="en">

<head><title>Earth</title></head>
<body>

 <dl class="place">
  <dt>name</dt> <dd>Earth</dd>
  <dt>maps</dt>
   <dd>
    <ul class="maps">
     <li><a class="map" href="/road/Earth">Road</a></li>
     <li><a class="map" href="/satellite/Earth">Satellite</a>
     ...
    </ul>
   </dd>
  <dt>type</dt> <dd>planet</dd>
  <dt>description</dt>
   <dd>
     Third planet from Sol. Inhabited by bipeds so amazingly primitive
     that they still think digital watches are a pretty neat idea.
   </dd>
 </dl>

</body>
</html>
```

I've chosen to represent places as lists of key-value pairs. Here, the "place" is the planet Earth itself. Earth in this system is a named place, just like San Francisco or Egypt. I'm representing it using the dd tag: HTML's standard way of presenting a set of key-value pairs. Like any place, Earth has a name, a type, a description, and a list of maps: links to all the resources that map this place.

Why am I representing a planet as a place? Because now my clients can parse the representation of a planet with the same code they use to parse the representation of a place. Example 5-8 is a representation for Mount Rushmore on Earth. You might get this XHTML file back in response to a GET request for /Earth/USA/Mount%20Rushmore.

Example 5-8. An XHTML representation of a place: Mount Rushmore

```
<!DOCTYPE html PUBLIC "-//W3C//DTD XHTML 1.1//EN"
    "http://www.w3.org/TR/xhtml11/DTD/xhtml11.dtd">
<html xmlns="http://www.w3.org/1999/xhtml" xml:lang="en">

<head><title>Mount Rushmore</title></head>
<body>

<ul class="places">

<li>
<dl class="place">
 <dt>name</dt> <dd>Mount Rushmore</dd>
 <dt>location</dt>
   <dd>
   <a class="coordinates" href="/Earth/43.9;-95.9">43.9&deg;N 95.8&deg;W</a>
   </dd>
 <dt>maps</dt>
   <ul class="maps">
   <li><a class="map" href="/road/Earth/43.9;-95.9">Road</a></dd>
   <li><a class="map" href="/satellite/Earth/43.9;-95.9">Satellite</a>
   ...
   </ul>
  </dd>
 <dt>type</dt> <dd>monument</dd>
 <dt>description</dt>
  <dd>
  Officially dedicated in 1991. Under the jurisdiction of the
  <a href="http://www.nps.gov/">National Park Service</a>.
  </dd>
</dl>
</li>

</body>
</html>
```

Rather than serve a map image of Mount Rushmore, or even an XHTML page that links to that image, this representation links to resources I've already defined: maps of the geographical point where Mount Rushmore happens to be located. Those resources take care of all the imagery and navigation details. The purpose of this resource is to talk about the state of the place, and what it looks like on a map is just one bit of that state. There's also its name, its type ("monument"), and its description. The only difference between the representation of a planet and that of a place is that a place has a location in its definition list, and a planet doesn't. A client can parse both representations with the same code.

You may also have noticed that you don't have to write a special client for this web service at all. You can use a plain old web browser. Starting at the home page (*http://maps.example.com/*), you click a link ("Earth") to select a planet. You get the representation shown in Example 5-7, and you click "Road" to see a road map of Earth. Then you navigate that map by clicking links ("North," "Zoom out"). My web service is also a web site! It's not a very pretty web site, because it's designed to be used by a computer program, but nothing prevents a human from consuming it (or debugging it) with a web browser.

If you get only one thing out of this book, I hope it's that this idea starts seeming natural to you (assuming it didn't before). Web services are just web sites for robots. My map service is particularly web site-like: it connects its resources together with hypermedia, the hypermedia representations happen to be HTML documents, and (so far) it doesn't use any features that web browsers don't support. But all RESTful resource-oriented web services partake of the nature of the Web, even if you can't use them with a standard web browser.

Example 5-9 shows one more representation: the representation of a point on the map.

Example 5-9. An XHTML representation of the point 43.9°N 103.46°W on Earth

```
<!DOCTYPE html PUBLIC "-//W3C//DTD XHTML 1.1//EN"
    "http://www.w3.org/TR/xhtml11/DTD/xhtml11.dtd">
<html xmlns="http://www.w3.org/1999/xhtml" xml:lang="en">

<head>
 <title>43.9&deg;N 103.46&deg;W on Earth</title>
</head>
<body>

<p>
 Welcome to
 <a class="coordinates" href="/Earth/43.9;-103.46">43.9&deg;N
  103.46&deg;W</a>
 on scenic <a class="place" href="/Earth">Earth</a>.
</p>

<p>See this location on a map:</p>

<ul class="maps">
 <li><a class="map" href="/road/Earth/43.9;-95.9">Road</a></li>
 <li><a class="map" href="/satellite/Earth/43.9;-95.9">Satellite</a></li>
 ...
</ul>

<p>Things that are here:</p>
```

```
<ul class="places">
 <li><a href="/Earth/43.9;-95.9/Mount%20Rushmore">Mount Rushmore</a></li>
</ul>

<form id="searchPlace" method="get" action="">
 <p>
  Show nearby places, features, or businesses:
  <input name="show" repeat="template" /> <input class="submit" />
 </p>
</form>

</body>
</html>
```

This representation consists entirely of links: links to maps centered around this point, and links to places located at this point. It has no state of its own. It's just a gateway to other, more interesting resources.

Representing Lists of Search Results

I've shown representations for the planet list, for a planet, for points and places on a planet, and for the maps themselves. What about my algorithmic resources, the search results? What's a good representation of the resource "diners near Mount Rushmore" (/Earth/USA/Mount%20Rushmore?show=diners)? What about "Areas of high arsenic near 24.9195°N 17.821°E" (/Earth/24.9195;17.821?show=arsenic)?

A list of search results is of course associated with the place being "searched," so a representation of "diners near Mount Rushmore" should link to the place "Mount Rushmore." That's a start.

When the client searches in or around a place, they're searching for more places. Whether the search string is an ambiguous place name ("Springfield") or a more general description of a place ("diners," "arsenic"), the results will be places on the map: cities named Springfield, diners, or sites with high arsenic readings. So a list of search results takes one place ("Mount Rushmore"), and associates certain other places ("Joe's Diner") with it.

A list of search results, then, can be nothing but a list of links to resources I've already defined: named places on the map. If the client is interested in a place, it can follow the appropriate link and find out about its state.

Example 5-10 shows the representation of a set of search results. The search is an attempt to find places called "Springfield" in the United States: its URI would be /Earth/USA?show=Springfield.

Example 5-10. The representation of "a list of places called Springfield in the United States"
```
<!DOCTYPE html PUBLIC "-//W3C//DTD XHTML 1.1//EN"
    "http://www.w3.org/TR/xhtml11/DTD/xhtml11.dtd">
<html xmlns="http://www.w3.org/1999/xhtml" xml:lang="en">
```

```
<head><title>Search results: "Springfield"</title></head>
<body>

<p>
 Places matching <span class="searchterm">Springfield</span>
 in or around
 <a class="place" href="/Earth/USA">the United States of America</a>:
</p>

<ul>
 <li>
  <a class="place" href="/Earth/USA/IL/Springfield">Springfield, IL</a>
 </li>
 <li>
  <a class="place" href="/Earth/USA/MA/Springfield">Springfield, MA</a>
 </li>
 <li>
  <a class="place" href="/Earth/USA/MO/Springfield">Springfield, MO</a>
 </li>
 ...
</body>
</html>
```

This representation is made up almost entirely of links to places. There's the link to the place that was searched, "the United States of America" (a place of type "country"). There are also links to various places that matched the search criteria. Each of these places is a resource, and exposes a representation that looks like Example 5-8. Each link contains enough scoping information to uniquely identify the Springfield in question.

A client can follow the links in the representations to find information about the places, as well as maps of them. Figure 5-3 shows some of the links you can follow from /Earth/USA?show=Springfield.

Google Maps presents search results by sewing image tiles together to make a large-scale map, and annotating the map with graphical markers. You can write a client for this web service that does the same thing. The first step is to build the large-scale map. The client follows the initial link to /Earth/USA and gets a representation like the one in Example 5-4. This gives the client the address of one graphical tile. The client can get adjacent tiles by following navigation links, and stitch them together into a large-scale tile map of the whole country.

The second step is to stick markers on the map, one for each search result. To find out where a marker should go, the client follows one of the search result links, fetching a representation like the one in Example 5-8. This representation lists the latitude and longitude of the appropriate Springfield.

That's potentially a lot of link following, but my representations are simple and so are the rules for going from one to another. I've spread out my data set over a huge number of resources, and made it easy to find the resource you want by following links. This strategy works on the human web, and it works on the programmable web too.

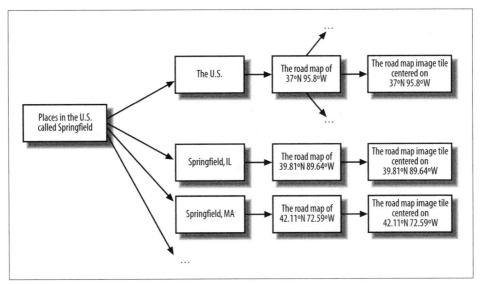

Figure 5-3. Where can you go from the list of search results?

Link the Resources to Each Other

Since I designed all my resources in parallel, they're already full of links to each other (see Figure 5-3). A client can get the service's "home page" (the planet list), follow a link to a specific planet, follow another link to a specific map, and then follow navigation and zoom links to jump around the map. A client can do a search for places that meet certain criteria, click one of the search results to find out more about the place, then follow another link to locate the place on a map.

One thing is still missing, though. How is the client supposed to get to a list of search results? I've set up rules for what the URI to a set of search results looks like, but if clients have to follow rules to generate URIs, my service isn't well connected.

I want to make it possible for a client to get from `/Earth/USA/Mount%20Rushmore` to `/Earth/USA/Mount%20Rushmore?show=diners`. But it does no good to link to "diners" specifically: that's just one of infinitely many things a client might search for. I can't put infinitely many links in the representation of `/Earth/USA/Mount%20Rushmore` just in case someone decides to search for pet stores or meteor craters near Mount Rushmore.

HTML solves this problem with forms. By sending an appropriate form in a representation, I can tell the client how to plug variables into a query string. The form represents infinitely many URIs, all of which follow a certain pattern. I'm going to extend my representations of places (like the one in Example 5-8) by including this HTML form (see Example 5-11).

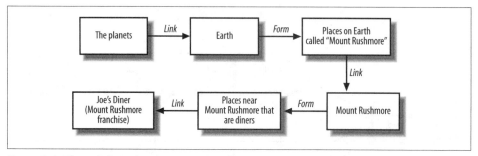

Figure 5-4. The path from the service root to a diner near Mount Rushmore

Example 5-11. An HTML form for searching a place

```
<form id="searchPlace" method="get" action="">
 <p>
  Show places, features, or businesses:
  <input id="term" repeat="template" name="show" />
  <input class="submit" />
 </p>
</form></screen>
```

A person using a web browser would see this form as a set of GUI elements: a text box, a button, and a set of labels. They'd put some data into the text box, click the button, and be taken to another URI. If they were at /Earth/USA/Mount%20Rushmore, and they'd typed in "diners," their web browser would make a GET request to /Earth/USA/Mount%20Rushmore?show=diners. An automatic client can't display the form to a human, but it would work the same way. Given a preprogrammed desire to search a place, it would look for the searchPlace form and use the form definition as a guide to constructing the URI /Earth/USA/Mount%20Rushmore?show=diners.

 You probably haven't seen the repeat="template" syntax before. It's a feature of XHTML 5, which is still being designed as this book goes to press. Occasionally in this chapter and the next, I'll introduce a feature of XHTML 5 to work around the shortcomings of XHTML 4 as a hypermedia format.

The problem here is that my service accepts any number of values for the query variable show. A client can make a simple search such as ?show=diners or perform a complicated search such as ?show=diners&show=arsenic&show=towns&show=oil+tankers.

A form in XHTML 4 could allow the latter request if it showed four text boxes, all called show. But an HTML form can never show an *arbitrary number* of text boxes, which is what I need to truly capture the capabilities of my service. XHTML 5 has a feature called the *repetition model*, which allows me to express an arbitrary number of text boxes without writing an infinitely long HTML page.

Now my service is better connected. It's now possible to get from the list of planets to a description of a diner near Mount Rushmore (assuming there is one). Figure 5-4 illustrates the journey. Starting at the service root (/), the client selects the planet Earth (/Earth). The client uses the HTML form in that representation to search for places called "Mount Rushmore" on Earth (/Earth?show=Mount%20Rushmore). Hopefully the top search result will be Mount Rushmore itself, and the client can follow the first search result link to /Earth/USA/Mount%20Rushmore. The representation of Mount Rushmore has a search form too, and the client enters "diners" in that. Assuming there are any nearby diners, the client can follow the first search result link to find a diner near Mount Rushmore.

The search function doesn't just keep clients from having to mint their own URIs. It resolves human place names, which are always fuzzy, into canonical resource URIs. A client should be also be able to search for "Mount Rushmore National Monument" and get /Earth/USA/Mount%20Rushmore as a search result, just like the client can search for "Springfield" and pick which Springfield they mean. This is a useful feature for any client that lets users type in their own place names.

The HTTP Response

I'm almost done with this design. I know what data I'm serving. I know which HTTP requests clients will send when asking for the data. I know how the data will be represented as I serve it. I still have to consider the HTTP response itself. I know what my possible representations will look like, and that's what's going in the entity-body, but I haven't yet considered the possible response codes or the HTTP headers I'll send. I also need to think about possible error conditions: cases where my response signals an error instead of delivering a representation.

What's Supposed to Happen?

This step of the design is conceptually simple, but it's the gateway to where you're going to spend much of your implementation time: making sure that client requests are correctly turned into responses.

Most read-only resources have a pretty simple typical course of events. The user sends a GET request to a URI, and the server sends back a happy response code like 200 ("OK"), some HTTP headers, and a representation. A HEAD request works the same way, but the server omits the representation. The only main question is which HTTP headers the client should send in the request, and which ones the server should send in the response.

The HTTP response headers are a fairly large toolkit, and most of them don't apply to this simple service. (For descriptions of the standard HTTP headers, see Appendix C.) In my service, the main HTTP response header is Content-Type, which tells the client the media type of the representation. My media types are application/xhtml+xml for the map representations and search results, and `image/png` for the map images. If you've done any server-side web programming you already know about `Content-Type`: every HTTP server and framework uses it.

I don't use HTTP request headers very often. I think it's best if the client can tweak the representation by tweaking the URI to the resource, rather than tweaking the request headers. But there is one set of headers that I think ought to be built into every HTTP client, every web service, and every service hacker's brain: the ones that make conditional GET possible.

Conditional HTTP GET

Conditional HTTP GET saves client and server time and bandwidth. It's implemented with two response headers (`Last-Modified` and `ETag`), and two request headers (`If-Modified-Since` and `If-None-Match`).

I cover conditional GET in detail in Chapter 8, but the discussion there is somewhat detached from specific services. This discussion is tied to the map service, and covers just enough to get you thinking about conditional GET as you design your services.

Certain resources are likely to be very popular: "A road map of the United States," "a satellite map of Earth," or "restaurants in New York City." A single client is likely to make a request for certain resources many times over its lifespan.

But this data is not constantly changing. Map data stays pretty constant over time. Satellite imagery is updated every few months at most. Restaurants come and go, but not on a minute-by-minute basis. Only a few resources are based on data that's constantly changing. Most of the time, the client's second and subsequent HTTP requests for a resource are wasted. They could have just reused the representation from their first request. But how are they supposed to know this?

This is where conditional GET comes in. Whenever a server serves a representation, it should include a time value for the `Last-Modified` HTTP header. This is the last time the data underlying the representation was changed. For "a road map of the United States," the `Last-Modified` is likely to be the time the map imagery was first imported into the service. For "restaurants in New York City," the `Last-Modified` may only be a few days old: whenever a restaurant was last added to the database of places. For "container ships near San Francisco," the value of `Last-Modified` may be only a few minutes prior.

The client can store this value of `Last-Modified` and use it later. Let's say the client requests "a road map of the United States" and gets a response that says:

    Last-Modified: Thu, 30 Nov 2006 20:00:51 GMT

The second time the client makes a GET request for that resource, it can provide that time in the `If-Modified-Since` header:

```
GET /road/Earth HTTP/1.1
Host: maps.example.com
If-Modified-Since: Thu, 30 Nov 2006 20:00:51 GMT
```

If the underlying data changed between the two requests, the server sends a response code of 200 ("OK") and provides the new representation in the entity-body. That's the same thing that happens during a normal HTTP request. But if the underlying data has not changed, the server sends a response code of 304 ("Not Modified"), and omits any entity-body. Then the client knows it's okay to reuse its cached representation: the underlying data hasn't changed since the first request.

There's a little more to it than that (again, I cover this in more detail in Chapter 8). But you can see the advantages. A client that fetches detailed maps is going to be making lots of HTTP requests. If most of those HTTP requests give a status code of 304, the client will be able to reuse old images and place lists instead of downloading new ones. Everyone saves time and bandwidth.

What Might Go Wrong?

I also need to plan for requests I can't fulfill. When I hit an error condition I'll send a response code in the 3xx, 4xx, or 5xx range, and I may provide supplementary data in HTTP headers. If they provide an entity-body, it'll be a document describing an error condition, not a representation of the requested resource (which, after all, couldn't be served).

I provide a full list of the HTTP response codes in Appendix B, along with examples where you might use each of them. Here are some likely error conditions for my map application:

- The client may try to access a map that doesn't exist, like /road/Saturn. I understand what the client is asking for, but I don't have the data. The proper response code in this situation is 404 ("Not Found"). I don't need to send an entity-body along with this response code, though it's helpful for debugging.

- The client may use a place name that doesn't exist in my database. The end user might have mistyped the name, or used a name the application doesn't recognize. They may have described the place instead of naming it, they might have the right name but the wrong planet. Or they might just be constructing URIs with random strings in them.

  I can return a 404 response code, as in the previous example, or I can try to be helpful. If I can't exactly match a requested place name, like /Earth/Mount%20Rush more%20National%20Monument, I might run it through my search engine and see if it comes up with a good match. If I do get a match, I can offer a redirect to that place: say, /Earth/43.9;-95.9/Mount%20Rushmore.

  The response code for the helpful case here would be 303 ("See Other"), and the HTTP response header Location would contain the URI of the resource I think the client was "really" trying to request. It's the client's responsibility to take the hint and request that URI, or not.

If I try a search and still have no idea what place the client is talking about, I'll return a response code of 404 ("Not Found").

• The client may use logically impossible latitudes or longitudes, like 500,-181 (500 degrees north latitude, 181 degrees west longitude). A 404 ("Not Found") is a good response here, just as it is for a place that doesn't exist. But a 400 ("Bad Request") would be more precise.

What's the difference between the two cases? Well, there's nothing obviously wrong with a request for a nonexistent place name like "Tanhoidfog." It just doesn't exist *right now*. Someone could name a town or a business "Tanhoidfog" and then it would be a valid place name. The client doesn't know there's no such place: one of the nice things a client can do with my map service is check to see which places really exist.

But there is something wrong with a request for the latitude/longitude pair 500,-181. The laws of geometry prevent such a place from ever existing. A minimally knowledgeable client could have figured that out before making the request. A 400 response code is appropriate in that case: the problem is the client's fault for even making the request.

• A search for places on a map might return no search results. There might be no racing speedways near Sebastopol, CA. This is disappointing, but it's not an error. I can treat this like any other search: send a 200 response code ("OK") and a representation. The representation would include a link to the place that was searched, along with an empty list of search results.

• The server may be overloaded with requests and unable to fulfil this particular request. The response code is 503 ("Service Unavailable"). An alternative is to refuse to handle the request at all.

• The server may not be functioning correctly. This might be due to missing or corrupted data, a software bug, a hardware failure, or any of the other things that can go wrong with a computer program. In this case the response code is 500 ("Internal Server Error").

This a frustrating response code (the whole 5xx series is frustrating, actually) because there's nothing the client can do about it. Many web application frameworks automatically send this error code when an exception happens on the server side.

Conclusion

I've now got a design for a map web service that's simple enough for a client to use without a lot of up-front investment, and useful enough to be the driver for any number of useful programs. It's so closely attuned to the philosophy of the Web that you can use it with a web browser. It's RESTful and resource-oriented. It's addressable, state-less, and well connected.

It's also read-only. It assumes that my clients have nothing to offer but their insatiable appetites for my data. Lots of existing web services work this way, but read-only web services are only half the story. In the next chapter I'll show you how clients can use HTTP's uniform interface to create new resources of their own.

## CHAPTER 6

Designing Read/Write Resource-Oriented Services

In Chapter 5 I designed a fantasy web service that serves map images of various planets,[*] navigation information for moving around the map, and information about places on the planets: restaurants, meteor craters, and so on. That's a huge amount of data to serve, but it can all be contained in a premade data set. There's nothing a user can do to put his own data on the server.

Clients for the map service in the previous chapter can do all sorts of interesting things with maps and places, but they can't rely on the server to track anything except the preset data. In this chapter I expand the scope of the map service. It becomes less like a search engine's web service and more like Amazon S3 and the Flickr and del.icio.us APIs. It not only serves data, it stores data on its clients' behalf.

How open should I make the new service? A totally open service would allow users to provide their own versions of everything in the standard data set. Clients could create their own planets, and upload custom maps and databases of places. If I was too lazy to find map data myself (I am), I could even start with an empty database and allow the community to populate my entire data set. That's what del.icio.us and Flickr did.

Is this a good idea? When designing a web service, which levers of state should you expose, and which should you keep to yourself? That depends on what your users want to do, and how much of their applications you're willing to write for them.

A client uses a web service because the service has something it wants: some data, a place to store data, or a secret algorithm. A web service is an abstraction layer, like an operating system API or a programming language library. If you wrote a math library for working with infinite series, and all your users started using it to estimate the value of π, you'd probably add that feature as a higher-level library function. That way all

---

[*] Remember, I'm using "planets" as a shorthand for "bodies that can be addressed with longitude and latitude." I don't just mean whatever 8 or 11 bodies the International Astronomical Union has decided are planets this week.

your users could use the same well-tested π-estimation code instead of each person writing his or her own implementation. Similarly, if all your users implement the same features on top of your web service, you might help them out by moving those features into the service. If all your users want to add certain kinds of custom data to the data set, you can start supporting a new kind of resource, so they don't have to define their own local structures.

My goal here is fairly modest: to illustrate the concepts of resource-oriented service design. It's certainly possible to design a mapping service that starts off with an empty data set and gets everything through user contributions, but such a service would have more moving parts than I've got concepts to explain. If I decided to show you that service, this chapter would start out well, but once I'd explained all the concepts I'd still have a lot of domain-specific design work to do, and it would get boring.

I want the map service to have about as many moving parts as I have new concepts to explain. I'm going to expand the previous chapter's service just enough so that clients can annotate the map with custom places. Every custom place is associated with a user account, and may be public or private to that account.

User Accounts as Resources

If I'm going to let anyone with a web service client annotate our worlds, I need some way of distinguishing his custom places from the standard places in my database. I'll also need a way to distinguish one user's places from everyone else's places. Basically, I need user accounts.

When a client annotates Earth or Mars with a custom place, the place he has created is associated with his user account. This way a client can find his place later. If the client chooses to expose that place publicly, other clients will see links to it in the representations they fetch.

Most existing web services have some kind of system for letting people sign up for user accounts or "API keys." Even services that only give read-only access often make you sign up for an account, so they can track and ration your usage. If you've followed along with all of the examples in the book, by this time you have an Amazon Web Services account, a del.icio.us account, and a Flickr account.

Yahoo! Web Services does things a little differently. Instead of tying the key to you personally, you can sign up for any number of application keys. You can distribute the application key with your application, and anyone can use it. Yahoo! tracks application usage, not individual usage. I registered the key "restbook" for a particular "application": this book. You and anyone else can use that key to run the sample Yahoo! Web Services code in this book.

The procedure for signing up for these web accounts doesn't vary much. You use your web browser to go to a web site and fill out some HTML forms. You usually have to click through a legal agreement, and maybe respond to a verification email. Sometimes your web service account is tied to your preexisting account on the corresponding web site.

The user account system I'm about to design works a little differently. In my map service, user accounts are resources, just like the maps themselves. In fact, they're my first read/write resources. My clients won't have to use their web browsers to sign up for a user account: they can create one with a generic web service client.

Why Should User Accounts Be Resources?

Why have I decided to design my user accounts differently from those of nearly every existing web service? I have two reasons. First: most web services make you sign up for an account through a web application. Web application design is a well-understood topic and it's not the topic of this book. Web services are indeed very similar to web applications, but resource creation is one of the places where they differ. The main difference here is that HTML forms currently support only GET and POST. This means web applications must use overloaded POST to convey any unsafe operation. If I tried to cover the typical method of getting a user account, I'd end up skimming the details as not relevant to web services. Treating user accounts as read/write resources means I can demonstrate the new resource-oriented design procedure on a data structure you're probably familiar with.

Second, I want to show that new possibilities open up when you treat everyday data structures as resources, subject to the uniform interface. Consider an Internet-connected GPS device that ties into my map service. Every hour or so, it annotates Earth (as exposed through my web service) with its current position, creating a record of where the GPS device is over time.

There will be thousands of these devices, and each one should only be able to see its own annotations. The person in charge of programming the device should not be limited to creating a single user account for personal use. Nor should everyone who buys the device have to go to my web site and fill out a form before they can use the device they bought.

Since user accounts are resources, every one of these devices can have its own account on my web service (possibly with a username based on the serial number), and these accounts can be created automatically. They might be created in batches as the devices are manufactured, or each one may create an account for itself when its owner first turns it on.

The end users may never know that they're using a web service, and they'll never have to sign up for a key. The device programmer does need to know how our web service works, and needs to write software that can create user accounts. If user accounts are resources, it's obvious how the device programmer can do this. HTTP's uniform interface gives most of the answers ahead of time.

Authentication, Authorization, Privacy, and Trust

Once I start exposing user accounts, I need some way of determining which user, if any, is responsible for a given HTTP request. *Authentication* is the problem of tying a request to a user. If you want to name a new place on Mars, I need some way of knowing that the new place should be associated with your user account instead of someone else's. *Authorization* is the problem of determining which requests to let through for a given user. There are some HTTP requests I'd accept from user A but reject from user B: requests like "DELETE user A" or "GET all of user A's private places." In my service, if you authenticate as user A, you're allowed to manipulate user A's account, but not anyone else's.

I'll have more to say about RESTful modes of authentication and authorization in Chapter 8, but here are the basics. When a web service client makes an HTTP request, it may include some credentials in the HTTP header `Authorization`. The service examines the credentials, and decides whether they correctly identify the client as a particular user (authentication), and whether that user is actually allowed to do what the client is trying to do (authorization). If both conditions are met, the server carries out the request. If the credentials are missing, invalid, or not good enough to provide authorization, then the server sends a response code of 401 ("Unauthorized"). It sets the `WWW-Authenticate` response header with instructions about how to send correct credentials in the future.

There are several standard kinds of authentication. The most common are HTTP Basic, HTTP Digest, and WSSE. Some web services implement custom forms of authentication: in Chapter 3 I showed how Amazon S3 implements authentication with a sophisticated request signing mechanism. It doesn't really matter which authentication mechanism I choose since I'm not actually implementing this service, but let's say I go with the simplest choice: HTTP Basic authentication.

There's also the notion of privacy. Given that user A's list of private annotations can't be accessed by any other user, the representation of that list still needs to be transmitted over the Internet. The data's going to go through a lot of computers before it gets to the client. What's to stop one of those computers from examining the supposedly private list? To solve this problem I'm going to encrypt each HTTP transaction over SSL. In the previous chapter I presented URIs that started with *http://maps.example.com/*. In this chapter my URIs all start with `https://maps.example.com/`.

Using HTTPS instead of HTTP prevents other computers from eavesdropping on the conversation between client and server. This is especially important when using HTTP Basic authentication, since that authentication mechanism involves the client sending its credentials in plain text.

Now I've got a secure, trusted means of communication between the client and the server. But there's one more relationship to consider: the relationship between the client software and the human end user. Why should the end user trust the client software with its authentication credentials? Let me ask you a question to clarify the problem.

Whenever you log in to a web site, you're trusting your web browser to send your username and password to that web site, and nowhere else. Why do you trust your browser with that information? How do you know your browser doesn't have a secret backdoor that broadcasts everything you type to some seedy IRC channel?

There are several possible answers. You might be using an open source browser like Firefox, which has good source control and a lot of people looking at the source code. You might say there's safety in numbers: that millions of people use your brand of browser and there haven't been any problems traceable to the browser itself. You might monitor your network traffic to make sure your browser is only sending the data you tell it to send. But most people just take it on faith that their web browser is trustworthy.

That's the human web. Now imagine I send you a cool new web service client for managing your del.icio.us bookmarks. Do you trust that client with your del.icio.us username and password? Do you trust it as much as you trust your web browser with the same information? Hopefully not! No web service client is as popular as a web browser, and no web service client has as many eyes on the source code. On the human web, we usually ignore the problem by taking a leap of faith and trusting our web browsers. On the programmable web the problem is more obvious. We don't necessarily trust our own clients with our authentication credentials.

There's nothing in the HTTP standard to deal with this problem, because it's a problem between the end user and the client: HTTP lives between the client and the server. Solving this problem requires forgoing all the standard ways of sending authentication information: Basic, Digest, and WSSE don't work because they require the client to know the credentials. (You can solve it with Digest or WSSE by having a tiny, trusted account manager send encrypted authentication strings to the actual, untrusted client. I don't know of any web service clients that use this architecture.)

Big names in web services like Google, Amazon, eBay, and Flickr have come up with ways for a client to make web service requests without knowing the actual authentication credentials. You saw a hint of this in Chapter 3: I showed how to sign an Amazon S3 request and give a special URI to someone else, which they could use without knowing your password. I'll have more to say about this in Chapter 8. For now I just want you to know that there's a complication on the programmable web you might never have considered. Because there's not yet any standard way of solving this problem, I'm going to punt on it for now and use HTTP Basic authentication for my services. My users will have to trust their clients as much as they trust their web browsers.

Turning Requirements into Read/Write Resources

Now that I've identified a new data set (user accounts), I'm going to go through the same design procedure I did for the data set I developed in the previous chapter (planets, places on the planets, maps of the planets, and points on the maps). But the procedure from the previous chapter only suffices for read-only resources. This chapter makes it possible for clients to create, modify, and delete resources. So I've added two steps to the procedure (steps 3 and 4).

1. Figure out the data set
2. Split the data set into resources
   For each kind of resource:
3. Name the resources with URIs
4. Expose a subset of the uniform interface
5. Design the representation(s) accepted from the client
6. Design the representation(s) served to the client
7. Integrate this resource into existing resources, using hypermedia links and forms
8. Consider the typical course of events: what's supposed to happen?
9. Consider error conditions: what might go wrong?

Figure Out the Data Set

Most sites with user accounts try to associate personal information with your account, like your name or email address. I don't care about any of that. In my map service, there are only two pieces of information associated with a user account:

- The name of the account
- A password used to access the account

Each user account also has some subordinate resources (custom places on planets) associated with it, but I'll figure that part out later. All I need for now is a way of identifying specific user accounts (a username), and a way for a client to present credentials that tie them to a certain user account (a password).

Since I don't track any personal information, there's no reason apart from tradition to even call this a "user account." I could call it a "password-protected set of annotations." But I'll stick to the traditional terminology. This makes it easier to visualize the service, and easier for you to come up with your own enhancements to the user account system.

Split the Data Set into Resources

This was a fairly large step back in Chapter 5, when my data set was large and vague: "planets, places, and maps." Here the data set is fairly constrained: "user accounts." I'll expose each user account as a resource. In terms of the Chapter 5 terminology, these new resources are resources of the second type. They're the portals through which my service exposes its underlying user objects. Another site might also expose the list of user accounts itself as a one-off resource, or expose algorithmic resources that let a client search the list of users. I won't bother.

Name the Resources with URIs

This part is also easy, since I only have one kind of resource. I'll expose a user account with a URI of the following form: `https://maps.example.com/user/{user-name}`.

Expose a Subset of the Uniform Interface

This is the first new step. I skipped it when designing read-only resources, because there was nothing to decide. By definition, read-only resources are the ones that expose no more than the HTTP methods GET, HEAD, and OPTIONS. Now that I're designing resources that can be created and modified at runtime, I also have PUT, POST, and DELETE to consider.

Even so, this step is pretty simple because the uniform interface is always the same. If you find yourself wishing there were more HTTP methods, the first thing to do is go back to step two, and try to split up your data set so you have more kinds of resources. Only if this fails should you consider introducing an element of the RPC style by making a particular resource support overloaded POST.

To reiterate the example from Chapter 5: if you have resources for "readers," and resources for "published columns," and you start thinking "it sure would be nice if there was a SUBSCRIBE method in HTTP," the best thing to do is to create a new kind of resource: the "subscription." As HTTP resources, subscriptions are subject to HTTP's uniform interface. If you decide to forgo the uniform interface and handle subscriptions through overloaded POST on your "reader" resources, defining the interface for those resources becomes much more difficult.

I can decide which bits of the uniform interface to expose by asking questions about intended usage:

- *Will clients be creating new resources of this type?* Of course they will. There's no other way for users to get on the system.
- *When the client creates a new resource of this type, who's in charge of determining the new resource's URI? Is it the client or the server?* The client is in charge, since the URI is made up entirely of constant strings (`https://maps.example.com/user/`) and variables under the client's control (`{user-name}`).

From those two questions I get my first result. To create a user account, a client will send a PUT request to the account's URI. If the answer to the second question was "the server's in charge of the final URI," I'd expect my clients to create a user by sending a POST request to some "factory" or "parent" URI. See the "Custom Places" section later in this chapter for a case where the answer to the second question is "the server's in charge."

- *Will clients be modifying resources of this type?* Yes. It's questionable whether or not a user should be allowed to change his username (I'm not going to allow it, for simplicity's sake), but a user should always be allowed to change his password.

- *Will clients be deleting resources of this type?* Sure. You can delete an account when you're done with it.

- *Will clients be fetching representations of resources of this type?* This is up for debate. Right now there's not much information associated with a user account: only the username, which is part of the URI, and the password, which I won't be giving out.

  I'm going to say yes, which means I will be exposing GET and HEAD on user account resources. If nothing else, clients will want to see whether or not their desired username already exists. And once I allow users to define custom places, clients will want to look at the public places defined by specific users.

Design the Representation(s) Accepted from the Client

My data set comes with no built-in user accounts: every one is created by some client. The obvious next step in this design is to specify how the client is supposed to create a user account.

Let's go back to Chapter 3 and Amazon S3 for a minute. A client creates an S3 bucket by sending an empty PUT request to the URI of the bucket. The client doesn't need to send an entity-body in the request, because the bucket has no state other than its name.

To create an S3 object inside a bucket takes a little more work. An S3 object has two bits of state: name and value. The name goes into the URI, the destination of the PUT request. But the value needs to go into the entity-body of the PUT request. S3 will accept any data at all in this entity-body, because the whole point is that the value of an S3 object can be anything, but there needs to be *something* there: you can't have an empty object.

Most web services are a little pickier about what goes into the entity-body: it has to be in a certain format and convey certain bits of resource state. My user accounts have two elements of resource state: the username and the password. If a PUT request is going to succeed in creating a user account, it needs to convey both pieces of state. The username is included in the scoping information: any PUT request that creates an account will have that account's username in the URI. What about the password?

The client will send the new user's password in an entity-body, as part of a *representation*. In Chapter 5, I introduced representations as documents the server sends the client: a way for the server to convey the state of a resource. Representations flow the other way, too. They're how a client suggests changes to the state of a resource. When you PUT an S3 object, the entity-body you send is a representation of the object. The representation you send with a PUT request is an assertion about the new state of a resource.

In "Representing the List of Planets" in Chapter 5 I considered several possible representation formats. I looked at plain text, JSON, XML using a made-up vocabulary, and Atom (XML again, but using a preexisting vocabulary). I decided on XHTML, a preexisting XML vocabulary oriented around marking up human-readable documents. In that chapter the question was what format would be most useful when served to the client. Now, the question is how the client should format its proposed state changes. What format makes it easiest for the client to convey a password to the server?

When the state is complex, it's helpful for the server to accept the same representation format it sends. The client can request a representation with GET, modify the representation, and then PUT it back, committing its changes to the underlying resource state. As we'll see in Chapter 9, the Atom Publishing Protocol uses this technique effectively. And, of course, S3 serves the representation of an object byte for byte the way it was when the client first PUT it into the system. S3 doesn't even pretend to know anything about the meaning of the representations it serves.

Here, I've only got one item of state (the password), and it's not one that the server will ever send to the client. Now's a good time to introduce a representation format for simple cases like these.

Form-encoding

This representation doesn't have an official name beyond its media type (`application/x-www-form-urlencoded`), but you've probably seen it before. It's sometimes called "CGI escaping." When you submit an HTML form in your web browser, this is the format the browser uses to marshal the form data into something that can go into an HTTP request. Consider an HTML form like the one in Example 6-1.

Example 6-1. A simple HTML form

```
<form action="http://www.example.com/color-pairs" method="POST">
 <input name="color1" type="text"/>
 <input name="color2" type="text"/>
</form>
```

If the user enters the values "blue" and "green" in the text fields `color1` and `color2` fields, a form-encoded representation of that data would be `color1=blue&color2=green`. When the form is submitted, the browser makes a POST request to *http://www.example.com/color-pairs*, and sends `color1=blue&color2=green` in the entity-body: that's a representation. If the form's "method" attribute were GET, then when the user submitted the form the browser would make a GET request to *http://www.example.com/color-pairs?color1=blue&color2=green*. That's got the same data in the same format, but there the data is scoping information that identifies a resource, not a representation.

When an object's state can be represented as key-value pairs, form-encoding is the simplest representation format. Almost every programming language has built-in facilities for doing form-encoding and -unencoding: they're usually located in the language's HTTP or CGI library.

My map service accepts a form-encoded representation when a client tries to create or edit a user. The only pieces of state I've associated with a user are its name and password. The name goes into the URI and I've decided it can't change, so my user representations just look like "password=*{the-password}*". Example 6-2 is hypothetical Ruby code for creating a user account with the map service.

Example 6-2. Hypothetical map client to create a user account

```ruby
require 'rubygems'
require 'rest-open-uri'
require 'cgi'
require 'uri'
def make_user(username, password)
  open("https://maps.example.com/user/#{URI.escape(username)}",
       :data => CGI::escape("password=#{password}"), :method => :put)
end
```

 A couple things to note here. First, I've started transmitting sensitive data (passwords) over the network, so I'm now using HTTPS. Second, I'm actually using two different kinds of encoding in this code sample. The username, which goes into the URI, is URI-encoded using `URI.escape`. The password, which goes into the representation, is form-encoded with `CGI::escape`. URI-encoding is similar to form-encoding, but it's not the same, and confusing them is a common source of subtle bugs.

Changing an account's password is the same as creating the account in the first place. The client sends a PUT request to the account URI, with a new representation of the account (that is, the new password). Of course, no one can change an account's password without authorization. To modify a user account, a client must also provide an `Authorization` header that convinces my service it has the right to modify that account. In short, changing a user's password requires knowing the current password. As I said earlier, my service expects incoming `Authorization` headers to conform to the HTTP Basic authentication standard.

A DELETE request never requires a representation, but deleting a user from my service will require a proper `Authorization` header. That is: to delete a user account you must know that user's password.

Design the Representation(s) to Be Served to the Client

A client will GET a user account's URI to retrieve a representation of a user account, just as a client GETs the URI of a map or a place to retrieve a representation of that map or place. What should the representation of a user account look like?

Right now it won't look like much, since I've only got two pieces of state to convey, and one of them (the password) I don't want to be sending out. Indeed, in a well-designed system I won't even have the password to send out. I'll only have an encrypted version of it, for use in authentication. Once I integrate custom places into this representation, it'll look better. For now, Example 6-3 is a fairly sparse XHTML document.

Example 6-3. A representation of "your" user's account

```
<!DOCTYPE html PUBLIC "-//W3C//DTD XHTML 1.1//EN"
    "http://www.w3.org/TR/xhtml11/DTD/xhtml11.dtd">
<html xmlns="http://www.w3.org/1999/xhtml" xml:lang="en">

<head>
 <title>User homepage for leonardr</title>
</head>
<body>

<p class="authenticated">
 You are currently logged in as
 <a class="user" href="/user/leonardr">leonardr</a>.
</p>

<p>User homepage for
    <a class="user" href="/user/leonardr">leonardr</a></p>

<form id="modifyUser" method="put" action="">
 <p>Change your password:
    <input class="password" name="password" /><br />
    <input class="submit" /></p>
</form>

</body>
</html>
```

Once again I'm using the representation to convey the current resource state, and to help the client drive to other states. I used an HTML form to describe a future PUT request the client might make if it wants to change the user's password (an item of resource state). Note that there's no form telling the client how to get a representation, or how to delete this user. It's taken for granted that you use HTTP GET and DELETE for that. I only need hypermedia for complicated things: links to other resources (so the client knows which URI to GET or DELETE), and descriptions of representations.

You may have noticed a problem in Example 6-3. Its form specifies an HTTP method of PUT, but HTML forms only allow GET and POST. As with the "repeat" syntax in Example 5-11, I'm using the as-yet-unreleased XHTML 5 to get around the shortcomings of the current version of HTML. Another way to handle this is to send a WADL snippet instead of an HTML form, or use the trick described in Chapter 8 to run PUT requests over overloaded POST.

If you GET someone else's user account, you'll be served a different representation, similar to the one in Example 6-4.

Example 6-4. A representation of someone else's user account

```
<!DOCTYPE html PUBLIC "-//W3C//DTD XHTML 1.1//EN"
    "http://www.w3.org/TR/xhtml11/DTD/xhtml11.dtd">
<html xmlns="http://www.w3.org/1999/xhtml" xml:lang="en">
```

```
<head>
 <title>User homepage for samruby</title>
</head>
<body>

<p class="authenticated">
 You are currently logged in as
 <a class="user" href="/user/leonardr">leonardr</a>.
</p>

<p>User homepage for <a class="user" href="/user/samruby">samruby</a></p>

</body>
</html>
```

This representation has no controls for altering the state of the resource, because the client isn't authorized to do that: the client authenticated as `leonardr` and this is `sam ruby`'s page. Right now the representation does nothing but confirm to `leonardr` that a user named `samruby` exists. If there was no such user, a GET request to /user/samruby would give a status code of 404 ("Not Found"), and the client would be free to create `samruby` with a PUT request.

Link This Resource to Existing Resources

In the previous chapter I defined several classes of resource: the list of maps, individual maps, places, and lists of places (that is, lists of search results). None of these are directly relevant to user accounts, but there are a couple of nice features I can add at this point.

One nice feature is to add the "authenticated" message (seen in the two sample representations above) to the representation of *every* resource. It'll be displayed whenever the client submits a request with valid credentials. The "authenticated" message is a piece of hypermedia that shows an authenticated client how to retrieve data about its user account. Every resource is now connected to the user account of the user who requested it.

Another nice piece of hypermedia would be one that shows an unauthenticated client how to *create* a user account. The best place for this bit of hypermedia would be the representation of the list of planets: after all, that's the service's "home page." It already contains links to the other main parts of the service, so it should contain a link to this new part.

Once again, HTML hypermedia isn't quite up to the job. And once again, I'm going to use XHTML 5, which makes minor changes to HTML, rather than introduce a totally new technology like WADL in the middle of a chapter. Example 6-5 is an XHTML 5 snippet that tells a client how to create a user.

Example 6-5. Hypermedia describing how to create a user account
```
<form id="createUser" method="PUT" template="/user/{username}">
 <p>Username: <input type="text" name="username" /><br />
```

```
<p>Password: <input type="password" name="password" /><br />
<input class="submit" />
</form>
```

 The two deviations from the HTML you're familiar with are in the method attribute (like Example 6-3, it specifies PUT where HTML 4 allows only GET and POST), and the brand-new template attribute, which inserts a form variable ("username") into the URI using the URI Templating standard (*http://www.ietf.org/internet-drafts/draft-gregorio-uritemplate-00.txt*).

As of the time of writing, URI Templating was a proposed addition to HTML 5, but it hadn't been approved. It's possible that it will be rejected, and that Example 6-5 won't be valid HTML 5 any more than it is valid HTML 4. In that case you can use URI Templating unofficially (forcing your users to write custom clients), or switch to WADL.

The hypermedia form talks about the syntax of the PUT request, but it can't say much about the semantics. A web service client can read the HTML form in Example 6-5, but its understanding is limited. It knows that the form is labelled "createUser" but it doesn't know what "createUser" means. It knows that if it PUTs a certain representation to a certain URI, the server will probably accept it. It knows what PUT means, because PUT always means the same thing. It knows that the representation should include a "username," but it doesn't know a username from an ostrich. It takes a human being—a programmer—to understand what a user is, that "createUser" means "create a user," what a username is, and all the rest. A programmer needs to set the rules about when and how user accounts are created. This piece of hypermedia does nothing but tell the client how to structure the PUT request when it comes time to "createUser," whatever that means. It's a promise from the web service to the client.

Many web services put all of this data up front, in a single WSDL or WADL file, for the ease of the client programmer. This is somewhat contrary to the REST design philosophy because it violates, or at the very least subverts, the principle of connectedness. But in web services, where the client must be programmed in advance, it's an understandable impulse, and often it doesn't cause any problems.

What's Supposed to Happen?

Let's consider what might happen when a client sends a PUT request to */user/leonardr*. As is usual with HTTP, the server reads this request, takes some action behind the scenes, and serves a response. I need to decide which numeric response code the response will have, and what HTTP headers and/or entity-body will be provided. I also need to decide how the request will affect resource state: that is, what real-world effects it will have.

It's not hard to see what happens if all goes well with a PUT request. If there's no user called "leonardr," the service creates one with the specified password. The response code is 201 ("Created"), and the Location header contains the URI of the newly created user.

If the user account already exists, the resource state is modified to bring it in line with the client's proposed new representation. That is, the account's password is modified. In this case the response code may be 200 ("OK"), and the response entity-body may contain a representation of the user account. Or, since the password change never affects the representation, the response code may be 205 ("Reset Content") and the response entity-body may be omitted altogether.

PUT requests are the only complicated ones, because they're the only ones that include a representation. GET and DELETE requests work exactly according to the uniform interface. A successful GET request has a response code of 200 ("OK") and a representation in the entity-body. A successful DELETE request also has a response code of 200 ("OK"). The server can send an entity-body in response to a successful DELETE, but it would probably contain just a status message: there's no longer a resource to send a representation of.

What Might Go Wrong?

A request that creates, modifies, or deletes a resource has more failure conditions than one that just retrieves a representation. Here are a few of the error conditions for this new resource.

The most obvious problem is that the client's representation might be unintelligible to the server. My server expects a representation in form-encoded format; the client might send an XML document instead. The status code in this case is 415 ("Unsupported Media Type").

Alternatively, the client might not have provided a representation at all. Or it might have provided a form-encoded representation that's ill-formed or full of nonsense data. The status code in this case is 400 ("Bad Request").

Maybe the representation makes sense but it tells the server to put the resource into an inconsistent or impossible state. Perhaps the representation is "password=", and I don't allow accounts with empty passwords. The exact status code depends on the error; in the case of the empty password it would probably be 400 ("Bad Request"). In another situation it might be 409 ("Conflict").

Maybe the client sends the wrong credentials, sends authorization credentials for a totally different user account, or doesn't send the Authorization header at all. A client can only modify or delete a user if it provides that user's credentials. The response code in this case is 401 ("Unauthorized"), and I'll set the WWW-Authenticate header with instructions to the client, giving a clue about how to format the Authorization header according to the rules of HTTP Basic authentication.

If the client tries to create a user that already exists, one possible response code is 409 ("Conflict"). This is appropriate because carrying out the PUT request would put the service's resources into an inconsistent state: there'd be two user resources with the same username. Another possibility is to treat the PUT request as an attempt to change an existing user's password without providing any authentication, and send a response code of 401 ("Unauthorized").

As in the previous chapter, there might be an unspecified problem on the server side: response code 500 ("Internal Server Error") or 503 ("Service Unavailable").

Custom Places

Now I'm ready to go through the resource design procedure all over again. This time I'm designing the custom places clients can create: places that will show up on maps alongside the built-in places. Hopefully you're getting the hang of the procedure by now (if not, take heart: I'll do it some more in the next chapter), so this trip through it will be somewhat abbreviated. This time I want to focus on what makes custom places different from user accounts.

Figure Out the Data Set

A web service client can create any number of places on any of the planets for which I have maps. Custom places will show up in lists of search results, just like the built-in places from the previous chapter. Custom places can have the same data as built-in places: a type ("city"), a name ("Springfield"), coordinates of latitude and longitude ("39.81E 89.64W"), and a textual description ("The capital of Illinois"). Many custom places may share the same coordinates ("My house" and "My current location"), and a custom place may share a location with a built-in place.

Every custom place is associated with some user account. Custom places may be public or private. A private place is visible and modifiable only to someone who provides the credentials for the user account that "owns" the place.

Split the Data Set into Resources

Each custom place will be a resource, just as every built-in place is. I also want to let clients get a list of their custom places. In my design, a user account is just a password-protected list of places, so I won't be exposing the place list as a separate resource. Instead I'll expand the "user account" resource so it encompasses a user's list of places. This is analogous to the way a bucket in Amazon S3 is represented as nothing but a list of objects.

Name the Resources with URIs

A custom place is clearly a subordinate resource, but subordinate to what? I could reasonably associate it with a user account, a geographic point on some planet, or an enclosing place like a city, country, or planet. Which of these relationships should I capture with my URIs?

I've chosen to name custom places much the same way I name built-in places. Each place is associated with a geographic point, and can be accessed with a URI of the form /user/{username}/{planet}/{latitude},{longitude}/{place name}. The new element is {username}, intended to distinguish between different people's views of the same place: for instance, Sam's review of Joe's Diner at /user/samruby/Earth/45.2;-114.2/Joe's%20Diner and Leonard's less glowing review at /user/leonardr/Earth/45.2;-114.2/Joe's%20Diner.

A URI like /Earth/USA?show=Joe's+Diner works like it did before: it returns search results for places called "Joe's Diner," anywhere in the U.S. The only difference is that now there are more possible places to search: not only the built-in database of places, but each user's public list of places, and your own private list.

Built-in places are still privileged. As it happens, there's a Japanese theme park that includes a one-third scale model of Mount Rushmore. If a client creates a custom place called "Mount Rushmore" north of Tokyo, /Earth/Mount%20Rushmore still points to the original in South Dakota. It doesn't suddenly become ambiguous which "Mount Rushmore" resource that URI refers to. However, /Earth?show=Mount+Rushmore will show both places.

Expose a Subset of the Uniform Interface

Clients can use GET and HEAD to retrieve representations of built-in places, their own places (whether public or private), and public places created by others. Clients can delete their own places with DELETE, and change the state of their places with PUT.

There are two ways a client might create a map annotation. The client might add a comment to an existing place on the map ("Mount Rushmore"), or it might give a new name to a certain point of latitude and longitude ("the cornfield where I kissed Betty").

In the first case, the resource being created is "Mount Rushmore (from leonardr's point of view)." When creating this resource the client shouldn't have to know exactly where on the map Mount Rushmore is. "Mount Rushmore" is a consensus name and there's a built-in place by that name. The client can rely on the server to look up the coordinates. In the second case, the resource being created is a brand new place that the server's never heard of, and the client is responsible for knowing the coordinates.

How can I work this feature into my resource-oriented design? "Mount Rushmore (from leonardr's point of view)" is a *subordinate resource* of another resource: the built-in place "Mount Rushmore." This resource already exists and has a URI: one of them is `/Earth/Mount%20Rushmore`. If the client wants to reuse the consensus name for a place, it shouldn't have to look up its location. Instead of figuring out the final URI of the annotation and sending a PUT request to it, the client can send a POST request to the "Mount Rushmore" URI and let the server figure out the ultimate URI.

Similarly, if the client wants to comment on the Alabama capitol building, it can POST to `/Earth/USA/AL/State%20capitol` instead of figuring out the exact coordinates or street address. Any URI that identifies a built-in place can be the target of a POST request that comments on that place.

What about custom names? What if a client wants to give the name "Mount Rushmore" not to the original in South Dakota, but to the scale model in Imaichi? What if the client wants to create an annotation for "the cornfield where I kissed Betty"?

Here the client must know the latitude and longitude of the place it wants to create. This means it'll have all the information necessary to create the URI of the new resource: the world, a geographic point on the world, the name of the place, and its own user-name. The client could make a PUT request to a URI like `/user/bob/Earth/42;-93.7/the%20cornfield%20where....` This would work just like creating a user account by sending a PUT request to `/user/bob`.

Even here, it's cleaner to use POST. A brand-new place on the map is a subordinate resource: it's subordinate to some point on the planet, just like a comment on a built-in place is subordinate to a place on the planet. So a client could also put a new place on the map by sending a POST request to `/Earth/42;-93.7`. It works the same way as a comment on existing places (a POST to `/Earth/Mount%20Rushmore`), except here the place is identified by latitude and longitude, not by consensus name.

My service will support POST for brand-new places because that's simpler. The interface will be the same whether you're adding a brand new place to the planet, or making a comment on some consensus place. Another service might support both methods: PUT to the final URI if the client is willing to figure out that URI, and POST to a parent URI if it's not.

Finally, note that although I'm using POST, it's not overloaded POST. Clients of my service use POST only when they want to create a resource "beneath" an existing one. The URI of the new resource (`/user/leonardr/Earth/43.9;-103.46/Mount%20Rushmore`) may not directly extend the URI of the old (`/Earth/Mount%20Rushmore`), but the resources have a conceptual relationship.

Design the Representation(s) Accepted from the Client

When the client sticks a pin into a planet and creates a custom place, what information does it need to provide? It must identify a planet and a place on that planet: the spot where the pin goes. The place can be identified either by latitude and longitude, or by reference to a canonical name like "Mount Rushmore." Call these variables `planet`, `latitude`, `longitude`, and `name`. The server must know what `type` of place the client is putting on the map. A place may be **public** or not, and the client may provide a custom **description** of the place. The final URI also incorporates a username, but the client is already providing that, in the **Authorization** header. There's no need to make the client send that information twice.

These are all key-value pairs. I can have clients represent places the way they represent user accounts: as form-encoded strings. There are no complex data structures here that might call for a JSON or XML representation.

Client requests may choose to send some key-value pairs and omit others. Information that's in the URI as scoping information doesn't need to be repeated in the representation. When the client sends a POST to **/Earth/43.9;-103.46** it doesn't need to specify **latitude** and **longitude**, because that information's in the URI. It does need to specify **name** and **type**.

When the client sends a POST to **/Earth/Mount%20Rushmore** it shouldn't specify **latitude**, **longitude**, or **name**. The client is making a new place based on a well-known existing place, and the new place will inherit the name and location of the existing place. The client may specify a custom **type** ("national-park," "political," "places in North Dakota") or inherit the default ("monument").

The client may always choose to omit **description** and **public**. My service sets default values for those variables: descriptions are empty by default, and places are public by default.

When the client modifies one of its custom places, anything and everything about the place might change: its name, its location, its type, its description, or its public status. The PUT request that modifies a place can specify the same key-value pairs used to create a place, in any combination. The server will make the appropriate changes, assuming the changes make sense.

Example 6-6 shows a sample HTTP POST request that creates a new custom place. Combined, the form-encoded representation and the scoping information in the URI convey all required states for the new resource. The name and location of the new resource come from the scoping information; its type and description come from the representation. Since the representation doesn't specify a value for **public**, the default takes over and this new resource is made public.

Example 6-6. An HTTP request that creates a subordinate resource

```
POST /Earth/USA/Mount%20Rushmore HTTP/1.1
Host: maps.example.com
Authorization: Basic dXNlcm5hbWU6cGFzc3dvcmQ=

type=national-park&description=We%20visited%20on%203/5/2005
```

Design the Representation(s) Served to the Client

Most of the work here is already done. In Chapter 5 I defined an XHTML-based representation format for places. Custom places look the same as places from the built-in database.

The only new part is this: when an authenticated client requests a representation of one of its custom places, our service will tack onto the representation some hypermedia showing the client how to edit that place (see Example 6-7). I don't need to tell clients how to delete the place: the uniform interface takes care of that. But I do need to convey the information I wrote in prose above: that a place is defined by planet, latitude, longitude, and so on.

Example 6-7. A hypermedia form showing the client how to edit one of its places

```
<form id="modifyPlace" method="PUT" action="">
 <p>Modify this place:</p>

 <p>
  Name: <input name="name" value="Mount Rushmore" type="text" /><br />
  Type: <input name="type" value="national-park" type="text" /><br />
  Position:
   <input name="latitude" value="43.9" type="text" />,
   <input name="longitude" value="-103.46" type="text" /><br />
  Description:
   <textarea name="description">We visited on 3/5/2005</textarea><br />
  Public?
   <input name="public" type="checkbox" value="on"/>
  <input type="submit" />
 </p>
</form>
```

The caveats from earlier apply here too. This isn't valid XHTML 4, though it is valid XHTML 5, because it specifies PUT as its method. Also, a client doesn't know what to do with this form unless it's been programmed in advance. Computers don't know what "modifyPlace" means or what data might be a good value for "latitude."

Because clients have to be programmed in advance to understand these forms, most of today's services don't include a form for modifying a resource in that resource's representation. They either serve all the forms up front (in a WSDL or WADL file), or they specify them in prose (as I did above) and leave it for the service programmer to figure out. It's debatable whether it's really helpful to serve forms along with representations, but serving them is better than just specifying the API in prose and making the programmer implement it.

Link This Resource to Existing Resources

I've got three kinds of integration to do. The first is data integration. When you DELETE a user account, the account's custom places—everything under /user/{user *name}*—should also be deleted. URIs to these resources used to work, but now they will return a response code of 410 ("Gone") or 404 ("Not Found").

The other kinds of integration should be familiar by now. They involve changing the representations of existing resources to talk about the new one. I want search results to link to custom places. I want points on the globe to show how the user can create a custom place at that point. I want to improve my connectedness by connecting "custom place" resources to the resources I defined already.

The rather empty-looking representation of a user's account, seen in Example 6-3, badly needs some link-based integration. This is the ideal place to list a user's custom places. I'll represent the place list with the same XHTML list of links I use to represent search results.

In the service defined in Chapter 5, a client that searched for places called "Mount Rushmore" (`/Earth?show=Mount+Rushmore`) would only find places from my built-in place database: probably only the "consensus" location of Mount Rushmore in South Dakota. In the new version of the service, there's likely to be more than one result. In the new version, that search will also return other users' annotations for Mount Rushmore, and other places that users have named "Mount Rushmore," like the scale model in Imaichi.

This is the same case as in Chapter 5, where the built-in place database contained more than one "Joe's diner." I present search results in a list, each linking to a specific resource. All I'm doing is expanding the search. A search result may be a place in the built-in database, a custom place created by some other user and exposed publicly, or a custom place created by the authenticated user (which may be public or private).

I also need to show the client how to create its own places on the map. Custom places are created as subordinate resources of existing places. The logical thing to do is to put that information in the representations of those places: places with URIs like `/Earth/Mount%20Rushmore` and `/Earth/42;-93.7`.

Example 6-8 is a possible representation of `/Earth/43.9;-103.46` that brings together most of what I've covered in the past two chapters. This representation abounds in hypermedia. It links to a certain point on several different maps, a place from the built-in database, custom places from other users, and a custom place created by the authenticated user. It also has a hypermedia form that will let the authenticated user create a new custom place at these coordinates. Compare this representation to the smaller representation of `/Earth/43.9;-103.46` back in Example 5-9.

Example 6-8. An XHTML representation of 43.9N 103.46W on Earth

```
<!DOCTYPE html PUBLIC "-//W3C//DTD XHTML 1.1//EN"
    "http://www.w3.org/TR/xhtml11/DTD/xhtml11.dtd">
<html xmlns="http://www.w3.org/1999/xhtml" xml:lang="en">

<head>
 <title>43.9&deg;N 103.46&deg;W on Earth</title>
</head>
```

```
<body>

<p class="authenticated">
 You are currently logged in as
 <a class="user" href="/user/leonardr">leonardr</a>.
</p>

<p>
 Welcome to
 <a class="coordinates" href="/Earth/43.9,-103.46">43.9&deg;N
  103.46&deg;W</a>
 on scenic <a class="place" href="/Earth">Earth</a>.
</p>

<p>See this location on a map:</p>

<ul class="maps">
 <li><a class="map" href="/road/Earth/43.9;-103.46">Road</a></li>
 <li><a class="map" href="/satellite/Earth/43.9;-103.46">Satellite</a></li>
  ...
</ul>

<p>Places at this location:</p>

<ul class="places">
 <li>
  <a class="builtin" href="Mount%20Rushmore">Mount Rushmore</a>
  System data says:
  <span class="description">The world's largest sculpture</span>
 </li>

 <li>
  <a class="custom" href="Mt.%20Rushmore/user1">Mt. Rushmore</a>
  <a class="user" href="/users/user1">user1</a> says:
  <span class="description">Built on land stolen from the Lakota tribe</span>
 </li>

 <li>
  <a class="custom" href="Mount%20Rushmore%20Gift%20Shop/user2">
   Mount Rushmore Gift Shop
  </a>
  <a class="user" href="/users/user1">user1</a> says:
  <span class="description">Best fudge I've ever had</span>
 </li>

 <li>
  <a class="custom-private" href="Mount%20Rushmore/leonardr">Mt. Rushmore</a>
  You said: <span class="description">We visited on 3/5/2005</span>
 </li>
</ul>

<form id="searchPlace" method="get" action="">
 <p>
  Show nearby places, features, or businesses:
  <input name="show" repeat="template" /> <input class="submit" />
```

```
    </p>
  </form>

  <form id="createPlace" method="post" action="">
   <p>Create a new place here:</p>

   <p>
    Name: <input name="name" value="" type="text" /><br />
    Type: <input name="type" value="" type="text" /><br />
    Description:
     <textarea name="description"></textarea><br />
    Public?
     <input name="public" type="checkbox" value="on"/>
    <input type="submit" />
   </p>
  </form>

  </body>
  </html>
```

What's Supposed to Happen?

This new resource, the custom place, mostly works like other resources I've already defined. A custom place responds to GET just like a built-in place. It responds to PUT (with a representation consisting of key-value pairs) and DELETE (with no representation) just like "user account" resources do. I only have a couple new edge cases to consider here.

When the client creates a custom place, the response code is 201 ("Created"). This works the same way as users. But it was never possible to cause a user's URI to change, because I prohibited users from changing their usernames. It's possible to change the name of a place, or to move one (say, a ship) from one point on the map to another. Either of these actions will change the URI.

When the client modifies a custom place without changing its location, the response code will be 200 ("OK"). If the location changes, the response code will be 301 ("Moved Permanently") and the `Location` header will contain the place's new URI. The client is responsible for updating its data structures to keep track of the new URI. This ties into a debate I'll revisit in Chapter 8, about whether it's more important to have URIs that contain useful information, or URIs that never change. My URIs describe a custom place using two pieces of resource state: coordinates and name (`/user/leonardr/Earth/43.9;-103.46/Mt.%20Rushmore`). If either of those changes, the old URI breaks.

Broken URIs are no fun on the human web, and they're even less fun on the programmable web. If my custom "place" is a ship or something else that's constantly moving, it effectively has no permanent URI. This is the single biggest design flaw in my system. If I were exposing this as a real web service, I'd probably give a "permalink" to every place: an alternate URI that doesn't incorporate any changeable resource state. Since everything about a place can change except the planet it's on and the person who owns it, these URIs will not look very friendly: my annotation of Mount Rushmore might be accessible from `/user/leonardr/Earth/36028efa8`. But at least they'll always refer to the same place.

What Might Go Wrong?

This new kind of resource introduces new error conditions, but most of them are variations of ones I've already covered, so I'll pass over them quickly. The client might try to move an existing place off of the map by providing an invalid latitude or longitude: the response code is 400 ("Bad Request"), just as it was in a similar case in Chapter 5. The 400 response code is also appropriate when a client tries to create a place without providing all the information the server needs. This is similar to the 400 response code the server sends if the client tells the server to change a user's password, but doesn't actually provide the new password.

My service doesn't allow a single user to define more than one place with the same name at the same coordinates. `/user/leonardr/Earth/43.9;-103.46/Mt.%20Rushmore` can only identify one place at a time. Suppose a client has two places called "My car," and makes a PUT request that would move one to the location of the other. My service rejects this request with a response code of 409 ("Conflict"). There's nothing wrong with moving a place to a certain set of coordinates; it's just that right now there happens to be another place with that name there. The same 409 response code would happen if the client had two custom places at the same coordinates, and tried to rename one to match the name of the other. In either case, the client is making a syntactically valid request that would put the system's resources into an inconsistent state. It's the same as trying to create a user that already exists.

There's one totally new error condition worthy of attention: the client may try to access a private place created by someone else. There are two possibilities. The first is to deny access with response code 403 ("Forbidden"). The 403 response code is used when the client provides no authentication, or insufficient authentication; the latter certainly applies in this case.

But a response code of 403 is a tacit admission that the resource exists. The server should not be giving out this information. If client A creates a custom place and marks it private, client B should not be able to figure out anything about it, even its name, even by guessing. When revealing the existence of a resource would compromise security, the HTTP standard allows the server to lie, and send a response code of 404 ("Not Found").

A Look Back at the Map Service

This is still a simple design but it's got quite a few features. In Chapter 5 my clients could get map images, navigate around a map, bookmark points on the globe, and do geographic searches against a built-in database of places. Now they can keep track of custom places, register comments on consensus places, and share places with other users. The representation in Example 5-6 shows off most of these features.

All of these features are made available through resources that expose the uniform interface. Occasionally I need to supplement the uniform interface with hypermedia forms (here, the XHTML 5 forms) that tell the client what representations can go with a PUT or POST request. The vast majority of requests will be GET requests. These need no hypermedia supplements, because GET always means the same thing.

A client can get right to its desired resource by constructing a URI, or it can get to that resource by navigating links in the hypermedia I serve. You can get anywhere from the service root (the list of planets) by following links and filling out forms. Each resource is fairly simple, but the service as a whole is very powerful. The power comes from the variety of resources, the links that connect them, and the fact that each resource is individually addressable.

The Resource-Oriented Architecture sets down a list of design questions you need to ask yourself. I embodied these questions in the previous chapter's seven-step design procedure, and this chapter's extended nine-step procedure. Like any architecture, the ROA imposes design constraints, but it doesn't make all the design decisions for you. There are many other ways to define a map service in a RESTful and resource-oriented way. It all depends on how you split the data set into resources, what representations you define for those resources, and how you tie them together with hypermedia.

What I've designed should work and be useful to clients, but I won't know for sure, because I don't have to implement it. I just designed it to illustrate concepts in a book. When designing a real service, you also have implementation issues to consider. You have to write code to back up every decision you make: decisions about what resources you expose, what parts of the uniform interface they respond to, what URIs you choose, and which representations you serve and accept. In the next chapter, I'll make all these decisions again for a different data set, and this time I'll back it up with a real implementation.

## CHAPTER 7

A Service Implementation

It's been a while since I presented any code. Indeed, coming up with the code is currently a general problem for REST advocates. Despite the simplicity of REST, right now there are few well-known services that show off its principles. The average web service has ang architecture that combines elements of REST with the RPC style. This is changing, of course, and this book is part of the wave of change. Another problem is that many services seem trivial when exposed through resources, even though they'd look very impressive as SOAP/WSDL services. See Appendix A for a partial list of real RESTful services with enough moving parts to learn from.

Until recently, web frameworks made few concessions to the lucrative REST market. They focus on applications for web browsers, using only the GET and POST methods of HTTP. You can implement RESTful services with just GET and POST, but the limitation seems to encourage the RPC style instead. New frameworks for RESTful services are showing up, though, and existing frameworks are changing to accommodate REST fans. Django (Python), Restlet (Java), and Ruby on Rails all make it easy to expose resources that respond to HTTP's uniform interface. I cover these frameworks in Chapter 12. In this chapter I use Ruby on Rails as a medium for demonstrating how to implement a real-world web service.

A Social Bookmarking Web Service

Back in Chapter 2 I introduced del.icio.us, a web site that lets you publicly post bookmarks, tag them with short metadata strings, and see which URIs other people have posted. There's also a del.icio.us web service, which I used as the target of the web service clients in Chapter 2.

I mentioned that the del.icio.us web service has a couple shortcomings. First, it's a REST-RPC hybrid, not a fully RESTful service. It only exposes resources by accident and it doesn't respect HTTP's uniform interface. Second, the web service only gives you access to your own bookmarks and tags. When you use the service, it looks like you're the only person on del.icio.us. In this chapter I use Ruby on Rails to develop a

RESTful web service has much of the functionality of the del.icio.us web service *and* the del.icio.us web site.

I've got three goals for this chapter. Previous chapters showed you service design from first principles. Here, I want to show you how to make a RESTful, resource-oriented service out of an *existing* RPC-style service. Second, I want to show you the sort of tradeoffs you might need to make to get a design that works within your chosen framework. Finally, I want to show you the complete code to a nontrivial web service, without boring you with page after page of implementation details. I chose Ruby on Rails as my framework because Ruby is a dynamic language, and Rails comes with a lot of helper classes. This makes it easy to illustrate the underlying concepts in just a few lines of code. What's more, the most recent version of Rails is explicitly designed around the principles of REST and resource-oriented design.

My challenge is to reconcile the constraints imposed by the Resource-Oriented Architecture, and my own design sensibilities, with the simplifying assumptions of the Rails framework. My resource design is heavily informed by what Rails itself considers good design, but at points I've had to hack Rails to get the behavior I want, instead of the behavior Rails creator David Heinemeier Hansson wants. Rails imposes more constraints than most frameworks (this is a big reason for its success, actually), but your choice of framework will always have some effect on your design.

I'm going to start with an empty Rails 1.2 application, and fill in the details as the design takes shape. I created a Rails application with the following command:

```
$ rails bookmarks
```

I installed two Rails plugins I know I'll need: `acts_as_taggable`, to implement tags on bookmarks, and `http_authentication`, to tie HTTP Basic authentication into my user model. I've also installed the `atom-tools` Ruby gem, so I can generate Atom feeds for representations.

```
$ cd bookmarks
$ script/plugin install acts_as_taggable
$ script/plugin install http_authentication
$ gem install atom-tools
```

I also created a SQL database called `bookmarks_development`, and configured *config/database.yaml* so that Rails can connect to the database.

Figuring Out the Data Set

Because I'm basing my service on an existing one, it's fairly easy to figure out the parameters of the data set. If what follows is confusing, feel free to flip back to "del.icio.us: The Sample Application" in Chapter 2 for an overview of del.icio.us.

The del.icio.us site has four main kinds of data: user accounts, bookmarks (del.icio.us calls them "posts"), tags (short strings that act as metadata for bookmarks), and bundles (collections of tags for a user). The web site and the web service track the same data set.

Unlike an S3 bucket, or a user account on my map service, a del.icio.us user account is not just a named list of subordinate resources. It's got state of its own. A del.icio.us account has a username and password, but it's supposed to correspond to a particular person, and it also tracks that person's full name and email address. A user account also has a list of subordinate resources: the user's bookmarks. All this state can be fetched and manipulated through HTTP.

A bookmark belongs to a user and has six pieces of state: a URI, a short and a long description, a timestamp, a collection of tags, and a flag that says whether or not it's public (the previous chapter's "custom place" resource has a similar flag). The client is in charge of specifying all of this information for each bookmark, though the URI and the short description are the only required pieces of state.

The URIs in users' bookmarks are the most interesting part of the data set. When you put a bunch of peoples' bookmarks together, you find that the URIs have emergent properties. On del.icio.us these properties include newness, a measure of how recently someone bookmarked a particular URI; "popularity," a measure of how many people have bookmarked that URI; and the "tag cloud," a generated vocabulary for the URI, based on which tags people tend to use to describe the URI. The del.icio.us web site also exposes a recommendation engine that relates URIs to each other, using a secret algorithm.

I'm not going to do much with the emergent properties of URIs, properties that account for much of del.icio.us's behind-the-scenes code. My implemented service will have a notion of newness but it won't have popularity, tag clouds, or recommendation algorithms. This is just so I can keep this book down to a manageable size instead of turning it into a book about recommendation algorithms.

Tags have only one piece of state: their name. They only exist in relation to bookmarks —and bundles, which I haven't described yet. A bundle is a user's decision to group particular tags together. A user with tags "recipes," "restaurants," and "food," might group those tags into a bundle called "gustation." I'll show the RESTful design of bundles, just for completeness, but I won't be implementing them when it comes time to write code.

At this point I know enough about the data set to create the database schema. I create an empty database called `bookmarks_development` in my MySQL installation, and put this data in the file *db/migrate/001_initial_schema.rb*, shown in Example 7-1.

Example 7-1. The bookmark database schema as a Rails migration

```
class InitialSchema < ActiveRecord::Migration

  # Create the database tables on a Rails migration.
  def self.up
    # The 'users' table, tracking four items of state
```

```ruby
  # plus a unique ID.
  create_table :users, :force => true do |t|
    t.column :name, :string
    t.column :full_name, :string
    t.column :email, :string
    t.column :password, :string
  end

  # The 'bookmarks' table, tracking six items of state,
  # plus a derivative field and a unique ID.
  create_table :bookmarks, :force => true do |t|
    t.column :user_id, :string
    t.column :uri, :string
    t.column :uri_hash, :string    # A hash of the URI.
                                   # See book text below.
    t.column :short_description, :string
    t.column :long_description, :text
    t.column :timestamp, :datetime
    t.column :public, :boolean
  end

  # This join table reflects the fact that bookmarks are subordinate
  # resources to users.
  create_table :user_bookmarks, :force => true do |t|
    t.column :user_id, :integer
    t.column :bookmark_id, :integer
  end

  # These two are standard tables defined by the acts_as_taggable
  # plugin, of which more later. This one defines tags.
  create_table :tags do |t|
    t.column :name, :string
  end

  # This one defines the relationship between tags and the things
  # tagged--in this case, bookmarks.
  create_table :taggings do |t|
    t.column :tag_id, :integer
    t.column :taggable_id, :integer
    t.column :taggable_type, :string
  end

  # Four indexes that capture the ways I plan to search the
  # database.
  add_index :users, :name
  add_index :bookmarks, :uri_hash
  add_index :tags, :name
  add_index :taggings, [:tag_id, :taggable_id, :taggable_type]
end
```

```
    # Drop the database tables on a Rails reverse migration.
    def self.down
      [:users, :bookmarks, :tags, :user_bookmarks, :taggings].each do |t|
        drop_table t
      end
    end
end
```

I've used Ruby code to describe five database tables and four indexes. I create the corresponding database schema by running this command:

```
$ rake db:migrate
```

Resource Design

In Chapters 5 and 6 I had a lot of leeway in turning my imaginary data set into resources. The idea for my map service came from the Google Maps application with its image tiles, but I took it off in another direction. I added user accounts, custom places, and other features not found in any existing map service.

This chapter works differently. I'm focusing on translating the ideas of del.icio.us into the Resource-Oriented Architecture. There are lots of ways of exposing a data set of tagged bookmarks, but I'm focusing on the ones del.icio.us actually uses. Let's start by taking a look at what the del.icio.us web service has to offer.

The del.icio.us web service is a REST-RPC hybrid service, described in English prose at *http://del.icio.us/help/api/*. The web service itself is rooted at *https://api.del.icio.us/ v1/*. The service exposes three RPC-style APIs, rooted at the relative URIs posts/, tags/, and bundles/. Beneath these URIs the web service exposes a total of twelve RPC functions that can be invoked through HTTP GET. I need to define RESTful resources that can expose at least the functionality of these three APIs:

First, the posts/ API, which lets the user fetch and manage her bookmark posts to del.icio.us:

- posts/get: Search your posts by tag or date, or search for a specific bookmarked URI.
- posts/recent: Fetch the *n* most recent posts by the authenticated user. The client may apply a tag filter: "fetch the *n* most recent posts that the authenticated user tagged with tag *t*".
- posts/dates: Fetch the number of posts by the authenticated user for each day: perhaps five posts on the 12th, two on the 15th, and so on. The client may apply a tag filter here, too.
- posts/all: Fetch all posts for the authenticated user, ever. The client may apply a tag filter.
- posts/update: Check when the authenticated user last posted a bookmark. Clients are supposed to check this before deciding to call the expensive posts/all.

- **posts/add**: Create a bookmark for a URI. The client must specify a short description. It may choose to specify a long description, a set of tags, and a timestamp. A bookmark may be public or private (the default is public). A client may not bookmark the same URI more than once: calling **posts/add** again overwrites the old post with new information.
- **posts/delete**: Deletes a user's post for a particular URI.

Second, the **tags/** API, which lets the authenticated user manage her tags separately from the bookmarks that use the tags:

- **tags/get**: Fetch a list of tags used by the authenticated user.
- **tags/rename**: Rename one of the authenticated user's tags. All posts tagged with the old name will now be tagged with the new name instead.

Finally, the **bundles** API, which lets the authenticated user group similar tags together.

- **tags/bundles/all**: Fetch the user's bundles. The resulting document lists the bundles, and each bundle lists the tags it contains.
- **tags/bundles/set**: Group several tags together into a (possibly new) bundle.
- **tags/bundles/delete**: Delete a bundle.

That's the web service. As I mentioned in Chapter 2, the service only gives you access to your own bookmarks and tags. The del.icio.us web site has social features as well, and I'm going to steal some of those features for my design.

Here are some interesting "functions" exposed by the del.icio.us web site but not the web service:

- **/{username}**: Fetch any user's bookmarks.
- **/{username}/{tag}**: Fetch any user's bookmarks, applying a tag filter.
- **/tag/{tag-name}**: Fetch bookmarks tagged with a particular tag, from all users.
- **/url/{URI-MD5}**: Fetch the list of users who have bookmarked a particular URI. The *{URI-MD5}* happens to be the MD5 hash of the URI, but from the average client's point of view that's not important: it's an opaque string of bytes that somehow identifies a URI within the del.icio.us system.
- **/recent**: Fetch the most recently posted bookmarks, from all users. The del.icio.us home page also shows this information.

Now that I know what the service has to do, arranging the features into resources is like working a logic puzzle. I want to expose as few kinds of resources as possible. But one kind of resource can only convey one concept, so sometimes I need to split a single feature across two kinds of resource. On the other hand, sometimes I can combine multiple RPC functions into one kind of resource, a resource that responds to several methods of HTTP's uniform interface.

REST in Rails

I'm not designing these resources in a vacuum: I'm going to implement them in a Rails application. It's worth taking a brief look at how RESTful applications work in Rails. Unlike some other frameworks, Rails doesn't let you define your resources directly. Instead, it divides up an application's functionality into *controllers*: it's the controllers that expose the resources. The first path variable in a request URI is used to route Rails to the appropriate controller class. For instance, in the URI /weblogs/4 the "weblogs" designates the controller: probably a class called WeblogController. The "4" designates the database ID of a particular weblog.

In previous versions of Rails, programmers defined RPC-style methods on controllers: methods like rename and delete. To rename a weblog you'd send a GET or an overloaded POST request to /weblogs/4/rename. Rails applications, like most web applications, were REST-RPC hybrids.

In Rails 1.2, programmers define special controller methods that correspond to the methods of HTTP's uniform interface. For instance, sending a GET to /weblogs triggers the WeblogController's index method, which is supposed to retrieve a list of the weblogs. Sending a POST to the same URI triggers the WeblogController#create method, which creates a subordinate resource beneath /weblogs: say, a weblog with a URI of /weblogs/4. The Rails controller exposes a resource—"the list of weblogs"—that responds to GET and POST. As you'd expect, when you POST to the "list" resource you get a subordinate resource: a new weblog.

The subordinate resource also supports the uniform interface. If you wanted to rename a weblog in an RPC-style service, you might POST a new name to /weblogs/4/rename. Under a RESTful regime, you PUT a new name to /weblogs/4, triggering the WeblogController#update method. To delete a weblog, you send a DELETE request to its URI, triggering the controller's WeblogController#destroy method. There's no need to expose an RPC-style URI /weblogs/4/delete, because HTTP's uniform interface already knows about deleting.

These two resources, a list and an item in the list, show up all the time. Every database table is a list that contains items. Anything that can be represented as an RSS or Atom feed is a list that contains items. Rails defines a RESTful architecture that makes a simplifying assumption: every resource you expose can be made to fit one of these two patterns. This makes things easy most of the time, but the cost is aggravation when you try to use Rails controllers to expose resources that don't fit this simple model.

I'm going to define my resources in terms of Rails controllers. These controllers impose constraints on my URI structure and my use of the uniform interface, and I need to design with those constraints in mind. By the time I'm done designing the controllers, I'll know which resources the controllers expose, which URIs they answer to, and which methods of the uniform interface correspond to which RPC functions from the del.icio.us service. Basically, I'll have completed steps 2 through 4 of the 9-step procedure from the "Turning Requirements into Read/Write Resources" section in

Chapter 6: "Split the data set into resources," "Name the resources with URIs," and "Expose a subset of the uniform interface." In Chapter 12 I give a variant of the service design procedure specifically for Rails services.

I'll only be accessing my Rails application from my local machine. The root URI will be *http://localhost:3000/v1*. When I give a relative URI below, like /users, understand that I'm talking about *http://localhost:3000/v1/users*. I only ever plan to write one version of this service, but I'm versioning the URIs, just in case. (When and how to version is discussed in Chapter 8).

The User Controller

Now I'm going to go back to that big list of RPC functions I found in the del.icio.us API and web site, and try to tease some Rails controllers out of it. One obvious controller is one that exposes information about user accounts. In Rails, this would be a class called `UsersController`. As soon as I say that, a lot of decisions are made for me. Rails sets up a path of least resistance that looks like this:

The user controller exposes a one-off "user list" resource, at the URI /users. It also exposes a resource for every user on the system, at a URI that incorporates the user's database ID: /users/52 and the like. These resources expose some subset of HTTP's uniform interface. Which subset? Rails defines this with a programming-language interface in the superclass of all controller classes: `ActionController::Base`. Table 7-1 shows how the two interfaces line up.

Table 7-1. How Rails wants my UsersController to look

Operation	HTTP action	Rails method
List the users	GET /users	UsersController#index
Create a user	POST /users	UsersController#create
View a user	GET /users/52	UsersController#show
Modify a user	PUT /users/52	UsersController#update
Delete a user	DELETE /users/52	UsersController#destroy

So if I want to let clients create new user accounts, I implement `UsersController#create`, and my "user list" resource starts calling that method in response to POST requests.

The path of least resistance is pretty good but I have a couple problems with it. First, I don't want to let clients fetch the list of users, because del.icio.us doesn't have that feature. (Presumably the del.icio.us administrative interface does have a feature like this.) That's fine: I don't have to expose GET on every resource, and I don't have to define `index` in every controller. My user list resource, at the URI /users, will only expose the POST method, for creating new users. My user list is a featureless container for user account resources, and the only thing a client can do with it is create a new account. This incorporates functionality like that at *https://secure.del.icio.us/register*, where you can use your web browser to sign up for a del.icio.us account.

User Account Creation

The real del.icio.us site doesn't expose user account creation through its web service. To create a user account you must prove you're a human being, by typing in the string you see in a graphic. This graphic (called a *CAPTCHA*) is an explicit attempt to move the human web off of the programmable web, to prevent automated clients (many of which are up to no good) from creating their own del.icio.us accounts.

This is legitimate. Not every piece of functionality has to be part of your web service, and it's your decision what to expose. But I don't want to get into the details of web site and CAPTCHA design in this book, so I'm exposing user account creation as part of the web service.

Another problem is that URIs like /users/52 look ugly. They certainly don't look like *http://del.icio.us/leonardr*, the URI to my corresponding page on del.icio.us. This URI format is the Rails default because every object in a Rails application's database can be uniquely identified by its table ("users") and its ID ("52"). This URI might go away (if user 52 DELETEs her account), but it will never change, because database unique IDs don't change.

I'd rather expose readable URIs that might change occasionally than permanent URIs that don't say anything, so I'm going to identify a user using elements of its resource state. I happen to know that users have unique names, so I'm going to expose my "user" resources at URIs like /users/leonardr. Each resource of this type will expose the methods GET, PUT, and DELETE. This incorporates the functionality of the del.icio.us web site's /{username} "function." It also incorporates the pages on the web site (I didn't mention these earlier) that let you edit and delete your own del.icio.us account.

To expose this RESTful interface, I just need to implement four special methods on UsersController. The create method implements POST on the "user list" resource at /users. The other three methods implement HTTP methods on the "user" resources at /users/{username}: show implements GET, update implements PUT, and destroy implements DELETE.

The Bookmarks Controller

Each user account has a number of subordinate resources associated with it: the user's bookmarks. I'm going to expose these resources through a second controller class, rooted beneath the "user account" resource.

The base URI of this controller will be /users/{username}/bookmarks. Like the users controller, the bookmarks controller exposes two types of resource: a one-off resource for the list of a user's bookmarks, and one resource for each individual bookmark.

Rails wants to expose an individual bookmark under the URI /users/{username}/book marks/{database-id}. I don't like this any more than I like /users/{database-id}. I'd like the URI to a bookmark to have some visible relationship to the URI that got bookmarked.

My original plan was to incorporate the target URI in the URI to the bookmark. That way if I bookmarked *http://www.oreilly.com/*, the bookmark resource would be available at /v1/users/leonardr/bookmarks/http://www.oreilly.com/. Lots of services work this way, including the W3C's HTML validator (*http://validator.w3.org/*). Looking at one of these URIs you can easily tell who bookmarked what. Rails didn't like this URI format, though, and after trying some hacks I decided to get back on Rails's path of least resistance. Instead of embedding external URIs in my resource URIs, I'm going to put the URI through a one-way hash function and embed the hashed string instead.

If you go to *http://del.icio.us/url/55020a5384313579a5f11e75c1818b89* in your web browser, you'll see the list of people who've bookmarked *http://www.oreilly.com/*. There's no obvious connection between the URI and its MD5 hash, but if you know one you can calculate the other. It's certainly better than a totally opaque database ID. And since it's a single alphanumeric string, Rails handles it with ease. My bookmark resources will have URIs like /v1/users/leonardr/bookmarks/ 55020a5384313579a5f11e75c1818b89. That URI identifies the time I bookmarked *http:// www.oreilly.com/* (see Example 7-2).

Example 7-2. Calculating an MD5 hash in Ruby

```
require 'digest/md5'
Digest::MD5.new("http://www.oreilly.com/").to_s
# => "55020a5384313579a5f11e75c1818b89"
```

When a user is first created it has no bookmarks. A client creates bookmarks by sending a POST request to its own "bookmark list" resource, just as it might create a user account by sending a POST to the "user list" resource. This takes care of the posts/add and posts/delete functions from the del.icio.us API.

Creating a New Bookmark

There are two other ways to expose the ability to create a new bookmark. Both are RESTful, but neither is on the Rails path of least resistance.

The first alternative is the one I chose for user accounts back in Chapter 6. In the fantasy map application, a client creates a user account by sending a PUT request to /users/ {username}. The corresponding solution for the user bookmark would be to have a client create a bookmark by sending a PUT request to /users/{username}/bookmarks/ {URI-MD5}. The client knows its own username and the URI it wants to bookmark, and it knows how to calculate MD5 hashes, so why not let it make the final URI itself?

This would work fine within the ROA, but it's not idiomatic for Rails. The simplest way to create new objects in RESTful Rails is to send a POST request to the corresponding "list" resource.

The other alternative treats bookmarks as a subordinate resource of user accounts. To create a bookmark you send a POST request, not to `/users/{username}/bookmarks` but to `/users/{username}`. The bookmark is made available at `/users/{username}/{URI-MD5}`. The "bookmarks" path fragment doesn't exist at all.

Those URIs are more compact, but Rails doesn't support them (at least not very easily), because it needs that extra path fragment `/bookmarks` to identify the `BookmarksController`. There's also no easy way of exposing POST on an individual user. The method `UsersController#create`, which responds to POST, is already being used to expose POST on the user *list*.

It's not a big deal in this case, but you can see how a framework can impose restrictions on the resource design, atop the rules and best practices of the Resource-Oriented Architecture.

Unlike with the list of users, I do want to let clients fetch the list of a user's bookmarks. This means `/users/{username}/bookmarks` will respond to GET. The individual bookmarks will respond to GET, PUT, and DELETE. This means the `BookmarksController`ler: `index`, `create`, `show`, `update`, and `delete`.

The "bookmark list" resource incorporates some of the functionality from the del.icio.us API functions `posts/get`, `posts/recent`, and `posts/all`.

The User Tags Controller

Bookmarks aren't the only type of resource that conceptually fits "beneath" a user account. There's also the user's tag vocabulary. I'm not talking about tags in general here: I'm asking questions about which tags a particular user likes to use. These questions are handled by the user tags controller.

This controller is rooted at `/users/{username}/tags`. That's the "user tag list" resource. It's an algorithmic resource, generated from the tags a user uses to talk about her bookmarks. This resource corresponds roughly to the del.icio.us `tags/get` function. It's a read-only resource: a user can't modify her vocabulary directly, only by changing the way she uses tags in bookmarks.

The resources at `/users/{username}/tags/{tag}` talk about the user's use of a specific tag. My representation will show which bookmarks a user has filed under a particular tag. This class of resource corresponds to the `/{username}/{tag}` "function" from the web site. It also incorporates some stuff of the del.icio.us API functions `posts/get`, `posts/recent`, and `posts/all`.

The "tag" resources are also algorithmic, but they're not strictly read-only. A user can't delete a tag except by removing it from all of her bookmarks, but I do want to let users rename tags. (Tag deletion is a plausible feature, but I'm not implementing it because, again, del.icio.us doesn't have it.) So each user-tag resource will expose PUT for clients who want to rename that tag.

Instead of PUT, I could have used overloaded POST to define a one-off "rename" method like the del.icio.us API's `tag/rename`. I didn't, because that's RPC-style thinking. The PUT method suffices to convey *any* state change, whether it's a rename or something else. There's a subtle difference between renaming the tag and changing its state so the name is different, but it's the difference between an RPC-style interface and a uniform, RESTful one. It's less work to program a computer to understand a generic "change the state" than to program it to understand "rename a tag."

The Calendar Controller

A user's posting history—her calendar— is handled by one more controller that lives "underneath" a user account resource. The posting history is another algorithmically generated, read-only resource: you can't change your posting history except by posting. The controller's root URI is `/users/{username}/calendar`, and it corresponds to the del.icio.us API's `posts/dates` function.

I'll also expose a variety of subresources, one for each tag in a user's vocabulary. These resources will give a user's posting history when only one tag is considered. These resources correspond to the del.icio.us API's `posts/dates` function with a tag filter applied. Both kinds of resource, posting history and filtered posting history, will expose only GET.

The URI Controller

I mentioned earlier that URIs in a social bookmarking system have emergent properties. The URI controller gives access to some of those properties. It's rooted at `/uris/`, and it exposes URIs as resources independent from the users who bookmark them.

I'm not exposing this controller's root URI as a resource, though I could. The logical thing to put there would be a huge list of all URIs known to the application. But again, the site I'm taking for my model doesn't have any feature like that. Instead, I'm exposing a series of resources at `/uris/{URI-MD5}`: one resource for each URI known to the application. The URI format is the same as `/users/{username}/bookmarks/{URI-MD5}` in the user bookmark controller: calculate the MD5 hash of the target URI and stick it onto the end of the controller's base URI.

These resources expose the application's knowledge about a specific URI, such as which users have bookmarked it. This corresponds to the `/url/{URI-MD5}` "function" on the del.icio.us web site.

The Recent Bookmarks Controller

My last implemented controller reveals another emergent property of the URIs. In this case the property is newness: which URIs were most recently posted.

This controller is rooted at /recent. The top-level "list" resource lists all the recently posted bookmarks. This corresponds to the /recent "function" on the del.icio.us web site.

The sub-resources at /recent/{tag} expose the list of recently posted bookmarks that were tagged with a particular tag. For instance, a client can GET /recent/recipes to find recently posted URIs that were tagged with "recipes". This corresponds to the /tag/{tag-name} function on the del.icio.us web site.

The Bundles Controller

Again, I'm not going to implement this controller, but I want to design it so you can see I'm not cheating. This controller is rooted at /user/{username}/bundles/. An alternative is /user/{username}/tags/bundles/, but that would prevent any user from having a tag named "bundles". A client can send a GET request to the appropriate URI to get any user's "bundle list". A client can POST to its own bundle list to create a new bundle. This takes care of tags/bundles/all and part of tags/bundles/set.

The sub-resources at /user/{username}/bundles/{bundle} expose the individual bundles by name. These respond to GET (to see which tags are in a particular bundle), PUT (to modify the tags associated with a bundle), and DELETE (to delete a bundle). This takes care of tags/bundles/delete and the rest of tags/bundles/set.

The Leftovers

What's left? I've covered almost all the functionality of the original del.icio.us API, but I haven't placed the posts/update function. This function is designed to let a client avoid calling posts/all when there's no new data there. Why bother? Because the posts/all function is extremely expensive on the server side. A del.icio.us client is supposed to keep track of the last time it called posts/all, and check that time against the "return value" of posts/update before calling the expensive function again.

There's already a solution for this built into HTTP: conditional GET. I cover it briefly in "Conditional HTTP GET" later in this chapter and I'll cover it in more detail in "Conditional GET," but in this chapter you'll see it implemented. By implementing conditional GET, I can give the time- and bandwidth-saving benefits of posts/update to most of of the resources I'm exposing, not just the single most expensive one.

Remodeling the REST Way

I've taken an RPC-style web service that was only RESTful in certain places and by accident, and turned it into a set of fully RESTful resources. I'd like to take a break now and illustrate how the two services line up with each other. Tables 7-2 through 7-6 show every social bookmarking operation I implemented, the HTTP request you'd send to invoke that operation on my RESTful web service, and how you'd invoke the corresponding operation on del.icio.us itself.

Table 7-2. Service comparison: user accounts

Operation	On my service	On del.icio.us
Create a user account	POST /users	POST /register (via web site)
View a user account	GET /users/{username}	GET /users/{username} (via web site)
Modify a user account	PUT /users/{username}	Various, via web site
Delete a user account	DELETE /users/{username}	POST /settings/{username}/profile/delete (via web site)

Table 7-3. Service comparison: bookmark management

Operation	On my service	On del.icio.us
Post a bookmark	POST /users/{username}/bookmarks	GET /posts/add
Fetch a bookmark	GET /users/{username}/bookmarks/{URI-MD5}	GET /posts/get
Modify a bookmark	PUT /users/{username}/bookmarks/{URI-MD5}	GET /posts/add
Delete a bookmark	DELETE /users/{username}/bookmarks/{URI-MD5}	GET /posts/delete
See when the user last posted a bookmark	Use conditional HTTP GET	GET /posts/update
Fetch a user's posting history	GET /users/{username}/calendar	GET /posts/dates (your history only)
Fetch a user's posting history, filtered by tag	GET /users/{username}/calendar/{tag}	GET /posts/dates with query string (your history only)

Table 7-4. Service comparison: finding bookmarks

Operation	On my service	On del.icio.us
Fetch a user's recent bookmarks	GET /users/{username}/bookmarks with query string	GET /posts/recent (your bookmarks only)
Fetch all of a user's bookmarks	GET /posts/{username}/bookmarks	GET /posts/all (your bookmarks only)
Search a user's bookmarks by date	GET /posts/{username}/bookmarks with query string	GET /posts/get with query string (your bookmarks only)
Fetch a user's bookmarks tagged with a certain tag	GET /posts/{username}/bookmarks/{tag}	GET /posts/get with query string (your bookmarks only)

Table 7-5. Service comparison: social features

Operation	On my service	On del.icio.us
See recently posted bookmarks	GET /recent	GET /recent (via web site)
See recently posted bookmarks for a certain tag	GET /recent/{tag}	GET /tag/{tag} (via web site)
See which users have bookmarked a certain URI	GET /uris/{URI-MD5}	GET /url/{URI-MD5} (via web site)

Table 7-6. Service comparison: tags and tag bundles

Operation	On my service	On del.icio.us
Fetch a user's tag vocabulary	GET /users/{username}/tags	GET /tags/get (your tags only)
Rename a tag	PUT /users/{username}/tags/{tag}	GET /tags/rename
Fetch the list of a user's tag bundles	GET /users/{username}/bundles	GET /tags/bundles/all (your bundles only)
Group tags into a bundle	POST /users/{username}/bundles	GET /tags/bundles/set
Fetch a bundle	GET /users/{username}/bundles/{bundle}	N/A
Modify a bundle	PUT /users/{username}/bundles/{bundle}	GET /tags/bundles/set
Delete a bundle	DELETE /users/{username}/bundles/{bundle}	GET /tags/bundles/delete

I think you'll agree that the RESTful service is more self-consistent, even accounting for the fact that some of the del.icio.us features come from the web service and some from the web site. Table 7-6 is probably the best for a straight-up comparison. There you can distinctly see the main advantage of my RESTful service: its use of the HTTP method to remove the operation name from the URI. This lets the URI identify an object in the object-oriented sense. By varying the HTTP method you can perform different operations on the object. Instead of having to understand some number of arbitrarily-named functions, you can understand a single class (in the object-oriented sense) whose instances expose a standardized interface.

My service also lifts various restrictions found in the del.icio.us web service. Most notably, you can see other peoples' public bookmarks. Now, sometimes restrictions are the accidental consequences of bad design, but sometimes they exist for a reason. If I were deploying this service commercially it might turn out that I want to add those limits back in. I might not want user A to have unlimited access to user B's bookmark list. I don't have to change my design to add these limits. I just have to change the authorization component of my service. I make it so that authenticating as userA doesn't authorize you to fetch userB's public bookmarks, any more than it authorizes you to delete userB's account. Or if bandwidth is the problem, I might limit how often any user can perform certain operations. I haven't changed my resources at all: I've just added additional rules about when operations on those resources will succeed.

Implementation: The routes.rb File

Ready for some more code? I've split my data set into Rails controllers, and each Rails controller has divided its data set further into one or two kinds of resources. Rails has also made decisions about what my URIs will look like. I vetoed some of these decisions (like /users/52, which I changed to /users/leonardr), but most of them I'm going to let stand.

I'll implement the controllers as Ruby classes, but what about the URIs? I need some way of mapping path fragments like bookmarks/ to controller classes like BookmarksController. In a Rails application, this is the job of the *routes.rb* file. Example 7-3 is a *routes.rb* that sets up URIs for the six controllers I'll implement later in the chapter.

Example 7-3. The routes.rb file

```
# service/config/routes.rb
ActionController::Routing::Routes.draw do |map|
  base = '/v1'

  ## The first controller I define is the UsersController. The call to
  ## map.resources sets it up so that all HTTP requests to /v1/users
  ## or /v1/users/{username} are routed to the UsersController class.

  # /v1/users => UsersController
  map.resources :users, :path_prefix => base

  ## Now I'm going to define a number of controllers beneath the
  ## UsersController. They will respond to requests for URIs that start out
  ## with /v1/users/{username}, and then have some extra stuff.
  user_base = base + '/users/:username'

  # /v1/users/{username}/bookmarks => BookmarksController
  map.resources :bookmarks, :path_prefix => user_base

  # /v1/users/{username}/tags => TagsController
  map.resources :tags, :path_prefix => user_base

  # /v1/users/{username}/calendar => CalendarController
  map.resources :calendar, :path_prefix => user_base

  ## Finally, two more controllers that are rooted beneath /v1.

  # /v1/recent => RecentController
  map.resources :recent, :path_prefix => base

  # /v1/uris => UrisController
  map.resources :uris, :path_prefix => base
end
```

Now I'm committed to defining six controller classes. The code in Example 7-3 determines the class names by tying into Rails' naming conventions. My six classes are called UsersController, BookmarksController, TagsController, CalendarController,

---

`RecentController`, and `UrisController`. Each class controls one or two kinds of resources. Each controller implements a specially-named Ruby method for each HTTP method the resources expose.

Design the Representation(s) Accepted from the Client

When a client wants to modify a user account or post a bookmark, how should it convey the resource state to the server? Rails transparently supports two incoming representation formats: form-encoded key-value pairs and the ActiveRecord XML serialization format.

Form-encoding should be familiar to you. I mentioned it back in Chapter 6, and it's everywhere in web applications. It's the `q=jellyfish` and `color1=blue&color2=green` you see in query strings on the human web. When a client makes a request that includes the query string `color1=blue&color2=green`, Rails gives the controller a hash that looks like this:

```
{"color1" => "blue", "color2" => "green"}
```

The service author doesn't have to parse the representation: they can work directly with the key-value pairs.

ActiveRecord is Rails's object-relational library. It gives a native Ruby interface to the tables and rows in a relational database. In a Rails application, most exposed resources correspond to these ActiveRecord tables and rows. That's the case for my service: all my users and bookmarks are database rows managed through ActiveRecord.

Any ActiveRecord object, and the database row that underlies it, can be represented as a set of key-value pairs. These key-value pairs can be form-encoded, but ActiveRecord also knows how to encode them into XML documents. Example 7-4 gives an XML depiction of an ActiveRecord object from this chapter: a user account. This is the string you'd get by calling **to_xml** on a (yet-to-be-defined) `User` object. Example 7-5 gives an equivalent form-encoded representation. Example 7-6 gives the hash that's left when Rails parses the XML document or the form-encoded string as an incoming representation.

Example 7-4. An XML representation of a user account

```
<user>
 <name>leonardr</body>
 <full-name>Leonard Richardson</body>
 <email>leonardr@example.com</body>
 <password>mypassword</body>
</user>
```

Example 7-5. A form-encoded representation of a user account

```
user[name]=leonardr&user[full-name]=Leonard%20Richardson
&user[email]=leonardr%40example.com&user[password]=mypassword
```

Example 7-6. A set of key-value pairs derived from XML or the form-encoded representation

```
{ "user[name]" => "leonardr",
  "user[full_name]" => "Leonard Richardson",
  "user[email]" => "leonardr@example.com",
  "user[password]" => "mypassword" }
```

I'm going to support both representation formats. I can do this by defining my keys for the form-encoded representation as user[name] instead of just name. This looks a little funny to the client, but it means that Rails will parse a form-encoded representation and an ActiveRecord XML representation into the same data structure: one that looks like the one in Example 7-6.

The keys for the key-value pairs of a user account representation are user[name], user [password], user[full_name], and user[email]. Not coincidentally, these are the names of the corresponding fields in my database table users.

The keys for a representation of a bookmark are bookmark[short_description], bookmark[long_description], bookmark[timestamp], bookmark[public], and bookmark [tag][]. These are all the names of database fields, except for bookmark[tag][], which corresponds to a bookmark's tags. I'll be handling tags specially, and you might recall they're kept in separate database tables. For now, just note that the extra "[]" in the variable name tells Rails to expect multiple tags in a single request.

> There are other ways of allowing the client to specify multiple tags. The del.icio.us service itself represents a list of tags as a single tags variable containing a space-separated string. This is good for a simple case, but in general I don't like that because it reimplements something you can already, do with the form-encoded format.
>
> A JSON data structure is another possible way of representing a bookmark. This would be a hash in which most keys correspond to strings, but where one key (tags) corresponds to a list.

The incoming representation of a tag contains only one key-value pair: the key is tag [name].

The incoming representation of a bundle contains two key-value pairs: bundle[name] and bundle[tag][]. The second one can show up multiple times in a single representation, since the point is to group multiple tags together. I'm approaching the implementation stage, so this is the last time I'll mention bundles.

Design the Representation(s) Served to the Client

I've got a huge number of options for outgoing representation formats: think back to the discussion in "Representing the List of Planets" in Chapter 5. Rails makes it easy to serve any number of representation formats, but the simplest to use is the XML representation you get when you call to_xml on an ActiveRecord object.

This is a very convenient format to serve from Rails, but it's got a big problem: it's not a hypermedia format. A client that gets the user representation in Example 7-4 knows enough to reconstruct the underlying row in the users table (minus the password). But that document says nothing about the relationship between that resource and other resources: the user's bookmarks, tag vocabulary, or calendar. It doesn't connect the "user" resource to any other resources. A service that serves only ActiveRecord XML documents isn't well-connected.

I'm going to serve to_xml representations in a couple places, just to keep the size of this chapter down. I'll represent a user account and a user's tag vocabulary with to_xml. I'll generate my own, custom to_xml-like document when representing a user's posting history.

When I think about the problem domain, another representation format leaps out at me: the Atom syndication format. Many of the resources I'm exposing are lists of bookmarks: recent bookmarks, bookmarks for a user, bookmarks for a tag, and so on. Syndication formats were designed to display lists of links. What's more, there are already lots of software packages that understand URIs and syndication formats. If I expose bookmark lists through a standard syndication format, I'll immediately gain a huge new audience for my service. Any program that manipulates syndication feeds can take my resources as input. What's more, syndication feeds can contain links. If a resource can be represented as a syndication feed, I can link it to other resources. My resources will form a *web*, not just an unrelated set.

My default representation will always be the to_xml one, but a client will be able to get an Atom representation of any list of bookmarks by tacking ".atom" onto the end of the appropriate URI. If a client GETs /users/leonardr/bookmarks/ruby, it'll see a link-less to_xml representation of the bookmarks belonging to the user "leonardr" and tagged with "ruby." The URI /users/leonardr/bookmarks/ruby.atom will give an Atom representation of the same resource, complete with links to related resources.

Connect Resources to Each Other

There are many, many relationships between my resources. Think about the relationship between a user and her bookmarks, between a bookmark and the tags it was posted under, or between a URI and the users who've bookmarked it. But a to_xml representation of a resource never links to the URI of another resource, so I can't show those relationships in my representations. On the other hand, an Atom feed can contain links, and can capture relationships between resources.

Figure 7-1 shows my problem. When I think about the bookmarking service, I envision lots of conceptual links between the resources. But links only exist in the actual service when they're embodied in representations. Atom representations contain lots of links, but to_xml documents don't. To give one example, the conceptual link between a user

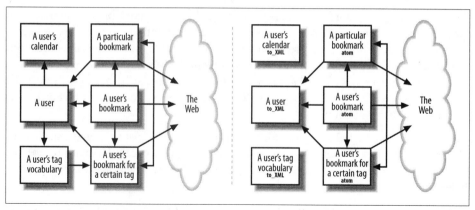

Figure 7-1. The bookmarking service in my head versus the actual service

and the user's bookmarks doesn't actually exist in my service. A client is just supposed to "know" how to get a user's bookmarks.

Also note that while the "user" resource is clearly the focal point of the service, neither diagram gives any clue as to how a client can get to that resource in the first place. I've described that in English prose. That means that my real audience is the people writing the web service clients, not the clients themselves.

This is a failure of connectivity, and it's the same failure you can see in Amazon S3 and some other RESTful services. As REST becomes more popular, this kind of failure will probably be the last remaining vestige of the RPC style. I dealt with this problem in Chapter 5 by defining a service home page that linked to a few top-level resources. These resources linked to more resources, and so on. My fantasy map application was completely connected.

What's Supposed to Happen?

Rails exposes every database-backed application using only two resource patterns: lists (the database tables) and list items (the rows in a table). All list resources work pretty much the same way, as do all list item resources. Every "creation" operation follows the same rules and has similar failure conditions, whether the database row being created is a user, a bookmark, or something else. I can consider these rules as a sort of generic control flow, a set of general guidelines for implementing the HTTP interface for list and list item resources. I'll start defining that control flow here, and pick it up again in Chapter 9.

When a resource is created, the response code should be 201 ("Created") and the Location header should point the way to the resource's location.

When a resource is modified, the response code should be 200 ("OK"). If the resource state changes in a way that changes the URI to the resource (for instance, a user account is renamed), the response code is 301 ("Moved Permanently") and the `Location` header should provide the new URI.

When an object is deleted, the response code should be 200 ("OK").

As far as possible, all resources that support GET should also support conditional GET. This means setting appropriate values for `ETag` and `Last-Modified`.

One final rule, a rule about data security. Unlike the del.icio.us API, I don't require authentication just to get information from the service. However, I do have a rule that no one should see a user's private bookmarks unless they're authenticated as that user. If you look at someone else's bookmarks, you'll get a representation that has her private bookmarks filtered out. You won't see the full resource state: just the part you're authorized to see. This principle extends past the bookmark lists themselves, and into things like the calendar and tag vocabulary. You should not see mysterious tags showing up in the representation of my tag vocabulary, tags that don't correspond to any of the tags I used in my visible bookmarks. This last rule is specific to my social bookmarking application, but its lessons can be applied more generally

What Might Go Wrong?

The main problem is unauthorized access. I can use the 401 response code ("Unauthorized") any time the client tries to do something (edit a user's account, rename a tag for a user) without providing the proper `Authorization` header.

A client might try to create a user account that already exists. From the point of view of the service, this looks like an attempt to modify the existing account without providing any authorization. The response code of 401 ("Unauthorized") is appropriate, but it might be confusing to the client. My service will send a 401 response code when the authorization is provided but incorrect, and a 409 ("Conflict") when no authorization at all is provided. This way, a client who thought she was creating a new account is less likely to be confused.

Similarly, a client might try to rename a user account to a name that already exists. The 409 response code is appropriate here as well.

Any resource that's a list of bookmarks will support query variables `limit` and `date`. These variables place restrictions on which bookmarks should show up in the representation: the client can set a maximum number of bookmarks to retrieve, or restrict the operation to bookmarks posted on a certain date. If the client sends a nonsensical `limit` or `date`, the appropriate response code is 400 ("Bad Request"). I'll also use 400 when a user tries to create or modify a resource, but doesn't provide a valid representation.

If the client tries to retrieve information about a nonexistent user, this service will do what del.icio.us does and send a response code of 404 ("Not Found"). This is the client's cue to create that user account if they wish. I'll do the same if the client tries to get information about a URI that no one has bookmarked.

A user can modify the URI listed in one of her bookmarks, but she can only have one bookmark for a given URI. If a user tries to change a bookmark's URI to one she's already bookmarked, a response code of 409 ("Conflict") is appropriate. 409 is also the correct response if the user tries to POST a URI she's already bookmarked. The uniform way to modify an existing bookmark is with PUT on the bookmark resource.

If the client tries to create a user account or bookmark, but provides an incomplete or nonsensical representation, the response is 400 ("Bad Request"). For instance, the client might try to POST a new bookmark, but forget to send the URI of the bookmark. Or it might try to bookmark a "URI" that's not a URI at all.

When creating a user, the client might send a JSON representation of a new user, instead of an ActiveRecord XML or form-encoded representation of the same data. In other words, it might send the totally wrong media type. The proper response code here is 415 ("Unsupported Media Type"). Rails handles this failure condition automatically.

Controller Code

Now we come to the heart of the application: the code that converts incoming HTTP requests into specific actions on the database. I'm going to define a base class called `ApplicationController`, which contains common code, including almost all of the tricky code. Then I'll define the six controller classes I promised earlier.

Each controller class will implement some `actions`: methods that are called to handle a HTTP request. Rails defines a list of standard actions that correspond to methods from HTTP's uniform interface. I mentioned these earlier: the `index` action is invoked in response to GET for a "list" type resource, and so on. Those are the actions I'll be defining, though many of them will delegate to other actions with nonstandard names.

There's a lot of code in this application, but relatively little of it needs to be published in this book. Most of the low-level details are in Rails, the plugins, and the `atom-tools` gem. I can express my high-level ideas almost directly in code. Of course, my reliance on external code occasionally has downsides, like the fact that some of my representations don't contain links.

What Rails Doesn't Do

There's one feature I want for my service that *isn't* built into Rails or plugins, and there's another that goes against Rails's path of least resistance. I'm going to be implementing these features myself. These two items account for much of the tricky code in the service.

Conditional GET

Wherever possible, a web service should send the response headers `Last-Modified` and `ETag` along with a representation. If the client makes future requests for the same resource, it can make its requests conditional on the representation having changed since the last GET. This can save time and bandwidth; see "Conditional GET" in Chapter 8 for more on this topic.

There are third-party Rails controllers that let the programmer provide values for `Last-Modified` and `ETag`. Core Rails doesn't do this, and I don't want to bring in the additional complexity of a third-party controller. I implement a fairly reusable solution for `Last-Modified` in Example 7-9.

param[:id] for things that aren't IDs

Rails assumes that resources map to ActiveRecord objects. Specifically, it assumes that the URI to a "list item" resource identifies a row in a database table by ID. For instance, it assumes the client will request the URI `/v1/users/4` instead of the more readable URI `/v1/users/leonardr`.

The client can still request `/users/leonardr`, and the controller can still handle it. This just means that the username will be available as `params[:id]` instead of something more descriptive, like `params[:username]`.

If a URI contains more than one path variable, then when I define that URI in *routes.rb* I get to choose the `params` name for all but the last one. The last variable always gets put into `params[:id]`, even if it's not an ID. The URI `/v1/users/leonardr/tags/food` has two path variables, for example. `params[:username]`, named back in Example 7-3, has a value of "leonardr". The tag name is the one that gets put into `params[:id]`. I'd rather call it `params[:tag]`, but there's no good way to do that in Rails. When you see `params[:id]` in the code below, keep in mind that it's never a database ID.

The ApplicationController

This class is the abstract superclass of my six controllers, and it contains most of the common functionality (the rest will go into the ActiveRecord model classes). Example 7-7 starts by defining an action for the single most common operation in this service: fetching a list of bookmarks that meet some criteria.

Example 7-7. app/controllers/application.rb

```
# app/controllers/application.rb
require 'digest/sha1'
require 'digest/md5'
require 'rubygems'
require 'atom/feed'

class ApplicationController < ActionController::Base
```

```
# By default, show 50 bookmarks at a time.
@@default_limit = 50

## Common actions

# This action takes a list of SQL conditions, adds some additional
# conditions like a date filter, and renders an appropriate list of
# bookmarks. It's used by BookmarksController, RecentController,
# and TagsController.
def show_bookmarks(conditions, title, feed_uri, user=nil, tag=nil)
  errors = []

  # Make sure the specified limit is valid. If no limit is specified,
  # use the default.
  if params[:limit] && params[:limit].to_i < 0
    errors << "limit must be >=0"
  end
  params[:limit] ||= @@default_limit
  params.delete(:limit) if params[:limit] == 0  # 0 means "no limit"

  # If a date filter was specified, make sure it's a valid date.
  if params[:date]
    begin
      params[:date] = Date.parse(params[:date])
    rescue ArgumentError
      errors << "incorrect date format"
    end
  end

  if errors.empty?
    conditions ||= [""]

    # Add a restriction by date if neccessary.
    if params[:date]
      conditions[0] << " AND " unless conditions[0].empty?
      conditions[0] << "timestamp >= ? AND timestamp < ?"
      conditions << params[:date]
      conditions << params[:date] + 1
    end

    # Restrict the list to bookmarks visible to the authenticated user.
    Bookmark.only_visible_to!(conditions, @authenticated_user)

    # Find a set of bookmarks that matches the given conditions.
    bookmarks = Bookmark.custom_find(conditions, tag, params[:limit])

    # Render the bookmarks however the client requested.
    render_bookmarks(bookmarks, title, feed_uri, user)
  else
    render :text => errors.join("\n"), :status => "400 Bad Request"
  end
end
```

The show_bookmarks method works like any Rails action: it gets query parameters like
limit from params, and verifies them. Then it fetches some data from the database and

renders it with a view. A lot of my RESTful action methods will delegate to this method. If the RESTful action specifies no conditions, `show_bookmarks` will fetch all the bookmarks that match the date and tag filters, up to the limit. Most of my actions will impose additional conditions, like only fetching bookmarks posted by a certain user.

The main difference between `show_bookmarks` and a traditional Rails action is in the view. Most Rails actions define the view with an ERb template like *show.rhtml*: a combination of HTML and Ruby code that works like JSP templates or PHP code. Instead, I'm passing the job off to the `render_bookmarks` function (see Example 7-8). This function uses code-based generators to build the XML and Atom documents that serve as representations for most of my application's resources.

Example 7-8. application.rb continued: render_bookmarks

```
# This method renders a list of bookmarks as a view in RSS, Atom, or
# ActiveRecord XML format. It's called by show_bookmarks
# above, which is used by three controllers. It's also used
# separately by UriController and BookmarksController.
#
# This view method supports conditional HTTP GET.
def render_bookmarks(bookmarks, title, feed_uri, user, except=[])
  # Figure out a current value for the Last-Modified header.
  if bookmarks.empty?
    last_modified = nil
  else
    # Last-Modified is the most recent timestamp in the bookmark list.
    most_recent_bookmark = bookmarks.max do |b1,b2|
      b1.timestamp <=> b2.timestamp
    end
    last_modified = most_recent_bookmark.timestamp
  end

  # If the bookmark list has been modified since it was last requested...
  render_not_modified_or(last_modified) do
    respond_to do |format|
      # If the client requested XML, serialize the ActiveRecord
      # objects to XML. Include references to the tags in the
      # serialization.
      format.xml { render :xml =>
        bookmarks.to_xml(:except => except + [:id, :user_id],
                         :include => [:tags]) }
      # If the client requested Atom, turn the ActiveRecord objects
      # into an Atom feed.
      format.atom { render :xml => atom_feed_for(bookmarks, title,
                                                 feed_uri, user) }
    end
  end
end
```

That method is also where I start handling conditional HTTP requests. I've chosen to use the timestamp of the most recent bookmark as the value of the HTTP header `Last-Modified`.

The rest of the conditional request handling is in the `render_not_modified_or` function (see Example 7-9). It's called just before `render_bookmarks` is about to write the list of bookmarks, and it applies the rules of conditional HTTP GET. If the list of bookmarks has changed since this client last requested it, this function calls the Ruby keyword `yield` and the rest of the code in `render_bookmarks` runs normally. If the list of bookmarks hasn't changed, this function short-circuits the Rails action, sending a response code of 304 ("Not Modified") instead of serving the representation.

Example 7-9. application.rb continued: render_not_modified_or

```
## Helper methods

# A wrapper for actions whose views support conditional HTTP GET.
# If the given value for Last-Modified is after the incoming value
# of If-Modified-Since, does nothing. If Last-Modified is before
# If-Modified-Since, this method takes over the request and renders
# a response code of 304 ("Not Modified").
def render_not_modified_or(last_modified)
  response.headers['Last-Modified'] = last_modified.httpdate if last_modified

  if_modified_since = request.env['HTTP_IF_MODIFIED_SINCE']
  if if_modified_since && last_modified &&
      last_modified <= Time.httpdate(if_modified_since)
    # The representation has not changed since it was last requested.
    # Instead of processing the request normally, send a response
    # code of 304 ("Not Modified").
    render :nothing => true, :status => "304 Not Modified"
  else
    # The representation has changed since it was last requested.
    # Proceed with normal request processing.
    yield
  end
end
```

Example 7-10 shows one more helper function used in multiple actions. The `if_found` method makes sure the client specified a URI that corresponds to an object in the database. If given a non-null object, nothing happens: `if_found` uses `yield` to return control to the action that called it. If given a null object, the function short-circuits the request with a response code of 404 ("Not Found"), and the action never gets a chance to run.

Example 7-10. application.rb continued: if_found.

```
# A wrapper for actions which require the client to have named a
# valid object. Sends a 404 response code if the client named a
# nonexistent object. See the user_id_from_username filter for an
# example.
def if_found(obj)
  if obj
    yield
```

```
    else
      render :text => "Not found.", :status => "404 Not Found"
      false
    end
  end
```

I've also implemented a number of *filters*: pieces of code that run before the Rails actions do. Some Rails filters perform common setup tasks (see Example 7-11). This is the job of `authenticate`, which checks the client's credentials. Filters may also check for a problem and short-circuit the request if they find one. This is the job of `must_authenticate`, and also `must_specify_user`, which depends on the `if_found` method defined above. Filters let me keep common code out of the individual actions.

Example 7-11. application.rb continued: filters
```
    ## Filters

    # All actions should try to authenticate a user, even those actions
    # that don't require authorization. This is so we can show an
    # authenticated user their own private bookmarks.
    before_filter :authenticate

    # Sets @authenticated_user if the user provides valid
    # credentials. This may be used to deny access or to customize the
    # view.
    def authenticate
      @authenticated_user = nil
      authenticate_with_http_basic do |user, pass|
        @authenticated_user = User.authenticated_user(user, pass)
      end
      return true
    end

    # A filter for actions that _require_ authentication. Unless the
    # client has authenticated as some user, takes over the request and
    # sends a response code of 401 ("Unauthorized").  Also responds with
    # a 401 if the user is trying to operate on some user other than
    # themselves. This prevents users from doing things like deleting
    # each others' accounts.
    def must_authenticate
      if @authenticated_user && (@user_is_viewing_themselves != false)
        return true
      else
        request_http_basic_authentication("Social bookmarking service")
        return false
      end
    end

    # A filter for controllers beneath /users/{username}. Transforms
    # {username} into a user ID. Sends a 404 response code if the user
    # doesn't exist.
    def must_specify_user
      if params[:username]
        @user = User.find_by_name(params[:username])
        if_found(@user) { params[:user_id] = @user.id }
```

```
      return false unless @user
    end
    @user_is_viewing_themselves = (@authenticated_user == @user)
    return true
  end
```

Finally, the application controller is where I'll implement my primary view method: atom_feed_for (see Example 7-12). This method turns a list of ActiveRecord Bookmark objects into an Atom document. The controller that wants to serve a list of bookmarks needs to provide a title for the feed (such as "Bookmarks for leonardr") and a URI to the resource being represented. The resulting document is rich in links. Every bookmark links to the external URI, to other people who bookmarked that URI, and to bookmarks that share tags with this one.

Example 7-12. application.rb concluded: atom_feed_for

```
    ## Methods for generating a representation

    # This method converts an array of ActiveRecord's Bookmark objects
    # into an Atom feed.
    def atom_feed_for(bookmarks, title, feed_uri, user=nil)
      feed = Atom::Feed.new
      feed.title = title
      most_recent_bookmark = bookmarks.max do |b1,b2|
        b1.timestamp <=> b2.timestamp
      end
      feed.updated = most_recent_bookmark.timestamp

      # Link this feed to itself
      self_link = feed.links.new
      self_link['rel'] = 'self'
      self_link['href'] = feed_uri + ".atom"

      # If this list is a list of bookmarks from a single user, that user is
      # the author of the feed.
      if user
        user_to_atom_author(user, feed)
      end

      # Turn each bookmark in the list into an entry in the feed.
      bookmarks.each do |bookmark|
        entry = feed.entries.new
        entry.title = bookmark.short_description
        entry.content = bookmark.long_description

        # In a real application, a bookmark would have a separate
        # "modification date" field which was not under the control of
        # the user. This would also make the Last-Modified calculations
        # more accurate.
        entry.updated = bookmark.timestamp

        # First, link this Atom entry to the external URI that the
        # bookmark tracks.
        external_uri = entry.links.new
```

```
        external_uri['href'] = bookmark.uri

        # Now we give some connectedness to this service. Link this Atom
        # entry to this service's resource for this bookmark.
        bookmark_resource = entry.links.new
        bookmark_resource['rel'] = "self"
        bookmark_resource['href'] = bookmark_url(bookmark.user.name,
                                          bookmark.uri_hash) + ".atom"
        bookmark_resource['type'] = "application/xml+atom"

        # Then link this entry to the list of users who've bookmarked
        # this URI.
        other_users = entry.links.new
        other_users['rel'] = "related"
        other_users['href'] = uri_url(bookmark.uri_hash) + ".atom"
        other_users['type'] = "application/xml+atom"

        # Turn this entry's user into the "author" of this entry, unless
        # we already specified a user as the "author" of the entire
        # feed.
        unless user
          user_to_atom_author(bookmark.user, entry)
        end

        # For each of this bookmark's tags...
        bookmark.tags.each do |tag|
          # ...represent the tag as an Atom category.
          category = entry.categories.new
          category['term'] = tag
          category['scheme'] = user_url(bookmark.user.name) + "/tags"

          # Link to this user's other bookmarks tagged using this tag.
          tag_uri = entry.links.new
          tag_uri['href'] = tag_url(bookmark.user.name, tag.name) + ".atom"
          tag_uri['rel'] = 'related'
          tag_uri['type'] = "application/xml+atom"

          # Also link to all bookmarks tagged with this tag.
          recent_tag_uri = entry.links.new
          recent_tag_uri['href'] = recent_url(tag.name) + ".atom"
          recent_tag_uri['rel'] = 'related'
          recent_tag_uri['type'] = "application/xml+atom"
        end
      end
      return feed.to_xml
  end

  # Appends a representation of the given user to an Atom feed or element
  def user_to_atom_author(user, atom)
    author = atom.authors.new
    author.name = user.full_name
    author.email = user.email
    author.uri = user_url(user.name)
  end
end
```

Example 7-13 shows what kind of Atom representation this method might serve.

Example 7-13. An Atom representation of a list of bookmarks

```
<feed xmlns='http://www.w3.org/2005/Atom'>
<title>Bookmarks for leonardr</title>
<screen>
<updated>2007-02-14T02:26:58-05:00</updated>
<link href="http://localhost:3000/v1/users/leonardr/bookmarks.atom" rel="self"/>
<author>
 <name>leonardr</name>
 <uri>http://localhost:3000/v1/users/leonardr</uri>
 <email>leonardr@example.com</email>
</author>

<entry>
 <title>REST and WS-*/title>
 <content>Joe Gregorio's lucid explanation of RESTful principles</content>
 <category term="rest" scheme="http://localhost:3000/v1/users/leonardr/rest"/>
 <link href="http://bitworking.org/news/125/REST-and-WS" rel="alternate"/>
 <link href="http://localhost:3000/v1/users/leonardr/bookmarks/68044f26e373de4a08ff343a7fa5f675.atom"
  rel="self" type="application/xml+atom"/>
 ...
 <link href="http://localhost:3000/v1/recent/rest.atom"
  rel="related" type="application/xml+atom"/>
 <updated>2007-02-14T02:26:58-05:00</updated>
</entry>
</feed>
```

The UsersController

Now I'm ready to show you some specific actions. I'll start with the controller that makes user accounts possible. In the code in Example 7-14, note the call to before_filter that sets up the must_authenticate filter. You don't need to authenticate to create (POST) a user account (as whom would you authenticate?), but you must authenticate to modify (PUT) or destroy (DELETE) an account.

Example 7-14. app/controllers/users_controller.rb

```
class UsersController < ApplicationController

  # A client must authenticate to modify or delete a user account.
  before_filter :must_authenticate, :only => [:modify, :destroy]

  # POST /users
  def create
    user = User.find_by_name(params[:user][:name])
    if user
      # The client tried to create a user that already exists.
      headers['Location'] = user_url(user.name)
      render :nothing => true, :status => "409 Conflict"
    else
      user = User.new(params[:user])
      if user.save
```

```
    headers['Location'] = user_path(user.name)
    render :nothing => true, :status => "201 Created"
  else
    # There was a problem saving the user to the database.
    # Send the validation error messages along with a response
    # code of 400.
    render :xml => user.errors.to_xml, :status => "400 Bad Request"
  end
 end
end
```

The conventions of RESTful Rails impose a certain structure on UsersController (and, indeed, on the name of the class itself). This controller exposes a resource for the list of users, and one resource for each particular user. The create method corresponds to a POST to the user list. The show, update, and delete methods correspond to a GET, PUT, or DELETE request on a particular user.

The create method follows a pattern I'll use for POST requests throughout this service. If the client tries to create a user that already exists, the response code is 409 ("Conflict"). If the client sends bad or incomplete data, the ActiveRecord validation rules (defined in the User) model) fail, and the call to User#save returns false. The response code then is 400 ("Bad Request"). If all goes well, the response code is 201 ("Created") and the Location header contains the URI of the newly created user. All I've done in Example 7-15 is put into code the things I said in "What's Supposed to Happen?" and "What Might Go Wrong?" earlier in this chapter. I'll mention this generic control flow again in Chapter 8.

Example 7-15. app/controllers/users_controller.rb continued
```
# PUT /users/{username}
def update
  old_name = params[:id]
  new_name = params[:user][:name]
  user = User.find_by_name(old_name)

  if_found user do
    if old_name != new_name && User.find_by_name(new_name)
      # The client tried to change this user's name to a name
      # that's already taken. Conflict!
      render :nothing => true, :status => "409 Conflict"
    else
      # Save the user to the database.
      user.update_attributes(params[:user])
      if user.save
        # The user's name changed, which changed its URI.
        # Send the new URI.
        if user.name != old_name
          headers['Location'] = user_path(user.name)
          status = "301 Moved Permanently"
        else
          # The user resource stayed where it was.
          status = "200 OK"
        end
```

```
      render :nothing => true, :status => status
    else
      # There was a problem saving the bookmark to the database.
      # Send the validation error messages along with a response
      # code of 400.
      render :xml => user.errors.to_xml, :status => "400 Bad Request"
    end
  end
 end
end
```

The **update** method has a slightly different flow, and it's a flow I'll use for PUT requests throughout the service. The general outline is the same as for POST. The twist is that instead of trying to create a user (whose name might already be in use), the client can rename an existing user (and their new name might already be in use).

I send a 409 response code ("Conflict") if the client proposes a new username that already exists, and a 400 response code ("Bad Request") if the data validation errors fail. If the client successfully edits a user, I send not a 201 response code ("Created") but a simple 200 ("OK").

The exception is if the client successfully changes a user's name. Now that resource is available under a different URI: say, **/users/leonard** instead of **/users/leonardr**. That means I need to send a response code of 301 ("Moved Permanently") and put the user's *new* URI in the **Location** header.

The GET and DELETE implementations are more straightforward, as shown in Example 7-16.

Example 7-16. app/controllers/users_controller.rb continued

```
# GET /users/{username}
def show
  # Find the user in the database.
  user = User.find_by_name(params[:id])
  if_found(user) do
    # Serialize the User object to XML with ActiveRecord's to_xml.
    # Don't include the user's ID or password when building the XML
    # document.
    render :xml => user.to_xml(:except => [:id, :password])
  end
end

# DELETE /users/{username}
def destroy
  user = User.find_by_name(params[:id])
  if_found user do
    # Remove the user from the database.
    user.destroy
    render :nothing => true, :status => "200 OK"
  end
 end
end
```

There is one hidden detail: the `if_found` method sends a response code of 404 ("Not Found") if the user tries to GET or DELETE a nonexistent user. Otherwise, the response code is 200 ("OK"). I have not implemented conditional HTTP GET for user resources: I figured the possible bandwidth savings wasn't big enough to justify the added complexity.

The BookmarksController

This is the other main controller in this application (see Example 7-17). It exposes a user's list of bookmarks and each individual bookmark. The filters are interesting here. This `BookmarksController` is for displaying a particular user's bookmarks, and any attempt to see a nonexistent user's bookmarks should be rebuffed with a stern 404 ("Not Found"). That's the job of the `must_specify_user` filter I defined earlier. The `must_authenticate` filter works like it did in `UsersController`: it prevents unauthenticated requests from getting through to Rails actions that require authentication. I've also got a one-off filter, `fix_params`, that enforces consistency in incoming representations of bookmarks.

Example 7-17. app/controllers/bookmarks_controller.rb

```
class BookmarksController < ApplicationController
  before_filter :must_specify_user
  before_filter :fix_params
  before_filter :must_authenticate, :only => [:create, :update, :destroy]

  # This filter cleans up incoming representations.
  def fix_params
    if params[:bookmark]
      params[:bookmark][:user_id] = @user.id if @user
    end
  end
```

The rest of `BookmarksController` is just like `UsersController`: fairly involved **create** (POST) and **update** (PUT) methods, simple **show** (GET) and **delete** (DELETE) methods (see Example 7-18). The only difference is that this controller's list resource responds to GET, so I start with a simple implementation of **index**. Like many of the Rails actions I'll define, **index** and **show** simply delegate to the **show_bookmarks** action.

Example 7-18. app/controllers/bookmarks_controller.rb continued

```
# GET /users/{username}/bookmarks
def index
  # Show this user's bookmarks by passing in an appropriate SQL
  # restriction to show_bookmarks.
  show_bookmarks(["user_id = ?", @user.id],
                 "Bookmarks for #{@user.name}",
                 bookmark_url(@user.name), @user)
end

# POST /users/{username}/bookmarks
def create
```

```ruby
  bookmark = Bookmark.find_by_user_id_and_uri(params[:bookmark][:user_id],
                                              params[:bookmark][:uri])
  if bookmark
    # This user has already bookmarked this URI. They should be
    # using PUT instead.
    headers['Location'] = bookmark_url(@user.name, bookmark.uri)
    render :nothing => true, :status => "409 Conflict"
  else
    # Enforce default values for 'timestamp' and 'public'
    params[:bookmark][:timestamp] ||= Time.now
    params[:bookmark][:public] ||= "1"

    # Create the bookmark in the database.
    bookmark = Bookmark.new(params[:bookmark])
    if bookmark.save
      # Add tags.
      bookmark.tag_with(params[:taglist]) if params[:taglist]

      # Send a 201 response code that points to the location of the
      # new bookmark.
      headers['Location'] = bookmark_url(@user.name, bookmark.uri)
      render :nothing => true, :status => "201 Created"
    else
      render :xml => bookmark.errors.to_xml, :status => "400 Bad Request"
    end
  end
end

# PUT /users/{username}/bookmarks/{URI-MD5}
def update
  bookmark = Bookmark.find_by_user_id_and_uri_hash(@user.id, params[:id])
  if_found bookmark do
    old_uri = bookmark.uri
    if old_uri != params[:bookmark][:uri] &&
        Bookmark.find_by_user_id_and_uri(@user.id, params[:bookmark][:uri])
      # The user is trying to change the URI of this bookmark to a
      # URI that they've already bookmarked. Conflict!
      render :nothing => true, :status => "409 Conflict"
    else
      # Update the bookmark's row in the database.
      if bookmark.update_attributes(params[:bookmark])
        # Change the bookmark's tags.
        bookmark.tag_with(params[:taglist]) if params[:taglist]
        if bookmark.uri != old_uri
          # The bookmark changed URIs. Send the new URI.
          headers['Location'] = bookmark_url(@user.name, bookmark.uri)
          render :nothing => true, :status => "301 Moved Permanently"
        else
          # The bookmark stayed where it was.
          render :nothing => true, :status => "200 OK"
        end
      else
        render :xml => bookmark.errors.to_xml, :status => "400 Bad Request"
      end
    end
```

```
      end
    end

  # GET /users/{username}/bookmarks/{uri}
  def show
    # Look up the requested bookmark, and render it as a "list"
    # containing only one item.
    bookmark = Bookmark.find_by_user_id_and_uri_hash(@user.id, params[:id])
    if_found(bookmark) do
      render_bookmarks([bookmark],
                       "#{@user.name} bookmarked #{bookmark.uri}",
                       bookmark_url(@user.name, bookmark.uri_hash),
                       @user)
    end
  end

  # DELETE /users/{username}/bookmarks/{uri}
  def destroy
    bookmark = Bookmark.find_by_user_id_and_uri_hash(@user.id, params[:id])
    if_found bookmark do
      bookmark.destroy
      render :nothing => true, :status => "200 OK"
    end
  end
end
```

The TagsController

This controller exposes a user's tag vocabulary, and the list of bookmarks she's filed under each tag (see Example 7-19). There are two twists here: the tag vocabulary and the "tag rename" operation.

The tag vocabulary is simply a list of a user's tags, along with a count of how many times this user used the tag. I can get this data fairly easily with ActiveResource, and format it as a representation with to_xml but what about security? If you tag two public and six private bookmarks with "ruby," when I look at your tag vocabulary, I should only see "ruby" used twice. If you tag a bunch of private bookmarks with "possible-acquisition," I shouldn't see "possible-acquisition" in your vocabulary at all. On the other hand, when you're viewing your own bookmarks, you should be able to see the complete totals. I use some custom SQL to count only the public tags when appropriate. Incidentally, this is another resource that doesn't support conditional GET.

Example 7-19. app/controllers/tags_controller.rb

```
class TagsController < ApplicationController
  before_filter :must_specify_user
  before_filter :must_authenticate, :only => [:update]

  # GET /users/{username}/tags
  def index
    # A user can see all of their own tags, but only tags used
    # in someone else's public bookmarks.
    if @user_is_viewing_themselves
```

```
    tag_restriction = ''
  else
    tag_restriction = " AND bookmarks.public='1'"
  end
  sql = ["SELECT tags.*, COUNT(bookmarks.id) as count" +
         " FROM tags, bookmarks, taggings" +
         " WHERE taggings.taggable_type = 'Bookmark'" +
         " AND tags.id = taggings.tag_id" +
         " AND taggings.taggable_id = bookmarks.id" +
         " AND bookmarks.user_id = ?" + tag_restriction +
         " GROUP BY tags.name", @user.id]
  # Find a bunch of ActiveRecord Tag objects using custom SQL.
  tags = Tag.find_by_sql(sql)

  # Convert the Tag objects to an XML document.
  render :xml => tags.to_xml(:except => [:id])
end
```

I said earlier I'd handle the "tag rename" operation with HTTP PUT. This makes sense since a rename is a change of state for an existing resource. The difference here is that this resource doesn't correspond to a specific ActiveRecord object. There's an Active-Record Tag object for every tag, but that object represents everyone's use of a tag. This controller doesn't expose tags, per se: it exposes a particular user's tag vocabulary.

Renaming a Tag object would rename it for everybody on the site. But if you rename "good" to "bad," then that should only affect your bookmarks. Any bookmarks I've tagged as "good" should stay "good." The client is not changing the tag, just one user's *use* of the tag.

From a RESTful perspective none of this matters. A resource's state is changed with PUT, and that's that. But the implementation is a bit tricky. What I need to do is find all the client's bookmarks tagged with the given tag, strip off the old tag, and stick the new tag on. Unlike with users or bookmarks, I won't be sending a 409 ("Conflict") response code if the user renames an old tag to a tag that already exists. I'll just merge the old tag into the new one (see Example 7-20).

Example 7-20. app/controllers/tags_controller.rb continued

```
# PUT /users/{username}/tags/{tag}
# This PUT handler is a little tricker than others, because we
# can't just rename a tag site-wide. Other users might be using the
# same tag.  We need to find every bookmark where this user uses the
# tag, strip the "old" name, and add the "new" name on.
def update
  old_name = params[:id]
  new_name = params[:tag][:name] if params[:tag]
  if new_name
    # Find all this user's bookmarks tagged with the old name
    to_change = Bookmark.find(["bookmarks.user_id = ?", @user.id],
                              old_name)
    # For each such bookmark...
    to_change.each do |bookmark|
      # Find its tags.
```

```
      tags = bookmark.tags.collect { |tag| tag.name }
      # Remove the old name.
      tags.delete(old_name)
      # Add the new name.
      tags << new_name
      # Assign the new set of tags to the bookmark.
      bookmark.tag_with tags.uniq
    end
    headers['Location'] = tag_url(@user.name, new_name)
    status = "301 Moved Permanently"
  end
  render :nothing => true, :status => status || "200 OK"
end

# GET /users/{username}/tags/{tag}
def show
  # Show bookmarks that belong to this user and are tagged
  # with the given tag.
  tag = params[:id]
  show_bookmarks(["bookmarks.user_id = ?", @user.id],
                 "#{@user.name}'s bookmarks tagged with '#{tag}'",
                 tag_url(@user.name, tag), @user, tag)
end
end
```

The Lesser Controllers

Every other controller in my application is read-only. This means it implements at most index and show. Hopefully by now you get the idea behind the controllers and their action methods, so I'll cover the rest of the controllers briefly.

The CalendarController

This resource, a user's posting history, is something like the one exposed by TagsController#show. I'm getting some counts from the database and rendering them as XML. This document doesn't directly correspond to any ActiveRecord object, or list of such objects; it's just a summary. As before, I need to be sure not to include other peoples' private bookmarks in the count.

The main body of code goes into the Bookmark.calendar method, defined in the Bookmark model class (see "The Bookmark Model). The controller just renders the data.

ActiveRecord's to_xml doesn't do a good job on this particular data structure, so I've implemented my own view function: calendar_to_xml (see Example 7-21). It uses Builder::XmlMarkup (a Ruby utility that comes with Rails) to generate an XML document without writing much code.

Example 7-21. app/controllers/calendar_controller.rb
```
class CalendarController < ApplicationController
  before_filter :must_specify_user
```

```
  # GET /users/{username}/calendar
  def index
    calendar = Bookmark.calendar(@user.id, @user_is_viewing_themselves)
    render :xml => calendar_to_xml(calendar)
  end

  # GET /users/{username}/calendar/{tag}
  def show
    tag = params[:id]
    calendar = Bookmark.calendar(@user.id, @user_is_viewing_themselves,
                                 tag)
    render :xml => calendar_to_xml(calendar, tag)
  end

  private

  # Build an XML document out of the data structure returned by the
  # Bookmark.calendar method.
  def calendar_to_xml(days, tag=nil)
    xml = Builder::XmlMarkup.new(:indent => 2)
    xml.instruct!
    # Build a 'calendar' element.
    xml.calendar(:tag => tag) do
      # For every day in the data structure...
      days.each do |day|
        # ...add a "day" element to the document
        xml.day(:date => day.date, :count => day.count)
      end
    end
  end
end
```

The RecentController

The controller in Example 7-22 shows recently posted bookmarks. Its actions are just
thin wrappers around the show_bookmarks method defined in *application.rb*.

Example 7-22. app/controllers/recent_controller.rb

```
# recent_controller.rb
class RecentController < ApplicationController

  # GET /recent
  def index
    # Take bookmarks from the database without any special conditions.
    # They'll be ordered with the most recently-posted first.
    show_bookmarks(nil, "Recent bookmarks", recent_url)
  end

  # GET /recent/{tag}
  def show
    # The same as above, but only fetch bookmarks tagged with a
    # certain tag.
    tag = params[:id]
    show_bookmarks(nil, "Recent bookmarks tagged with '#{tag}'",
```

```
                    recent_url(tag), nil, tag)
      end
    end
```

The UrisController

The controller in Example 7-23 shows what the site's users think of a particular URI. It shows a list of bookmarks, all for the same URI but from different people and with different tags and descriptions.

Example 7-23. app/controllers/uris_controller.rb

```
# uris_controller.rb
class UrisController < ApplicationController
  # GET /uris/{URI-MD5}
  def show
    # Fetch all the visible Bookmark objects that correspond to
    # different people bookmarking this URI.
    uri_hash = params[:id]
    sql = ["SELECT bookmarks.*, users.name as user from bookmarks, users" +
           " WHERE users.id = bookmarks.user_id AND bookmarks.uri_hash = ?",
           uri_hash]
    Bookmark.only_visible_to!(sql, @authenticated_user)
    bookmarks = Bookmark.find_by_sql(sql)

    if_found(bookmarks) do

      # Render the list of Bookmark objects as XML or a syndication feed,
      # depending on what the client requested.
      uri = bookmarks[0].uri
      render_bookmarks(bookmarks, "Users who've bookmarked #{uri}",
                       uri_url(uri_hash), nil)
    end
  end
end
```

Model Code

Those are the controllers. I've also got three "model" classes, corresponding to my three main database tables: User, Bookmark, and Tag. The Tag class is defined entirely through the acts_as_taggable Rails plugin, so I've only got to define User and Bookmark.

The model classes define validation rules for the database fields. If a client sends bad data (such as trying to create a user without specifying a name), the appropriate validation rule is triggered and the controller method sends the client a response code of 400 ("Bad Request"). The same model classes could be used in a conventional web application, or a GUI application. The validation errors would be displayed differently, but the same rules would always apply.

The model classes also define a few methods which work against the database. These methods are used by the controllers.

The User Model

This is the simpler of the two models (see Example 7-24). It has some validation rules, a one-to-many relationship with Bookmark objects, and a few methods (called by the controllers) for validating passwords.

Example 7-24. app/models/user.rb

```
class User < ActiveRecord::Base
  # A user has many bookmarks. When the user is destroyed,
  # all their bookmarks should also be destroyed.
  has_many :bookmarks, :dependent => :destroy

  # A user must have a unique username.
  validates_uniqueness_of :name

  # A user must have a username, full name, and email.
  validates_presence_of :name, :full_name, :email

  # Make sure passwords are never stored in plaintext, by running them
  # through a one-way hash as soon as possible.
  def password=(password)
    super(User.hashed(password))
  end

  # Given a username and password, returns a User object if the
  # password matches the hashed one on file. Otherwise, returns nil.
  def self.authenticated_user(username, pass)
    user = find_by_name(username)
    if user
      user = nil unless hashed(pass) == user.password
    end
    return user
  end

  # Performs a one-way hash of some data.
  def self.hashed(password)
    Digest::SHA1.new(password).to_s
  end
end
```

The Bookmark Model

This is a more complicated model (see Example 7-25). First, let's define the relationships between Bookmark and the other model classes, along with some validation rules and a rule for generating the MD5 hash of a URI. We have to keep this information because the MD5 calculation only works in one direction. If a client requests **/v1/uris/ 55020a5384313579a5f11e75c1818b89**, we can't reverse the MD5 calculation. We need to be able to look up a URI by its MD5 hash.

Example 7-25. app/models/bookmark.rb

```ruby
class Bookmark < ActiveRecord::Base
  # Every bookmark belongs to some user.
  belongs_to :user

  # A bookmark can have tags. The relationships between bookmarks and
  # tags are managed by the acts_as_taggable plugin.
  acts_as_taggable

  # A bookmark must have an associated user ID, a URI, a short
  # description, and a timestamp.
  validates_presence_of :user_id, :uri, :short_description, :timestamp

  # The URI hash should never be changed directly: only when the URI
  # changes.
  attr_protected :uri_hash

  # And.. here's the code to update the URI hash when the URI changes.
  def uri=(new_uri)
    super
    self.uri_hash = Digest::MD5.new(new_uri).to_s
  end

  # This method is triggered by Bookmark.new and by
  # Bookmark#update_attributes. It replaces a bookmark's current set
  # of tags with a new set.
  def tag_with(tags)
    Tag.transaction do
      taggings.destroy_all
      tags.each { |name| Tag.find_or_create_by_name(name).on(self) }
    end
  end
end
```

That last method makes it possible to associate tags with bookmarks. The `acts_as_tag gable` plugin allows me to do basic queries like "what bookmarks are tagged with 'ruby'?" Unfortunately, I usually need slightly more complex queries, like "what bookmarks belonging to `leonardr` are tagged with 'ruby'?", so I can't use the plugin's `find_tagged_with` method. I need to define my own method that attaches a tag restriction to some preexisting restriction like "bookmarks belonging to `leonardr`."

This `custom_find` method is the workhorse of the whole service, since it's called by the `ApplicationController#show_bookmarks` method, which is called by many of the REST-ful Rails actions (see Example 7-26).

Example 7-26. app/models/bookmark.rb continued

```ruby
  # This method finds bookmarks, possibly ones tagged with a
  # particular tag.
  def self.custom_find(conditions, tag=nil, limit=nil)
    if tag
      # When a tag restriction is specified, we have to find bookmarks
      # the hard way: by constructing a SQL query that matches only
      # bookmarks tagged with the right tag.
      sql = ["SELECT bookmarks.* FROM bookmarks, tags, taggings" +
```

```
        " WHERE taggings.taggable_type = 'Bookmark'" +
        " AND bookmarks.id = taggings.taggable_id" +
        " AND taggings.tag_id = tags.id AND tags.name = ?",
        tag]
  if conditions
    sql[0] << " AND " << conditions[0]
    sql += conditions[1..conditions.size]
  end
  sql[0] << " ORDER BY bookmarks.timestamp DESC"
  sql[0] << " LIMIT " << limit.to_i.to_s if limit
  bookmarks = find_by_sql(sql)
else
  # Without a tag restriction, we can find bookmarks the easy way:
  # with the superclass find() implementation.
  bookmarks = find(:all, {:conditions => conditions, :limit => limit,
                          :order => 'timestamp DESC'})
end
return bookmarks
end
```

There are two more database-related methods (see Example 7-27). The
Bookmark.only_visible_to! method manipulates a set of ActiveRecord conditions so
that they only apply to bookmarks the given user can see. The Bookmark.calendar
method groups a user's bookmarks by the date they were posted. This implementation
may not work for you, since it uses a SQL function (DATE) that's not available for all
databases.

Example 7-27. app/models/bookmark.rb concluded

```
# Restricts a bookmark query so that it only finds bookmarks visible
# to the given user. This means public bookmarks, and the given
# user's private bookmarks.
def self.only_visible_to!(conditions, user)
  # The first element in the "conditions" array is a SQL WHERE
  # clause with variable substitutions. The subsequent elements are
  # the variables whose values will be substituted. For instance,
  # if "conditions" starts out empty: [""]...

  conditions[0] << " AND " unless conditions[0].empty?
  conditions[0] << "(public='1'"
  if user
    conditions[0] << " OR user_id=?"
    conditions << user.id
  end
  conditions[0] << ")"

  # ...its value might now be ["(public='1' or user_id=?)", 55].
  # ActiveRecord knows how to turn this into the SQL WHERE clause
  # "(public='1' or user_id=55)".
end

# This method retrieves data for the CalendarController. It uses the
# SQL DATE() function to group together entries made on a particular
# day.
def self.calendar(user_id, viewed_by_owner, tag=nil)
```

```
    if tag
      tag_from = ", tags, taggings"
      tag_where = "AND taggings.taggable_type = 'Bookmark'" +
        " AND bookmarks.id = taggings.taggable_id" +
        " AND taggings.tag_id = tags.id AND tags.name = ?"
    end

    # Unless a user is viewing their own calendar, only count public
    # bookmarks.
    public_where = viewed_by_owner ? "" : "AND public='1'"

    sql = ["SELECT date(timestamp) AS date, count(bookmarks.id) AS count" +
        " FROM bookmarks#{tag_from} " +
        " WHERE user_id=? #{tag_where} #{public_where} " +
        " GROUP BY date(timestamp)", user_id]
    sql << tag if tag

    # This will return a list of rather bizarre ActiveRecord objects,
    # which CalendarController knows how to turn into an XML document.
    find_by_sql(sql)
  end
end
```

Now you should be ready to start your Rails server in a console window, and start using the web service.

```
$ script/server
```

What Does the Client Need to Know?

Of course, using the web service just means writing more code. Unlike a Rails service generated with script/generate scaffold_resource (see "Clients Made Transparent with ActiveResource" in Chapter 3), this service can't be used as a web site. I didn't create any HTML forms or HTML-based views of the data. This was done mainly for space reasons. Look back at Example 7-8 and the call to respond_to. It's got a call to format.xml and a call to format.atom, and so on. That's the sort of place I'd put a call to format.html, to render an ERb template as HTML.

Eventually the site will be well-populated with peoples' bookmarks, and the site will expose many interesting resources as interlinked Atom representations. Any program, including today's web browsers, can take these resources as input: the client just needs to speak HTTP GET and know what to do with a syndication file.

But how are those resources supposed to get on the site in the first place? The only existing general-purpose web service client is the web browser, and I haven't provided any HTML forms for creating users or posting bookmarks. Even if I did, that would only take care of situations where the client is under the direct control of a human being.

Natural-Language Service Description

There are three possibilities for making it easy to write clients; they're more or less the ones I covered in Chapters 2 and 3. The simplest is to publish an English description of the service's layout. If someone wants to use my service they can study my description and write custom HTTP client code.

Most of today's RESTful and hybrid web services work this way. Instead of specifying the levers of state in hypermedia, they specify the levers in regular media—English text —which a human must interpret ahead of time. You'll need a basic natural-language description of your service anyway, to serve as advertisement. You want people to immediately see what your service does and want to use it.

I've already got a prose description of my social bookmarking service: it takes up much of this chapter. Example 7-28 is a simple command-line Ruby client for the service, based on that prose description. This client knows enough to create user accounts and post bookmarks.

Example 7-28. A rest-open-uri client for the bookmark service

```ruby
#!/usr/bin/ruby
#open-uri-bookmark-client.rb
require 'rubygems'
require 'rest-open-uri'
require 'uri'
require 'cgi'

# An HTTP-based Ruby client for my social bookmarking service
class BookmarkClient

  def initialize(service_root)
    @service_root = service_root
  end

  # Turn a Ruby hash into a form-encoded set of key-value pairs.
  def form_encoded(hash)
    encoded = []
    hash.each do |key, value|
      encoded << CGI.escape(key) + '=' + CGI.escape(value)
    end
    return encoded.join('&')
  end

  # Create a new user.
  def new_user(username, password, full_name, email)
    representation = form_encoded({ "user[name]" => username,
                                    "user[password]" => password,
                                    "user[full_name]" => full_name,
                                    "user[email]" => email })
    puts representation
    begin
      response = open(@service_root + '/users', :method => :post,
                      :body => representation)
```

```ruby
      puts "User #{username} created at #{response.meta['location']}"
    rescue OpenURI::HTTPError => e
      response_code = e.io.status[0].to_i
      if response_code == "409" # Conflict
        puts "Sorry, there's already a user called #{username}."
      else
        raise e
      end
    end
  end

  # Post a new bookmark for the given user.
  def new_bookmark(username, password, uri, short_description)
    representation = form_encoded({ "bookmark[uri]" => uri,
                                    "bookmark[short_description]" =>
                                    short_description })
    begin
      dest = "#{@service_root}/users/#{URI.encode(username)}/bookmarks"
      response = open(dest, :method => :post, :body => representation,
                      :http_basic_authentication => [username, password])
      puts "Bookmark posted to #{response.meta['location']}"
    rescue OpenURI::HTTPError => e
      response_code = e.io.status[0].to_i
      if response_code == 401 # Unauthorized
        puts "It looks like you gave me a bad password."
      elsif response_code == 409 # Conflict
        puts "It looks like you already posted that bookmark."
      else
        raise e
      end
    end
  end
end

# Main application
command = ARGV.shift
if ARGV.size != 4 || (command != "new-user" && command != "new-bookmark")
  puts "Usage: #{$0} new-user [username] [password] [full name] [email]"
  puts "Usage: #{$0} new-bookmark [username] [password]" +
    " [URI] [short description]"
  exit
end

client = BookmarkClient.new('http://localhost:3000/v1')
if command == "new-user"
  username, password, full_name, email = ARGV
  client.new_user(username, password, full_name, email)
else
  username, password, uri, short_description = ARGV
  client.new_bookmark(username, password, uri, short_description)
end
```

Description Through Standardization

One alternative to explaining everything is to make your service like other services. If all services exposed the same representation formats, and mapped URIs to resources in the same way... well, we can't get rid of client programming altogether, but clients could work on a higher level than HTTP.* Conventions are powerful tools: in fact, they're the same tools that REST uses. Every RESTful resource-oriented web service uses URIs to designate resources, and expresses operations in terms of HTTP's uniform interface. The idea here is to apply higher-level conventions than REST's, so that the client programmer doesn't have to write as much code.

Take the Rails architecture as an example. Rails is good at gently imposing its design preferences on the programmer. The result is that most RESTful Rails services do the same kind of thing in the same way. At bottom, the job of almost every Rails service is to send and accept representations of ActiveRecord objects. These services all map URIs to Rails controllers, Rails controllers to resources, resources to ActiveRecord objects, and ActiveRecord objects to rows in the database. The representation formats are also standardized: either as XML documents like the one in Example 7-4, or form-encoded key-value pairs like the ones in Example 7-5. They're not the best representation formats, because it's difficult to make connected services out of them, but they're OK.

The ActiveResource library, currently under development, is a client library that takes advantage of these similarities between Rails services. I first mentioned ActiveResource in Chapter 3, where I showed it in action against a very simple Rails service. It doesn't replace custom client code, but it hides the details of HTTP access behind an interface that looks like ActiveRecord. The ActiveResource/ActiveRecord approach won't work for all web services, or even all Rails web services. It doesn't work very well on this service. But it's not quite fair for me to judge ActiveResource by these standards, since it's still in development. As of the time of writing, it's more a promising possiblity than a real-world solution to a problem.

Hypermedia Descriptions

Even when the Ruby ActiveResource client is improved and officially released, it will be nothing more than the embodiment of some high-level design conventions. The conventions are useful: another web service framework might copy these conventions, and then Ruby's ActiveResource client would work with it. An ActiveResource library written in another language will work with Rails services. But if a service doesn't follow the conventions, ActiveResource can't talk to it.

What we need is a general framework, a way for each individual service to tell the client about its resource design, its representation formats, and the links it provides between

---

* There will always be client-side code for translating the needs of the user into web service operations. The only exception is in a web browser, where the user is right there, guiding the client through every step.

resources. That will give us some of the benefits of standardized conventions, without forcing all web services to comply with more than a few minimal requirements.

This brings us full circle to the REST notion of connectedness, of "hypermedia as the engine of application state." I talk about connectedness so much because hypermedia links and forms *are* these machine-readable conventions for describing the differences between services. If your service only serves serialized data structures that show the current resource state, then of course you start thinking about additional standards and conventions. Your representations are only doing half a job.

We don't think the human web needs these additional standards, because the human web serves *documents* full of links and forms, not serialized data structures that need extra interpretation. The links and forms on the human web tell our web browsers how to manipulate application and resource state, in response to our expressed desires. It doesn't matter that every web site was designed by a different person, because the differences between them are represented in machine-readable format.

The XHTML links and forms in Chapters 5 and 6 are machine-readable descriptions of what makes the fantasy map service different from other services. In this chapter, the links embedded in the Atom documents are machine-readable descriptions of the connections that distinguish this service from others that serve Atom documents. In Chapter 9 I'll consider three major hypermedia formats that can describe these differences between services: XHTML 4, XHTML 5, and WADL. For now, though, it's time to take a step back and take a look at REST and the ROA as a whole.

## CHAPTER 8

REST and ROA Best Practices

By now you should have a good idea of how to build resource-oriented, RESTful web services. This chapter is a pause to gather in one place the most important ideas so far, and to fill in some of the gaps in my coverage.

The gaps exist because the theoretical chapters have focused on basics, and the practical chapters have worked with specific services. I've implemented conditional HTTP GET but I haven't explained it. I've implemented HTTP Basic authentication and a client for Amazon's custom authentication mechanism, but I haven't compared them to other kinds of HTTP authentication, and I've glossed over the problem of authenticating a client *to its own user*.

The first part of this chapter is a recap of the main ideas of REST and the ROA. The second part describes the ideas I haven't already covered. I talk about specific features of HTTP and tough cases in resource design. In Chapter 9 I discuss the building blocks of services: specific technologies and patterns that have been used to make successful web services. Taken together, this chapter and the next form a practical reference for RESTful web services. You can consult them as needed when making technology or design decisions.

Resource-Oriented Basics

The only differences between a web service and a web site are the audience (preprogrammed clients instead of human beings) and a few client capabilities. Both web services and web sites benefit from a resource-oriented design based on HTTP, URIs, and (usually) XML.

Every interesting thing your application manages should be exposed as a *resource*. A resource can be anything a client might want to link to: a work of art, a piece of information, a physical object, a concept, or a grouping of references to other resources.

A URI is the name of a resource. Every resource must have at least one name. A resource should have as few names as possible, and every name should be meaningful.

The client cannot access resources directly. A web service serves *representations* of a resource: documents in specific data formats that contain information about the resource. The difference between a resource and its representation is somewhat academic for static web sites, where the resources are just files on disk that are sent verbatim to clients. The distinction takes on greater importance when the resource is a row in a database, a physical object, an abstract concept, or a real-world event in progress.

All access to resources happens through HTTP's uniform interface. These are the four basic HTTP verbs (GET, POST, PUT, and DELETE), and the two auxiliaries (HEAD and OPTIONS). Put complexity in your representations, in the variety of resources you expose, and in the links between resources. Don't put it in the access methods.

The Generic ROA Procedure

Reprinted from Chapter 6, this is an all-purpose procedure for splitting a problem space into RESTful resources.

This procedure only takes into account the constraints of REST and the ROA. Your choice of framework may impose additional constraints. If so, you might as well take those into account while you're designing the resources. In Chapter 12 I give a modified version of this procedure that works with Ruby on Rails.

1. Figure out the data set
2. Split the data set into resources
   For each kind of resource:
3. Name the resources with URIs
4. Expose a subset of the uniform interface
5. Design the representation(s) accepted from the client
6. Design the representation(s) served to the client
7. Integrate this resource into existing resources, using hypermedia links and forms
8. Consider the typical course of events: what's supposed to happen? Standard control flows like the Atom Publishing Protocol can help (see Chapter 9).
9. Consider error conditions: what might go wrong? Again, standard control flows can help.

Addressability

A web service is addressable if it exposes the interesting aspects of its data set through resources. Every resource has its own unique URI: in fact, URI just stands for "Universal Resource Identifier." Most RESTful web services expose an infinite number of URIs. Most RPC-style web services expose very few URIs, often as few as one.

Representations Should Be Addressable

A URI should never represent more than one resource. Then it wouldn't be a *Universal* Resource Identifier. Furthermore, I suggest that every *representation* of a resource should have its own URI. This is because URIs are often passed around or used as input to other web services. The expectation then is that the URI designates a particular representation of the resource.

Let's say you've exposed a press release at `/releases/104`. There's an English and a Spanish version of the press release, an HTML and plain-text version of each. Your clients should be able set the `Accept-Language` request header to choose an English or Spanish representation of `/releases/104`, and the `Accept` request header to choose an HTML or plain-text representation. But you should also give each representation a separate URI: maybe URIs like `/releases/104.en`, `/releases/104.es.html`, and `/releases/104.txt`.

When a client requests one of the representation-specific URIs, you should set the `Content-Location` response header to `/releases/104`. This lets the client know the canonical location of the "press release" resource. If the client wants to talk about the press release independent of any particular language and format, it can link to that canonical URI. If it wants to talk about the press release in a particular language and/or format, the client can link to the URI it requested.

In the bookmarking service from Chapter 7, I exposed two representations of a set of bookmarks: a generic XML representation at `/v1/users/leonardr/bookmarks.xml`, and an Atome representation at `/v1/users/leonardr/bookmarks.atom`. I also exposed a canonical URI for the resource at `/v1/users/leonardr/bookmarks`. A client can set its `Accept` request header to distinguish between Atom and generic XML representations of `/v1/users/leonardr/bookmarks`, or it can tweak the URI to get a different representation. Both techniques work, and both techniques are RESTful, but a URI travels better across clients if it specifies a resource *and* a representation.

It's OK for a client to send information in HTTP request headers, so long as the server doesn't make that the only way of selecting a resource or representation. Headers can also contain sensitive information like authentication credentials, or information that's different for every client. But headers shouldn't be the only tool a client has to specify which representation is served or which resource is selected.

State and Statelessness

There are two types of state in a RESTful service. There's resource state, which is information about resources, and application state, which is information about the path the client has taken through the application. Resource state stays on the server and is only sent to the client in the form of representations. Application state stays on the client until it can be used to create, modify, or delete a resource. Then it's sent to the server as part of a POST, PUT, or DELETE request, and becomes resource state.

A RESTful service is "stateless" if the server never stores any application state. In a stateless application, the server considers each client request in isolation and in terms of the current resource state. If the client wants any application state to be taken into consideration, the client must submit it as part of the request. This includes things like authentication credentials, which are submitted with every request.

The client manipulates resource state by sending a representation as part of a PUT or POST request. (DELETE requests work the same way, but there's no representation.) The server manipulates client state by sending representations in response to the client's GET requests. This is where the name "Representational State Transfer" comes from.

Connectedness

The server can guide the client from one application state to another by sending links and forms in its representations. I call this *connectedness* because the links and forms connect the resources to each other. The Fielding thesis calls this "hypermedia as the engine of application state."

In a well-connected service, the client can make a path through the application by following links and filling out forms. In a service that's not connected, the client must use predefined rules to construct every URI it wants to visit. Right now the human web is very well-connected, because most pages on a web site can be reached by following links from the main page. Right now the programmable web is not very well-connected.

The server can also guide the client from one *resource* state to another by sending forms in its representations. Forms guide the client through the process of modifying resource state with a PUT or POST request, by giving hints about what representations are acceptable.

Links and forms reveal the levers of state: requests the client might make in the future to change application or resource state. Of course, the levers of state can be exposed only when the representation format supports links or forms. A hypermedia format like XHTML is good for this; so is an XML format that can have XHTML or WADL embedded in it.

The Uniform Interface

All interaction between clients and resources is mediated through a few basic HTTP methods. Any resource will expose some or all of these methods, and a method does the same thing on every resource that supports it.

A GET request is a request for information about a resource. The information is delivered as a set of headers and a representation. The client never sends a representation along with a GET request.

A HEAD request is the same as a GET request, except that only the headers are sent in response. The representation is omitted.

A PUT request is an assertion about the state of a resource. The client usually sends a representation along with a PUT request, and the server tries to create or change the resource so that its state matches what the representation says. A PUT request with no representation is just an assertion that a resource should exist at a certain URI.

A DELETE request is an assertion that a resource should no longer exist. The client never sends a representation along with a DELETE request.

A POST request is an attempt to create a new resource from an existing one. The existing resource may be the parent of the new one in a data-structure sense, the way the root of a tree is the parent of all its leaf nodes. Or the existing resource may be a special "factory" resource whose only purpose is to generate other resources. The representation sent along with a POST request describes the initial state of the new resource. As with PUT, a POST request doesn't need to include a representation at all.

A POST request may also be used to append to the state of an existing resource, without creating a whole new resource.

An OPTIONS request is an attempt to discover the levers of state: to find out which subset of the uniform interface a resource supports. It's rarely used. Today's services specify the levers of state up front, either in human-readable documentation or in hypermedia documents like XHTML and WADL files.

If you find yourself wanting to add another method or additional features to HTTP, you can overload POST (see "Overloading POST"), but you probably need to add another kind of resource. If you start wanting to add transactional support to HTTP, you should probably expose transactions as resources that can be created, updated, and deleted. See "Resource Design" later in this chapter for more on this technique.

Safety and Idempotence

A GET or HEAD request should be *safe*: a client that makes a GET or HEAD request is not requesting any changes to server state. The server might decide on its own to change state (maybe by logging the request or incrementing a hit counter), but it should not hold the client responsible for those changes. Making any number of GET requests to a certain URI should have the same practical effect as making no requests at all.

A PUT or DELETE request should be *idempotent*. Making more than one PUT or DELETE request to a given URI should have the same effect as making only one. One common problem: PUT requests that set resource state in relative terms like "increment value by 5." Making 10 PUT requests like that is a lot different from just making one. PUT requests should set items of resource state to specific values.

The safe methods, GET and HEAD, are automatically idempotent as well. POST requests for resource creation are neither safe nor idempotent. An overloaded POST request might or might not be safe or idempotent. There's no way for a client to tell, since overloaded POST can do anything at all. You can make POST idempotent with POST Once Exactly (see Chapter 9).

New Resources: PUT Versus POST

You can expose the creation of new resources through PUT, POST, or both. But a client can only use PUT to create resources when it can calculate the final URI of the new resource. In Amazon's S3 service, the URI path to a bucket is /{bucket-name}. Since the client chooses the bucket name, a client can create a bucket by constructing the corresponding URI and sending a PUT request to it.

On the other hand, the URI to a resource in a typical Rails web service looks like /{database-table-name}/{database-ID}. The name of the database table is known in advance, but the ID of the new resource won't be known until the corresponding record is saved to the database. To create a resource, the client must POST to a "factory" resource, located at /{database-table-name}. The server chooses a URI for the new resource.

Overloading POST

POST isn't just for creating new resources and appending to representations. You can also use it to turn a resource into a tiny RPC-style message processor. A resource that receives an overloaded POST request can scan the incoming representation for additional method information, and carry out any task whatsoever. This gives the resource a wider vocabulary than one that supports only the uniform interface.

This is how most web applications work. XML-RPC and SOAP/WSDL web services also run over overloaded POST. I strongly discourage the use of overloaded POST, because it ruins the uniform interface. If you're tempted to expose complex objects or processes through overloaded POST, try giving the objects or processes their own URIs, and exposing them as resources. I show several examples of this in "Resource Design" later in this chapter.

There are two noncontroversial uses for overloaded POST. The first is to *simulate* HTTP's uniform interface for clients like web browsers that don't support PUT or DELETE. The second is to work around limits on the maximum length of a URI. The HTTP standard specifies no limit on how long a URI can get, but many clients and servers impose their own limits: Apache won't respond to requests for URIs longer than 8 KB. If a client can't make a GET request to *http://www.example.com/numbers/ 1111111* because of URI length restrictions (imagine a million more ones there if you like), it can make a POST request to *http://www.example.com/numbers? _method=GET* and put "1111111" in the entity-body.

If you want to do without PUT and DELETE altogether, it's entirely RESTful to expose safe operations on resources through GET, and all other operations through overloaded

POST. Doing this violates my Resource-Oriented Architecture, but it conforms to the less restrictive rules of REST. REST says you should use a uniform interface, but it doesn't say which one.

If the uniform interface really doesn't work for you, or it's not worth the effort to make it work, then go ahead and overload POST, but don't lose the resource-oriented design. Every URI you expose should still be a resource: something a client might want to link to. A lot of web applications create new URIs for operations exposed through overloaded POST. You get URIs like `/weblog/myweblog/rebuild-index`. It doesn't make sense to link to that URI. Instead of putting method information in the URI, expose overloaded POST on your existing resources (`/weblog/myweblog`) and ask for method information in the incoming representation (`method=rebuild-index`). This way, `/weblog/myweblog` still acts like a resource, albeit one that doesn't totally conform to the uniform interface. It responds to GET, PUT, DELETE... and also "rebuild-index" through overloaded POST. It's still an object in the object-oriented sense.

A rule of thumb: if you're using overloaded POST, and you never expose GET and POST on the same URI, you're probably not exposing resources at all. You've probably got an RPC-style service.

This Stuff Matters

The principles of REST and the ROA are not arbitrary restrictions. They're simplifying assumptions that give advantages to resource-oriented services over the competition. RESTful resource-oriented services are simpler, easier to use, more interoperable, and easier to combine than RPC-style services. As I introduced the principles of the ROA in Chapter 4, I gave brief explanations of the ideas underlying the principles. In addition to recapping these ideas to help this chapter serve as a summary, I'd like to revisit them now in light of the real designs I've shown for resource-oriented services: the map service of Chapters 5 and 6, and the social bookmarking service of Chapter 7.

Why Addressability Matters

Addressability means that every interesting aspect of your service is immediately accessible from outside. Every interesting aspect of your service has a URI: a unique identifier in a format that's familiar to every computer-literate person. This identifier can be bookmarked, passed around between applications, and used as a stand-in for the actual resource. Addressability makes it possible for others to make *mashups* of your service: to use it in ways you never imagined.

In Chapter 4 I compared URIs to cell addresses in a spreadsheet, and to file paths in a command-line shell. The web is powerful in the same way that spreadsheets and command-line shells are powerful. Every piece of information has a structured name that can be used as a reference to the real thing.

Why Statelessness Matters

Statelessness is the simplifying assumption to beat all simplifying assumptions. Each of a client's requests contains all application states necessary to understand that request. None of this information is kept on the server, and none of it is implied by previous requests. Every request is handled in isolation and evaluated against the current resource state.

This makes it trivial to scale your application up. If one server can't handle all the requests, just set up a load balancer and make a second server handle half the requests. Which half? It doesn't matter, because every request is self-contained. You can assign requests to servers randomly, or with a simple round-robin algorithm. If two servers can't handle all the requests, you add a third server, ad infinitum. If one server goes down, the others automatically take over for it. When your application is stateless, you don't need to coordinate activity between servers, sharing memory or creating "server affinity" to make sure the same server handles every request in a "session." You can throw web servers at the problem until the bottleneck becomes access to your *resource* state. Then you have to get into database replication, mirroring, or whatever strategy is most appropriate for the way you've chosen to store your resource state.

Stateless applications are also more reliable. If a client makes a request that times out, statelessness means the client can resend the request without worrying that its "session" has gone into a strange state that it can't recover from. If it was a POST request, the client might have to worry about what the request did to the *resource* state, but that's a different story. The client has complete control over the application state at all times.

There's an old joke. Patient: "Doctor, it hurts when I try to scale a system that keeps client state on the server!" Doctor: "Then don't do that." That's the idea behind statelessness: don't do the thing that causes the trouble.

Why the Uniform Interface Matters

I covered this in detail near the end of Chapter 4, so I'll just give a brief recap here. If you say to me, "I've exposed a resource at `http://www.example.com/myresource`," that gives me no information about what that resource is, but it tells me a whole lot about how I can manipulate it. I know how to fetch a representation of it (GET), I know how to delete it (DELETE), I know roughly how to modify its state (PUT), and I know roughly how to spawn a subordinate resource from it (POST).

There are still details to work out: which of these activities the resource actually supports,[*] which representation formats the resource serves and expects, and what this resource represents in the real world. But every resource works basically the same way and can be accessed with a universal client. This is a big part of the success of the Web.

---

[*] In theory, I know how to find out which of these activities are supported: send an OPTIONS request. But right now, nobody supports OPTIONS.

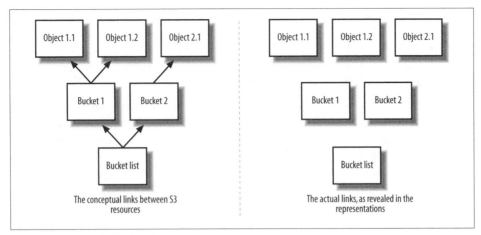

The conceptual links between S3 resources

The actual links, as revealed in the representations

Figure 8-1. We see links, but there are none

The restrictions imposed by the uniform interface (safety for GET and HEAD, idempotence for PUT and DELETE), make HTTP more reliable. If your request didn't go through, you can keep resending it with no ill effects. The only exception is with POST requests. (See "POST Once Exactly" in Chapter 9 for ways of making POST idempotent.)

The power of the uniform interface is not in the specific methods exposed. The human web has a different uniform interface—it uses GET for safe operations, and POST for everything else—and it does just fine. The power is the uniformity: everyone uses the same methods for everything. If you deviate from the ROA's uniform interface (say, by adopting the human web's uniform interface, or WebDAV's uniform interface), you switch communities: you gain compatibility with certain web services at the expense of others.

Why Connectedness Matters

Imagine the aggravation if instead of hypertext links, web pages gave you English instructions on how to construct the URI to the next page. That's how most of today's RESTful web services work: the resources aren't connected to each other. This makes web services more brittle than human-oriented web sites, and it means that emergent properties of the Web (like Google's PageRank) don't happen on the programmable web.

Look at Amazon S3. It's a perfectly respectable resource-oriented service. It's addressable, it's stateless, and it respects the uniform interface. But it's not connected at all. The representation of the S3 bucket list gives the name of each bucket, but it doesn't link to the buckets. The representation of a bucket gives the name of each object in the bucket, but it doesn't link to the objects. We humans know these objects are conceptually linked, but there are no actual links in the representations (see Figure 8-1).

An S3 client can't get from one resource to another by following links. Instead it must internalize rules about how to construct the URI to a given bucket or object. These rules are given in the S3 technical documentation, not anywhere in the service itself. I demonstrated the rules in "Resources" in Chapter 3. This wouldn't work on the human web, but in a web service we don't complain. Why is that?

In general, we expect less from web services than from the human web. We experience the programmable web through customized clients, not generic clients like web browsers. These customized clients can be programmed with rules for URI construction. Most information on the programmable web is also available on the human web, so a lack of connectedness doesn't hide data from generic clients like search engines. Or else the information is hidden behind an authentication barrier and you don't want a search engine seeing it anyway.

The S3 service gets away with a lack of connectedness because it only has three simple rules for URI construction. The URI to a bucket is just a slash and the URI-escaped name of the bucket. It's not difficult to program these rules into a client. The only bug that's at all likely is a failure to URI-escape the bucket or object name. Of course, there are additional rules for filtering and paginating the contents of buckets, which I skimmed over in Chapter 3. Those rules are more complex, and it would be better for S3 representations to provide hypermedia forms instead of making clients construct these URIs on their own.

More importantly, the S3 resources have simple and stable relationships to each other. The bucket list contains buckets, and a bucket contains objects. A link is just an indication of a relationship between two resources. A simple relationship is easy to program into a client, and "contains" is one of the simplest. If a client is preprogrammed with the relationships between resources, links that only serve to convey those relationships are redundant.

The social bookmarking service I implemented in Chapter 7 is a little better-connected than S3. It represents lists of bookmarks as Atom documents full of internal and external links. But it's not totally connected: its representation of a user doesn't link to that user's bookmarks, posting history, or tag vocabulary (look back to Figure 7-1). And there's no information about where to find a user in the service, or how post a bookmark. The client is just supposed to know how to turn a username into a URI, and just supposed to know how to represent a bookmark.

It's easy to see how this is theoretically unsatisfying. A service ought to be self-describing, and not rely on some auxiliary English text that tells programmers how to write clients. It's also easy to see that a client that relies on rules for URI construction is more brittle. If the server changes those rules, it breaks all the clients. It's less easy to see the problems that stem from a lack of connectedness when the relationships between resources are complex or unstable. These problems can break clients even when the rules for URI construction never change.

Let's go back to the mapping service from Chapter 5. My representations were full of hyperlinks and forms, most of which were not technically necessary. Take this bit of markup from the representation of a road map that was in Example 5-6:

```
<a class="zoom_in" href="/road.1/Earth/37.0;-95.8" />Zoom out</a>
<a class="zoom_out" href="/road.3/Earth/37.0;-95.8" />Zoom in</a>
```

Instead of providing these links everywhere, the service provider could put up an English document telling the authors of automated clients how to manipulate the zoom level in the first path variable. That would disconnect some related resources (the road map at different zoom levels), but it would save some bandwidth in every representation and it would have little effect on the actual code of any automated client. Personally, if I was writing a client for this service, I'd rather get from zoom level 8 to zoom level 4 by setting `road.4` directly, than by following the "Zoom out" link over and over again. My client will break if the URI construction rule ever changes, but maybe I'm willing to take that risk.

Now consider this bit of markup from the representation of the planet Earth. It's reprinted from Example 5-7:

```
<dl class="place">
 <dt>name</dt> <dd>Earth</dd>
 <dt>maps</dt>
   <ul class="maps">
    <li><a class="map" href="/road/Earth">Road</a></li>
    <li><a class="map" href="/satellite/Earth">Satellite</a></li>
    ...
   </ul>
```

The URIs are technically redundant. The name of the place indicates that these are maps of Earth, and the link text indicate that there's a satellite and a road map. Given those two pieces of information, a client can construct the corresponding map URI using a rule like the one for S3 objects: slash, map type, slash, planet name. Since the URIs can be replaced by a simple rule, the service might follow the S3 model and save some bandwidth by presenting the representation of Earth in an XML format like this:

```
<place name="Earth" type="planet">
 <map type="satellite" />
 <map type="road" />
 ...
</place>
```

If I was writing a client for this service, I would rather be given those links than have to construct them myself, but it's up for debate.

Here's another bit of markup from Example 5-6. These links are to help the client move from one tile on the map to another.

```
<a class="map_nav" href="46.0518,-95.8">North</a>
<a class="map_nav" href="41.3776,-89.7698">Northeast</a>
<a class="map_nav" href="36.4642,-84.5187">East</a>
<a class="map_nav" href="32.3513,-90.4459">Southeast</a>
```

It's technically possible for a client to generate these URIs based on rules. After all, the server is generating them based on rules. But the rules involve knowing how latitude and longitude work, the scale of the map at the current zoom level, and the size and shape of the planet. Any client programmer would agree it's easier to navigate a map by following the links than by calculating the coordinates of tiles. We've reached a point at which the relationships between resources are too complex to be expressed in simple rules. Connectedness becomes very important.

This is where Google Maps's tile-based navigation system pays off (I described that system back in "Representing Maps and Points on Maps" in Chapter 5, if you're curious). Google Maps addresses its tiles by arbitrary X and Y coordinates instead of latitude and longitude. Finding the tile to the north is usually as easy as subtracting one from the value of Y. The relationships between tiles are much simpler. Nobody made me design my tile system in terms of latitude and longitude. If latitude/longitude calculations are why I have to send navigation links along with every map representation, maybe I should rethink my strategy and expose simpler URIs, so that my clients can generate them more easily.

But there's another reason why connectedness is valuable: it makes it possible for the client to handle relationships that change over time. Links not only hide the rules about how to build a URI for a given resource, they embody the rules of how resources are related to each other. Here's a terrifying example to illustrate the point.

A terrifying example

Suppose I get some new map data for my service. It's more accurate than the old data, but the scale is a little different. At zoom level 8, the client sees a slightly smaller map than it did before. Let's say at zoom level 8, a tile 256 pixels square now depicts an area three-quarters of a mile square, instead of seven-eigths of a mile square.

At first glance, this has no effect on anything. Latitude and longitude haven't changed, so every point on the old map is in the same place on the new map. Google Maps-style tile URIs would break at this point, because they use X and Y instead of latitude and longitude. When the map data was updated, I'd have to recalculate all the tile images. Many points on the map would suddenly shift to different tiles, and get different X and Y coordinates. But all of my URIs still work. Every point on the map has the same URI it did before.

In this new data set, the URI `/road.8/Earth/40.76;-73.98.png` still shows part of the island of Manhattan, and the URI `/road.8/Earth/40.7709,-73.98` still shows a point slightly to the north. But the rules have changed for finding the tile *directly* to the north of another tile. Those two tile graphics are centered on the same coordinates as before, but now each tile depicts a slightly smaller space. They used to be adjacent on the map, but now there's a gap between them (see Figure 8-2).

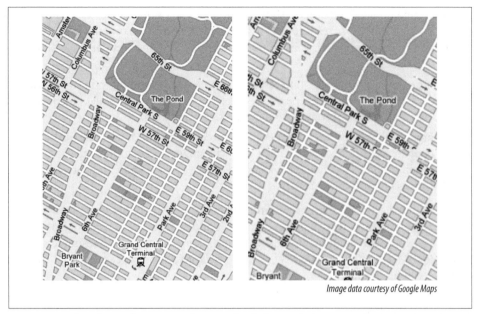

Image data courtesy of Google Maps

Figure 8-2. When clients choose URIs for map tiles: before and after

If a client application finds nearby tiles by following the navigation links I provide, it will automatically adapt to the new map scale. But an application that "already knows" how to turn latitude and longitude into image URIs will suddenly start showing maps that look like *MAD Magazine* fold-ins.

I made a reasonable change to my service that didn't change any URIs, but it broke clients that always construct their own URIs. What changed was not the resources but the relationships between them: not the rules for constructing URIs but the rules for driving the application from one state to another. Those rules are embedded in my navigation links, and a client duplicates those rules at its own peril.

And that's why it's important to connect your resources to each other. It's fine to expect your clients to use your rules to construct an initial URI (say, a certain place on the map at a certain zoom level), but if they need to navigate from one URI to another, you should provide appropriate links. As the programmable web matures, connectedness will become more and more important.

Resource Design

You'll need one resource for each "thing" exposed by your service. "Resource" is about as vague as "thing," so any kind of data or algorithm you want to expose can be a resource. There are three kinds of resources:

- Predefined one-off resources, such as your service's home page or a static list of links to resources. A resource of this type corresponds to something you've only got a few of: maybe a class in an object-oriented system, or a database table in a database-oriented system.

- A large (possibly infinite) number of resources corresponding to individual items of data. A resource of this type might correspond to an object in an object-oriented system, or a database row in a database-oriented system.

- A large (probably infinite) number of resources corresponding to the possible outputs of an algorithm. A resource of this type might correspond to the results of a query in a database-oriented system. Lists of search results and filtered lists of resources fall into this category.

There are some difficult cases in resource design, places where it seems you must manipulate a resource in a way that doesn't fit the uniform interface. The answer is almost always to expose the thing that's causing the problem as a new set of resources. These new resources may be more abstract then the rest of your resources, but that's fine: a resource can be anything.

Relationships Between Resources

Suppose Alice and Bob are resources in my service. That is, they're people in the real world, but my service gives them URIs and offers representations of their state. One day Alice and Bob get married. How should this be represented in my service?

A client can PUT to Alice's URI, modifying her state to reflect the fact that she's married to Bob, and then PUT to Bob's URI to say he's married to Alice. That's not very satisfying because it's two steps. A client might PUT to Alice's URI and forget to PUT to Bob's. Now Alice is married to Bob but not vice versa.

Instead I should treat the marriage, this relationship between two resources, as a thing in itself: a third resource. A client can declare two people married by sending a PUT request to a "marriage" URI or a POST request to a "registrar" URI (it depends on how I choose to do the design). The representation includes links to Alice and Bob's URIs: it's an assertion that the two are married. The server applies any appropriate rules about who's allowed to get married, and either sends an error message or creates a new resource representing the marriage. Other resources can now link to this resource, and it responds to the uniform interface. A client can GET it or DELETE it (though hopefully DELETEing it won't be necessary).

Asynchronous Operations

HTTP has a synchronous request-response model. The client opens an Internet socket to the server, makes its request, and keeps the socket open until the server has sent the response. If the client doesn't care about the response it can close the socket early, but to get a response it must leave the socket open until the server is ready.

The problem is not all operations can be completed in the time we expect an HTTP request to take. Some operations take hours or days. An HTTP request would surely be timed out after that kind of inactivity. Even if it didn't, who wants to keep a socket open for days just waiting for a server to respond? Is there no way to expose such operations asynchronously through HTTP?

There is, but it requires that the operation be split into two or more synchronous requests. The first request spawns the operation, and subsequent requests let the client learn about the status of the operation. The secret is the status code 202 ("Accepted").

I'll demonstrate one strategy for implementing asynchronous requests with the 202 status code. Let's say we have a web service that handles a queue of requests. The client makes its service request normally, possibly without any knowledge that the request will be handled asynchronously. It sends a request like this one:

```
POST /queue HTTP/1.1
Host: jobs.example.com
Authorization: Basic mO1Tcm4hbAr3gBUzv3kcceP=

Give me the prime factorization of this 100000-digit number:
...
```

The server accepts the request, creates a new job, and puts it at the end of the queue. It will take a long time for the new job to be completed, or there wouldn't be a need for a queue in the first place. Instead of keeping the client waiting until the job finally runs, the server sends this response right away:

```
202 Accepted
Location: http://jobs.example.com/queue/job11a4f9
```

The server has created a new "job" resource and given it a URI that doesn't conflict with any other job. The asynchronous operation is now in progress, and the client can make GET requests to that URI to see how it's going— that is, to get the current state of the "job" resource. Once the operation is complete, any results will become available as a representation of this resource. Once the client is done reading the results it can DELETE the job resource. The client may even be able to cancel the operation by DELETEing its job prematurely.

Again, I've overcome a perceived limitation of the Resource-Oriented Architecture by exposing a new kind of resource corresponding to the thing that was causing the problem. In this case, the problem was how to handle asynchronous operations, and the solution was to expose each asynchronous operation as a new resource.

There's one wrinkle. Because every request to start an asynchronous operation makes the server create a new resource (if only a transient one), such requests are neither safe nor idempotent. This means you can't spawn asynchronous operations with GET, DELETE, or (usually) PUT. The only HTTP method you can use and still respect the uniform interface is POST. This means you'll need to expose different resources for asynchronous operations than you would for synchronous operations. You'll probably do something like the job queue I just demonstrated. You'll expose a single resource

—the job queue—to which the client POSTs to create a subordinate resource—the job. This will hold true whether the purpose of the asynchronous operation is to read some data, to make a calculation (as in the factoring example), or to modify the data set.

Batch Operations

Sometimes clients need to operate on more than one resource at once. You've already seen this: a list of search results is a kind of batch GET. Instead of fetching a set of resources one at a time, the client specifies some criteria and gets back a document containing abbreviated representations of many resources. I've also mentioned "factory" resources that respond to POST and create subordinate resources. The factory idea is easy to scale up. If your clients need to create resources in bulk, you can expose a factory resource whose incoming representation describes a set of resources instead of just one, and creates many resources in response to a single request.

What about modifying or deleting a set of resources at once? Existing resources are identified by URI, but addressability means an HTTP request can only point to a single URI, so how can you DELETE two resources at once? Remember that URIs can contain embedded URI paths, or even whole other URIs (if you escape them). One way to let a client modify multiple resources at once is to expose a resource for every *set* of resources. For instance, *http://www.example.com/sets/resource1;subdir/resource2* might refer to a set of two resources: the one at *http://www.example.com/resource1* and the one at *http://www.example.com/subdir/resource2*. Send a DELETE to that "set" resource and you delete both resources in the set. Send a PUT instead, with a representation of each resource in the set, and you can modify both resources with a single HTTP request.

You might be wondering what HTTP status code to send in response to a batch operation. After all, one of those PUTs might succeed while the other one fails. Should the status code be 200 ("OK") or 500 ("Internal Server Error")? One solution is to make a batch operation spawn a series of asynchronous jobs. Then you can send 202 ("Accepted"), and show the client how to check on the status of the individual jobs. Or, you can use an extended HTTP status code created by the WebDAV extension to HTTP: 207 ("Multi-Status").

The 207 status code tells the client to look in the entity-body for a *list* of status codes like 200 ("OK") and 500 ("Internal Server Error"). The entity-body is an XML document that tells the client which operations succeeded and which failed. This is not an ideal solution, since it moves information about what happened out of the status code and into the response entity-body. It's similar to the way overloaded POST moves the method information out of the HTTP method and into the request entity-body. But since there might be a different status code for every operation in the batch, you're really limited in your options here. Appendix B has more information about the 207 status code.

Transactions

In the Resource-Oriented Architecture, every incoming HTTP request has some resource as its destination. But some services expose operations that span multiple resources. The classic example is an operation that transfers money from a checking to a savings account. In a database-backed system you'd use a transaction to prevent the possibility of losing or duplicating money. Is there a resource-oriented way to implement transactions?

You can expose simple transactions as batch operations, or use overloaded POST, but here's another way. It involves (you guessed it) exposing the transactions themselves as resources. I'll show you a sample transaction using the account transfer example. Let's say the "checking account" resource is exposed at /accounts/checking/11, and the "savings account" resource is exposed at /accounts/savings/55. Both accounts have a current balance of $200, and I want to transfer $50 from checking to savings.

I'll quickly walk you through the requests and then explain them. First I create a transaction by sending a POST to a transaction factory resource:

```
POST /transactions/account-transfer HTTP/1.1
Host: example.com
```

The response gives me the URI of my newly created transaction resource:

```
201 Created
Location: /transactions/account-transfer/11a5
```

I PUT the first part of my transaction: the new, reduced balance of the checking account.

```
PUT /transactions/account-transfer/11a5/accounts/checking/11 HTTP/1.1
Host: example.com

balance=150
```

I PUT the second part of my transaction: the new, increased balance of the savings account.

```
PUT /transactions/account-transfer/11a5/accounts/savings/55 HTTP/1.1
Host: example.com

balance=250
```

At any point up to this I can DELETE the transaction resource to roll back the transaction. Instead, I'm going to commit the transaction:

```
PUT /transactions/account-transfer/11a5 HTTP/1.1
Host: example.com

committed=true
```

This is the server's chance to make sure that the transaction doesn't create any inconsistencies in resource state. For an "account transfer" transaction the server should check whether the transaction tries to create or destroy any money, or whether it tries to move money from one person to another without authorization. If everything checks out, here's the response I might get from my final PUT:

```
200 OK
Content-Type: application/xhtml+xml

...
<a href="/accounts/checking/11">Checking #11</a>: New balance $150
<a href="/accounts/savings/55">Savings #55</a>: New balance $250
...
```

At this point I can DELETE the transaction and it won't be rolled back. Or the server might delete it automatically. More likely, it will be archived permanently as part of an audit trail. It's an addressable resource. Other resources, such as a list of transactions that affected checking account #11, can link to it.

The challenge in representing transactions RESTfully is that every HTTP request is supposed to be a self-contained operation that operates on one resource. If you PUT a new balance to /accounts/checking/11, then either the PUT succeeds or it doesn't. But during a transaction, the state of a resource is in flux. Look at the checking account from inside the transaction, and the balance is $150. Look at it from outside, and the balance is still $200. It's almost as though there are two different resources.

That's how this solution presents it: as two different resources. There's the actual checking account, at /accounts/checking/11, and there's one transaction's view of the checking account, at /transactions/account-transfer/11a5/accounts/checking/11. When I POSTed to create /transactions/account-transfer/11a5/, the service exposed additional resources beneath the transaction URI: probably one resource for each account on the system. I manipulated those resources as I would the corresponding account resources, but my changes to resource state didn't go "live" until I committed the transaction.

How would this be implemented behind the scenes? Probably with something that takes incoming requests and builds a queue of actions associated with the transaction. When the transaction is committed the server might start a database transaction, apply the queued actions, and then try to commit the database transaction. A failure to commit would be propagated as a failure to commit the web transaction.

A RESTful transaction is more complex to implement than a database or programming language transaction. Every step in the transaction comes in as a separate HTTP request. Every step identifies a resource and fits the uniform interface. It might be easier to punt and use overloaded POST. But if you implement transactions RESTfully, your transactions have the benefits of resources: they're addressable, operations on them are transparent, and they can be archived or linked to later. Yet again, the way to deal with an action that doesn't fit the uniform interface is to expose the action itself as a resource.

When In Doubt, Make It a Resource

The techniques I've shown you are not the official RESTful or resource-oriented ways to handle transactions, asynchronous operations, and so on. They're just the best ones I could think up. If they don't work for you, you're free to try another arrangement.

The larger point of this section is that when I say "anything can be a resource" I do mean *anything*. If there's a concept that's causing you design troubles, you can usually fit it into the ROA by exposing it as a new kind of resource. If you need to violate the uniform interface for performance reasons, you've always got overloaded POST. But just about anything can be made to respond to the uniform interface.

URI Design

URIs should be meaningful and well structured. Wherever possible, a client should be able to construct the URI for the resource they want to access. This increases the "surface area" of your application. It makes it possible for clients to get directly to any state of your application without having to traverse a bunch of intermediate resources. (But see "Why Connectedness Matters" earlier in this chapter; links are the most reliable way to convey the relationships between resources.)

When designing URIs, use path variables to separate elements of a hierarchy, or a path through a directed graph. Example: `/weblogs/myweblog/entries/100` goes from the general to the specific. From a list of weblogs, to a particular weblog, to the entries in that weblog, to a particular entry. Each path variable is in some sense "inside" the previous one.

Use punctuation characters to separate multiple pieces of data at the same level of a hierarchy. Use commas when the order of the items matters, as it does in latitude and longitude: `/Earth/37.0,-95.2`. Use semicolons when the order doesn't matter: `/color-blends/red;blue`.

Use query variables only to suggest arguments being plugged into an algorithm, or when the other two techniques fail. If two URIs differ only in their query variables, it implies that they're the different sets of inputs into the same underlying algorithm.

URIs are supposed to designate resources, not operations on the resources. This means it's almost never appropriate to put the names of operations in your URIs. If you have a URI that looks like `/object/do-operation`, you're in danger of slipping into the RPC style. Nobody wants to link to `do-operation`: they want to link to the `object`. Expose the operation through the uniform interface, or use overloaded POST if you have to, but make your URIs designate objects, not operations on the objects.

I can't make this an ironclad rule, because a resource can be anything. Operations on objects can be first-class objects, similar to how methods in a dynamic programming language are first-class objects. `/object/do-operation` might be a full-fledged resource that responds to GET, PUT, and DELETE. But if you're doing this, you're well ahead of the current web services curve, and you've got weightier issues on your mind than whether you're contravening some best practice I set down in a book.

Outgoing Representations

Most of the documents you serve will be representations of resources, but some of them will be error conditions. Use HTTP status codes to convey how the client should regard the document you serve. If there's an error, you should set the status code to indicate an appropriate error condition, possibly 400 ("Bad Request"). Otherwise, the client might treat your error message as a representation of the resource it requested.

The status code says what the document is for. The Content-Type response header says what format the document is in. Without this header, your clients won't know how to parse or handle the documents you serve.

Representations should be human-readable, but computer-oriented. The job of the human web is to present information for direct human consumption. The main job of the programmable web is to present the same information for manipulation by computer programs. If your service exposes a set of instrument readings, the focus should be on providing access to the raw data, not on making human-readable graphs. Clients can make their own graphs, or pipe the raw data into a graph-generation service. You can provide graphs as a convenience, but a graph should not be the main representation of a set of numbers.

Representations should be useful: that is, they should expose interesting data instead of irrelevant data that no one will use. A single representation should contain all relevant information necessary to fulfill a need. A client should not have to get several representations of the same resource to perform a single operation.

That said, it's difficult to anticipate what part of your data set clients will use. When in doubt, expose all the state you have for a resource. This is what a Rails service does by default: it exposes representations that completely describe the corresponding database rows.

A resource's representations should change along with its state.

Incoming Representations

I don't have a lot to say about incoming representations, apart from talking about specific formats, which I'll do in the next chapter. I will mention the two main kinds of incoming representations. Simple representations are usually key-value pairs: set this item of resource state to that value: username=leonardr. There are lots of representations for key-value pairs, form-encoding being the most popular.

If your resource state is too complex to represent with key-value pairs, your service should accept incoming representations in the same format it uses to serve outgoing representations. A client should be able to fetch a representation, modify it, and PUT it back where it found it. It doesn't make sense to have your clients understand one complex data format for outgoing representations and another, equally complex format for incoming representations.

Service Versioning

Web sites can (and do) undergo drastic redesigns without causing major problems, because their audience is made of human beings. Humans can look at a web page and understand what it means, so they're good at adapting to changes. Although URIs on the Web are not supposed to change, in practice they can (and do) change all the time. The consequences are serious—external links and bookmarks still point to the old URIs —but your everyday use of a web site isn't affected. Even so, after a major redesign, some web sites keep the old version around for a while. The web site's users need time to adapt to the new system.

Computer programs are terrible at adapting to changes. A human being (a programmer) must do the adapting for them. This is why connectedness is important, and why extensible representation formats (like Atom and XHTML) are so useful. When the client's options are described by hypermedia, a programmer can focus on the high-level semantic meaning of a service, rather than the implementation details. The implementations of resources, the URIs to the resources, and even the hypermedia representations themselves can change, but as long as the semantic cues are still there, old clients will still work.

The mapping service from Chapter 5 was completely connected and served representations in an extensible format. The URI to a resource followed a certain pattern, but you didn't need that fact to use the service: the representations were full of links, and the links were annotated with semantic content like "zoom_in" and "coordinates." In Chapter 6 I added new resources and added new features to the representations, but a client written against the Chapter 5 version would still work. Except for the protocol change: the Chapter 5 service was served through HTTP, and the Chapter 6 service through HTTPS. All the semantic cues stayed the same, so the representations still "meant" the same thing.

By contrast, the bookmarking service from Chapter 7 isn't well connected. You can't get a representation of a user except by applying a URI construction rule I described in English prose. If I change that rule, any clients you wrote will break. In a situation like this, the service should allow for a transitional period where the old resources work alongside the new ones. The simplest way is to incorporate version information into the resources' URIs. That's what I did in Chapter 7: my URIs looked like `/v1/users/leonardr` instead of `/users/leonardr`.

Even a well-connected service might need to be versioned. Sometimes a rewrite of the service changes the meaning of the representations, and all the clients break, even ones that understood the earlier semantic cues. When in doubt, version your service.

You can use any of the methods developed over the years for numbering software releases. Your URI might designate the version as v1, or 1.4.0, or 2007-05-22. The simplest way to incorporate the version is to make it the first path variable: /v1/resource versus /v2/resource. If you want to get a little fancy, you can incorporate the version number into the hostname: v1.service.example.com versus v2.service.example.com.

Ideally, you would keep the old versions of your services around until no more clients use them, but this is only possible in private settings where you control all the clients. More realistically, you should keep old versions around until architectural changes make it impossible to expose the old resources, or until the maintenance cost of the old versions exceeds the cost of actively helping your user base migrate.

Permanent URIs Versus Readable URIs

I think there should be an intuitive correspondence between a URI and the resource it identifies. REST doesn't forbid this, but it doesn't require it either. REST says that resources should have names, not that the names should mean anything. The URI /contour/Mars doesn't have to be the URI to the contour map of Mars: it could just as easily be the URI to the radar map of Venus, or the list of open bugs in a bug tracker. But making a correspondence between URI and resource is one of the most useful things you can do for your clients. Usability expert Jakob Nielsen recommends this in his essay "URL as UI" (*http://www.useit.com/alertbox/990321.html*). If your URIs are intuitive enough, they form part of your service's user interface. A client can get right to the resource they want by constructing an appropriate URI, or surf your resources by varying the URIs.

There's a problem, though. A meaningful URI talks about the resource, which means it contains elements of resource state. What happens when the resource state changes? Nobody will ever successfully rename the planet Mars (believe me, I've tried), but towns change names occasionally, and businesses change names all the time. I ran into trouble in Chapter 6 because I used latitude and longitude to designate a "place" that turned out to be a moving ship. Usernames change. People get married and change their names. Almost any piece of resource state that might add meaning to a URI can change, breaking the URI.

This is why Rails applications expose URIs that incorporate database table IDs, URIs like /weblogs/4. I dissed those URIs in Chapter 7, but their advantage is that they're based on a bit of resource state that never changes. It's state that's totally useless to the client, but it never changes, and that's worth something too.

Jakob Nielsen makes the case for meaningful URIs, but Tim Berners-Lee makes the case for *URI opacity*: "meaningless" URIs that never change. Berners-Lee's "Axioms of

Web Architecture" (*http://www.w3.org/DesignIssues/Axioms.html*) describes URI opacity like this: "When you are not dereferencing you should not look at the contents of the URI string to gain other information." That is: you can use a URI as the name of a resource, but you shouldn't pick the URI apart to see what it says, and you shouldn't assume that you can vary the resource by varying the URI. Even if a URI really looks meaningful, you can't make any assumptions.

This is a good rule for a general web client, because there are no guarantees about URIs on the Web as a whole. Just because a URI ends in ".html" doesn't mean there's an HTML document on the other side. But today's average RESTful web service is built around rules for URI construction. With URI templates, a web service can make promises about whole *classes* of URIs that fit a certain pattern. The best argument for URI opacity on the programmable web is the fact that a non-opaque URI incorporates resource state that might change. To use another of Tim Berners-Lee's coinages, opaque URIs are "cool."[†]

So which is it? URI as UI, or URI opacity? For once in this book I'm going to give you the cop-out answer: it depends. It depends on which is worse for your clients: a URI that has no visible relationship to the resource it names, or a URI that breaks when its resource state changes. I almost always come down on the side of URI as UI, but that's just my opinion.

To show you how subjective this is, I'd like to break the illusion of the authorial "I" for just a moment. The authors of this book both prefer informative URIs to opaque ones, but Leonard tries to choose URIs using the bits of resource state that are least likely to change. If he designed a weblog service, he'd put the date of a weblog entry in that entry's URI, but he wouldn't put the entry title in there. He thinks the title's too easy to change. Sam would rather put the title in the URI, to help with search engine optimization and to give the reader a clue what content is behind the URI. Sam would handle retitled entries by setting up a permanent redirect at the old URI.

Standard Features of HTTP

HTTP has several features designed to solve specific engineering problems. Many of these features are not widely known, either because the problems they solve don't come up very often on the human web, or because today's web browsers implement them transparently. When working on the programmable web, you should know about these features, so you don't reinvent them or prematurely give up on HTTP as an application protocol.

[†] Hypertext Style: Cool URIs Don't Change (*http://www.w3.org/Provider/Style/URI*)

Authentication and Authorization

By now you probably know that HTTP authentication and authorization are handled with HTTP headers—"stickers" on the HTTP "envelope." You might not know that these headers were designed to be extensible. HTTP defines two authentication schemes, but there's a standard way of integrating other authentication schemes into HTTP, by customizing values for the headers `Authorization` and `WWW-Authenticate`. You can even define custom authentication schemes and integrate them into HTTP: I'll show you how that's done by adapting a small portion of the WS-Security standard to work with HTTP authentication. But first, I'll cover the two predefined schemes.

Basic authentication

Basic authentication is a simple challenge/response. If you try to access a resource that's protected by basic authentication, and you don't provide the proper credentials, you receive a challenge and you have to make the request again. It's used by the del.icio.us web service I showed you in Chapter 2, as well as my mapping service in Chapter 6 and my del.icio.us clone in Chapter 7.

Here's an example. I make a request for a protected resource, not realizing it's protected:

```
GET /resource.html HTTP/1.1
Host: www.example.com
```

I didn't include the right credentials. In fact, I didn't include any credentials at all. The server sends me the following response:

```
401 Unauthorized
WWW-Authenticate: Basic realm="My Private Data"
```

This is a challenge. The server dares me to repeat my request with the correct credentials. The `WWW-Authenticate` header gives two clues about what credentials I should send. It identifies what kind of authentication it's using (in this case, Basic), and it names a *realm*. The realm can be any name you like, and it's generally used to identify a collection of resources on a site. In Chapter 7 the realm was "Social bookmarking service" (I defined it in Example 7-11). A single web site might have many sets of protected resources guarded in different ways: the realm lets the client know which authentication credentials it should provide. The realm is the *what*, and the authentication type is the *how*.

To meet a Basic authentication challenge, the client needs a username and a password. This information might be filed in a cache under the name of the realm, or the client may have to prompt an end user for this information. Once the client has this information, username and password are combined into a single string and encoded with base 64 encoding. Most languages have a standard library for doing this kind of encoding: Example 8-1 uses Ruby to encode a username and password.

Example 8-1. Base 64 encoding in Ruby

```ruby
#!/usr/bin/ruby
# calculate-base64.rb
USER="Alibaba"
PASSWORD="open sesame"

require 'base64'
puts Base64.encode64("#{USER}:#{PASSWORD}")
# QWxpYmFiYTpvcGVuIHNlc2FtZQ==
```

This seemingly random string of characters is the value of the `Authorization` header. Now I can send my request again, using the username and password as Basic auth credentials.

```
GET /resource.html HTTP/1.1
Host: www.example.com
Authorization: Basic QWxpYmFiYTpvcGVuIHNlc2FtZQ==
```

The server decodes this string and matches it against its user and password list. If they match, the response is processed further. If not, the request fails, and once again the status code is 401 ("Unauthorized").

Of course, if the server can decode this string, so can anyone who snoops on your network traffic. Basic authentication effectively transmits usernames and passwords in plain text. One solution to this is to use HTTPS, also known as Transport Level Security or Secure Sockets Layer. HTTPS encrypts all communications between client and server, incidentally including the `Authorization` header. When I added authentication to my map service in Chapter 6, I switched from plain HTTP to encrypted HTTPS.

Digest authentication

HTTP Digest authentication is another way to hide the authorization credentials from network snoops. It's more complex than Basic authentication, but it's secure even over unencrypted HTTP. Digest follows the same basic pattern as Basic: the client issues a request, and gets a challenge. Here's a sample challenge:

```
401 Unauthorized
WWW-Authenticate: Digest realm="My Private Data",
  qop="auth",
  nonce="0cc175b9c0f1b6a831c399e269772661",
  opaque="92eb5ffee6ae2fec3ad71c777531578f"
```

This time, the `WWW-Authenticate` header says that the authentication type is `Digest`. The header specifies a realm as before, but it also contains three other pieces of information, including a *nonce*: a random string that changes on every request.

The client's responsibility is to turn this information into an encrypted string that proves the client knows the password, but that doesn't actually contain the password. First the client generates a client-side nonce and a sequence number. Then the client makes a single "digest" string out of a huge amount of information: the HTTP method and path from the request, the four pieces of information from the challenge, the username and password, the client-side nonce, and the sequence number. The formula for doing this is considerably more complicated than for Basic authentication (see Example 8-2).

Example 8-2. HTTP digest calculation in Ruby

```
#!/usr/bin/ruby
# calculate-http-digest.rb
require 'md5'

#Information from the original request
METHOD="GET"
PATH="/resource.html"

# Information from the challenge
REALM="My Private Data"
NONCE="0cc175b9c0f1b6a831c399e269772661",
OPAQUE="92eb5ffee6ae2fec3ad71c777531578f"
QOP="auth"

# Information calculated by or known to the client
NC="00000001"
CNONCE="4a8a08f09d37b73795649038408b5f33"
USER="Alibaba"
PASSWORD="open sesame"

# Calculate the final digest in three steps.
ha1 = MD5::hexdigest("#{USER}:#{REALM}:#{PASSWORD}")
ha2 = MD5::hexdigest("#{METHOD}:#{PATH}")
ha3 = MD5::hexdigest("#{ha1}:#{NONCE}:#{NC}:#{CNONCE}:#{QOP}:#{ha2}")

puts ha3
# 2370039ff8a9fb83b4293210b5fb53e3
```

The digest string is similar to the S3 request signature in Chapter 3. It proves certain things about the client. You could never produce this string unless you knew the client's username and password, knew what request the client was trying to make, and knew which challenge the server had sent in response to the first request.

Once the digest is calculated, the client resends the request and passes back all the constants (except, of course, the password), as well as the final result of the calculation:

```
GET /resource.html HTTP/1.1
Host: www.example.com
Authorization: Digest username="Alibaba",
  realm="My Private Data",
  nonce="0cc175b9c0f1b6a831c399e269772661",
  uri="/resource.html",
  qop=auth,
  nc=00000001,
  cnonce="4a8a08f09d37b73795649038408b5f33",
  response="2370039ff8a9fb83b4293210b5fb53e3",
  opaque="92eb5ffee6ae2fec3ad71c777531578f"
```

The cryptography is considerably more complicated, but the process is the same as for HTTP Basic auth: request, challenge, response. One key difference is that even the server can't figure out your password from the digest. When a client initially sets a password for a realm, the server needs to calculate the hash of `user:realm:password` (`ha1` in the example above), and keep it on file. That gives the server the information it needs to calculate the final value of `ha3`, without storing the user's actual password.

A second difference is that every request the client makes is actually two requests. The point of the first request is to get a challenge: it includes no authentication information, and it always fails with a status code of 401 ("Unauthorized"). But the `WWW-Authenti cate` header includes a unique nonce, which the client can use to construct an appropriate `Authorization` header. It makes a second request, using this header, and this one is the one that succeeds. In Basic auth, the client can avoid the challenge by sending its authorization credentials along with the first request. That's not possible in Digest.

Digest authentication has some options I haven't shown here. Specifying `qop=auth-int` instead of `qop-auth` means that the calculation of `ha2` above must include the request's entity-body, not just the HTTP method and the URI path. This prevents a man-in-the-middle from tampering with the representations that accompany PUT and POST requests.

My goal here isn't to dwell on the complex mathematics— that's what libraries are for. I want to demonstrate the central role the `WWW-Authenticate` and `Authorization` headers play in this exchange. The `WWW-Authenticate` header says, "Here's everything you need to know to authenticate, assuming you know the secret." The `Authorization` header says, "I know the secret, and here's the proof." Everything else is parameter parsing and a few lines of code.

WSSE username token

What if neither HTTP Basic or HTTP Digest work for you? You can define your own standards for what goes into `WWW-Authenticate` and `Authorization`. Here's one real-life example. It turns out that, for a variety of technical reasons, users with low-cost hosting accounts can't take advantage of either HTTP Basic or HTTP Digest.[‡] At one time, this was important to a segment of the Atom community. Coming up with an entirely new cryptographically secure option was beyond the ability of the Atom working group. Instead, they looked to the WS-Security specification, which defines several different ways of authenticating SOAP messages with SOAP headers. (SOAP headers are the "stickers" on the SOAP envelope I mentioned back in Chapter 1.) They took a single idea—WS-Security UsernameToken—from this standard and ported it from SOAP headers to HTTP headers. They defined an extension to HTTP that used `WWW-Authenticate` and `Authorization` in a way that people with low-cost hosting accounts could use. We call the resulting extension WSSE UsernameToken, or WSSE for

[‡] Documented by Mark Pilgrim in "Atom Authentication" (*http://www.xml.com/pub/a/2003/12/17/dive.html*) on *xml.com*.

short. (WSSE just means WS-Security Extension. Other extensions would have a claim to the same name, but there aren't any others right now.)

WSSE is like Digest in that the client runs their password through a hash algorithm before sending it across the network. The basic pattern is the same: the client makes a request, gets a challenge, and formulates a response. A WSSE challenge might look like this:

```
HTTP/1.1 401 Unauthorized
WWW-Authenticate: WSSE realm="My Private Data", profile="UsernameToken"
```

Instead of Basic or Digest, the authentication type is WSSE. The realm serves the same purpose as before, and the "profile" tells the client that the server expects it to generate a response using the UsernameToken rules (as opposed to some other rule from WS-Security that hasn't yet been ported to HTTP headers). The UsernameToken rules mean that the client generates a nonce, then hashes their password along with the nonce and the current date (see Example 8-3).

Example 8-3. Calculating a WSSE digest

```ruby
#!/usr/bin/ruby
# calculate-wsse-digest.rb
require 'base64'
require 'sha1'

PASSWORD = "open sesame"
NONCE = "EFD89F06CCB28C89",
CREATED = "2007-04-13T09:00:00Z"

puts Base64.encode64(SHA1.digest("#{NONCE}#{CREATED}#{PASSWORD}"))
# Z2Y59TewHV6r9BWjtHLkKfUjm2k=
```

Now the client can send a response to the WSSE challenge:

```
GET /resource.html HTTP/1.1
Host: www.example.com
Authorization: WSSE profile="UsernameToken"
X-WSSE: UsernameToken Username="Alibaba",
  PasswordDigest="Z2Y59TewHV6r9BWjtHLkKfUjm2k=",
  Nonce="EFD89F06CCB28C89",
  Created="2007-04-13T09:00:00Z"
```

Same headers. Different authentication method. Same message flow. Different hash algorithm. That's all it takes to extend HTTP authentication. If you're curious, here's what those authentication credentials would look like as a SOAP header under the original WS-Security UsernameToken standard.

```
<wsse:UsernameToken
  xmlns:wsse="http://schemas.xmlsoap.org/ws/2002/xx/secext"
  xmlns:wsu="http://schemas.xmlsoap.org/ws/2002/xx/utility">
  <wsse:Username>Alibaba</wsse:Username>
  <wsse:Password Type="wsse:PasswordDigest">
```

```
    Z2Y59TewHV6r9BWjtHLkKfUjm2k=
  </wsse:Password>
  <wsse:Nonce>EFD89F06CCB28C89</wsse:Nonce>
  <wsu:Created>2007-04-13T09:00:00Z</wsu:Created>
</wsse:UsernameToken>
```

WSSE UsernameToken authentication has two big advantages. It doesn't send the password in the clear over the network, the way HTTP Basic does, and it doesn't require any special setup on the server side, the way HTTP Digest usually does. It's got one big disadvantage. Under HTTP Basic and Digest, the server can keep a one-way hash of the password instead of the password itself. If the server gets cracked, the passwords are still (somewhat) safe. With WSSE UsernameToken, the server must store the password in plain text, or it can't verify the responses to its challenges. If someone cracks the server, they've got all the passwords. The extra complexity of HTTP Digest is meant to stop this from happening. Security always involves tradeoffs like these.

Compression

Textual representations like XML documents can be compressed to a fraction of their original size. An HTTP client library can request a compressed version of a representation and then transparently decompress it for its user. Here's how it works: along with an HTTP request the client sends an `Accept-Encoding` header that says what kind of compression algorithms the client understands. The two standard values for `Accept-Encoding` are compress and gzip.

```
GET /resource.html HTTP/1.1
Host: www.example.com
Accept-Encoding: gzip,compresss
```

If the server understands one of the compression algorithms from `Accept-Encoding`, it can use that algorithm to compress the representation before serving it. The server sends the same `Content-Type` it would send if the representation wasn't compressed. But it also sends the `Content-Encoding` header, so the client knows the document has been compressed:

```
200 OK
Content-Type: text/html
Content-Encoding: gzip

[Binary representation goes here]
```

The client decompresses the data using the algorithm given in `Content-Encoding`, and then treats it as the media type given as `Content-Type`. In this case the client would use the gzip algorithm to decompress the binary data back into an HTML document. This technique can save a lot of bandwidth, with very little cost in additional complexity.

You probably remember that I think different representations of a resource should have distinct URIs. Why do I recommend using HTTP headers to distinguish between compressed and uncompressed versions of a representation? Because I don't think the compressed and uncompressed versions are different representations. Compression, like encryption, is something that happens to a representation in transit, and must be undone before the client can use the representation. In an ideal world, HTTP clients and servers would compress and decompress representations automatically, and programmers should not have to even think about it. Today, most web browsers automatically request compressed representations, but few programmable clients do.

Conditional GET

Conditional HTTP GET allows a server and client to work together to save bandwidth. I covered it briefly in Chapter 5, in the context of the mapping service. There, the problem was sending the same map tiles over and over again to clients who had already received them. This is a more general treatment of the same question: how can a service keep from sending representations to clients that already have them?

Neither client nor server can solve this problem alone. If the client retrieves a representation and never talks to the server again, it will never know when the representation has changed. The server keeps no application state, so it doesn't know when a client last retrieved a certain representation. HTTP isn't a reliable protocol anyway, and the client might not have received the representation the first time. So when the client requests a representation, the server has no idea whether the client has done this before —unless the client provides that information as part of the application state.

Conditional HTTP GET requires client and server to work together. When the server sends a representation, it sets some HTTP response headers: `Last-Modified` and/or `ETag`. When the client requests the same representation, it should send the values for those headers as `If-Modified-Since` and/or `If-None-Match`. This lets the server make a decision about whether or not to resend the representation. Example 8-4 gives a demonstration of conditional HTTP GET.

Example 8-4. Make a regular GET request, then a conditional GET request

```
#!/usr/bin/ruby
# fetch-oreilly-conditional.rb

require 'rubygems'
require 'rest-open-uri'
uri = 'http://www.oreilly.com'

# Make an HTTP request and then describe the response.
def request(uri, *args)
  begin
    response = open(uri, *args)
  rescue OpenURI::HTTPError => e
    response = e.io
  end

  puts " Status code: #{response.status.inspect}"
  puts " Representation size: #{response.size}"
  last_modified = response.meta['last-modified']
```

```
    etag = response.meta['etag']
    puts " Last-Modified: #{last_modified}"
    puts " Etag: #{etag}"
    return last_modified, etag
  end

  puts "First request:"
  last_modified, etag = request(uri)

  puts "Second request:"
  request(uri, 'If-Modified-Since' => last_modified, 'If-None-Match' => etag)
```

If you run that code once, it'll fetch *http://www.oreilly.com* twice: once normally and once conditionally. It prints information about each request. The printed output for the first request will look something like this:

```
First request:
  Status code: ["200", "OK"]
  Representation size: 41123
  Last-Modified: Sun, 21 Jan 2007 09:35:19 GMT
  Etag: "7359b7-a37c-45b333d7"
```

The `Last-Modified` and `Etag` headers are the ones that make HTTP conditional GET possible. To use them, I make the HTTP request again, but this time I use the value of `Last-Modified` as `If-Modified-Since`, and the value of `ETag` as `If-None-Match`. Here's the result:

```
Second request:
  Status code: ["304", "Not Modified"]
  Representation size: 0
  Last-Modified:
  Etag: "7359b7-a0a3-45b5d90e"
```

Instead of a 40-KB representation, the second request gets a 0-byte representation. Instead of 200 ("OK"), the status code is 304 ("Not Modified"). The second request saved 40 KB of bandwidth because it made the HTTP request conditional on the representation of *http://www.oreilly.com/* actually having changed since last time. The representation didn't change, so it wasn't resent.

`Last-Modified` is a pretty easy header to understand: it's the last time the representation of this resource changed. You may be able to view this information in your web browser by going to "view page info" or something similar. Sometimes humans check a web page's `Last-Modified` time to see how recent the data is, but its main use is in conditional HTTP requests.

`If-Modified-Since` makes an HTTP request conditional. If the condition is met, the server carries out the request as it would normally. Otherwise, the condition fails and the server does something unusual. For `If-Modified-Since`, the condition is: "the representation I'm requesting must have changed after this date." The condition succeeds when the server has a newer representation than the client does. If the client and server have the same representation, the condition fails and the server does something unusual: it omits the representation and sends a status code of 304 ("Not Modified").

That's the server's way of telling the client: "reuse the representation you saved from last time."

Both client and server benefit here. The server doesn't have to send a representation of the resource, and the client doesn't have to wait for it. Both sides save bandwidth. This is one of the tricks underlying your web browser's cache, and there's no reason not to use it in custom web clients.

How does the server calculate when a representation was last modified? A web server like Apache has it easy: it mostly serves static files from disk, and filesystems already track the modification date for every file. Apache just gets that information from the filesystem. In more complicated scenarios, you'll need to break the representation down into its component parts and see when each bit of resource state was last modified. In Chapter 7, the Last-Modified value for a list of bookmarks was the most recent timestamp in the list. If you're not tracking this information, the bandwidth savings you get by supporting Last-Modified might make it worth your while to start tracking it.

Even when a server provides Last-Modified, it's not totally reliable. Let's say a client GETs a representation at 12:30:00.3 and sees a Last-Modified with the time "12:30:00." A tenth of a second later, the representation changes, but the Last-Modified time is still "12:30:00." If the client tries a conditional GET request using If-Modified-Since, the server will send a 304 ("Not Modified") response, even though the resource was modified after the original GET. One second is not a high enough resolution to keep track of when a resource changes. In fact, no resolution is high enough to keep track of when a resource changes with total accuracy.

This is not quite satisfactory. The world cries out for a completely reliable way of checking whether or not a representation has been modified since last you retrieved it. Enter the Etag response header. The Etag (it stands for "entity tag") is a nonsensical string that must change whenever the corresponding representation changes.

The If-None-Match request header is to Etag as the If-Modified-Since request header is to Last-Modified. It's a way of making an HTTP request conditional. In this case, the condition is "the representation has changed, as embodied in the entity tag." It's supposed to be a totally reliable way of identifying changes between representations.

It's easy to generate a good ETag for any representation. Transformations like the MD5 hash can turn any string of bytes into a short string that's unique except in pathological cases. The problem is, by the time you can run one of those transformations, you've already created the representation as a string of bytes. You may save bandwidth by not sending the representation over the wire, but you've already done everything necessary to build it.

The Apache server uses filesystem information like file size and modification time to generate Etag headers for static files without reading their contents. You might be able to do the same thing for your representations: pick the data that tends to change, or summary data that changes along with the representation. Instead of doing an MD5 sum of the entire representation, just do a sum of the important data. The `Etag` header doesn't need to incorporate every bit of data in the representation: it just has to change whenever the representation changes.

If a server provides both `Last-Modified` and `Etag`, the client can provide both `If-Modified-Since` and `If-None-Match` in subsequent requests (as I did in Example 8-4). The server should make both checks: it should only send a new representation if the representation has changed *and* the `Etag` is different.

Caching

Conditional HTTP GET gives the client a way to refresh a representation by making a GET request that uses very little bandwidth if the representation has not changed. Caching gives the client some rough guidelines that can make it unnecessary to make that second GET request at all.

HTTP caching is a complex topic, even though I'm limiting my discussion to client-side caches and ignoring proxy caches that sit between the client and the server.§ The basics are these: when a client makes an HTTP GET or HEAD request, it might be able to cache the HTTP response document, headers and all. The next time the client is asked to make the same GET or HEAD request, it may be able to return the cached document instead of actually making the request again. From the perspective of the user (a human using a web browser, or a computer program using an HTTP library), caching is transparent. The user triggers a request, but instead of making an actual HTTP request, the client retrieves a cached response from the server and presents it as though it were freshly retrieved. I'm going to focus on three topics from the point of view of the service provider: how you can tell the client to cache, how you can tell the client *not* to cache, and when the client might be caching without you knowing it.

Please cache

When the server responds to a GET or HEAD request, it may send a date in the response header `Expires`. For instance:

```
Expires: Tue, 30 Jan 2007 17:02:06 GMT
```

This header tells the client (and any proxies between the server and client) how long the response may be cached. The date may range from a date in the past (meaning the response has expired by the time it gets to the client) to a date a year in the future (which means, roughly, "the response will never expire"). After the time specified in `Expires`, the response becomes *stale*. This doesn't mean that it must be removed from the cache

---

§ For more detailed coverage, see section 13 of RFC 2616, and Chapter 7 of *HTTP: The Definitive Guide*, by Brian Totty and David Gourley (O'Reilly).

immediately. The client might be able to make a conditional GET request, find out that the response is actually still fresh, and update the cache with a new expiration date.

The value of Expires is a rough guide, not an exact date. Most services can't predict to the second when a response is going to change. If Expires is an hour in the future, that means the server is pretty sure the response won't change for at least an hour. But something could legitimately happen to the resource the second after that response is sent, invalidating the cached response immediately. When in doubt, the client can make another HTTP request, hopefully a conditional one.

The server should not send an Expires that gives a date more than a year in the future. Even if the server is totally confident that a particular response will never change, a year is a long time. Software upgrades and other events in the real world tend to invalidate cached responses sooner than you'd expect.

If you don't want to calculate a date at which a response should become stale, you can use Cache-Control to say that a response should be cached for a certain number of seconds. This response can be cached for an hour:

```
Cache-Control: max-age=3600
```

Thank you for not caching

That covers the case when the server would like the client to cache. What about the opposite? Some responses to GET requests are dynamically generated and different every time: caching them would be useless. Some contain sensitive information that shouldn't be stored where someone else might see it: caching them would cause security problems. Use the Cache-Control header to convey that the client should not cache the representation at all:

```
Cache-Control: no-cache
```

Where Expires is a fairly simple response header, Cache-Control header is very complex. It's the primary interface for controlling client-side caches, and proxy caches between the client and server. It can be sent as a request or as a response header, but I'm just going to talk about it use as a response header, since my focus is on how the server can work with a client-side cache.

I already showed how specifying "max-age" in Cache-Control controls how long a response can stay fresh in a cache. A value of "no-cache" prevents the client from caching a response at all. A third value you might find useful is "private," which means that the response may be cached by a client cache, but not by any proxy cache between the client and server.

Default caching rules

In the absence of Expires or Cache-Control, section 13 of the HTTP standard defines a complex set of rules about when a client can cache a response. Unless you're going to set caching headers on every response, you'll need to know when a client is likely to cache what you send, so that you can override the defaults when appropriate. I'll summarize the basic common-sense rules here.

In general, the client may cache the responses to its successful HTTP GET and HEAD requests. "Success" is defined in terms of the HTTP status code: the most common success codes are 200 ("OK"), 301 ("Moved Permanently"), and 410 ("Gone").

Many (poorly-designed) web applications expose URIs that trigger side effects when you GET them. These dangerous URIs usually contain query strings. The HTTP standard recommends that if a URI contains a query string, the response from that URI should not be automatically cached: it should only be cached if the server explicitly says caching is OK. If the client GETs this kind of URI twice, it should trigger the side effects twice, not trigger them once and then get a cached copy of the response from last time.

If the client then finds itself making a PUT, POST, or DELETE request to a URI, any cached responses from that URI immediately become stale. The same is true of any URI mentioned in the `Location` or `Content-Location` of a response to a PUT, POST, or DELETE request. There's a wrinkle here, though: site A can't affect how the client caches responses from site B. If you POST to *http://www.example.com/resource*, then any cached response from `resource` is automatically stale. If the response comes back with a `Location` of *http://www.example.com/resource2*, then any cached response from `http://www.example.com/resource2` is also stale. But if the `Location` is *http://www.oreilly.com/resource2*, it's not OK to consider a cached response from `http://www.oreilly.com/resource2` to be stale. The site at `www.example.com` doesn't tell `www.oreilly.com` what to do.

If none of these rules apply, and if the server doesn't specify how long to cache a response, the decision falls to the client side. Responses may be removed at any time or kept forever. More realistically, a client-side cache should consider a response to be stale after some time between an hour and a day. Remember that a stale response doesn't have to be removed from the cache: the client might make a conditional GET request to check whether the cached response can still be used. If the condition succeeds, the cached response is still fresh and it can stay in the cache.

Look-Before-You-Leap Requests

Conditional GET is designed to save the server from sending enormous representations to a client that already has them. Another feature of HTTP, less often used, can save the *client* from fruitlessly sending enormous (or sensitive) representations to the *server*. There's no official name for this kind of request, so I've came up with a silly name: look-before-you-leap requests.

To make a LBYL request, a client sends a PUT or POST request normally, but omits the entity-body. Instead, the client sets the `Expect` request header to the string "100-continue". Example 8-5 shows a sample LBYL request.

Example 8-5. A sample look-before-you-leap request

```
PUT /filestore/myfile.txt HTTP/1.1
Host: example.com
Content-length: 524288000
Expect: 100-continue
```

This is not a real PUT request: it's a question about a possible future PUT request. The client is asking the server: "would you allow me to PUT a new representation to the resource at `/filestore/myfile.txt`?" The server makes its decision based on the current state of that resource, and the HTTP headers provided by the client. In this case the server would examine `Content-length` and decide whether it's willing to accept a 500 MB file.

If the answer is yes, the server sends a status code of 100 ("Continue"). Then the client is expected to resend the PUT request, omitting the `Expect` and including the 500-MB representation in the entity-body. The server has agreed to accept that representation.

If the answer is no, the server sends a status code of 417 ("Expectation Failed"). The answer might be no because the resource at `/filestore/myfile.txt` is write-protected, because the client didn't provide the proper authentication credentials, or because 500 MB is just too big. Whatever the reason, the initial look-before-you-leap request has saved the client from sending 500 MB of data only to have that data rejected. Both client and server are better off.

Of course, a client with a bad representation can lie about it in the headers just to get a status code of 100, but it won't do any good. The server won't accept a bad representation on the second request, any more than it would have on the first request.

Partial GET

Partial HTTP GET allows a client to fetch only a subset of a representation. It's usually used to resume interrupted downloads. Most web servers support partial GET for static content; so does Amazon's S3 service.

Example 8-6 is a bit of code that makes two partial HTTP GET requests to the same URI. The first request gets bytes 10 through 20, and the second request gets everything from byte 40,000 to the end.

Example 8-6. Make two partial HTTP GET requests

```
#!/usr/bin/ruby
# fetch-oreilly-partial.rb

require 'rubygems'
require 'rest-open-uri'
uri = 'http://www.oreilly.com/'

# Make a partial HTTP request and describe the response.
def partial_request(uri, range)
  begin
```

```
    response = open(uri, 'Range' => range)
  rescue OpenURI::HTTPError => e
    response = e.io
  end

  puts " Status code: #{response.status.inspect}"
  puts " Representation size: #{response.size}"
  puts " Content Range: #{response.meta['content-range']}"
  puts " Etag: #{response.meta['etag']}"
end

puts "First request:"
partial_request(uri, "bytes=10-20")

puts "Second request:"
partial_request(uri, "bytes=40000-")
```

When I run that code I see this for the first request:

```
First request:
 Status code: ["206", "Partial Content"]
 Representation size: 11
 Content Range: bytes 10-20/41123
 Etag: "7359b7-a0a3-45b5d90e"
```

Instead of 40 KB, the server has only sent me the 11 bytes I requested. Similarly for the second request:

```
Second request:
 Status code: ["206", "Partial Content"]
 Representation size: 1123
 Content Range: bytes 40000-41122/41123
 Etag: "7359b7-a0a3-45b5d90e"
```

Note that the Etag is the same in both cases. In fact, it's the same as it was back when I ran the conditional GET code back in Example 8-4. The value of Etag is always a value calculated for the whole document. That way I can combine conditional GET and partial GET.

Partial GET might seem like a way to let the client access subresources of a given resource. It's not. For one thing, a client can only address part of a representation by giving a byte range. That's not very useful unless your representation is a binary data structure. More importantly, if you've got subresources that someone might want to talk about separately from the containing resource, guess what: you've got more resources. A resource is anything that might be the target of a hypertext link. Give those subresources their own URIs.

Faking PUT and DELETE

Not all clients support HTTP PUT and DELETE. The action of an XHTML 4 form can only be GET or POST, and this has made a lot of people think that PUT and DELETE aren't real HTTP methods. Some firewalls block HTTP PUT and DELETE but not

POST. If the server supports it, a client can get around these limitations by tunneling PUT and DELETE requests through overloaded POST. There's no reason these techniques can't work with other HTTP actions like HEAD, but PUT and DELETE are the most common.

I recommend a tunneling technique pioneered by today's most RESTful web frameworks: include the "real" HTTP method in the query string. Ruby on Rails defines a hidden form field called _method which references the "real" HTTP method. If a client wants to delete the resource at /my/resource but can't make an HTTP DELETE request, it can make a POST request to /my/resource?_method=delete, or include _method=delete in the entity-body. Restlet uses the method variable for the same purpose.

The second way is to include the "real" HTTP action in the X-HTTP-Method-Override HTTP request header. Google's GData API recognizes this header. I recommend appending to the query string instead. A client that doesn't support PUT and DELETE is also likely to not support custom HTTP request headers.

The Trouble with Cookies

A web service that sends HTTP cookies violates the principle of statelessness. In fact, it usually violates statelessness twice. It moves application state onto the server even though it belongs on the client, and it stops clients from being in charge of their own application state.

The first problem is simple to explain. Lots of web frameworks use cookies to implement sessions. They set cookies that look like the Rails cookie I showed you back in Chapter 4:

```
Set-Cookie: _session_id=c1c934bbe6168dcb904d21a7f5644a2d; path=/
```

That long hexadecimal number is stored as client state, but it's not application state. It's a meaningless key into a session hash: a bunch of application state stored on the server. The client has no access to this application state, and doesn't even know what's being stored. The client can only send its cookie with every request and let the server look up whatever application state the server thinks is appropriate. This is a pain for the client, and it's no picnic for the server either. The server has to keep this application state all the time, not just while the client is making a request.

OK, so cookies shouldn't contain session IDs: that's just an excuse to keep application state on the server. What about cookies that really do contain application state? What if you serialize the actual session hash and send it as a cookie, instead of just sending a reference to a hash on the server?

This can be RESTful, but it's usually not. The cookie standard says that the client can get rid of a cookie when it expires, or when the client terminates. This is a pretty big restriction on the client's control over application state. If you make 10 web requests and suddenly the server sends you a cookie, you have to start sending this cookie with your future requests. You can't make those 10 precookie requests unless you quit and start over. To use a web browser analogy, your "Back" button is broken. You can't put the application in any of the states it was in before you got the cookie.

Realistically, no client follows the cookie standard that slavishly. Your web browser lets you choose which cookies to accept, and lets you destroy cookies without restarting your browser. But clients aren't generally allowed to *modify* the server's cookies, or even understand what they mean. If the client sends application state without knowing what it means, it doesn't really know what request it's making. The client is just a custodian for whatever state the server thinks it should send. Cookies are almost always a way for the server to force the client to do what it wants, without explaining why. It's more RESTful for the server to guide the client to new application states using hypermedia links and forms.

The only RESTful use of cookies is one where the client is in charge of the cookie value. The server can suggest values for a cookie using the `Set-Cookie` header, just like it can suggest links the client might want to follow, but the client chooses what cookie to send just as it chooses what links to follow. In some browser-based applications, cookies are created by the client and never sent to the server. The cookie is just a convenient container for application state, which makes its way to the server in representations and URIs. That's a very RESTful use of cookies.

Why Should a User Trust the HTTP Client?

HTTP authentication covers client-server authentication: the process by which the web service client proves to the server that it has some user's credentials. What HTTP doesn't cover is why the user should trust the web service client with its credentials. This isn't usually a problem on the human web, because we implicitly trust our web browsers (even when we shouldn't, like when there's spyware present on the system). If I'm using a web application on `example.com`, I'm comfortable supplying my `example.com` username and password.

But what if, behind the scenes, the web application on `example.com` is a client for eBay's web services? What if it asks me for my eBay authentication information so it can make hidden web service requests to `ebay.com`? Technically speaking, there's no difference between this application and a phishing site that pretends to be `ebay.com`, trying to trick me into giving it my eBay username and password.

The standalone client programs presented in this book authenticate by encoding the end user's username and password in the `Authorization` header. That's how many web services work. It works fine on the human web, because the HTTP clients are our own trusted web browsers. But when the HTTP client is an untrusted program, possibly running on a foreign computer, handing it your username and password is naive at best. There's another way. Some web services attack phishing by preventing their clients from handling usernames and passwords at all.

In this scenario, the end user uses her web browser (again, trusted implicitly) to get an *authorization token*. She gives this token to the web service client instead of giving her username and password, and the web service client sends this token in the `Authorization` header. The end user is basically delegating the ability to make web service calls as herself. If the web service client abuses that ability, its authorization token can be revoked without making the user change her password.

Google, eBay, Yahoo!, and Flickr all have user-client authorization systems of this type. Amazon's request signing, which I showed you in Chapter 3, fulfills the same function. There's no official standard, but all four systems are similar in concept, so I'll discuss them in general terms. When I need to show you specific URIs, I'll use Google's and Flickr's user-client authorization systems as examples.

Applications with a Web Interface

Let's start with the simplest case: a web application that needs to access a web service such as Google Calendar. It's the simplest case because the web application has the same user interface as the application that gives out authorization tokens: a web browser. When a web application needs to make a Google web service call, it serves an HTTP redirect that sends the end user to a URI at `google.com`. The URI might look something like this:

```
https://www.google.com/accounts/AuthSubRequest
 ?scope=http%3A%2F%2Fwww.google.com%2Fcalendar%2Ffeeds%2F
 &next=http%3A%2F%2Fcalendar.example.com%2Fmy
```

That URI has two other URIs embedded in it as query variables. The `scope` variable, with a value of *http://www.google.com/calendar/feeds/*, is the base URI of the web service we're trying to get an authorization token for. The `next` variable, value *http://calendar.example.com/my*, will be used when Google hands control of the end user's web browser back to the web application.

When the end user's browser hits this URI, Google serves a web page that tells the end user that `example.com` wants to access her Google Calendar account on her behalf. If the user decides she trusts `example.com`, she authenticates with Google. She never gives her Google username or password to `example.com`.

After authenticating the user, Google hands control back to the original web application by redirecting the end user's browser to a URI based on the value of the query variable `next` in the original request. In this example, `next` was *http://calendar.example.com/my*, so Google might redirect the end user to *http://calendar.example.com/my?token=IFM29SdTSpKL77INCn*. The new query variable `token` contains a one-time authorization token. The web application can put this token the `Authorization` header when it makes a web service call to Google Calendar:

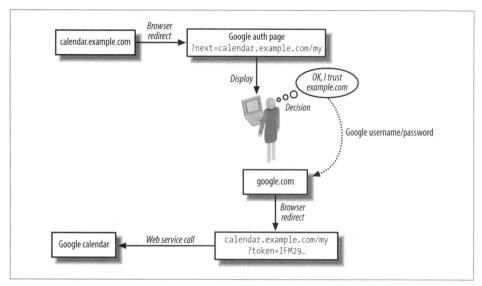

Figure 8-3. How a web application gets authorization to use Google Calendar

```
Authorization: AuthSub token="IFM29SdTSpKL77INCn"
```

Now the web application can make a web-service call as the end user, without actually knowing anything about the end user. The authentication information never leaves `google.com`, and the authorization token is only good for one request.

Those are the basics. Google's user-client authorization mechanism has lots of other features. A web service client can use the one-time authorization token to get a "session token" that's good for more than one request. A client can digitally sign requests, similarly to how I signed Amazon S3 requests back in Chapter 3. These features are different for every user-client authorization mechanism, so I won't dwell on them here. The point is this flow (shown graphically in Figure 8-3): control moves from the web application's domain to the web service's domain. The user authenticates with the web service, and authorizes the foreign web application to act on her behalf. Then control moves back to the web application's domain. Now the web app has an authorization token that it can use in the `Authorization` header. It can make web service calls without knowing the user's username and password.

Applications with No Web Interface

For applications that expose a web interface, browser-based user-client authorization makes sense. The user is already in her web browser, and the application she's using is running on a faraway server. She doesn't trust the web application with her password, but she does trust her own web browser. But what if the web service client is a standalone application running on the user's computer? What if it's got a GUI or command-line interface, but it's not a web browser?

There are two schools of thought on this. The first is that the end user should trust any client-side application as much as she trusts her web browser. Web applications run on an untrusted computer, but I control every web service client that runs on my computer. I can keep track of what the clients are doing and kill them if they get out of control.

If you as a service designer subscribe to this philosophy, there's no need to hide the end user's username and password from desktop clients. They're all just as trustworthy as the web browser. Google takes this attitude. Its authentication mechanism for client-side applications (*http://code.google.com/apis/accounts/AuthForInstalledApps.html*) is different from the web-based one I described above. Both systems are based on tokens, but desktop applications get an authorization token by gathering the user's username and password and "logging in" as them—not by redirecting the user's browser to a Google login page. This token serves little purpose from a security standpoint. The client needs a token to make web service requests, but it can only get one if it knows the user's username and password—a far more valuable prize.

If you don't like this, then you probably think the web browser is the only client an end user should trust with her username and password. This creates a problem for the programmer of a desktop client. Getting an authentication token means starting up a trusted client—the web browser—and getting the end user to visit a certain URI. For the Flickr service the URI might look like this:

```
http://flickr.com/services/auth/?perms=write&api_sig=925e1&api_key=1234&frob=abcd
```

The most important query variable here is `frob`. That's a predefined ID, obtained through an earlier web service call, and I'll use it in a moment. The first thing the end user sees is that her browser suddenly pops up and visits this URI, which shows a Flickr login screen. The end user gives her authentication credentials and authorizes the client with `api_key=1234` to act on her behalf. In the Google example above, the web service client was the web application at `example.com`. Here, the web service client is the application running on the end user's own desktop.

Without the `frob`, the desktop client at this point would have to cajole the end user to copy and paste the authorization token from the browser into the desktop client. But the client and the service agreed on a `frob` ahead of time, and the desktop client can use this `frob` to get the authorization token. The end user can close his browser at this point, and the desktop client makes a GET request to a URI that looks like this:

```
http://flickr.com/services/rest/?method=flickr.auth.getToken
&api_sig=1f348&api_key=1234&frob=abcd
```

The eBay and Flickr web services use a mechanism like this: what Flickr calls a frob, eBay calls an runame. The end user can authorize a standalone client to make web service requests on her behalf, without ever telling it her username or password. I've diagrammed the whole process in Figure 8-4.

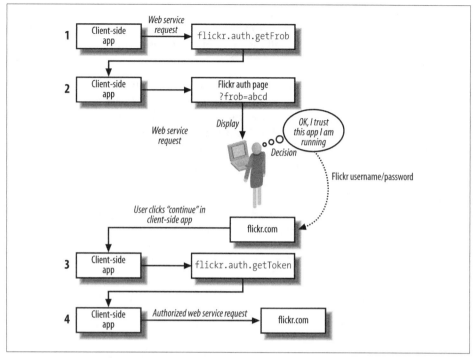

Figure 8-4. How a web application gets authorization to use Flickr

Some mobile devices have network connectivity but no web browser. A web service that thinks the only trusted client is a web browser must make special allowances for such devices, or live with the fact that it's locking them out.

What Problem Does this Solve?

Despite appearances, I've gone into very little detail: just enough to give you a feel for the two ways an end user might delegate her authority to make web service calls. Even in the high-level view it's a complex system, and it's worth asking what problem it actually solves. After all, the end user still has to type her username and password into a web form, and nothing prevents a malicious application writer from sending the browser to a fake authorization page instead of the real page. Phishers redirect people to fake sign-in pages all the time, and a lot of people fall for it. So what does this additional infrastructure really buy?

If you look at a bank or some other web site that's a common target of phishing attacks, you'll see a big warning somewhere that looks like this: "Never type in your mybank.com username and password unless you're using a web browser and visiting a URI that starts with *https://www.mybank.com/*." Common sense, right? It's not the most ironclad guarantee of security, but if you're careful you'll be all right. Yet most web services can't even provide this milquetoast cover. The standalone applications presented throughout this book take your service username and password as input. Can you trust them? If the web site at `example.com` wants to help you manage your del.icio.us bookmarks, you need to give it your del.icio.us username and password. Do you trust `example.com`?

The human web has a universal client: the web browser. It's not a big leap of faith to trust a single client that runs on your computer. The programmable web has different clients for different purposes. Should the end user trust all those clients? The mechanisms I described in this section let the end user use her web browser—which she already trusts—as a way of bestowing lesser levels of trust on other clients. If a client abuses the trust, it can be blocked from making future web service requests. These strategies don't eliminate phishing attacks, but they make it possible for a savvy end user to avoid them, and they allow service providers to issue warnings and disclaimers. Without these mechanisms, it's technically impossible for the end user to tell the difference between a legitimate client and a phishing site. They both take your password: the only difference is what they do with it.

## CHAPTER 9

The Building Blocks of Services

Throughout this book I've said that web services are based on three fundamental technologies: HTTP, URIs, and XML. But there are also lots of technologies that build on top of these. You can usually save yourself some work and broaden your audience by adopting these extra technologies: perhaps a domain-specific XML vocabulary, or a standard set of rules for exposing resources through HTTP's uniform interface. In this chapter I'll show you several technologies that can improve your web services. Some you're already familiar with and some will probably be new to you, but they're all interesting and powerful.

Representation Formats

What representation formats should your service actually send and receive? This is the question of how data should be represented, and it's an epic question. I have a few suggestions, which I present here in a rough order of precedence. My goal is to help you pick a format that says something about the semantics of your data, so you don't find yourself devising yet another one-off XML vocabulary that no one else will use.

I assume your clients can accept whatever representation format you serve. The known needs of your clients take priority over anything I can say here. If you know your data is being fed directly into Microsoft Excel, you ought to serve representations in Excel format or a compatible CSV format. My advice also does not extend to document formats that can only be understood by humans. If you're serving audio files, I've got nothing to say about which audio format you should choose. To a first approximation, a programmed client finds all audio files equally unintelligible.

XHTML

Media type: `application/xhtml+xml` The common `text/html` media type is deprecated for XHTML. It's also the only media type that Internet Explorer handles as HTML. If your service might be serving XHTML data directly to web browsers, you might want to serve it as `text/html`.

My number-one representation recommendation is the format I've been using in my own services throughout this book, and the one you're probably most familiar with. HTML drives the human web, and XHTML can drive the programmable web. The XHTML standard (*http://www.w3.org/TR/xhtml1/*) relies on the HTML standard to do most of the heavy lifting (*http://www.w3.org/TR/html401/*).

XHTML is HTML under a few restrictions that make every XHTML document also valid XML. If you know HTML, you know most of what there is to know about XHTML, but there are some syntactic differences, like how to present self-closing tags. The tag names and attributes are the same: XHTML is expressive in the same ways as HTML. Since the XHTML standard just points to the HTML standard and then adds some restrictions to it, I tend to refer to "HTML tags" and the like except where there really is a difference between XHTML and HTML.

I don't actually recommend HTML as a representation format, because it can't be reliably parsed with an XML parser. There are many excellent and liberal HTML parsers, though (I mentioned a few in Chapter 2), so your clients have options if you can't or don't want to serve XHTML. Right now, XHTML is a better choice if you expect a wide variety of clients to handle your data.

HTML can represent many common types of data: nested lists (tags like `ul` and `li`), key-value pairs (the `dl` tag and its children), and tabular data (the `table` tag and its children). It supports many different kinds of hypermedia. HTML does have its shortcomings: its hypermedia forms are limited, and won't fully support HTTP's uniform interface until HTML 5 is released.

HTML is also poor in semantic content. Its tag vocabulary is very computer-centric. It has special tags for representing computer code and output, but nothing for the other structured fruits of human endeavor, like poetry. One resource can link to another resource, and there are standard HTML attributes (`rel` and `rev`) for expressing the relationship between the linker and the linkee. But the HTML standard defines only 15 possible relationships between resources, including "alternate," "stylesteet," "next," "prev," and "glossary." See *http://www.w3.org/TR/html401/types.html#type-links* for a complete list.

Since HTML pages are representations of resources, and resources can be anything, these 15 relationships barely scratch the surface. HTML might be called upon to represent the relationship between any two things. Of course, I can come up with my own values for `rel` and `rev` to supplement the official 15, but if everyone does that confusion will reign: we'll all pick different values to represent the same relationships. If I link my web page to my wife's web page, should I specify my relationship to her as husband, spouse, or sweetheart? To a human it doesn't matter much, but to a computer program (the real client on the programmable web) it matters a lot. Similarly, HTML can easily represent a list, and there's a standard HTML attribute (`class`) for expressing what kind of list it is. But HTML doesn't say what kinds of lists there are.

This isn't HTML's fault, of course. HTML is supposed to be used by people who work in any field. But once you've chosen a field, everyone who works in that field should be able to agree on what kinds of lists there are, or what kinds of relationships can exist between resources. This is why people have started getting together and adding standard semantics to XHTML with microformats.

XHTML with Microformats

Media type: `application/xhtml+xml`

Microformats (*http://microformats.org/*) are lightweight standards that extend XHTML to give domain-specific semantics to HTML tags. Instead of reinventing data storage techniques like lists, microformats use existing HTML tags like `ol`, `span`, and `abbr`. The semantic content usually lives in custom values for the attributes of the tags, such as `class`, `rel`, and `rev`. Example 9-1 shows an example: someone's home telephone number represented in the microformat known as hCard.

Example 9-1. A telephone number represented in the hCard microformat

```
<span class="tel">
 <span class="type">home</span>:
 <span class="value">+1.415.555.1212</span>
</span>
```

Microformat adoption is growing, especially as more special-purpose devices get on the web. Any microformat document can be embedded in an XHTML page, because it is XHTML. A web service can serve an XHTML representation that contains microformat documents, along with links to other resources and forms for creating new ones. This document can be automatically parsed for its microformat data, or rendered for human consumption with a standard web browser.

As of the time of writing there were nine microformat specifications. The best-known is probably `rel-nofollow`, a standard value for the `rel` attribute invented by engineers at Google as a way of fighting comment spam on weblogs. Here's a complete list of official microformats:

hCalendar

A way of representing events on a calendar or planner. Based on the IETF iCalendar format.

hCard

A way of representing contact information for people and organizations. Based on the vCard standard defined in RFC 2426.

rel-license

A new value for the `rel` attribute, used when linking to the license terms for a XHTML document. For example:

```
<a href="http://creativecommons.org/licenses/by-nd/" rel="license">
 Made avaliable under a Creative Commons Attribution-NoDerivs license.
 </a>
```

That's standard XHTML. The only thing the microformat does is define a meaning for the string `license` when it shows up in the `rel` attribute.

rel-nofollow

A new value for the `rel` attribute, used when linking to URIs without neccessarily endorsing them.

rel-tag

A new value for the `rel` attribute, used to label a web page according to some external classification system.

VoteLinks

A new value for the `rev` attribute, an extension of the idea behind `rel-nofollow`. VoteLinks lets you say how you feel about the resource you're linking to by casting a "vote." For instance:

```
<a rev="vote-for" href="http://www.example.com">The best webpage ever.</a>
<a rev="vote-against" href="http://example.com/">
A shameless ripoff of www.example.com</a>
```

XFN

Stands for XHTML Friends Network. A new set of values for the `rel` attribute, for capturing the relationships between people. An XFN value for the `rel` attribute captures the relationship between this "person" resource and another such resource. To bring back the "Alice" and "Bob" resources from "Relationships Between Resources" in Chapter 8, an XHTML representation of Alice might include this link:

```
<a rel="spouse" href="Bob">Bob</a>
```

XMDP

Stands for XHTML Meta Data Profiles. A way of describing your custom values for XHTML attributes, using the XHTML tags for definition lists: `DL`, `DD`, and `DT`. This is a kind of meta-microformat: a microformat like `rel-tag` could itself be described with an XMDP document.

XOXO

Stands (sort of) for Extensible Open XHTML Outlines. Uses XHTML's list tags to represent outlines. There's nothing in XOXO that's not already in the XHTML standard, but declaring a document (or a list in a document) to be XOXO signals that a list is an outline, not just a random list.

Those are the official microformat standards; they should give you an idea of what microformats are for. As of the time of writing there were also about 10 microformat drafts and more than 50 discussions about possible new microformats. Here are some of the more interesting drafts:

geo

A way of marking up latitude and longitude on Earth. This would be useful in the mapping application I designed in Chapter 5. I didn't use it there because there's still a debate about how to represent latitude and longitude on other planetary bodies: extend geo or define different microformats for each body?

hAtom

A way of representing in XHTML the data Atom represents in XML.

hResume

A way of representing resumés.

hReview

A way of representing reviews, such as product reviews or restaurant reviews.

xFolk

A way of representing bookmarks. This would make an excellent representation format for the social bookmarking application in Chapter 7. I chose to use Atom instead because it was less code to show you.

You get the idea. The power of microformats is that they're based on HTML, the most widely-deployed markup format in existence. Because they're HTML, they can be embedded in web pages. Because they're also XML, they can be embedded in XML documents. They can be understood at various levels by human beings, specialized microformat processors, dumb HTML processors, and even dumber XML processors.

Even if the microformats wiki (*http://microformats.org/wiki/Main_Page*) shows no microformat standard or draft for your problem space, you might find an open discussion on the topic that helps you clarify your data structures. You can also create your own microformat (see "Ad Hoc XHTML" later in this chapter).

Atom

Media type: `application/atom+xml`

Atom is an XML vocabulary for describing lists of timestamped entries. The entries can be anything, but they usually contain pieces of human-authored text like you'd see on a weblog or a news site. Why should you use an Atom list instead of a regular XHTML list? Because Atom provides special tags for conveying the semantics of publishing: authors, contributors, languages, copyright information, titles, categories, and so on. (Of course, as I mentioned earlier, there's a microformat called hAtom that brings all of these semantics into XHTML.) Atom is a useful XML vocabulary because so many web services are, in the broad sense, ways of publishing information. What's more, there are a lot of web service clients that understand the semantics of Atom documents. If your web service is addressable and your resources expose Atom representations, you've immediately got a huge audience.

Atom lists are called *feeds*, and the items in the lists are called *entries*.

Some feeds are written in some version of RSS, a different XML vocabulary with similar semantics. All versions of RSS have the same basic
structure as Atom: a feed that contains a number of entries. There are a
number of variants of RSS but you shouldn't have to worry about it at
all. Today, every major tool for consuming feeds understands Atom.

These days, most weblogs and news sites expose a special resource whose representation is an Atom feed. The entries in the feed describe and link to other resources: weblog
entries or news stories published on the site. You, the client, can consume these resources with a feed reader or some other external program. In Chapter 7, I represented
lists of bookmarks as Atom feeds. Example 9-2 shows a simple Atom feed document.

Example 9-2. A simple Atom feed containing one entry

```
<?xml version="1.0" encoding="utf-8"?>
  <feed xmlns="http://www.w3.org/2005/Atom">
    <title>RESTful News</title>
    <link rel="alternate" href="http://example.com/RestfulNews" />
    <updated>2007-04-14T20:00:39Z</updated>
    <author><name>Leonard Richardson</name></author>
    <contributor><name>Sam Ruby</name></contributor>
    <id>urn:1c6627a0-8e3f-0129-b1a6-003065546f18</id>

    <entry>
      <title>New Resource Will Respond to PUT, City Says</title>
      <link rel="edit" href="http://example.com/RestfulNews/104" />
      <id>urn:239b2f40-8e3f-0129-b1a6-003065546f18</id>
      <updated>2007-04-14T20:00:39Z</updated>

      <summary>
      After long negotiations, city officials say the new resource
      being built in the town square will respond to PUT. Earlier
      criticism of the proposal focused on the city's plan to modify
      the resource through overloaded POST.
      </summary>
      <category scheme="http://www.example.com/categories/RestfulNews"
                term="local" label="Local news" />
    </entry>
  </feed>
```

In that example you can see some of the tags that convey the semantics of publishing:
author, title, link, summary, updated, and so on. The feed as a whole is a joint project:
it has an author tag and a contributor tag. It's also got a link tag that points to an
alternate URI for the underlying "feed" resource: the news site. The single entry has no
author tag, so it inherits author information from the feed. The entry does have its own
link tag, which points to *http://www.example.com/RestfulNews/104*. That URI identifies the entry as a resource in its own right. The entry also has a textual summary of the
story. To get the remainder, the client must presumably GET the entry's URI.

An Atom document is basically a directory of published resources. You can use Atom
to represent photo galleries, albums of music (maybe a link to the cover art plus one to

each track on the album), or lists of search results. Or you can omit the LINK tags and use Atom as a container for original content like status reports or incoming emails. Remember: the two reasons to use Atom are that it represents the semantics of publishing, and that a lot of existing clients can consume it.

If your application *almost* fits in with the Atom schema, but needs an extra tag or two, there's no problem. You can embed XML tags from other namespaces in an Atom feed. You can even define a custom namespace and embed its tags in your Atom feeds. This is the Atom equivalent of XHTML microformats: your Atom feeds can use conventions not defined in Atom, without becoming invalid. Clients that don't understand your tag will see a normal Atom feed with some extra mysterious data in it.

OpenSearch

OpenSearch (*http://www.opensearch.org/*) is one XML vocabulary that's commonly embedded in Atom documents. It's designed for representing lists of search results. The idea is that a service returns the results of a query as an Atom feed, with the individual results represented as Atom entries. But some aspects of a list of search results can't be represented in a stock Atom feed: the total number of results, for instance. So OpenSearch defines three new elements, in the opensearch namespace:[*]

totalResults
> The total number of results that matched the query.

itemsPerPage
> How many items are returned in a single "page" of search results.

startindex
> If all the search results are numbered from zero to totalResults, then the first result in this feed document is entry number startindex. When combined with itemsPerPage you can use this to figure out what "page" of results you're on.

SVG

Media type: image/svg+xml

Most graphic formats are just ways of laying pixels out on the screen. The underlying content is opaque to a computer: it takes a skilled human to modify a graphic or reuse part of one in another. Scalable Vector Graphics is an XML vocabulary that makes it possible for programs to understand and manipulate graphics. It describes graphics in terms of primitives like shapes, text, colors, and effects.

It would be a waste of time to represent a photograph in SVG, but using it to represent a graph, a diagram, or a set of relationships gives a lot of power to the client. SVG images can be scaled to arbitrary size without losing any detail. SVG diagrams can be edited

---

[*] OpenSearch also defines a simple control flow: a special kind of resource called a "description document." I'm not covering OpenSearch description documents in this book, mainly for space reasons.

or rearranged, and bits of them can be seamlessly snipped out and incorporated into other graphics. In short, SVG makes graphic documents work like other sorts of documents. Web browsers are starting to get support for SVG: newer versions of Firefox support it natively.

Form-Encoded Key-Value Pairs

Media type: `application/x-www-form-urlencoded`

I covered this simple format in Chapter 6. This format is mainly used in representations the client sends to the server. A filled-out HTML form is represented in this format by default, and it's an easy format for an Ajax application to construct. But a service can also use this format in the representations it sends. If you're thinking of serving comma-separated values or RFC 822-style key-value pairs, try form-encoded values instead. Form-encoding takes care of the tricky cases, and your clients are more likely to have a library that can decode the document.

JSON

Media type: `application/json`

JavaScript Object Notation is a serialization format for general data structures. It's much more lightweight and readable than an equivalent XML document, so I recommend it for most cases when you're transporting a serialized data structure rather than a hypermedia document.

I introduced JSON in "JSON Parsers: Handling Serialized Data" in Chapter 2, and showed a simple JSON document in Example 2-11. Example 9-3 shows a more complex JSON document: a hash of lists.

Example 9-3. A complex data type in JSON format
```
{"a":["b","c"], "1":[2,3]}
```

As I show in Chapter 11, JSON has special advantages when it comes to Ajax applications. It's useful for any kind of application, though. If your data structures are more complex than key-value pairs, or you're thinking of defining an ad hoc XML format, you might find it easier to define a JSON structure of nested hashes and arrays.

RDF and RDFa

The Resource Description Framework (*http://www.w3.org/RDF/*) is a way of representing knowledge about resources. Resource here means the same thing as in Resource-Oriented-Architecture: a resource is anything important enough to have a URI. In RDF, though, the URIs might not be `http:` URIs. Abstract URI schemas like `isbn:` (for books) and `urn:` (for just about anything) are common. Example 9-4 is a simple RDF assertion, which claims that the title of this book is *RESTful Web Services*.

Example 9-4. An RDF assertion

```
<span about="isbn:9780596529260" property="dc:title">
RESTful Web Services
</span>
```

There are three parts to an RDF assertion, or *triple*, as they're called. There's the *subject*, a resource identifier: in this case, `isbn:9780596529260`. There's the *predicate*, which identifies a property of the resource: in this case, `dc:title`. Finally there's the *object*, which is the value of the property: in this case, "RESTful Web Services." The assertion as a whole reads: "The book with ISBN 9780596529260 has a title of 'RESTful Web Services.'"

I didn't make up the `isbn:` URI space: it's a standard way of addressing books as resources. I didn't make up the `dc:title` predicate, either. That comes from the Dublin Core Metadata Initiative (*http://www.dublincore.org/documents/dcmi-terms/*). DCMI defines a set of useful predicates that apply to published works like books and weblogs. An automated client that understands the Dublin Core can scan RDF documents that use those terms, evaluate the assertions they contain, and even make logical deductions about the data.

Example 9-4 looks a lot like an XHTML snippet, because that's what it is. There are a couple ways of representing RDF assertions, and I've chosen to show you RDFa (*http://rdfa.info/about*), a microformat-like standard for embedding RDF in XHTML. RDF/XML is a more popular RDF representation format, but I think it makes RDF look more complicated than it is, and it's difficult to integrate RDF/XML documents into the web. RDF/A documents can go into XHTML files, just like microformat documents. However, since RDFa takes some ideas from the unreleased XHTML 2 standard, a document that includes it won't be valid XHTML for a while. A third way of representing RDF assertions is eRDF (*http://research.talis.com/2005/erdf/wiki*), which results in valid XHTML.

RDF in its generic form is the basis for the W3C's Semantic Web project. On the human web, there are no standards for how we talk about the resources we link to. We describe resources in human language that's difficult or impossible for machines to understand. RDF is a way of constraining human speech so that we talk about resources using a standard vocabulary—not one that machines "understand" natively, but one they can be programmed to understand. A computer program doesn't understand the Dublin Core's "dc:title" any more than it understands "title." But if everyone agrees to use "dc:title," we can program standard clients to reason about the Dublin Core in consistent ways.

Here's the thing: I think microformats do a good job of adding semantics to the web we already have, and they add less complexity than RDF's general subject-predicate-object form. I recommend using RDF only when you want interoperability with existing RDF processors, or are treating RDF as a general-purpose microformat for representing assertions about resources.

One very popular use of RDF is FOAF (*http://www.foaf-project.org/*), a way of representing information about human beings and the relationships between them.

Framework-Specific Serialization Formats

Media type: `application/xml`

I'm talking here about informal XML vocabularies used by frameworks like Ruby's ActiveRecord and Python's Django to serialize database objects as XML. I gave an example back in Example 7-4. It's a simple data structure: a hash or a list of hashes.

These representation formats are very convenient if you happen to be writing a service that gives you access to one. In Rails, you can just call **to_xml** on an ActiveRecord object or a list of such objects. The Rails serialization format is also useful if you're not using Rails, but you want your service to be usable by ActiveResource clients. Otherwise, I don't really recommend these formats, unless you're just trying to get something up and running quickly (as I am in Chapters 7 and 12). The major downside of these formats is that they look like documents, but they're really just serialized data structures. They never contain hypermedia links or forms.

Ad Hoc XHTML

Media type: `application/xhtml+xml`

If none of the work that's already been done fits your problem space... well, first, think again. Just as you should think again before deciding you can't fit your resources into HTTP's uniform interface. If you think your resources can't be represented by stock HTML or Atom or RDF or JSON, there's a good chance you haven't looked at the problem in the right way.

But it's quite possible that your resources won't fit any of the representation formats I've mentioned so far. Or maybe you can represent most of your resource state with XHTML plus some well-chosen microformats, but there's still something missing. The next step is to consider creating your own microformat.

The high-impact way of creating a microformat is to go through the microformat process (*http://microformats.org/wiki/process*), hammer it out with other microformat enthusiasts, and get it published as an official microformat. This is most appropriate when lots of people are trying to represent the same kind of data. Ideally, you're in a situation where the human web is littered with ad hoc HTML representations of the data, and where there are already a couple of big standards that can serve as a model for a more agile microformat. This is how the hCard and hCalendar microformats were developed. There were many people trying to put contact information and upcoming events on the human web, and preexisting standards (vCard and iCalendar) to steal ideas from. The representation of "places on a map" that I devised in Chapter 5 might be a starting point for an official microformat. There are lots of mapping sites on the human web, and lots of heavyweight standards for representing GIS data. If I wanted to build a microformat, I'd have a lot of ideas to work from.

The low-impact way of creating a microformat is to add semantic content to the XHTML you were going to write anyway. This is suitable for representation formats that no one else is likely to use, or as a starting point so you can get a real web service running while you're going through the microformat process. The representation of the list of planets from Chapter 5 works better as an ad hoc set of semantics than as an official microformat. All it's doing is saying that one particular list is a list of planets.

The microformat design patterns (*http://microformats.org/wiki/ Main_Page#Design_Patterns*) and naming principles (*http://microformats.org/wiki/ naming-principles*) give a set of sensible general rules for adding semantics to HTML. Their advice is useful even if you're not trying to create an official microformat. The semantics you choose for your "micromicroformat" won't be standardized, but you can present them in a standard way: the way microformats do it. Here are some of the more useful patterns.

- If there's an HTML tag that conveys the semantics you want, use it. To represent a set of key-value pairs, use the dl tag. To represent a list, use one of the list tags. If nothing fits, use the span or div tag.

- Give a tag additional semantics by specifying its class attribute. This is especially important for span and div, which have no real meaning on their own.

- Use the rel attribute in a link to specify another resource's relationship to this one. Use the rev attribute to specify this page's relationship to another one. If the relationship is symmetric, use rel. See "Hypermedia Technologies" later in this chapter for more on this.

- Consider providing an XMDP file that describes your custom values for class, rel, and rev.

Other XML Standards and Ad Hoc Vocabularies

Media type: application/xml

In addition to XHTML, Atom, and SVG, there are a lot of specialized XML vocabularies I haven't covered: MathML, OpenDocument, Chemical Markup Language, and so on. There are also specialized vocabularies you can use in RDF assertions, like Dublin Core and FOAF. A web service might serve any of these vocabularies as standalone representations, embed them into Atom feeds, or even wrap them in SOAP envelopes. If none of these work for you, you can define a custom XML vocabulary to represent your resource state, or maybe the parts that Atom doesn't cover.

Although I've presented this as the last resort, that's certainly not the common view. People come up with custom XML vocabularies all the time: that's how there got to be so many of them. Almost every real web service mentioned in this book exposes its representations in a custom XML vocabulary. Amazon S3, Yahoo!'s search APs, and the del.icio.us API all serve representations that use custom XML vocabularies, even though they could easily serve Atom or XHTML and reuse an existing vocabulary.

Part of this is tech culture. The microformats idea is fairly new, and a custom XML vocabulary still looks more "official." But this is an illusion. Unless you provide a schema definition for your vocabulary, your custom tags have exactly the same status as a custom value for the HTML "class" attribute. Even a definition does nothing but codify the vocabulary you made up: it doesn't confer any legitimacy. Legitimacy can only come "from the consent of the governed": from other people adopting your vocabulary.

That said, there is a space for custom XML vocabularies. It's usually easy to use XHTML instead of creating your own XML tags, but it's not so easy when you need tags with a lot of custom attributes. In that situation, a custom XML vocabulary makes sense. All I ask is that you seriously think about whether you really need to define a new XML vocabulary for a given problem. It's possible that in the future, people will err in the opposite direction, and create ad hoc microformats when they shouldn't. Then I'll urge caution before creating a microformat. But right now, the problem is too many ad hoc XML vocabularies.

Encoding Issues

It's a global world (I actually heard someone say that once), and any service you expose must deal with the products of people who speak different languages from you and use different writing systems. You don't have to understand all of these languages, but to handle multilingual data without mangling it, you do need to know something about character encodings: the conventions that let us represent human-readable text as strings of bytes.

Every text file you've ever created has some character encoding, even though you probably never made a decision about which encoding to use (it's usually a system property). In the United States the encoding is usually UTF-8, US-ASCII, or Windows-1252. In western Europe it might also be ISO 8859-1. The default for HTML on the web is ISO 8859-1, which is almost but not quite the same as Windows-1252. Japanese documents are commonly encoded with EUC-JP, Shift_JIS, or UTF-8. If you're curious about what character encodings are used in different places, most web browsers list the encodings they understand. My web browser supports five different encodings for simplified Chinese, five for Hebrew, nine for the Cyrillic alphabet, and so on. Most of these encodings are mutually incompatible, even when they encode the same language. It's insane!

Fortunately there is a way out of this confusion. We as a species have come up with Unicode, a way of representing every human writing system. Unicode isn't a character encoding, but there are two good encodings for it: UTF-8 (more efficient for alphabetic languages like English) and UTF-16 (more efficient for logographic languages like Japanese). Either of these encodings can handle text written in any combination of human languages. The best single decision you can make when handling multilingual data is to *keep all of your data in one of these encodings*: probably UTF-8 unless you live or do a lot of business in east Asia, then maybe UTF-16 with a byte-order mark.

This might be as simple as making a decision when you start the project, or you may have to convert an existing database. You might have to install an encoding converter to work on incoming data, or write encoding detection code. The Universal Encoding Detector (*http://chardet.feedparser.org/*) is an excellent autodetection library for Python. It's got a Ruby port, available as the `chardet` gem. It might be easy or difficult. But once you're keeping all of this data in one of the Unicode encodings, most of your problems will be over. When your clients send you data in a weird encoding, you'll be able to convert it to your chosen UTF-* encoding. If they send data that specifies no format at all, you'll be able to guess its encoding and convert it, or reject it as unintelligible.

The other half of the equation is communicating with your clients: how do you tell them which encoding you're using in your outgoing representations? Well, XML lets you specify a character encoding on the very first line:

```
<?xml version="1.0" encoding="UTF-8"?>
```

All but one of my recommended representation formats is based on XML, so that solves most of the problem. But there is an encoding problem with that one outlier, and there's a further problem in the relationship between XML and HTTP.

XML and HTTP: Battle of the encodings

An XML document can and should define a character encoding in its first line, so that the client will know how to interpret the document. An HTTP response can and should specify a value for the `Content-Type` response header, so that the client knows it's being given an XML document and not some other kind. But the `Content-type` can also specify a document character encoding with "charset," and this encoding might conflict with what it actually says in the document.

```
Content-Type: application/xml; charset="ebcdic-fr-297+euro"

<?xml version="1.0" encoding="UTF-8"?>
```

Who wins? Surprisingly, HTTP's character encoding takes precedence over the encoding in the document itself.[†] If the document says "UTF-8" and `Content-Type` says "ebcdic-fr-297+euro," then extended French EBCDIC it is. Almost no one expects this kind of surprise, and most programmers write code first and check the RFCs later. The result is that the character encoding, as specified in `Content-Type`, tends to be unreliable. Some servers claim everything they serve is UTF-8, even though the actual documents say otherwise.

[†] This is specified, and argued for, in RFC 3023.

When serving XML documents, I don't recommend going out of your way to send a character encoding as part of Content-type. You can do it if you're absolutely sure you've got the right encoding, but it won't do much good. What's really important is that you specify a document encoding. (Technically you can do without a document encoding if you're using UTF-8, or if you're using UTF-16 with a byte-order mark. But if you have that much control over the data, you should be able to specify a document encoding.) If you're writing a web service client, be aware that any character encoding specified in Content-Type may be incorrect. Use common sense to decide which encoding declaration to believe, rather than relying on a counterintuitive rule from an RFC a lot of people haven't read.

Another note: when you serve XML documents, you should serve them with a media type of application/xml, not text/xml. If you serve a document as text/xml with no charset, the correct client behavior is to totally ignore the encoding specified in the XML document and interpret the XML document as US-ASCII.[‡] Avoid these complications altogether by always serving XML as application/xml, and always specifying an encoding in the first line of the XML documents you generate.

The character encoding of a JSON document

I didn't mention plain text in my list of recommended representation formats, mostly because plain text is not a structured format, but also because the lack of structure means there's no way to specify the character encoding of "plain text." JSON is a way of structuring plain text, but it doesn't solve the character encoding problem. Fortunately, you don't have to solve it yourself: just follow the standard convention.

RFC 4627 states that a JSON file must contain Unicode characters, encoded in one of the UTF-* encodings. Practically, this means either UTF-8, or UTF-16 with a byte-order mark. Plain US-ASCII will also work, since ASCII text happens to be valid UTF-8. Given this restriction, a client can determine the character encoding of a JSON document by looking at the first four bytes (the details are in RFC 4627), and there's no need to specify an explicit encoding. You should follow this convention whenever you serve plain text, not just JSON.

Prepackaged Control Flows

Not only does HTTP have a uniform interface, it has a standard set of response codes —possible ways a request can turn out. Though resources can be anything at all, they usually fall into a few broad categories: database tables and their rows, publications and the articles they publish, and so on. When you know what sort of resource a service

---

[‡] Again, according to RFC 3023, which few developers have read. For a lucid explanation of these problems, see Mark Pilgrim's article "XML on the Web Has Failed" (*http://www.xml.com/pub/a/2004/07/21/dive.html*).

exposes, you can often anticipate the possible responses to an HTTP request without knowing too much about the resource.

In one sense the standard HTTP response codes (see Appendix B) are just a suggested control flow: a set of instructions about what to do when you get certain kinds of requests. But that's pretty vague advice, and we can do better. Here I present several prepackaged control flows: patterns that bring together advice about resource design, representation formats, and response codes to help you design real-world services.

General Rules

These snippets of control flow can be applied to almost any service. I can make very general statements about them because they have nothing to do with the actual nature of your resources. All I'm doing here is picking out a few important HTTP status codes and telling you when to use them.

You should be able to implement these rules as common code that runs before your normal request handling. In Example 7-11 I implemented most of them as Rails filters that run before certain actions, or as Ruby methods that short-circuit a request unless a certain condition is met.

If the client tries to do something without providing the correct authorization, send a response code of 401 ("Unauthorized") along with instructions for correctly formatting the `Authorization` header.

If the client tries to access a URI that doesn't correspond to any existing resource, send a response code of 404 ("Not Found"). The only possible exception is when the client is trying to PUT a new resource to that URI.

If the client tries to use a part of the uniform interface that a resource doesn't support, send a response code of 405 ("Method Not Allowed"). This is the proper response when the client tries to DELETE a read-only resource.

Database-Backed Control Flow

In many web services there's a strong connection between a resource and something in a SQL database: a row in the database, a table, or the database as a whole. These services are so common that entire frameworks like Rails are oriented to making them easy to write. Since these services are similar in design, it makes sense that their control flows should also be similar.

For instance, if an incoming request contains a nonsensical representation, the proper response is almost certainly 415 ("Unsupported Media Type") or 400 ("Bad Request"). It's up to the application to decide which representations make sense, but the HTTP standard is pretty strict about the possible responses to "nonsensical representation."

With this in mind, I've devised a standard control flow for the uniform interface in a database-backed application. It runs on top of the general rules I mentioned in the previous section. I used this control flow in the controller code throughout Chapter 7. Indeed, if you look at the code in that chapter you'll see that I implemented the same ideas multiple times. There's space in the REST ecosystem for a higher-level framework that implements this control flow, or some improved version of it.

GET

If the resource can be identified, send a representation along with a response code of 200 ("OK"). Be sure to support conditional GET!

PUT

If the resource already exists, parse the representation and turn it into a series of changes to the state of this resource. If the changes would leave the resource in an incomplete or inconsistent state, send a response code of 400 ("Bad Request").

If the changes would cause the resource state to conflict with some other resource, send a response code of 409 ("Conflict"). My social bookmarking service sends a response code of 409 if you try to change your username to a name that's already taken.

If there are no problems with the proposed changes, apply them to the existing resource. If the changes in resource state mean that the resource is now available at a different URI, send a response code of 301 ("Moved Permanently") and include the new URI in the `Location` header. Otherwise, send a response code of 200 ("OK"). Requests to the old URI should now result in a response code of 310 ("Moved Permanently"), 404 ("Not Found"), or 410 ("Gone").

There are two ways to handle a PUT request to a URI that doesn't correspond to any resource. You can return a status code of 404 ("Not Found"), or you can create a resource at that URI. If you want to create a new resource, parse the representation and use it to form the initial resource state. Send a response code of 201 ("Created"). If there's not enough information to create a new resource, send a response code of 400 ("Bad Request").

POST for creating a new resource

Parse the representation, pick an appropriate URI, and create a new resource there. Send a response code of 201 ("Created") and include the URI of the new resource in the `Location` header. If there's not enough information provided to create the resource, send a response code of 400 ("Bad Request"). If the provided resource state would conflict with some existing resource, send a response code of 409 ("Conflict"), and include a `Location` header that points to the problematic resource.

POST for appending to a resource

Parse the representation. If it doesn't make sense, send a response code of 400 ("Bad Request"). Otherwise, modify the resource state so that it incorporates the information in the representation. Send a response code of 200 ("OK").

DELETE

Send a response code of 200 ("OK").

The Atom Publishing Protocol

Earlier I described Atom as an XML vocabulary that describes the semantics of publishing: authors, summaries, categories, and so on. The Atom Publishing Protocol (*http://tools.ietf.org/wg/atompub/*) (APP) defines a set of resources that capture the *process* of publishing: posting a story to a site, editing it, assigning it to a category, deleting it, and so on.

The obvious applications for the APP are those for Atom and online publishing in general: weblogs, photo albums, content management systems, and the like. The APP defines four kinds of resources, specifies some of their behavior under the uniform interface, and defines the representation documents they should accept and serve. It says nothing about URI design or what data should go into the documents: that's up to the individual application.

The APP takes HTTP's uniform interface and puts a higher-level uniform interface on top of it. Many kinds of applications can conform to the APP, and a generic APP client should be able to access all of them. Specific applications can extend the APP by exposing additional resources, or making the APP resources expose more of HTTP's uniform interface, but they should all support the minimal features mentioned in the APP standard.

The ultimate end of the APP is to serve Atom documents to the end user. Of course, the Atom documents are just the representations of underlying resources. The APP defines what those resources are. It defines two resources that correspond to Atom documents, and two that help the client find and modify APP resources.

Collections

An APP *collection* is a resource whose representation is an Atom feed. The document in Example 9-2 has everything it takes to be a representation of an Atom collection. There's no neccessary difference between an Atom feed you subscribe to in your feed reader, and an Atom feed that you manipulate with an APP client. A collection is just a list or grouping of pieces of data: what the APP calls *members*. The APP is heavily oriented toward manipulating "collection" type resources.

The APP defines a collection's response to GET and POST requests. GET returns a representation: the Atom feed. POST adds a new member to the collection, which (usually) shows up as a new entry in the feed. Maybe you can also DELETE a collection, or modify its settings with a PUT request. The APP doesn't cover that part: it's up to your application.

Members

An APP collection is a collection *of* members. A member corresponds roughly to an entry in an Atom feed: a weblog entry, a news article, or a bookmark. But a member can also be a picture, song, movie, or Word document: a binary format that can't be represented in XML as part of an Atom document.

A client creates a member inside a collection by POSTing a representation of the member to the collection URI. This pattern should be familiar to you by now: the member is created as a subordinate resource of the collection. The server assigns the new member a URI. The response to the POST request has a response code of 201 ("Created"), and a Location header that lets the client know where to find the new resource.

Example 9-5 shows an Atom entry document: a representation of a member. This is the same sort of entry tag I showed you in Example 9-2, presented as a standalone XML document. POSTing this document to a collection creates a new member, which starts showing up as a child of the collection's feed tag. A document like this one might be how the entry tag in Example 9-2 got where it is today.

Example 9-5. A sample Atom entry document, suitable for POSTing to a collection

```
<?xml version="1.0" encoding="utf-8"?>
<entry>
 <title>New Resource Will Respond to PUT, City Says</title>
 <summary>
   After long negotiations, city officials say the new resource
   being built in the town square will respond to PUT. Earlier
   criticism of the proposal focused on the city's plan to modify the
   resource through overloaded POST.
 </summary>
 <category scheme="http://www.example.com/categories/RestfulNews"
          term="local" label="Local news" />
</entry>
```

Service document

This vaguely-named type of resource is just a grouping of collections. A typical move is to serve a single service document, listing all of your collections, as your service's "home page." A service document is an XML document written using a particular vocabulary, and its media type is application/atomserv+xml (see Example 9-6).

Example 9-6 shows a representation of a typical service document. It describes three collections. One of them is a weblog called "RESTful news," which accepts a POST request if the representation is an Atom entry document like the one in Example 9-5.

The other two are personal photo albums, which accept a POST request if the representation is an image file.

Example 9-6. A representation of a service document that describes three collections

```
<?xml version="1.0" encoding='utf-8'?>
<service xmlns="http://purl.org/atom/app#"
         xmlns:atom="http://www.w3.org/2005/Atom">
  <workspace>
    <atom:title>Weblogs</atom:title>
    <collection href="http://www.example.com/RestfulNews">
      <atom:title>RESTful News</atom:title>
      <categories href="http://www.example.com/categories/RestfulNews" />
    </collection>
  </workspace>

  <workspace>
    <atom:title>Photo galleries</atom:title>
    <collection
        href="http://www.example.com/samruby/photos" >
      <atom:title>Sam's photos</atom:title>
      <accept>image/*</accept>
      <categories href="http://www.example.com/categories/samruby-photo" />
    </collection>

    <collection
        href="http://www.example.com/leonardr/photos" >
      <atom:title>Leonard's photos</atom:title>
      <accept>image/*</accept>
      <categories href="http://www.example.com/categories/leonardr-photo" />
    </collection>
  </workspace>
</service>
```

How do I know what kind of POST requests a collection will accept? From the accept tags. The accept tag works something like the HTTP Accept header, only in reverse. The Accept header is usually sent by the client with a GET request, to tell the server which representation formats the client understands. The accept tag is the APP server's way of telling the client which incoming representations a collection will accept as part of a POST request that creates a new member.

My two photo gallery collections specify an accept of image/*. Those collections will only accept POST requests where the representation is an image. On the other hand, the RESTful News weblog doesn't specify an accept tag at all. The APP default is to assume that a collection only accepts POST requests when the representation is an Atom entry document (like the one in Example 9-5). The accept tag defines what the collections are for: the weblog is for textual data, and the photo collections are for images.

The other important thing about a service document is the categories tag, which links to a "category document" resource. The category document says what categories are allowed.

The APP doesn't say much about service documents. It specifies their representation format, and says that they must serve a representation in response to GET. It doesn't specify how service documents get on the server in the first place. If you write an APP application you can hardcode your service documents in advance, or you can make it possible to create new ones by POSTing to some new resource not covered by the APP. You can expose them as static files, or you can make them respond to PUT and DE-LETE. It's up to you.

 As you can see from Example 9-6, a service document's representation doesn't just describe collections: it groups collections into *workspaces*. When I wrote that representation I put the weblog in a workspace of its own, and grouped the photo galleries into a second workspace. The APP standard devotes some time to workspaces, but I'm going to pass over them, because the APP doesn't define workspaces *as resources*. They don't have their own URIs, and they only exist as elements in the representation of a service document. You can expose workspaces as resources if you want. The APP doesn't prohibit it, but it doesn't tell you how to do it, either.

Category documents

APP members (which correspond to Atom elements) can be put into categories. In Chapter 7, I represented a bookmark's tags with Atom categories. The Atom entry described in Example 9-5 put the entry into a category called "local." Where did that category come from? Who says which categories exist for a given collection? This is the last big question the APP answers.

The Atom entry document in Example 9-5 gave its category a "scheme" of *http://www.example.com/categories/RestfulNews*. The representation of the RESTful News collection, in the service document, gave that same URI in its `categories` tag. That URI points to the final APP resource: a category document (see Example 9-7). A category document lists the category vocabulary for a particular APP collection. Its media type is `application/atomcat+xml`.

Example 9-7 shows a representation of the category document for the collection "RESTful News." This category document defines three categories: "local," "international," and "lighterside," which can be referenced in Atom `entry` entities like the one in Example 9-5.

Example 9-7. A representation of a category document

```
<?xml version="1.0" ?>
<app:categories
    xmlns:app="http://purl.org/atom/app#"
    xmlns="http://www.w3.org/2005/Atom"
    scheme="http://www.example.com/categories/RestfulNews"
    fixed="no">
  <category term="local" label="Local news"/>
```

```
<category term="international" label="International news"/>
<category term="lighterside" label="The lighter side of REST"/>
</app:categories>
```

The scheme is not fixed, meaning that it's OK to publish members to the collection even if they belong to categories not listed in this document. This document might be used in an end-user application to show a selectable list of categories for a new "RESTful news" story.

As with service documents, the APP defines the representation format for a category document, but says nothing about how category documents are created, modified, or destroyed. It only defines GET on the category document resource. Any other operations (like automatically modifying the category document when someone files an entry under a new category) are up to you to define.

Binary documents as APP members

There's one important wrinkle I've glossed over. It has to do with the "photo gallery" collections I described in Example 9-6. I said earlier that a client can create a new member in a photo gallery by POSTing an image file to the collection. But an image file can't go into an Atom feed: it's a binary document. What exactly happens when a client POSTs a binary document to an APP collection? What's in those photo galleries, really?

Remember that a resource can have more than one representation. Each photo I upload to a photo collection has two representations. One representation is the binary photo, and the other is an XML document containing metadata. The XML document is an Atom entry, the same as the news item in Example 9-5, and that's the data that shows up in the Atom feed.

Here's an example. I POST a JPEG file to my "photo gallery" collection, like so:

```
POST /leonardr/photos HTTP/1.1
Host: www.example.com
Content-type: image/jpeg
Content-length: 62811
Slug: A picture of my guinea pig

[JPEG file goes here]
```

The Slug is a custom HTTP header defined by the APP, which lets me specify a title for the picture while uploading it. The slug can show up in several pieces of resource state, as you'll see in a bit.

The HTTP response comes back as I described it in "Members" earlier in this chapter. The response code is 201 and the Location header gives me the URI of the newly created APP member.

```
201 Created
Location: http://www.example.com/leonardr/photos/my-guinea-pig.atom
```

But what's at the other end of the URI? Not the JPEG file I uploaded, but an Atom entry document describing and linking to that file:

```
<![CDATA[ <?xml version="1.0" encoding="utf-8"?>
<entry>
  <title>A picture of my guinea pig</title>
  <updated>2007-01-24T11:52:29Z</updated>
  <id>urn:f1ef2e50-8ec8-0129-b1a7-003065546f18</id>
  <summary></summary>
  <link rel="edit-media" type="image/jpeg"
      href="http://www.example.com/leonardr/photos/my-guinea-pig.jpg" />
</entry>
```

The actual JPEG I uploaded is at the other end of that `link`. I can GET it, of course, and I can PUT to it to overwrite it with another image. My POST created a new "member" resource, and my JPEG is a representation of some of its resource state. But there's also this other representation of resource state: the metadata. These other elements of resource state include:

- The title, which I chose (the server decided to use my `Slug` as the title) and can change later.
- The summary, which starts out blank but I can change.
- The "last update" time, which I sort of chose but can't change arbitrarily.
- The URI to the image representation, which the server chose for me based on my `Slug`.
- The unique ID, which the server chose without consulting me at all.

This metadata document can be included in an Atom feed: I'll see it in the representation of the "photo gallery" collection. I can also modify this document and PUT it back to *http://www.example.com/leonardr/photos/20070124-1.atom* to change the resource state. I can specify myself as the `author`, add categories, change the title, and so on. If I get tired of having this member in the collection, I can delete it by sending a DELETE request to either of its URIs.

That's how the APP handles photos and other binary data as collection members. It splits the representation of the resource into two parts: the binary part that can't go into an Atom feed and the metadata part that can. This works because the metadata of publishing (categories, summary, and so on) applies to photos and movies just as easily as to news articles and weblog entries.

 If you read the APP standard (which you should, since this section doesn't cover everything), you'll see that it describes this behavior in terms of two different resources: a "Media Link Entry," whose representation is an Atom document, and a "Media Resource," whose representation is a binary file. I've described one resource that has two representations. The difference is purely philosophical and has no effect on the actual HTTP requests and responses.

Summary

That's a fairly involved workflow, and I haven't even covered everything that the APP specifies, but the APP is just a well-thought-out way of handling a common web service problem: the list/feed/collection that keeps having items/elements/members added to it. If your problem fits this domain, it's easier to use the APP design—and get the benefits of existing client support—than to reinvent something similar (see Table 9-1).

Table 9-1. APP resources and their methods

	GET	POST	PUT	DELETE
Service document	Return a representation (XML)	Undefined	Undefined	Undefined
Category document	Return a representation (XML)	Undefined	Undefined	Undefined
Collection	Return a representation (Atom feed)	Create a new member	Undefined	Undefined
Member	Return the representation identified by this URI. (This is usually an Atom entry document, but it might be a binary file.)	Undefined	Update the representation identified by this URI	Delete the member

GData

I said earlier that the Atom Publishing Protocol defines only a few resources and only a few operations on those resources. It leaves a lot of space open for extension. One extension is Google's GData (*http://code.google.com/apis/gdata*), which adds a new kind of resource and some extras like an authorization mechanism. As of the time of writing, the Google properties Blogger, Google Calendar, Google Code Search, and Google Spreadsheets all expose RESTful web service interfaces. In fact, all four expose the *same* interface: the Atom Publishing Protocol with the GData extensions.

Unless you work for Google, you probably won't create any services that expose the precise GData interface, but you may encounter GData from the client side. It's also useful to see how the APP can be extended to handle common cases. See how Google used the APP as a building block, and you'll see how you can do the same thing.

Querying collections

The biggest change GData makes is to expose a new kind of resource: the list of search results. The APP says what happens when you send a GET request to a collection's URI. You get a representation of some of the members in the collection. The APP doesn't say anything about finding specific subsets of the collection: finding members older than a certain date, written by a certain author, or filed under a certain category. It doesn't specify how to do full-text search of a member's text fields. GData fills in these blanks.

GData takes every APP collection and exposes an infinite number of additional resources that slice it in various ways. Think back to the "RESTful News" APP collection I showed in Example 9-2. The URI to that collection was *http://www.example.com/RestfulNews*. If that collection were exposed through a GData interface, rather than just an APP interface, the following URIs would also work:

- *http://www.example.com/RestfulNews?q=stadium*: A subcollection of the members where the content contains the word "stadium."
- *http://www.example.com/RestfulNews/-/local*: A subcollection of the members categorized as "local."
- *http://www.example.com/RestfulNews?author=Tom%20Servo&max-results=50*: At most 50 of the members where the author is "Tom Servo."

Those are just three of the search possibilities GData exposes. (For a complete list, see the GData developer's guide (*http://code.google.com/apis/gdata/reference.html*). Note that not all GData applications implement all query mechanisms.) Search results are usually represented as Atom feeds. The feed contains a **entry** element for every member of the collection that matched the query. It also contains OpenSearch elements (q.v.) that specify how many members matched the query, and how many members fit on a page of search results.

Data extensions

I mentioned earlier that an Atom feed can contain markup from arbitrary other XML namespaces. In fact, I just said that GData search results include elements from the OpenSearch namespace. GData also defines a number of new XML entities in its own "gd" namespace, for representing domain-specific data from the Google web services.

Consider an event in the Google Calendar service. The collection is someone's calendar and the member is the event itself. This member probably has the typical Atom fields: an author, a summary, a "last updated" date. But it's also going to have calendar-specific data. When does the event take place? Where will it happen? Is it a one-time event or does it recur?

Google Calendar's GData API puts this data in its Atom feeds, using tags like `gd:when`, `gd:who`, and `gd:recurrence`. If the client understands Google Calendar's extensions it can act as a calendar client. If it only understands the APP, it can act as a general APP client. If it only understands the basic Atom feed format, it can treat the list of events as an Atom feed.

POST Once Exactly

POST requests are the fly in the ointment that is reliable HTTP. GET, PUT, and DE-LETE requests can be resent if they didn't go through the first time, because of the restrictions HTTP places on those methods. GET requests have no serious side effects, and PUT and DELETE have the same effect on resource state whether they're sent once or many times. But a POST request can do anything at all, and sending a POST request twice will probably have a different effect from sending it once. Of course, if a service committed to accepting only POST requests whose actions were safe or idempotent, it would be easy to make reliable HTTP requests to that service.

POST Once Exactly (POE) is a way of making HTTP POST idempotent, like PUT and DELETE. If a resource supports Post Once Exactly, then it will only respond success-fully to POST once over its entire lifetime. All subsequent POST requests will give a response code of 405 ("Method Not Allowed"). A POE resource is a one-off resource exposed for the purpose of handling a single POST request.

> POE was defined by Mark Nottingham in an IETF draft that expired in 2005. I think POE was a little ahead of its time, and if real services start implementing it, there could be another draft.
>
> You can see the original standard at *http://www.mnot.net/drafts/draft-nottingham-http-poe-00.txt*.

Think of a "weblog" resource that responds to POST by creating a new weblog entry. How would we change this design so that no resource responds to POST more than once? Clearly the weblog can't expose POST anymore, or there could only ever be one weblog entry. Here's how POE does it. The client sends a GET or HEAD request to the "weblog" resource, and the response includes the special POE header:

```
HEAD /weblogs/myweblog HTTP/1.1
Host: www.example.com
POE: 1
```

The response contains the URI to a POE resource that hasn't yet been POSTed to. This URI is nothing more than a unique ID for a future POST request. It probably doesn't even exist on the server. Remember that GET is a safe operation, so the original GET request couldn't have changed any server state.

```
200 OK
POE-Links: /weblogs/myweblog/entry-factory-104a4ed
```

POE and POE-Links are custom HTTP headers defined by the POE draft. POE just tells the server that the client is expecting a link to a POE resource. POE-Links gives one or more links to POE resources. At this point the client can POST a representation of its new weblog entry to /weblogs/myweblog/entry-factory-104a4ed. After the POST goes through, that URI will start responding to POST with a response code of 405 ("Oper-ation Not Supported"). If the client isn't sure whether or not the POST request went through, it can safely resend. There's no possiblity that the second POST will create a second weblog entry. POST has been rendered idempotent.

The nice thing about Post Once Exactly is that it works with overloaded POST. Even if you're using POST in a way that totally violates the Resource-Oriented Architecture, your clients can use HTTP as a reliable protocol if you expose the overloaded POST operations through POE.

An alternative to making POST idempotent is to get rid of POST altogether. Remember, POST is only neccessary when the client doesn't know which URI it should PUT to. POE works by generating a unique ID for each of the client's POST operations. If you allow clients to generate their own unique IDs, they can use PUT instead. You can get the benefits of POE without exposing POST at all. You just need to make sure that two clients will never generate the same ID.

Hypermedia Technologies

There are two kinds of hypermedia: links and forms. A link is a connection between the current resource and some target resource, identified by its URI. Less formally, a link is any URI found in the body of a representation. Even JSON and plain text are hypermedia formats of a sort, since they can contain URIs in their text. But throughout this book when I say "hypermedia format," I mean a format with some kind of *structured* support for links and forms.

There are two kinds of forms. The simplest kind I'll call *application forms*, because they show the client how to manipulate application state. An application form is a way of handling resources whose names follow a pattern: it basically acts as a link with more than one destination. A search engine doesn't link to every search you might possibly make: it gives you a form with a space for you to type in your search query. When you submit the form, your browser constructs a URI from what you typed into the form (say, *http://www.google.com/search?q=jellyfish*), and makes a GET request to that URI. The application form lets one resource link to an infinite number of others, without requiring an infinitely large representation.

The second kind of form I'll call *resource forms*, because they show the client how to format a representation that modifies the state of a resource. GET and DELETE requests don't need representations, of course, but POST and PUT requests often do. Resource forms say what the client's POST and PUT representations should look like.

Links and application forms implement what I call connectedness, and what the Fielding thesis calls "hypermedia as the engine of application state." The client is in charge of the application state, but the server can send links and forms that suggest possible next states. By contrast, a resource form is a guide to changing the *resource* state, which is ultimately kept on the server.

I cover four hypermedia technologies in this section. As of the time of writing, XHTML 4 is the only hypermedia technology in active use. But this is a time of rapid change, thanks in part to growing awareness of RESTful web services. XHTML 5 is certain to be widely used once it's finally released. My guess is that URI Templates will also catch on, whether or not they're incorporated into XHTML 5. WADL may catch on, or it may be supplanted by a combination of XHTML 5 and microformats.

URI Templates

URI Templates (currently an Internet Draft (*http://www.ietf.org/internet-drafts/draft-gregorio-uritemplate-00.txt*)) are a technology that makes simple resource forms look like links. I've used URI Template syntax whenever I want to show you an infinite variety of similar URIs. There was this example from Chapter 3, when I was showing you the resources exposed by Amazon's S3 service:

```
https://s3.amazonaws.com/{name-of-bucket}/{name-of-object}
```

That string is not a valid URI, because curly brackets aren't valid in URIs, but it is a valid URI Template. The substring *{name-of-bucket}* is a blank to be filled in, a placeholder to be replaced with the value of the variable `name-of-bucket`. There are an infinite number of URIs lurking in that one template, including *https://s3.amazonaws.com/bucket1/object1*, *https://s3.amazonaws.com/my-other-bucket/subdir/SomeObject.avi*, and so on.

URI templating gives us a precise way to play fill-in-the-blanks with URIs. Without URI Templates, a client must rely on preprogrammed URI construction rules based on English descriptions like `https://s3.amazonaws.com/`, and then the bucket name.

URI Templates are not a data format, but any data format can improve its hypermedia capabilities by allowing them. There is currently a proposal to support URI Templates in XHTML 5, and WADL supports them already.

XHTML 4

HTML is the most successful hypermedia format of all time, but its success on the human web has typecast it as sloppy, and sent practitioners running for the more structured XML. The compromise standard is XHTML, an XML vocabulary for describing documents which uses the same tags and attributes found in HTML. Since it's basically the same as HTML, XHTML has a powerful set of hypermedia features, though its forms are somewhat anemic.

XHTML 4 links

A number of HTML tags can be used to make hypertext links (consider `img`, for example), but the two main ones are `link` and `a`. A `link` tag shows up in the document's `head`, and connects the document to some resource. The `link` tag contains no text or other tags: it applies to the entire document. An **a** tag shows up in the document's **body**. It can contain text and other tags, and it links its contents (not the document as a whole) to another resource (see Example 9-8).

Example 9-8. An XHTML 4 document with some links

```
<!DOCTYPE html
PUBLIC "-//W3C//DTD XHTML 1.0 Strict//EN"
"http://www.w3.org/TR/xhtml1/DTD/xhtml1-strict.dtd">
<html xmlns="http://www.w3.org/1999/xhtml" xml:lang="en">
 <head>
  <link rel="alternate" type="application/atom+xml" href="atom.xml">
  <link rel="stylesheet" href="display.css">
 </head>

 <body>
  <p>
   Have you read
   <a href="Great-Expectations.html"><i>Great Expectations</i></a>?
  </p>
 </body>
</html>
```

Example 9-8 shows a simple HTML document that contains both sorts of hyperlinks. There are two links that use **link** to relate the document as a whole to other URIs, and there's one link that uses **a** to relate part of the document (the italicized phrase "Great Expectations") to another URI.

The three important attributes of **link** and **a** tags are **href**, **rel**, and **rev**. The **href** attribute is the most important: it gives the URI of the resource that's being linked to. If you don't have an **href** attribute, you don't have a hyperlink.

The **rel** attribute adds semantics that explain the foreign URI's relationship to this document. I mentioned this attribute earlier when I was talking about microformats. In Example 9-8, the relationship of the URI **atom.xml** to this document is "alternate". The relationship of the URI **display.css** to this document is "stylesheet". These particular values for **rel** are among the 15 defined in the HTML 4 standard. The value "alternate" means that the linked URI is an alternate representation of the resource this document represents. The value "stylesheet" means that the linked URI contains instructions on how to format this document for display. Microformats often define additional values for **rel**. The **rel-nofollow** microformat defines the relationship "nofollow", to show that a document doesn't trust the resource it's linking to.

The **rev** attribute is the exact opposite of **rel**: it explains the relationship of this document to the foreign URI. The VoteLinks microformat lets you express your opinion of a URI by setting **rev** to "vote-for" or "vote-against". In this case, the foreign URI probably has no relationship to you, but you have a relationship to it.

A simple example illustrates the difference between **rel** and **rev**. Here's an HTML snippet of a user's home page, which contains two links to his father's home page.

```
<a rel="parent" href="/Dad">My father</a>
<a rev="child" href="/Dad">My father</a>
```

XHTML 4 forms

These are the forms that drive the human web. You might not have known about the
`rel` and `rev` attributes, but if you've done any web programming, you should be familiar
with the hypermedia capabilities of XHTML forms.

To recap what you might already know: HTML forms are described with the `form` tag.
A `form` tag has a `method` attribute, which names the HTTP method the client should use
when submitting the form. It has an `action` attribute, which gives the (base) URI of the
resource the form is accessing. It also has an `enctype` attribute, which gives the media
type of any representation the client is supposed to send along with the request.

A `form` tag can contain form elements: children like `input` and `select` tags. These show
up in web browsers as GUI elements: text inputs, checkboxes, buttons, and the like.
In application forms, the values entered into the form elements are used to construct
the ultimate destination of a GET request. Here's an application form I just made up:
an interface to a search engine.

```
<form method="GET" action="http://search.example.com/search">
 <input name="query" type="text" />
 <input type="submit" />
</form>
```

Since this is an application form, it's not designed to operate on any particular resource.
The point of the form is to use the URI in the `action` as a jumping-off point to an infinity
of resources with user-generated URIs: *http://search.example.com/search?q=jellyfish*,
http://search.example.com/search?q=chocolate, and so on.

A resource form in HTML 4 identifies one particular resource, and it specifies an action
of POST. The form elements are used to build up a representation to be sent along with
the POST request. Here's a resource form I just made up: an interface to a file upload
script.

```
<form method="POST" action="http://files.example.com/dir/subdir/"
enctype="multipart/form-data">
 <input type="text" name="description" />
 <input type="file" name="newfile" />
</form>
```

This form is designed to manipulate resource state, to create a new "file" resource as a
subordinate resource of the "directory" resource at *http://files.example.com/dir/sub-
dir/*. The representation format is a "multipart/form-data" document that contains a
textual description and a (possibly binary) file.

Shortcomings of XHTML 4

HTML 4's hypermedia features are obviously good enough to give us the human web we enjoy today, but they're not good enough for web services. I have five major problems with HTML's forms.

1. Application forms are limited in the URIs they can express. You're limited to URIs that take a base URI and then tack on some key-value pairs. With an HTML application form you can "link" to *http://search.example.com/search?q=jellyfish*, but not *http://search.example.com/search/jellyfish*. The variables must go into the URI's query string as key-value pairs.

2. Resource forms in HTML 4 are limited to using HTTP POST. There's no way to use a form to tell a client to send a DELETE request, or to show a client what the representation of a PUT request should look like. The human web, which runs on HTML forms, has a different uniform interface from web services as a whole. It uses GET for safe operations, and overloaded POST for everything else. If you want to get HTTP's uniform interface with HTML 4 forms, you'll need to simulate PUT and DELETE with overloaded POST (see "Faking PUT and DELETE" in Chapter 8 for the standard way).

3. There's no way to use an HTML form to describe the HTTP headers a client should send along with its request. You can't define a form entity and say "the value of this entity goes into the HTTP request header `X-My-Header`." I generally don't think services should require this of their clients, but sometimes it's neccessary. The Atom Publishing Protocol defines a special request header (`Slug`, mentioned above) for POST requests that create a new member in a collection. The APP designers defined a new header, instead of requiring that this data go into the entity-body, because the entity-body might be a binary file.

4. You can't use an HTML form to specify a representation more complicated than a set of key-value pairs. All the form elements are designed to be turned into key-value pairs, except for the "file" element, which doesn't help much. The HTML standard defines two content types for form representations: `application/x-www-form-urlencoded`, which is for key-value pairs (I covered it in "Form-encoding" in Chapter 6); and `multipart/form-data`, which is for a combination of key-value pairs and uploaded files.

   You can specify any content type you want in `enctype`, just as you can put anything you want in a tag's `class` and `rel` attributes. So you can tell the client it should POST an XML file by setting a form's `enctype` to `application/xml`. But there's no way of conveying what should go into that XML file, unless it happens to be an XML representation of a bunch of key-value pairs. You can't nest form elements, or define new ones that represent data structures more complex than key-value pairs. (You can do a little better if the XML vocabulary you're using has its own media type, like `application/atom+xml` or `application/rdf+xml`.)

5. As I mentioned in "Link the Resources to Each Other" in Chapter 5, you can't define a repeating field in an HTML form. You can define the same field twice, or ten times, but eventually you'll have to stop. There's no way to tell the client: "you can specify as many values as you want for this key-value pair."

XHTML 5

HTML 5 solves many of the problems that turn up when you try to use HTML on the programmable web. The main problem with HTML 5 is the timetable. The official estimate has HTML 5 being adopted as a W3C Proposed Recommendation in late 2008. More conservative estimates push that date all the way to 2022. Either way, HTML 5 won't be a standard by the time this book is published. That's not really the issue, though. The issue is when real clients will start supporting the HTML 5 features I describe below. Until they do, if you use the features of HTML 5, your clients will have to write custom code to interpret them.

HTML 5 forms support all four basic methods of HTTP's uniform interface: GET, POST, PUT, and DELETE. I took advantage of this when designing my map application, if you'll recall Example 6-3. This is the easiest HTML 5 feature to support today, especially since (as I'll show in Chapter 11) most web browsers can already make PUT and DELETE requests.

There's a proposal (not yet incorporated into HTML 5; see *http://blog.welldesignedurls.org/2007/01/11/proposing-uri-templates-for-webforms-2/*) that would allow forms to use URI Templates. Under this proposal, an application form can have its `template` attribute (*not* its `action` attribute) be a URI Template like `http://search.example.com/search/{q}`. It could then define q as a text field within the form. This would let you use an application form to "link" to `http://search.example.com/search/jellyfish`.

HTML 4 forms can specify more than one form element with the same name. This lets clients know they can submit the same key with 2 or 10 values: as many values as there are form elements. HTML 5 forms support the "repetition model," a way of telling the client it's allowed to submit the same key as many times as it wants. I used a simple repetition block in Example 5-11.

Finally, HTML 5 defines two new ways of serializing key-value pairs into representations: as plain text, or using a newly defined XML vocabulary. The content type for the latter is `application/x-www-form+xml`. This is not as big an advance as you might think. Form entities like `input` are still ways of getting data in the form of key-value pairs. These new serialization formats are just new ways of representing those key-value pairs. There's still no way to show the client how to format a more complicated representation, unless the client can figure out the format from just the content type.

WADL

The Web Application Description Language is an XML vocabulary for expressing the behavior of HTTP resources (see the development site for the Java client (*https://wadl.dev.java.net/*)). It was named by analogy with the Web *Service* Description Language, a different XML vocabulary used to describe the SOAP-based RPC-style services that characterize Big Web Services.

Look back to "Service document" earlier in this chapter where I describe the Atom Publishing Protocol's service documents. The representation of a service document is an XML document, written in a certain vocabulary, which describes a set of resources (APP collections) and the operations you're allowed to perform on those resources. WADL is a standard vocabulary that can do for any resource at all what APP service documents do for APP collection resources.

You can provide a WADL file that describes every resource exposed by your service. This corresponds roughly to a WSDL file in a SOAP/WSDL service, and to the "site map" pages you see on the human web. Alternatively, you can embed a snippet of WADL in an XML representation of a particular resource, the way you might embed an HTML form in an HTML representation. The WADL snippet tells you how to manipulate the state of the resource.

As I said way back in Chapter 2, WADL makes it easy to write clients for web services. A WADL description of a resource can stand in for any number of programming-language interfaces to that resource: all you need is a WADL client written in the appropriate language. WADL abstracts away the details of HTTP requests, and the building and parsing of representations, without hiding HTTP's uniform interface.

As of the time of writing, WADL is more talked about than used. There's a Java client implementation (*http://wadl.dev.java.net/*), a rudimentary Ruby client (*http://www.crummy.com/software/wadl.rb/*), and that's about it. Most existing WADL files are bootleg descriptions of other peoples' RESTful and REST-RPC services.

WADL does better than HTML 5 as a hypermedia format. It supports URI Templates and every HTTP method there is. A WADL file can also tell the client to populate certain HTTP headers when it makes a request. More importantly, WADL can describe representation formats that aren't just key-value pairs. You can specify the format of an

XML representation by pointing to a schema definition. Then you can point out which parts of the document are most important by specifying key-value pairs where the "keys" are XPath statements. This is a small step, but an important one. With HTML you can only specify the format of an XML representation by giving it a different content type.

Of course, the "small step" only applies to XML. You can use WADL to say that a certain resource serves or accepts a JSON document, but unless that JSON document happens to be a hash (key-value pairs again!), there's no way to specify what the JSON document ought to look like. This is a general problem which was solved in the XML world with schema definitions. It hasn't been solved for other formats.

Describing a del.icio.us resource

Example 9-9 shows a Ruby client for the del.icio.us web service based on Ruby's WADL library. It's a reprint of the code from "Clients Made Easy with WADL" in Chapter 2.

Example 9-9. A Ruby/WADL client for del.icio.us

```
#!/usr/bin/ruby
# delicious-wadl-ruby.rb
require 'wadl'

if ARGV.size != 2
  puts "Usage: #{$0} [username] [password]"
  exit
end
username, password = ARGV

# Load an application from the WADL file
delicious = WADL::Application.from_wadl(open("delicious.wadl"))

# Give authentication information to the application
service = delicious.v1.with_basic_auth(username, password)

begin
  # Find the "recent posts" functionality
  recent_posts = service.posts.recent

  # For every recent post...
  recent_posts.get.representation.each_by_param('post') do |post|
    # Print its description and URI.
    puts "#{post.attributes['description']}: #{post.attributes['href']}"
  end
rescue WADL::Faults::AuthorizationRequired
  puts "Invalid authentication information!"
end
```

The code's very short but you can see what's happening, especially now that we're past Chapter 2 and I've shown you how resource-oriented services work. The del.icio.us web service exposes a resource that the WADL library identifies with **v1**. That resource has a subresource identified by **posts.recent**. If you recall the inner workings of del.icio.us from Chapter 2, you'll recognize this as corresponding to the URI *https://api.del.icio.us/v1/posts/recent*. When you tell the WADL library to make a GET request to that resource, you get back some kind of response object which includes an XML `representation`. Certain parts of this representation, the `post`s, are especially interesting, and I process them as XML elements, extracting their `description`s and `href`s.

Let's look at the WADL file that makes this code possible. I've split it into three sections: resource definition, method definition, and representation definition. Example 9-10 shows the resource definition. I've defined a nested set of WADL resources: `v1` inside `posts` inside `recent`. The `recent` WADL resource corresponds to the HTTP resource the del.icio.us API exposes at *https://api.del.icio.us/v1/posts/recent*.

Example 9-10. WADL file for del.icio.us: the resource

```
<?xml version="1.0"?>
<!-- This is a partial bootleg WADL file for the del.icio.us API. -->

<application xmlns="http://research.sun.com/wadl/2006/07">

  <!-- The resource -->
  <resources base="https://api.del.icio.us/">
    <doc xml:lang="en" title="The del.icio.us API v1">
      Post or retrieve your bookmarks from the social networking website.
      Limit requests to one per second.
    </doc>

    <resource path="v1">
      <param name="Authorization" style="header" required="true">
      <doc xml:lang="en">All del.icio.us API calls must be authenticated
      using Basic HTTP auth.</doc>
      </param>

      <resource path="posts">
      <resource path="recent">
        <method href="#getRecentPosts" />
      </resource>
      </resource>
    </resource>
  </resources>
</resources>
```

That HTTP resource exposes a single method of the uniform interface (GET), so I define a single WADL method inside the WADL resource. Rather than define the method inside the `resource` tag and clutter up Example 9-10, I've defined it by reference. I'll get to it next.

Every del.icio.us API request must include an `Authorization` header that encodes your del.icio.us username and password using HTTP Basic Auth. I've represented this with a `param` tag that tells the client it must provide an `Authorization` header. The `param` tag is the equivalent of an HTML form element: it tells the client about a blank to be filled in.[§]

Example 9-11 shows the definition of the method `getRecentPosts`. A WADL method corresponds to a request you might make using HTTP's uniform interface. The `id` of the method can be anything, but its `name` is always the name of an HTTP method: here, "GET". The method definition models both the HTTP `request` and `response`.

Example 9-11. WADL file for del.icio.us: the method

```
<!-- The method -->
<method id="getRecentPosts" name="GET">

  <doc xml:lang="en" title="Returns a list of the most recent posts." />

  <request>
    <param name="tag" style="form">
  <doc xml:lang="en" title="Filter by this tag." />
    </param>

    <param name="count" style="form" default="15">
  <doc xml:lang="en" title="Number of items to retrieve.">
    Maximum: 100
  </doc>
    </param>
  </request>

  <response>
    <representation href="#postList" />
    <fault id="AuthorizationRequired" status="401" />
  </response>
</method>
```

This particular `request` defines two more `param`s: two more blanks to be filled in by the client. These are "query" `param`s, which in a GET request means they'll be tacked onto the query string—just like elements in an HTML form would be. These `param` definitions make it possible for the WADL client to access URIs like *https://api.del.icio.us/v1/posts/recent?count=100* and *https://api.del.icio.us/v1/posts/recent?tag=rest&count=20*.

This WADL `method` defines an application form: not a way of manipulating resource state, but a pointer to possible new application states. This `method` tag tells the client about an infinite number of GET requests they *can* make to a set of related resources, without having to list infinitely many URIs. If this method corresponded to a PUT or POST request, its `request` might be a resource form, a way of manipulating resource state. Then it might describe a `representation` for you to send along with your request.

The `response` does describe a `representation`: the response document you get back from del.icio.us when you make one of these GET requests. It also describes a possible fault condition: if you submit a bad `Authorization` header, you'll get a response code of 401 ("Unauthorized") instead of a representation.

---

§ Marc Hadley, the primary author of the WADL standard, is working on more elegant ways of representing the need to authenticate.

Take a look at Example 9-12, which defines the representation. This is WADL's description of the XML document you receive when you GET *https://api.del.icio.us/v1/posts/recent*: a document like the one in Example 2-3.

Example 9-12. WADL file for del.icio.us: the representation

```
    <!-- The representation -->
    <representation id="postList" mediaType="text/xml" element="posts">
      <param name="post" path="/posts/post" repeating="true" />
    </representation>

  </application>
```

The WADL description gives the most important points about this document: its content type is `text/xml`, and it's rooted at the `posts` tag. The `param` tag points out that the the `posts` tag has a number of interesting children: the `post` tags. The `param`'s `path` attribute gives an XPath expression which the client can use on the XML document to fetch all the del.icio.us posts. My client's call to `each_by_param('post')` runs that XPath expression against the document, and lets me operate on each matching element without having to know anything about XPath or the structure of the representation.

There's no schema definition for this kind of XML representation: it's a very simple document and del.icio.us just assumes you can figure out the format. But for the sake of demonstration, let's pretend this representation has an XML Schema Definition (XSD) file. The URI of this imaginary definition is *https://api.del.icio.us/v1/posts.xsd*, and it defines the schema for the `posts` and `post` tags. In that fantasy situation, Example 9-13 shows how I might define the `representation` in terms of the schema file.

Example 9-13. WADL file for del.icious: the resource

```
    <?xml version="1.0"?>
    <!-- This is a partial bootleg WADL file for the del.icio.us API. -->

    <application xmlns="http://research.sun.com/wadl/2006/07"
                 xmlns:delicious="https://api.del.icio.us/v1/posts.xsd">

      <grammars>
       <include "https://api.del.icio.us/v1/posts.xsd" />
      </grammars>

      ...

       <representation id="postList" mediaType="text/xml" element="delicious:posts" />
       ...

    </application>
```

I no longer need a `param` to say that this document is full of `post` tags. That information's in the XSD file. I just have to define the representation in terms of that file. I do this by referencing the XSD file in this WADL file's `grammars`, assigning it to the `delicious:` namespace, and scoping the representation's `element` attribute to that namespace. If the client is curious about what a `delicious:posts` tag might contain, it can check the

XSD. Even though the XSD completely describes the representation format, I might define some param tags anyway to point out especially important parts of the document.

Describing an APP collection

That was a pretty simple example. I used an application form to describe an infinite set of related resources, each of which responds to GET by sending a simple XML document. But I can use WADL to describe the behavior of any resource that responds to the uniform interface. If a resource serves an XML representation, I can reach into that representation with param tags: show where the interesting bits of data are, and where the links to other resources can be found.

Earlier I compared WADL files to the Atom Publishing Protocol's service documents. Both are XML vocabularies for describing resources. Service documents describe APP collections, and WADL documents describe any resource at all. You've seen how a service document describes a collection (Example 9-6). What would a WADL description of the same resources look like?

As it happens, the WADL standard gives just this example. Section A.2 of the standard shows an APP service document and then a WADL description of the same resources. I'll present a simplified version of this idea here.

The service document in Example 9-6 describes three Atom collections. One accepts new Atom entries via POST, and the other two accept image files. These collections are pretty similar. In an object-oriented system I might factor out the differences by defining a class hierarchy. I can do something similar in WADL. Instead of defining all three resources from scratch, I'm going to define two *resource types*. Then it'll be simple to define individual resources in terms of the types (see Example 9-14).

Example 9-14. A WADL file for APP: resource types

```
<?xml version="1.0"?>
<!-- This is a description of two common types of resources that respond
     to the Atom Publishing Protocol. -->

<application xmlns="http://research.sun.com/wadl/2006/07"
             xmlns:app="http://purl.org/atom/app">

  <!-- An Atom collection accepts Atom entries via POST. -->
  <resource_type id="atom_collection">
    <method href="#getCollection" />
    <method href="#postNewAtomMember" />
  </resource_type>

  <!-- An image collection accepts image files via POST. -->
  <resource_type id="image_collection">
    <method href="#getCollection" />
    <method href="#postNewImageMember" />
  </resource_type>
```

There are my two resource types: the Atom collection and the image collection. These don't correspond to any specific resources: they're equivalent to classes in an object-oriented design. Both "classes" support a method identified as getCollection, but the Atom collection supports a method postNewAtomMember where the image collection supports postNewImageMember. Example 9-15 shows those three methods:

Example 9-15. A WADL file for APP: methods

```
<!-- Three possible operations on resources. -->
<method name="GET" id="getCollection">
  <response>
    <representation href="#feed" />
  </response>
</method>

<method name="POST" id="postNewAtomMember">
  <request>
    <representation href="#entry" />
  </request>
</method>

<method name="POST" id="postNewImageMember">
  <request>
    <representation id="image"  mediaType="image/*" />
    <param name="Slug" style="header" />
  </request>
</method>
```

The getCollection WADL method is revealed as a GET operation that expects an Atom feed (to be described) as its representation. The postNewAtomMember method is a POST operation that sends an Atom entry (again, to be described) as its representation. The postNewImageMember method is also a POST operation, but the representation it sends is an image file, and it knows how to specify a value for the HTTP header Slug.

Finally, Example 9-16 describes the two representations: Atom feeds and atom entries. I don't need to describe these representations in great detail because they're already described in the XML Schema Document for Atom: I can just reference the XSD file. But I'm free to annotate the XSD by defining param elements that tell a WADL client about the links between resources.

Example 9-16. A WADL file for APP: the representations

```
<!-- Two possible XML representations. -->
<representation id="feed" mediaType="application/atom+xml"
      element="atom:feed" />

<representation id="entry" mediaType="application/atom+xml"
      element="atom:entry" />

</application>
```

I can make the file I just defined available on the Web: say, at http://www.example.com/app-resource-types.wadl. Now it's a resource. I can use it in my services by referencing its URI. So can anyone else. It's now possible to define certain APP collections in terms of these resource types. My three collections are defined in just a few lines in Example 9-17.

Example 9-17. A WADL file for a set of APP collections

```xml
<?xml version="1.0"?>
<!-- This is a description of three "collection" resources that respond
     to the Atom Publishing Protocol. -->

<application xmlns="http://research.sun.com/wadl/2006/07"
             xmlns:app="http://purl.org/atom/app">
  <resources base="http://www.example.com/">
    <resource path="RESTfulNews"
     type="http://www.example.com/app-resource-types.wadl#atom_collection" />
    <resource path="samruby/photos"
     type="http://www.example.com/app-resource-types.wadl#image_collection" />
    <resource path="leonardr/photos"
     type="http://www.example.com/app-resource-types.wadl#image_collection"/>
  </resources>
</application>
```

The Atom Publishing Protocol is popular because it's such a general interface. The major differences between two APP services are described in the respective service documents. A generic APP client can read these documents and reprogram itself to act as a client for many different services. But there's an even more general interface: the uniform interface of HTTP. An APP service document uses a domain-specific XML vocabulary, but hypermedia formats like HTML and WADL can be used to describe any web service at all. Their clients can be even more general than APP clients.

Hypermedia is how one service communicates the ways it differs from other services. If that intelligence is embedded in hypermedia, the programmer needs to hardwire less of it in code. More importantly, hypermedia gives you access to the link: the second most important web technology after the URI. The potential of REST will not be fully exploited until web services start serving their representations as link-rich hypermedia instead of plain media.

Is WADL evil?

In Chapter 10 I'll talk about how WSDL turned SOAP from a simple XML envelope format to a name synonymous with the RPC style of web services. WSDL abstracts away the details of HTTP requests and responses, and replaces them with a model based on method calls in a programming language. Doesn't WADL do the exact same thing? Should we worry that WADL will do to plain-HTTP web services what WSDL did to SOAP web services: tie them to the RPC style in the name of client convenience?

I think we're safe. WADL abstracts away the details of HTTP requests and responses, but—this is the key point—it doesn't add any new abstraction on top. Remember, REST isn't tied to HTTP. When you abstract HTTP away from a RESTful service, you've still got REST. A resource-oriented web service exposes resources that respond to a uniform interface: that's REST. A WADL document describes resources that respond to a uniform interface: that's REST. A program that uses WADL creates objects that correspond to resources, and accesses them with method calls that embody a uniform interface: that's REST. RESTfulness doesn't live in the protocol. It lives in the interface.

About the worst you can do with WADL is hide the fact that a service responds to the uniform interface. I've deliberately not shown you how to do this, but you should be able to figure it out. You may need to do this if you're writing a WADL file for a web application or REST-RPC hybrid service that doesn't respect the uniform interface.

I'm fairly sure that WADL itself won't tie HTTP to an RPC model, the way WSDL did to SOAP. But what about those push-button code generators, the ones that take your procedure-call-oriented code and turn it into a "web service" that only exposes one URI? WADL makes you define your resources, but what if tomorrow's generator creates a WADL file that only exposes a single "resource", the way an autogenerated WSDL file exposes a single "endpoint"?

This is a real worry. Fortunately, WADL's history is different from WSDL's. WSDL was introduced at a time when SOAP was still officially associated with the RPC style. But WADL is being introduced as people are becoming aware of the advantages of REST, and it's marketed as a way to hide the details while keeping the RESTful interface. Hopefully, any tool developers who want to make their tools support WADL will also be interested in making their tools support RESTful design.

## CHAPTER 10

The Resource-Oriented Architecture Versus Big Web Services

Throughout this book I've focused on technologies and architectures that work with the grain of the Web. I've shown you how to arrange resources into services that are very powerful, but conceptually simple and accessible from a wide variety of standard clients. But I've hardly said a word about the technologies that most people think of when they think web services: SOAP, WSDL, and the WS-* stack. These technologies form a competing paradigm for web services: one that doesn't really work like the Web. Rather than letting these technologies claim the entire field of web services for themselves, I've given them a not entirely kind, but fairly mild nickname: Big Web Services. In this chapter I'll compare the two paradigms.

The web is based on resources, but Big Web Services don't expose resources. The Web is based on URIs and links, but a typical Big Web Service exposes one URI and zero links. The Web is based on HTTP, and Big Web Services hardly use HTTP's features at all. This isn't academic hair-splitting, because it means Big Web Services don't get the benefits of resource-oriented web services. They're not addressable, cacheable, or well connected, and they don't respect any uniform interface. (Many of them are stateless, though.) They're opaque, and understanding one doesn't help you understand the next one. In practice, they also tend to have interoperability problems when serving a variety of clients.

In this chapter I apply the same analytical tools to Big Web Services as I've been using to explain the REST architectural style and the Resource-Oriented Architecture. I'll be covering a lot of ideas in just a few pages—there are already whole books about these technologies—but my goal is not to give you a complete introduction. I just want to show you how the two philosophies line up. I'll examine technologies like SOAP on a technical level, and not in terms of how they've been hyped or demonized. I'll focus on these specifications as they're widely deployed, and less on the unrealized potential of newer versions.

The vision of Big Web Services has evolved over time and not all practitioners are up to date on the latest concepts. To make sure I get everybody, I'm going to take a chronological approach to my analysis. I'll start with the original "publish, find, and bind" vision, move on to "secure, reliable transactions," and finally touch on more recent developments like the Enterprise Server Bus, Business Process Execution Language, and Service-Oriented Architecture.

What Problems Are Big Web Services Trying to Solve?

As I said, the Web is resource-oriented. To implement the RPC style atop it is to go against the grain of the Web. But the Web wasn't designed to support general-purpose distributed programming. Sometimes your application has a natural grain of its own, and going against *that* is problematic.

Here's a concrete example that I'll come back to throughout this chapter: a service that sets up travel reservations. Booking a trip might require booking a flight, a hotel, and a rental car. These tasks are interrelated: getting a rental car and a seat on a flight may be of little use to the client if you can't find a hotel. Each task requires coordinating with external authorities to find the best deal: the airlines, the rental car companies, the hotels. Each of these external authorities may be a separate service, and dealing with them involves making commitments. You may be able to have the airline service hold a seat on a plane for five minutes while you try to line up the rest of the deal. You may need to make a hotel reservation that will bill the customer for the first night's stay whether or not they show up. These time-limited commitments represent shared state.

The resource-oriented approach I advocate in this book is Turing-complete. It can model any application, even a complex one like a travel broker. If I implemented this travel broker as a set of resource-oriented services, I'd expose resources like "a five-minute hold on seat 24C." This would work, but there's probably little value in that kind of resource. I don't pretend to know what emergent properties might show up in a resource-oriented system like this, but it's not likely that someone would want to bookmark that resource's URI and pass it around.

The travel agency service has a different grain than the rest of the Web. This doesn't mean that it can't be made into a successful web application. Nor does it imply that SOAP and related specifications are a better fit. But this is the main problem that Big Web Services are trying to solve: the design of process-oriented, brokered distributed services. For whatever reason, this kind of application tends to be more prevalent in businesses and government applications, and less prevalent in technical and academic areas.

SOAP

SOAP is the foundation on which the plethora of WS-* specifications is built. Despite the hype and antihype it's been subjected to, there's amazingly little to this specification. You can take any XML document (so long as it doesn't have a DOCTYPE or processing instructions), wrap it in two little XML elements, and you have a valid SOAP document. For best results, though, the document's root element should be in a namespace.

Here's an XML document:

```
<hello-world xmlns="http://example.com"/>
```

Here's the same document, wrapped in a SOAP envelope:

```
<soap:Envelope xmlns:soap="http://schemas.xmlsoap.org/soap/envelope/">
 <soap:Body>
   <hello-world xmlns="http://example.com"/>
 </soap:Body>
</soap:Envelope>
```

The only catch is that the SOAP `Envelope` must have the same character encoding as the document it encloses. That's pretty much all there is to it. Wrapping an XML document in two extra elements is certainly not an unreasonable or onerous task, but it doesn't exactly solve all the world's problems either.

Seem too simple? Here's a real-world example. In Example 1-8 I showed you an elided version of a SOAP document you might submit to Google's web search service. Example 10-1 shows the whole document.

Example 10-1. A SOAP envelope to be submitted to Google's SOAP search service

```
<soap:Envelope xmlns:soap="http://schemas.xmlsoap.org/soap/envelope/">
  <soap:Body>
    <gs:doGoogleSearch xmlns:gs="urn:GoogleSearch">
      <key>00000000000000000000000000000000</key>
      <q>REST book</q>
      <start>0</start>
      <maxResults>10</maxResults>
      <filter>true</filter>
      <restrict/>
      <safeSearch>false</safeSearch>
      <lr/>
      <ie>latin1</ie>
      <oe>latin1</oe>
    </gs:doGoogleSearch>
  </soap:Body>
</soap:Envelope>
```

This document describes a Call to the Remote Procedure `gs:doGoogleSearch`. All of the query parameters are neatly tucked into named elements. This example is fully functional, though if you POST it to Google you'll get back a fault document saying that the `key` is not valid.

This style of encoding parameters to a remote function is sometimes called RPC/literal or Section 5 encoding. That's the section in the SOAP 1.1 specification that shows how to use SOAP for RPC. But over time, fashions change. Later versions of the specification made support of this encoding optional, and so it's now effectively deprecated. It was largely replaced by an encoding called document/literal, and then by wrapped document/literal. Wrapped document/literal looks largely the same as section 5 encoding, except that the parameters tend to be scoped to a namespace.

One final note about body elements: the parameters may be annotated with data type information based on XML Schema Data Types. This annotation goes into attributes, and generally reduces the readability of the document. Instead of `<ie>latin1</ie>` you might see `<ie xsi:type="xsd:string">latin1</ie>`. Multiply that by the number of arguments in Example 10-1 and you may start to see why many recoil in horror when they hear "SOAP."

In Chapter 1 I said that HTTP and SOAP are just different ways of putting messages in envelopes. HTTP's main moving parts are the entity-body and the headers. With a SOAP element named `Body`, you might expect to also find a `Header` element. You'd be right. Anything that can go into the `Body` element—any namespaced document which has no DOCTYPE or processing instructions—can go into the `Header`. But while you tend to only find a single element inside the `Body`, the `Header` can contain any number of elements. `Header` elements also tend to be small.

Recalling the terminology used in "HTTP: Documents in Envelopes" in Chapter 1, headers are like "stickers" on an envelope. SOAP headers tend to contain information about the data in the body, such as security and routing information. The same is true of HTTP headers.

SOAP defines two attributes for header entities: `actor` and `mustUnderstand`. If you know in advance that your message is going to pass through intermediaries on the way to its destination, you can identify (via a URI) the `actor` that's the target of any particular header. The `mustUnderstand` attribute is used to impose restrictions on those intermediaries (or on the final destination). If the `actor` doesn't understand a header addressed to it, and `mustUnderstand` is true, it must reject the message—even if it thinks it could handle the message otherwise. An example of this would be a header associated with a two-phase commit operation. If the destination doesn't understand two-phase commit, you don't want the operation to proceed.

Beyond that, there isn't much to SOAP. Requests and responses have the same format, similar to HTTP. There's a separate format for a SOAP `Fault`, used to signify an error condition. Right now the only thing that can go into a SOAP document is an XML document. There have been a few attempts to define mechanisms for attaching binary data to messages, but no clear winner has emerged.

Given this fairly simple protocol, what's the basis for the hype and controversy? SOAP is mainly infamous for the technologies built on top of it, and I'll cover those next. It does have one alleged benefit of its own: transport independence. The headers are inside the message, which means they're independent of the protocol used to transport the message. You don't have to send a SOAP envelope inside an HTTP envelope. You can send it over email, instant messaging, raw TCP, or any other protocol. In practice, this feature is rarely used. There's been some limited public use of SMTP transports, and some use of JMS transports behind the corporate firewall, but the overwhelming majority of SOAP traffic is over HTTP.

The Resource-Oriented Alternative

SOAP is almost always sent over HTTP, but SOAP toolkits make little use of HTTP status codes, and tend to coerce all operations into POST methods. This is not technically disallowed by the REST architectural style, but it's a degenerate sort of RESTful architecture that doesn't get any of the benefits REST is supposed to provide. Most SOAP services support multiple operations on diverse data, all mediated through POST on a single URI. This isn't resource-oriented: it's RPC-style.

The single most important change you can make is to split your service into resources: identify every "thing" in your service with a separate URI. Pretty much every SOAP toolkit in existence provides access to this information, so use it! Put the object reference up front. Such usages may not feel idiomatic at first, but if you stop and think about it, this is what you'd expect to be doing if SOAP were really a Simple *Object* Access Protocol. It's the difference between object-oriented programming in a function-oriented language like C:

```
my_function(object, argument);
```

and in an object-oriented language like C++:

```
object->my_method(argument);
```

When you move the scoping information outside the parentheses (or, in this case, the `Envelope`), you'll soon find yourself identifying large numbers of resources with common functionality. You'll want to refactor your logic to exploit these commonalities.

The next most important change has to do with the object-oriented concept of polymorphism. You should try to make objects of different types respond to method calls with the same name. In the world of the Web, this means (at a minimum) supporting HTTP's `GET` method. Why is this important? Think about a programming language's standard library. Pretty much every object-oriented language defines a standard class hierarchy, and at its root you find an `Object` class which defines a `toString` method. The details are different for every language, but the result is always the same: every object has a method that provides a canonical representation of the object. The `GET` method provides a similar function for HTTP resources.

Once you do this, you'll inevitably notice that the `GET` method is used more heavily than all the other methods you have provided. Combined. And by a wide margin. That's where conditional GET and caching come in. Implement these standard features of HTTP, make your representations cacheable, and you make your application more scalable. That has direct and tangible economic benefits.

Once you've done these three simple things, you may find yourself wanting more. Chapter 8 is full of advice on these topics.

WSDL

SOAP provides an envelope for your messages, but little else. Beyond section 5 (which is falling out of favor), SOAP doesn't constrain the structure of the message one bit. Many environments, especially those that depend on static typing, need a bit more definition up front. That's where WSDL comes in.

I'm going to illustrate the concepts behind WSDL using the weblogs.com SOAP 1.1 interface (*http://www.soapware.org/weblogsCom*). I chose it because it's pretty much the simplest deployed SOAP interface out there. Any service you encounter or write will undoubtedly be more complicated, but the basic steps are the same.

The weblogs.com interface exposes a single RPC-style function called ping. The function takes two arguments, both strings, and returns a pingResult structure. This custom structure contains two elements: flerror, a Boolean, and message, a string. Strings and Booleans are standard primitive data types, but to use a pingResult I need to define it as an XML Schema complexType. I'll do this within the types element of my WSDL file in Example 10-2.

Example 10-2. XML Schema definition of the pingResult struct

```
<types>
  <s:schema targetNamespace="uri:weblogscom">
    <s:complexType name="pingResult">
      <s:sequence>
        <s:element minOccurs="1" maxOccurs="1" name="flerror" type="s:boolean"/>
        <s:element minOccurs="1" maxOccurs="1" name="message" type="s:string" />
      </s:sequence>
    </s:complexType>
  </s:schema>
</types>
```

Now that I've defined the custom type, I'll move on to defining the messages that can be sent between client and server. There are two messages here: the ping request and the ping response. The request has two parts, and the response has only one (see Example 10-3).

Example 10-3. WSDL definitions of the ping messages

```
<message name="pingRequest">
  <part name="weblogname" type="s:string"/>
  <part name="weblogurl" type="s:string"/>
</message>

<message name="pingResponse">
  <part name="result" type="tns:pingResult"/>
</message>
```

Now I can use these messages in the definition of an WSDL *operation*, which is defined as a part of a *port type*. A *port* is simply a collection of operations. A programming language would refer to this as a library, a module, or a class. But this is the world of messaging, so the connection points are called ports, and an abstract definition of a port is called a port type. In this case, I'm defining a port type that supports a single operation: ping (see Example 10-4).

Example 10-4. WSDL definition of the portType for the ping operation

```
<portType name="pingPort">
  <operation name="ping">
    <input message="tns:pingRequest"/>
    <output message="tns:pingResponse"/>
  </operation>
</portType>
```

At this point, the definition is still abstract. There are any number of ways to implement this ping operation that takes two strings and returns a struct. I haven't specified that the message is going to be transported via SOAP, or even that the message is going to be XML. Vendors of WSDL implementations are free to support other transports, but in Example 10-5, the intended *binding* is to section 5 compliant SOAP messages, send over HTTP. This is the SOAP/HTTP binding for the port type, which will be presented without commentary.

Example 10-5. Binding the ping portType to a SOAP/HTTP implementation

```
<binding name="pingSoap" type="tns:pingPort">
  <soap:binding style="rpc" transport="http://schemas.xmlsoap.org/soap/http" />
  <operation name="ping">
    <soap:operation soapAction="/weblogUpdates" style="rpc"/>
    <input>
      <soap:body use="encoded" namespace="uri:weblogscom"
        encodingStyle="http://schemas.xmlsoap.org/soap/encoding/"/>
    </input>
    <output>
      <soap:body use="encoded" namespace="uri:weblogscom"
        encodingStyle="http://schemas.xmlsoap.org/soap/encoding/"/>
    </output>
  </operation>
</binding>
```

We're still not done. The final piece to the puzzle is to define a service, which connects a portType with a binding and (since this is SOAP over HTTP) with an endpoint URI (see Example 10-6).

Example 10-6. Defining a SOAP service that exposes the ping port

```
<service name="weblogscom">
  <document>
    For a complete description of this service, go to the following URL:
    http://www.soapware.org/weblogsCom
  </document>

  <port name="pingPort" binding="tns:pingSoap">
    <soap:address location="http://rpc.weblogs.com:80/"/>
  </port>
</service>
```

The full WSDL for this single-function service is shown in Example 10-7.

Example 10-7. The complete WSDL file

```
<?xml version="1.0" encoding="utf-8"?>

<definitions
  xmlns:soap="http://schemas.xmlsoap.org/wsdl/soap/"
  xmlns:s="http://www.w3.org/2001/XMLSchema"
  xmlns:tns="uri:weblogscom"
  targetNamespace="uri:weblogscom"
  xmlns="http://schemas.xmlsoap.org/wsdl/">

  <types>
    <s:schema targetNamespace="uri:weblogscom">
     <s:complexType name="pingResult">
    <s:sequence>
      <s:element minOccurs="1" maxOccurs="1"
        name="flerror" type="s:boolean"/>
      <s:element minOccurs="1" maxOccurs="1"
        name="message" type="s:string" />
    </s:sequence>
     </s:complexType>
    </s:schema>
  </types>

  <message name="pingRequest">
    <part name="weblogname" type="s:string"/>
    <part name="weblogurl" type="s:string"/>
  </message>

  <message name="pingResponse">
    <part name="result" type="tns:pingResult"/>
  </message>

  <portType name="pingPort">
    <operation name="ping">
      <input message="tns:pingRequest"/>
      <output message="tns:pingResponse"/>
    </operation>
  </portType>

  <binding name="pingSoap" type="tns:pingPort">
    <soap:binding style="rpc"
      transport="http://schemas.xmlsoap.org/soap/http"/>
    <operation name="ping">
      <soap:operation soapAction="/weblogUpdates" style="rpc"/>
      <input>
    <soap:body use="encoded" namespace="uri:weblogscom"
      encodingStyle="http://schemas.xmlsoap.org/soap/encoding/"/>
      </input>
      <output>
    <soap:body use="encoded" namespace="uri:weblogscom"
      encodingStyle="http://schemas.xmlsoap.org/soap/encoding/"/>
      </output>
    </operation>
```

```
    </binding>

    <service name="weblogscom">
      <document>
        For a complete description of this service, go to the following
        URL: http://www.soapware.org/weblogsCom
      </document>

      <port name="pingPort" binding="tns:pingSoap">
        <soap:address location="http://rpc.weblogs.com:80/"/>
      </port>
    </service>

  </definitions>
```

Frankly, that's a lot of work for a single operation that accepts two string parameters and returns a Boolean and a string. I had to do all this work because WSDL makes no simplifying assumptions. I started off specifying the request and response in the abstract. Then I had to bind them together into an operation. I exposed the operation as a portType, I defined a port of that type that accepted SOAP messages through HTTP, and then I had to expose that port at a specific URI. For this simple case, creating the WSDL by hand is possible (I just did it) but difficult. That's why most WSDL is generated by automated tools. For simple services you can start from a generated WSDL file and tweak it slightly, but beyond that you're at the mercy of your tools.

The tools then become the real story. It abstracts away the service, the binding, the portType, the messages, the schema, and even the network itself. If you are coding in a statically typed language, like C# or Java, you can have all this WSDL generated for you at the push of a button. Generally all you have to do is select which methods in which classes you want exposed as a web service. Almost all WSDL today is generated by tools and can only be understood by tools. After some setup, the client's tools can call your methods through a web service and it looks like they're calling native-language methods.

What's not to like? How is this different from a compiler, which turns high-level concepts into machine code?

What ought to concern you is that you're moving further and further away from the Web. Machine code is no substitute for a high-level language, but the Web is already a perfectly good platform for distributed programming. That's the whole point of this book. This way of exposing programming-language methods as web services encourages an RPC style that has the overhead of HTTP, but doesn't get any of the benefits I've been talking about.

Even new WSDL features like document/literal encoding (which I haven't covered here) encourage the RPC style of web services: one where every method is a POST, and one where URIs are overloaded to support multiple operations. It's theoretically possible to define a fully RESTful and resource-oriented web service in WSDL (something that's even more possible with WSDL 2.0). It's also theoretically possible to stand an egg on end on a flat surface. You can do it, but you'll be fighting your environment the whole way.

Generated SOAP/WSDL interfaces also tend to be brittle. Different Big Web Services stacks interpret the standards differently, generate slightly different WSDL files, and can't understand each other's messages. The result is that clients are tightly bound to servers that use the same stack. Web services ought to be loosely coupled and resilient: they're being exposed across a network to clients who might be using a totally different set of software tools. The web has already proven its ability to meet this goal.

Worst of all, none of the complexities of WSDL help address the travel broker scenario. Solving the travel broker problem requires solving a number of business problems, like getting "a five-minute hold on seat 24C." Strong typing and protocol independence aren't the solution to any of these problems. Sometimes these requirements can be justified on their own terms, but a lot of the time they go unnoticed and unchallenged, silently dragging on other requirements like simplicity and scalability.

The Resource-Oriented Alternative

WSDL serves two main purposes in real web services. It describes which interface (which RPC-style functions) the service exposes. It also describes the representation formats: the schemas for the XML documents the service accepts and sends. In resource-oriented services, these functions are often unnecessary or can be handled with much simpler standards.

From a RESTful perspective, the biggest problem with WSDL is what kind of interface it's good at describing. WSDL encourages service designers to group many custom operations into a single "endpoint" that doesn't respond to any uniform interface. Since all this functionality is accessible through overloaded POST on a single endpoint URI, the resulting service isn't addressable. WADL is an alternative service description language that's more in line with the Web. Rather than describing RPC-style function calls, it describes resources that respond to HTTP's uniform interface.

WSDL also has no provisions for defining hypertext links, beyond the *anyURI* data type built into XML Schema. SOAP services aren't well connected. How could they be, when an entire service is hidden behind a single address? Again, WADL solves this problem, describing how one resource links to another.

A lot of the time you don't need to describe your representation formats at all. In many Ajax applications, the client and server ends are written by the same group of people. If all you're doing is serializing a data structure for transport across the wire (as happens in the `weblogs.com` ping service), consider JSON as your representation format. You can represent fairly complex data structures in JSON without defining a schema; you don't even need to use XML.

Even when you do need XML, you often find yourself not needing a formally defined schema. Sprinkled throughout this book are numerous examples of clients that use

XPath expressions like "/posts/post" to extract a desired chunk out of a larger XML document. These short strings are often the only description of an XML document a client needs.

There's nothing unRESTful or un-resource-oriented about XML Schema definitions. A schema definition is often overkill, but if it's the right tool for the job, use it. I just think it shouldn't be required.

UDDI

A full description of UDDI is way beyond the scope of this book. Think of it as a yellow pages for WSDL, a way for clients to look up a service that fits their needs. UDDI is even more complex than WSDL. The UDDI specification defines a four-tier hierarchical XML schema that provides metadata about web service descriptions. The data structure types you'll find in a UDDI registry are a *businessEntity*, a *businessService*, a *binding-Template*, and a *tModel*.

The vision of UDDI was one of multiple registries: a fully-replicated Internet-scale registry for businesses, and a private registry behind the firewall of every company that wanted to host one. In 2006, IBM and Microsoft shut down their public UDDI registry after publicly declaring it a success. The IBM/Microsoft registry was reported to describe 50,000 businesses, but privately it was recognized that not all of that data was properly vetted, which inhibited adoption.

So sheer complexity is not the only reason why public adoption of UDDI never caught on. This is just speculation, but additional factors were probably the relatively small number of public SOAP services, successful companies' general desire to not commoditize themselves, and WSDL's tendency to promote a unique interface for every web service. Which is a shame, as UDDI could definitely have helped travel brokers find independently operated hotels. UDDI has seen greater success within companies, where it's practical to impose quality controls and impose uniform interfaces.

The Resource-Oriented Alternative

There's no magic bullet here. Any automated system that helps people find hotels has a built-in economic incentive for hotel chains to game the system. This doesn't mean that computers can't assist in the process, but it does mean that a human needs to make the ultimate decision.

The closest RESTful equivalents to UDDI are the search engines, like Google, Yahoo!, and MSN. These help (human) clients find the resources they're looking for. They take advantage of the uniform interface and common data formats promoted by REST. Even this isn't perfect: spammers try to game the search engines, and sometimes they succeed. But think of the value of search engines and you'll see the promise of UDDI, even if its complexity turns you off.

As RESTful web services grow in popularity and become better-connected (both internally and to the Web at large), something like today's search engines may fulfill the promise of the public UDDI registry. Instead of searching for services that expose certain APIs, we'll search for resources that accept or serve representations with certain semantics. Again, this is speculation. Right now, the public directories of web services (I list a few in Appendix A) are oriented toward use by human beings.

Security

"Security" evokes a lot of related concepts: signatures, encryption, keys, trust, federation, and identity. HTTP's security techniques focus pretty much exclusively on authentication and the transfer of messages. The collection of WS-* specifications related to security (and they are numerous) attempt to cover a more complete picture.

The simplest application of WS-Security is the UserName token profile. This is a SOAP "sticker" that goes on the envelope to give some context to the request: in this case, the sticker explains who's making the request (see Example 10-8).

Example 10-8. The UserName token: a SOAP sticker

```
<Security wsse="http://schemas.xmlsoap.org/ws/2002/xx/secext">
    <UsernameToken>
        <Username>Zoe</Username>
        <Password>ILoveDogs</Password>
    </UsernameToken>
</Security>
```

When placed inside of the `Header` section of a SOAP message, this conveys a set of authentication credentials. It has the same qualities as HTTP Basic authentication, an HTTP sticker which goes into the `Authorization` HTTP header.

Passing passwords in clear text is not exactly best practice, especially if the channel isn't secure. WS-Security defines a number of alternatives. To oversimplify considerably, the WS-Security specification defines a consistent set of XML element names for conveying concepts defined in other standards: passwords, SAML tokens, X.509 tokens, Kerberos tokens, and the like. There's no reason that a similar effort couldn't be undertaken to map similar concepts to HTTP headers. HTTP authentication is extensible, and in the early days of the development of Atom, some WS-Security concepts were ported to HTTP as WSSE (again, see "Authentication and Authorization" in Chapter 8).

But Big Web Services security involves more than the WS-Security standard. Two examples:

- *Signatures* can enable nonrepudiation. It's possible to prove the originator of a given message was long after it sent, and that the message was not modified after it was received. These concepts are important in contracts and checks.

- *Federation* enables a third party to broker trust of identities. This would allow a travel broker to verify that a given person works for one of the travel broker's customers: this might affect billing and discounts.

More examples are well beyond the scope of this book. Suffice it to say that security concepts are much better specified and deployed in SOAP-based protocols than in native HTTP protocols. That doesn't mean that this gap can't be closed, that SOAP stickers can't be ported to HTTP stickers, or that one-off solutions are possible without SOAP. Right now, though, SOAP has many security-related stickers that HTTP doesn't have, and these stickers *are* useful when implementing applications like the travel broker.

As a caution, many of these areas are not areas where amateurs can productively dabble. Nobody should try to add new security concepts to HTTP all by themselves.

The Resource-Oriented Alternative

An application is only as secure as its weakest link. If you encrypt a credit card number for transport over the wire and then simply store it in a database, all you've done is ensure that attackers will target your database. Your view of security needs to encompass the entire system, not just the bits transmitted over the network.

That said, the WS-Security family of specifications are not the only tools for securing those bits. HTTPS (a.k.a Transport Layer Security [TLS], a.k.a. Secure Sockets Layer [SSL]) has proven sufficient in practice for securing credit card information as it's sent across the network. People trust their credit cards to SSL all the time, and the vast majority of attacks don't involve breaking SSL. The use of XML signatures and encryption is also not limited to WS-*. Section 5 of the Atom Syndication Format standard shows how to use these features in Atom documents. You've also seen how S3 implements request signing and access control in Chapter 3. These aspects of security are possible, and have been deployed, in RESTful resource-oriented services. But no one's done the work to make these features available in general.

When all is said and done, your best protection may be the fact that resource-oriented architectures promote simplicity and uniformity. When you're trying to build a secure application, neither complexity nor a large number of interfaces turn out to be advantages.

Reliable Messaging

The WS-ReliableMessaging standard tries to provide assurances to an application that a sequence of messages will be delivered AtMostOnce, AtLeastOnce, ExactlyOnce, or InOrder. It defines some new headers (that is, stickers on the envelope) that track sequence identifiers and message numbers, and some retry logic.

The Resource-Oriented Alternative

Again, these are areas where the specification and implementation for SOAP-based protocols are further advanced than those for native HTTP. In this case, there is an important difference. When used in a certain way, HTTP doesn't need these stickers at all.

As I said earlier, almost all of the HTTP methods are idempotent. If a GET, HEAD, PUT, or DELETE operation doesn't go through, or you don't know whether or not it went through, the appropriate course of action is to just retry the request. With idempotent operations, there's no difference between AtMostOnce, AtLeastOnce, and ExactlyOnce. To get InOrder you just send the messages in order, making sure that each one goes through.

The only nonidempotent method is POST, the one that SOAP uses. SOAP solves the reliable delivery problem from scratch, by defining extra stickers. In a RESTful application, if you want reliable messaging for all operations, I recommend implementing POST Once Exactly (covered back in Chapter 9) or getting rid of POST altogether. The WS-ReliableMessaging standard is motivated mainly by complex scenarios that RESTful web services don't address at all. These might be situations where a message is routed through multiple protocols on the way to its destination, or where both source and destination are cell phones with intermittent access to the network.

Transactions

Transactions are simple to describe, but insanely difficult to implement, particularly in a distributed environment. The idea is that you have a set of operations: say, "transfer $50 from bank A to bank B," and the entire operation must either succeed or fail. Bank A and bank B compete with each other and expose separate web services. You either want bank A to be debited and bank B to be credited, or you want nothing to happen at all. Neither debiting without crediting, or crediting without debiting are desirable outcomes.

There are two basic approaches. The WS-AtomicTransaction standard specifies a common algorithm called a *two-phase commit*. In general, this is only wise between parties that trust one another, but it's the easiest to implement, it falls within the scope of existing products, and therefore it's the one that is most widely deployed.

The second approach is defined by WS-BusinessActivity, and it more closely follows how businesses actually work. If you deposit a check from a foreign bank, your bank may put a hold on it and seek confirmation from the foreign bank. If it hears about a problem before the hold expires, it rolls back the transaction. Otherwise, it accepts the check. If it happens to hear about a problem after it's committed the transaction, it creates a compensating transaction to undo the deposit. The focus is on undoing mistakes in an auditable way, not just preventing them from happening.

The Resource-Oriented Alternative

Again, there's not much that corresponds to this level of specification and deployment in native HTTP applications. It's usually not necessary at all. In Chapter 8 I implemented a transaction system by exposing the transactions as resources, but I didn't need two-phase commit because there was only one party to the transaction. I was transferring money between accounts in a single bank. But if a number of web services supported this kind of transaction, I could stick a little bit of infrastructure on top and then orchestrate them with RESTful two-phase commit.

Two-phase commit requires a level of control over and trust in the services you're coordinating. This works well when all the services are yours, but not so well when you need to work with a competing bank. SOA architects think two-phase commit is inappropriate for web service-based interactions in general, and I think it's usually inappropriate for RESTful web services. When you don't control the services you're coordinating, I recommend implementing the ideas behind WS-BusinessActivity with asynchronous operations (again, from Chapter 8).

To go back to the example of the check from a foreign bank: your bank might create a "job" resource on the foreign bank's web service, asking if the check is valid. After a week with no updates to that resource, your bank might provisionally accept the check. If two days later the foreign bank updates the "job" resource saying that the check is bad, your bank can create a compensating transaction, possibly triggering an overdraft and other alerts. You probably won't need to create a complex scenario like this, but you can see how patterns I've already demonstrated can be used to implement these new ideas.

BPEL, ESB, and SOA

Implemented on top of the foundation I just described are some concepts that are controversial even in the world of Big Web Services. I'll cover them briefly here.

Business Process Execution Language (BPEL) is an XML grammar that makes it possible to describe business processes that span multiple parties. The processes can be orchestrated automatically via software and web services.

The definition of an Enterprise Service Bus (ESB) varies, but tends to include discovery, load balancing, routing, bridging, transformation, and management of web service requests. This often leads to a separation of operations from development, making each simpler and easier to run.

The downside of BPEL and ESB is that they tend to increase coupling with, and reliance on, common third-party middleware. One upside is that you have a number of choices in middleware, varying from well-supported open source offerings to ones provided by established and recognized proprietary vendors.

Service-Oriented Architecture (SOA) is perhaps the least well-defined term of all, which is why I called it out in Chapter 1 as a term I wasn't going to use. I know of no litmus test which indicates whether a given implementation is SOA or not. Sometimes a discussion of SOA starts off saying that SOA encompasses all REST/HTTP applications, but inevitably the focus turns to the Big Web Services standards I described in this chapter.

That said, one aspect of SOA is noteworthy. To date, many approaches to distributed programming focus on remote procedure calls, striving to make them as indistinguishable from local procedure calls as humanly possible. An example is a WSDL file generated from a preexisting application. The SOA idea at least returns the focus to interfaces: in particular, to interfaces that span machine boundaries. Machine boundaries tend to not happen by accident. They often correlate to trust boundaries, and they're the places where message reliability tends to be an issue. Machine boundaries should be studied, not abstracted away

Some other aspects of SOA are independent of the technical architecture of a service. They can be implemented in resource-oriented environments, environments full of Remote Procedure Call services, or heterogeneous environments. "Governance," for example, has to do with auditing and conformance to policies. These "policies" can be anything from government regulations to architectural principles. One possible policy might be: "Don't make RPC-style web service calls."

Conclusion

Both REST and web services have become buzzwords. They are chic and fashionable. These terms are artfully woven into PowerPoint presentations by people who have no real understanding of the subject. This chapter, and indeed this book, is an attempt to dispel some of the confusion.

In this chapter you've seen firsthand the value that SOAP brings (not so much), and the complexity that WSDL brings (way too much). You've also seen resource-oriented alternatives listed every step of the way. Hopefully this will help you make better choices. If you can see you'll need some of the features described in this chapter which are only available as stickers on SOAP envelopes, getting started on the SOAP path from the beginning will provide a basis for you to build on.

The alternative is to start lightweight and apply the YAGNI (You Aren't Gonna Need It) principle, adding only the features that you know you actually need. If it turns out you need some of the stickers that only Big Web Services can provide, you can always wrap your XML representations in SOAP envelopes, or cherry-pick the stickers you need and port them to HTTP headers. Given the proven scalability of the Web, starting simple is usually a safe choice—safe enough, I think, to be the default.

## CHAPTER 11

Ajax Applications as REST Clients

Ajax applications have become very hot during the past couple of years. Significantly hotter, in fact, than even knowing what Ajax applications are. Fortunately, once you understand the themes of this book it's easy to explain Ajax in those terms. At the risk of seeming old-fashioned, I'd like to present a formal definition of Ajax:

> An Ajax application is a web service client that runs inside a web browser.

Does this make sense? Consider two examples widely accepted not to be Ajax applications: a JavaScript form validator and a Flash graphics demo. Both run inside the web browser, but they don't make programmatic HTTP requests, so they're not Ajax applications. On the flip side: the standalone clients I wrote in Chapters2 and 3 aren't Ajax applications because they don't run inside a web browser.

Now consider Gmail, a site that everyone agrees uses Ajax. If you log into Gmail you can watch your browser make background requests to the web service at `mail.google.com`, and update the web page you're seeing with new data. That's exactly what a web service client does. The Gmail web service has no public-facing name and is not intended for use by clients other than the Gmail web page, but it's a web service nonetheless. Don't believe it? There are libraries like libgmail (*http://libgmail.sourceforge.net/*) that act as unofficial, non-Ajax clients to the Gmail web service. Remember, if it's on the Web, it's a web service.

This chapter covers client programming, and it picks up where Chapter 2 left off. Here I'm focusing on the special powers and needs of web service clients that run in a browser environment. I cover JavaScript's `XMLHttpRequest` class and the browser's DOM, and show how security settings affect which web service clients you can run in a browser.

From AJAX to Ajax

Every introduction to Ajax will tell you that it used to be AJAX, an acronym for Asynchronous JavaScript And XML. The acronym has been decommissioned and now Ajax is just a word. It's worth spending a little time exploring why this happened. Programmers didn't suddenly lose interest in acronyms. AJAX had to be abandoned because what it says isn't necessarily true. Ajax is an architectural style that doesn't need to involve JavaScript or XML.

The JavaScript in AJAX actually means whatever browser-side language is making the HTTP requests. This is *usually* JavaScript, but it can be any language the browser knows how to interpret. Other possibilities are ActionScript (running within a Flash application), Java (running within an applet), and browser-specific languages like Internet Explorer's VBScript.

XML actually means whatever representation format the web service is sending. This can be any format, so long as the browser side can understand it. Again, this is *usually* XML, because it's easy for browsers to parse, and because web services tend to serve XML representations. But JSON is also very common, and it can be also be HTML, plain text, or image files: anything the browser can handle or the browser-side script can parse.

So AJAX hackers decided to become Ajax hackers, rather than always having to explain that JavaScript needn't mean JavaScript and XML might not be XML, or becoming Client-Side Scripting And Representation Format hackers. When I talk about Ajax in this book I mostly talk in terms of JavaScript and XML, but I'm not talking *about* those technologies: I'm talking about an application architecture.

The Ajax Architecture

The Ajax architecture works something like this:

1. A user, controlling a browser, makes a request for the main URI of an application.

2. The server serves a web page that contains an embedded script.

3. The browser renders the web page and either runs the script, or waits for the user to trigger one of the script's actions with a keyboard or mouse operation.

4. The script makes an asynchronous HTTP request to some URI on the server. The user can do other things while the request is being made, and is probably not even aware that the request is happening.

5. The script parses the HTTP response and uses the data to modify the user's view. This might mean using DOM methods to change the tag structure of the original HTML page. It might mean modifying what's displayed inside a Flash application or Java applet.

    From the user's point of view, it looks like the GUI just modified itself.

This architecture looks a lot like that of a client-side GUI application. In fact, that's what this is. The web browser provides the GUI elements (as described in your initial HTML file) and the event loop (through JavaScript events). The user triggers events, which get data from elsewhere and alter the GUI elements to fit. This is why Ajax applications are often praised as working like desktop applications: they have the same architecture.

A standard web application has the same GUI elements but a simpler event loop. Every click or form submission causes a refresh of the entire view. The browser gets a new HTML page and constructs a whole new set of GUI elements. In an Ajax application, the GUI can change a little bit at a time. This saves bandwidth and reduces the psychological effects on the end user. The application appears to change incrementally instead of in sudden jerks.

The downside is that every application state has the same URI: the first one the end user visited. Addressability and statelessness are destroyed. The underlying web service may be addressable and stateless, but the end user can no longer bookmark a particular state, and the browser's "Back" button stops working the way it should. The application is no longer on the Web, any more than a SOAP+WSDL web service that only exposes a single URI is on the Web. I discuss what to do about this next.

A del.icio.us Example

Back in Chapter 2 I showed clients in various languages for a REST-RPC hybrid service: the API for the del.icio.us social bookmarking application. Though I implemented my own, fully RESTful version of that service in Chapter 7, I'm going to bring the original service out one more time to demonstrate a client written in JavaScript. Like most JavaScript programs, this one runs in a web browser, and since it's a web service client, that makes it an Ajax application. Although simple, this program brings up almost all of the advantages of and problems with Ajax that I discuss in this chapter.

The first part of the application is the user interface, implemented in plain HTML. This is quite different from my other del.icio.us clients, which ran on the command line and wrote their data to standard output (see Example 11-1).

Example 11-1. An Ajax client to the del.icio.us web service

```
<!DOCTYPE HTML PUBLIC "-//W3C//DTD HTML 4.0
 Transitional//EN" "http://www.w3.org/TR/REC-html40/transitional.dtd">
<!--delicious-ajax.html-->
<!--An Ajax application that uses the del.icio.us web service. This
    application will probably only work when saved as a local
    file. Even then, your browser's security policy might prevent it
    from running.-->

<html>
 <head>
  <title>JavaScript del.icio.us</title>
 </head>
 <body>
  <h1>JavaScript del.icio.us example</h1>

  <p>Enter your del.icio.us account information, and I'll fetch and
  display your most recent bookmarks.</p>

  <form onsubmit="callDelicious(); return false;">
    Username: <input id="username" type="text" /><br />
```

```
    Password: <input id="password" type="password" /><br />
    <input type="submit" value="Fetch del.icio.us bookmarks"/>
</form>

<div id="message"></div>

<ul id="links"></ul>
```

My user interface is an HTML form that doesn't point anywhere, and some tags (div and ul) that don't contain anything. I'm going to manipulate these tags with JavaScript functions. The first is setMessage, which puts a given string into the div tag (see Example 11-2).

Example 11-2. Ajax client continued: definition of setMessage

```
<script type="text/javascript">
 function setMessage(newValue) {
   message = document.getElementById("message");
   message.firstChild.textContent = newValue;
 }
```

And it's not quite fair to say that the HTML form doesn't point anywhere. Sure, it doesn't have an "action" attribute like a normal HTML form, but it does have an onsubmit event handler. This means the web browser will call the JavaScript function callDelicious whenever the end user clicks the submit button. Instead of going through the page request loop of a web browser, I'm using the GUI-like event loop of a JavaScript program.

The callDelicious function uses the JavaScript library XMLHttpRequest to fetch data from *https://api.del.icio.us/v1/posts/recent/*. This is the URI used throughout Chapter 2 to fetch a user's most recent del.icio.us bookmarks. First we need to do some housekeeping: get permission from the browser to send the request, and gather whatever data the user entered into the HTML form (see Example 11-3).

Example 11-3. Ajax client continued: definition of callDelicious

```
function callDelicious() { // Get permission from the browser to send the request.
  try {
    if (netscape.security.PrivilegeManager.enablePrivilege)
     netscape.security.PrivilegeManager.enablePrivilege("UniversalBrowserRead");
  } catch (e) {
    alert("Sorry, browser security settings won't let this program run.");
    return;
  }

  // Fetch the user-entered account information
  var username = document.getElementById("username").value;
  var password = document.getElementById("password").value;

  // Remove any old links from the list.
  var links = document.getElementById("links");
  while (links.firstChild)
    links.removeChild(links.firstChild)
  setMessage("Please wait...");
```

Now we're ready to send the HTTP request, as shown in Example 11-4.

Example 11-4. callDelicious definition continued

```
// Send the request.
// See "Working Around the Corner Cases" for a cross-browser
// "createXMLHttpRequest" implementation.
request = new XMLHttpRequest();
request.open("GET", "https://api.del.icio.us/v1/posts/recent", true,
             username, password);
request.onreadystatechange = populateLinkList;
request.send(null);
```

The third JavaScript function I'll define is populateLinkList. I've already referenced this function, in the line request.onreadystatechange = populateLinkList. That line sets up populateLinkList as a callback function. The idea is that while api.del.icio.us is processing the request, the user can go about her business, surfing the web in another browser window. Once the request completes, the browser calls populateLinkList, which handles the response. You can do JavaScript programming without these callback functions, but it's a bad idea. Without callbacks, the web browser will go nonresponsive while the XMLHttpRequest object is making an HTTP request. Not very asynchronous.

The job of populateLinkList is to parse the XML document from the del.icio.us web service. The representation in Example 11-5 represents a list of bookmarks, and populateLinkList turns each bookmark into a list item of the formerly empty ul list tag.

Example 11-5. Ajax client concluded: definition of populateLinkList

```
// Called when the HTTP request has completed.
function populateLinkList() {
  if (request.readyState != 4) // Request has not yet completed
    return;

  setMessage("Request complete.");
  if (netscape.security.PrivilegeManager.enablePrivilege)
    netscape.security.PrivilegeManager.enablePrivilege("UniversalBrowserRead");
  // Find the "post" tags in the representation
  posts = request.responseXML.getElementsByTagName("post");

  setMessage(posts.length + " link(s) found:");
  // For every "post" tag in the XML document...
  for (var i = 0; i < posts.length; i++) {
    post = posts[i];
    // ...create a link that links to the appropriate URI.
    var link = document.createElement("a");
    var description = post.getAttribute('description');
    link.setAttribute("href", post.getAttribute('href'));
    link.appendChild(document.createTextNode(description));

    // Stick the link in an "li" tag...
    var listItem = document.createElement("li");
    // ...and make the "li" tag a child of the "ul" tag.
    listItem.appendChild(link); links.appendChild(listItem)
```

```
      }
     }
    }
   </script>
  </body>
 </html>
```

The Advantages of Ajax

If you try out the del.icio.us client you'll notice some nice features that come from the web browser environment. Most obviously: unlike the examples in Chapter 2, this application has a GUI. And as GUI programming goes, this is pretty easy. Method calls that seem to do nothing but manipulate a mysterious document data structure, actually change the end user's view of the application. The document is just the thing the user sees rendered in the browser. Since the browser knows how to turn changes to the document into GUI layout changes, there's no widget creation and layout specification, as you'd see in conventional GUI programs.

This client also never explicitly parses the XML response from the del.icio.us web service. A web browser has an XML parser built in, and `XMLHttpRequest` automatically parses into a DOM object any XML document that comes in on a web service response. You access the DOM object through the `XMLHttpRequest.responseXML` member. The DOM standard for web browsers defines the API for this object: you can iterate over its children, search it with methods like `getElementsByTagName`, or hit it with XPath expressions.

More subtly: try loading this HTML file and clicking the submit button without providing a username and password. You'll get a dialog box asking you for a del.icio.us username and password: the same dialog box you get whenever your browser accesses a page that requires HTTP basic auth. This is exactly what you're doing: visiting *https://api.del.icio.us/v1/posts/recent*, which requires HTTP basic auth, in your web browser. But now you're doing it by triggering an action in an Ajax application, rather than clicking on a link to the URI.

Web browsers are by far the most popular HTTP clients out there, and they've been written to handle the corner cases of HTTP. You could remove both text fields from the HTML form in Example 11-1, and the Ajax application would still work, because real web browsers have their own user interface for gathering basic HTTP auth information.

The Disadvantages of Ajax

Unfortunately, thanks to the wide variety of web browsers in use, you'll need to deal with a whole new set of corner cases if you want your application to work in all browsers. Later on I'll show you code libraries and code snippets that work around the corner cases.

If you try out this program, you'll also run into the problem I talked about at the end of Chapter 8: why should the end user trust the web service client? You'd trust your browser with your del.icio.us username and password, but this isn't your browser. It's a web service client that uses your browser to make HTTP requests, and it could be doing anything in those requests. If this was an official web page that was itself served from `api.del.icio.us`, then your browser would trust it to make web service calls to the server it came from. But it's a web page that comes from a file on your hard drive, and wants to call out to the Web at large. To a web browser, this is very suspicious behavior.

From a security standpoint, this is no different from the standalone del.icio.us clients I wrote in other programming languages. But there's no real reason why you should trust a standalone web service client, either. We just tend to assume they're safe. A web browser is constantly loading untrusted web pages, so it has a security model that restricts what those pages can do in JavaScript. If strangers were always dumping executables into your home directory, you'd probably think twice before running them.

Which is why I called `netscape.security.PrivilegeManager.enablePrivilege`, asking the browser if it won't let me make an HTTP request to a foreign domain ("Universal-BrowserRead"), and won't it also let me use the browser's XML parser on some data from a foreign domain ("UniversalBrowserRead" again, but in a different JavaScript function). Even with these calls in place, you're likely to get browser security messages asking you if you want to accept this risky behavior. (These are not like the browser messages you might get when you do something innocuous like submit an HTML form, messages that Justin Mason once characterized as "are you sure you want to *send stuff on the intarweb?*". These are more serious.) And that's with this file sitting on your (presumably trusted) filesystem. If I tried to serve this Ajax application from `oreilly.com`, there's no way your browser would let it make an HTTP request to `api.del.icio.us`.

So why don't we see these problems all the time in Ajax applications? Because right now, most Ajax applications are served from the same domain names as the web services they access. This is the fundamental difference between JavaScript web service clients and clients written in other languages: the client and the server are usually written by the same people and served from the same domain.

The browser's security model doesn't totally prevent you from writing an `XMLHttpRequest` application against someone else's web service, but it does make it difficult. According to the web browser, the only Ajax application safe enough to run without a warning is one that only makes requests against the domain it was served from. At the end of this chapter I'll show you ways of writing Ajax clients that can consume foreign web services. Note, though, that these techniques rely heavily on cheating.

REST Goes Better

Ajax applications are web service clients, but why should they be clients of RESTful web services in particular? Most Ajax applications consume a web service written by the same people who wrote the application, mainly because the browser security model makes it difficult to do anything else. Why should it matter whether a service used by one client is fully RESTful or just a resource-oriented/RPC hybrid? There are even programs that turn a WSDL file into a JavaScript library for making RPC SOAP calls through XMLHttpRequest. What's wrong with that?

Well, in general, the interface between two parts of an application matters. If RESTful architectures yield better web services, then you'll benefit from using them, even if you're the only one consuming the service. What's more, if your application does something useful, people *will* figure out your web service and write their own clients —just as if your web site exposes useful information, people will screen-scrape it. Unless you want to obfuscate your web service so only you can use it, I think the Resource-Oriented Architecture is the best design.

The web services that Ajax applications consume should be RESTful for the same reasons almost all web services should be RESTful: addressability, statelessness, and the rest. The only twist here is that Ajax clients are embedded inside a web browser. And in general, the web browser environment strengthens the argument for REST. You probably don't need me to reiterate my opinion of Big Web Services in this chapter, but SOAP, WSDL, and the rest of the gang look even more unwieldy inside a web browser. Maybe you're a skeptic and you think the REST paradigm isn't suitable as a general platform for distributed programming—but it should at least be suitable for the communication between a web browser and a web server!

Outside of a web browser, you might decide to limit yourself to the human web's interface of GET and POST. Many client libraries support only the basic features of HTTP. But every Ajax application runs inside a capable HTTP client. The chart below has the details, but almost every web browser gives XMLHttpRequest access to the five basic HTTP methods, and they all let you customize the request headers and body.

What's more, Ajax calls take place in the same environment as the end user's other web browsing. If the client needs to make HTTP requests through a proxy, you can assume they've already configured it. An Ajax request sends the same cookies and Basic auth headers as do other browser requests to your domain. You can usually use the same authentication mechanisms and user accounts for your web site and your Ajax services.

Look back at steps 4 and 5 of the Ajax architecture—basically "GET a URI" and "use data from the URI to modify the view." That fits in quite well with the Resource-Oriented Architecture. An Ajax application can aggregate information about a large number of resources, and incrementally change the GUI as the resource state changes. The architectural advantages of REST apply to Ajax clients just as they do to other clients. One example: you don't need to coordinate the browser's application state with the server if the server never keeps any application state.

Making the Request

Now I'd like to look at the technical details underlying the most common client language for Ajax: JavaScript. The major web browsers all implement a JavaScript HTTP client library called `XMLHttpRequest`. Its interface is simple because the browser environment handles the hairy edge cases (proxies, HTTPS, redirects, and so on). Because `XMLHttpRequest` is so simple, and because I want to drive home the point that it's fundamentally no different from (say) Ruby's `open-uri`, I'm going to cover almost the whole interface in this section and the next. If you're already familiar with `XMLHttpRequest`, feel free to skim this section, or skip to the end where there's a nice chart.

To build an HTTP request you need to create an `XMLHttpRequest` object. This seemingly simple task is actually one of the major points of difference between the web browsers. This simple constructor works in Mozilla-family browsers like Firefox:

    request = new XMLHttpRequest();

The second step is to call the `XMLHttpRequest.open` method with information about the request. All but the first two arguments in this sample call are optional:

    request.open([HTTP method], [URI], true, [Basic auth username], [Basic auth password]);

Pretty self-explanatory, except for the third argument, which I've hard-coded to `true`. This argument controls whether the browser carries out the request asynchronously (letting the user do other things while it's going on) or synchronously (locking up the whole browser until it gets and parses the server response). Locking up the browser never creates a good user experience, so I never recommend it, even in simple applications. This does mean you have to set up a handler function to be called when the request completes:

    request.onReadyStateChange = [Name of handler function];

If you want to set any HTTP request headers, you use `setrequestHeader`:

    request.setRequestHeader([Header name], [Header value]);

Then you send the request to the HTTP server by calling `send`. If the request is a POST or PUT request, you should pass the entity-body you want to send as an argument to `send`. For all other requests, it should be `null`.

    request.send([Entity-body]);

If all goes well, your handler function (the one you set to `request.onReadyStateChange`) will be called four times over the lifetime of the HTTP request, and the value of `request.readyState` will be different every time. The value you're looking for is the last one, 4, which means that the request has completed and it's time to manipulate the response. If `request.readyState` doesn't equal 4, you'll just `return` from the handler function.

`XMLHttpRequest` uses the underlying web browser code to make its requests. Since the major web browsers are among the most complete HTTP client implementations around, this means that `XMLHttpRequest` does pretty well on the feature matrix I introduced for HTTP clients back in Chapter 2. Cookies, proxies, and authentication tend to work in Ajax applications as they do in normal web access.

Handling the Response

Eventually the request will complete and the browser will call your handler function for the last time. At this point your `XMLHttpRequest` instance gains some new and interesting abilities:

- The `status` property contains the numeric status code for the request.
- The `responseXML` property contains a preparsed DOM object representing the response document—assuming it was served as XML and the browser can parse it. HTML, even XHTML, will *not* be parsed into `responseXML`, unless the document was served as an XML media type like `application/xml` or `application/xhtml+xml`.
- The `responseText` property contains the response document as a raw string—useful when it's JSON or some other non-XML format.
- Passing the name of an HTTP header into the `getResponseHeader` method looks up the value of that header.

Web browsers epitomize the tree-style parsing strategy that turns a document into a data structure. When you make a web service request from within JavaScript, the `responseXML` property gives you your response document as a tree. You can access the representation with a standardized set of DOM manipulation methods.

 Unlike the `XMLHttpRequest` interface, the DOM interface is extremely complex and I won't even think about covering it all here. See the official standard (*http://www.w3.org/DOM*), the Mozilla DOM reference (*http://www.mozilla.org/docs/dom/*), or a book like *Dynamic HTML: The Definitive Reference* by Danny Goodman (O'Reilly).

You can navigate the tree with methods like `getElementByID`, and run XPath queries against it with `evaluate`.

But there's another treelike data structure in town: the HTML document being displayed in the end user's web browser. In an Ajax application, this document is your user interface. You manipulate it with the same DOM methods you use to extract data from an XML web service representation. An Ajax application acts as glue between the raw data the web service sends, and the HTML GUI the end user sees. Useful DOM methods here are `createTextNode` and `createElement`, both of which I used in Example 11-5.

JSON

I covered JSON briefly in Chapter 2. I brought it up again in Chapter 9 as one of my recommended representation formats. But since it comes from JavaScript, I want to show it in action in the Ajax chapter.

Example 11-6 shows of an Ajax client for Yahoo!'s image search web service.

Example 11-6. An Ajax client that calls out to a service that serves JSON representations

```
<!DOCTYPE HTML PUBLIC "-//W3C//DTD HTML 4.0 Transitional//EN"
"http://www.w3.org/TR/REC-html40/transitional.dtd">
<!--yahoo-ajax.html-->
<!--An Ajax application that uses the JSON output feature of Yahoo!
    Web Services-->

<html>
<head><title>Javascript Yahoo! JSN</title></head>
<body>
<h1>Javascript Yahoo! JSON example</h1>

<p id="message">Loading pictures of baby elephants!</p>

<div id="images">
</div>

<script type="text/javascript">
function formatImages(result)
{
  var images = document.getElementById("images");
  items = result["ResultSet"]["Result"];
  document.getElementById("message").firstChild.textContent =
    items.length + " baby elephant pictures:";
  for (var i = 0; i < items.length; i++)
  {
    image = items[i];

    // Create a link
    var link = document.createElement("a");
    link.setAttribute("href", image["ClickUrl"]);

    // Put a thumbnail image in the link.
    var img = document.createElement("img");
    var thumbnail = image["Thumbnail"];
    img.setAttribute("src", thumbnail["Url"]);
    img.setAttribute("width", thumbnail["Width"]);
    img.setAttribute("height", thumbnail["Height"]);
    img.setAttribute("title", image["Height"]);
    link.appendChild(img);
```

```
    images.appendChild(link);
  }
}
</script>

<script type="text/javascript"
 src="http://api.search.yahoo.com/ImageSearchService/V1/imageSearch
?appid=restbook&query=baby+elephant&output=json&callback=formatImages" />

</body>
</html>
```

If you load this HTML file in your web browser you'll see some cute pictures of baby elephants, courtesy of Yahoo! Image Search. What you won't see is a browser security warning. The del.icio.us example had to ask the browser if it was OK to make an `XMLHttpRequest` to another domain, and even then the browser imposes strict rules about when it is OK. But this Ajax client just makes the web service call. That's because it doesn't make the call through `XMLHttpRequest`. It uses a technique described as Java-Script on Demand (JoD). JoD bypasses the browser's security policy by fetching custom-generated JavaScript from a web service. Because any JSON data structure is a valid JavaScript program, this works especially well with web services that serve JSON representations.

Don't Bogart the Benefits of REST

It's easy for an Ajax application to take all the advantages of REST for itself, and leave none of them for the end user. Gmail is a good example of this. The Gmail Ajax application benefits greatly from its use of an addressable, stateless web service. But in terms of user experience, all the end user sees is one constantly changing HTML page. No addressability for you! If you want to bookmark a search or a particular email message, you need to start off at Gmail's plain HTML interface (*https://mail.google.com/mail/?ui=html*).

Ordinarily, your browser's back and forward buttons move you back and forth through application state. This works because the Web is stateless. But if you start using a typical Ajax application, your back button breaks. Clicking it doesn't take you backward in application state: it takes you to the page you were on before you started using the Ajax application. No statelessness for you!

The underlying cause is the same thing that gives Ajax applications their polished look. Ajax applications disconnect the end user from the HTTP request-response cycle. When you visit the URI of an Ajax application, you leave the Web. From that point on you're using a GUI application that makes HTTP requests for you, behind the scenes, and folds the data back into the GUI. The GUI application just happens to be running in the same piece of software you use to browse the Web. But even an Ajax application can give its users the benefits of REST, by incorporating them into the user interface.

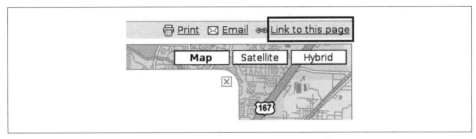

Figure 11-1. An entry point into a web service (that is, a URI), maintained through Ajax

I'm basically asking you to reinvent some of the features of the web browser within your application.

The best example of this is Google Maps, the application that started the Ajax craze. At first glimpse, Google Maps looks about as addressable as Gmail. You visit *http://maps.google.com/* and are presented with a large-scale map. You can use Ajax to zoom in and navigate to any point on the globe, but the URI in your browser's address bar never changes.

But Google Maps also uses Ajax to maintain a "permalink" for whatever point on the globe you're currently at. This URI is kept not in your browser's address bar but in an a tag in the HTML document (see Figure 11-1). It represents all the information Google Maps needs to identify a section of the globe: latitude, longitude, and map scale. It's a new entry point into the Ajax application. This link is the Google Maps equivalent of your browser's address bar.

Thanks to the extra DOM work that keeps this a tag up to date as you navigate the map, every point on every map is on the Web. Any point can be bookmarked, blogged about, and emailed around. Anyone who visits one of these URIs enters the Google Maps Ajax application at the right point, instead of getting a view centered on the continental US (as would happen if you navigated to a place on a map and then reloaded *http://maps.google.com/*). Addressability, destroyed by Ajax but added back by good application design, has allowed communities like Google Sightseeing (*http://googlesightseeing.com/*) to grow up around the Google Maps application.

Your Ajax applications can give statelessness back by reproducing the functionality of the browser's back and forward buttons. You don't have to reproduce the browser's behavior slavishly. The point is to let the end user move back and forth in his application state, instead of having to start from the beginning of a complex operation if he makes a mistake or gets lost.

Cross-Browser Issues and Ajax Libraries

As always when web browsers are involved, different clients have different levels of support for XMLHttpRequest. And as always seems to happen, Internet Explorer is the major outlier. This isn't quite fair, because XMLHttpRequest was a Microsoft invention and Internet Explorer was the first browser to support Ajax at all. But until the release of Internet Explorer 7, Ajax was implemented as Windows-specific technology: an ActiveX control called `XMLHttp`.

The cross-platform Mozilla project adopted the API of the `XMLHttp` control, but implemented it as a class you could instantiate directly from JavaScript. Other browsers followed this lead, and all current browsers now use the `XMLHttpRequest` name (including the new Internet Explorer). But old versions of Internet Explorer still make up a big portion of the user base, so cross-browser issues are still a problem.

Example 11-7 is a JavaScript function that always creates an object that acts like an `XMLHttpRequest`, even though under the covers it may be an ActiveX control. It was written by Bret Taylor and comes from his site at *http://ajaxcookbook.org/*.

Example 11-7. A cross-browser wrapper for XMLHttpRequest

```
function createXMLHttpRequest() {
  if (typeof XMLHttpRequest != "undefined") {
    return new XMLHttpRequest();
  } else if (typeof ActiveXObject != "undefined") {
    return new ActiveXObject("Microsoft.XMLHTTP");
  } else {
    throw new Error("XMLHttpRequest not supported");
  }
}
```

This function is a drop-in replacement for the `XMLHttpRequest` constructor in Example 11-3, instead of this:

```
request = new XMLHttpRequest();
```

you might write this:

```
request = createXMLHttpRequest();
```

I know of two other major cross-browser issues. First, the Safari browser doesn't support the PUT and DELETE methods. If you want your service to be accessible from Safari, you'll need to allow your clients to simulate PUT and DELETE requests with overloaded POST. Second, Microsoft Internet Explorer caches successful responses indefinitely. This makes it look to the user like your resources haven't changed, even when they have. The best way to get around this is to send proper `ETag` response headers with your representations, or to disable caching altogether with `Cache-Control`. You can use the `XMLHttpRequest` test suite (*http://www.mnot.net/javascript/xmlhttprequest/*) to find out about more minor cross-browser quirks.

Because Ajax is a very important niche for JavaScript applications, some JavaScript libraries include wrappers for hiding the differences between browsers. I'm not going to cover these frameworks in detail, because they act more as standard libraries for JavaScript than tools for building web service clients. I will show how to make simple HTTP requests with two popular libraries, Prototype and Dojo. Another popular library, script.aculo.us (*http://script.aculo.us/*), is based on Prototype.

Prototype

Prototype (*http://prototype.conio.net/*) introduces three classes for making HTTP requests:

- `Ajax.Request`: a wrapper around `XMLHttpRequest` that takes care of cross-browser issues and can call different JavaScript functions on the request's success or failure. The actual `XMLHttpRequest` object is available as the `transport` member of the `Request` object, so `responseXML` will be through `request.transport.responseXML`.

- `Ajax.Updater`: a subclass of `Request` that makes an HTTP request and inserts the response document into a specified element of the DOM.

- `Ajax.PeriodicalUpdater`, which makes the same HTTP request at intervals, refreshing a DOM element each time.

I've implemented the del.icio.us Ajax client in Prototype, and it was mostly the same as the client I showed you starting in Example 11-1. The code snippet below mostly replaces the code in Example 11-3 where the `XMLHttpRequest` constructor used to be. Note the new `script` tag, the use of `request.transport` instead of `request`, and the use of Prototype's `onFailure` hook to signal a failure (such as an authorization failure) to the user.

Example 11-8. A portion of ajax-delicious-prototype.html

```
...
<script src="prototype.js"></script>
<script type="text/javascript">
  ...
  var request = new Ajax.Request("https://api.del.icio.us/v1/posts/recent",
                                 {method: 'get', onSuccess: populateLinkList,
                                  onFailure: reportFailure});
  function reportFailure() {
    setMessage("An error occured: " + request.transport.status);
  }

  // Called when the HTTP request has completed.
  function populateLinkList() {
    setMessage("Request complete.");
    if (netscape.security.PrivilegeManager.enablePrivilege) {
      netscape.security.PrivilegeManager.enablePrivilege("UniversalBrowserRead");
    }

    posts = request.transport.responseXML.getElementsByTagName("post");
    ...
```

In its quest to simplify `XMLHttpRequest`, Prototype hides some of the features. You can't set request headers, or specify a username and password for basic HTTP auth. So even if you're using Prototype, you might want to keep around a snippet of code like the one in Example 11-7. On the other hand, the Prototype implementation of the del.icio.us client doesn't need the username and password text fields at all: it just needs a button.

The end user's browser will prompt her anyway for her del.icio.us username and password.

Dojo

The Dojo library (*http://dojotoolkit.org/*) provides a uniform API that not only hides the differences between browsers when it comes to XMLHttpRequest, it hides the difference between XMLHttpRequest and other ways of getting the browser to send an HTTP request. These "transports" include tricks that use HTML tags, such as JoD. All the variants on XMLHttpRequest are kept in the dojo.io.XMLHttp transport class. For all transports, the bind method is the one that makes the HTTP request.

As with Prototype, I've implemented the del.icio.us Ajax client with Dojo, and it's mostly the same as the original, except for the section in Example 11-3 where the XMLHttpRequest constructor used to be. Example 11-9 shows the relevant portions of *ajax-delicious-dojo.html*.

Example 11-9. Some portions of ajax-delicious-dojo.html

```
...
    <script src="dojo/dojo.js"></script>
    <script type="text/javascript">
      ...
      dojo.require("dojo.io.*");
      dojo.io.bind({ url: "https://api.del.icio.us/v1/posts/recent", load:
                     populateLinkList, error: reportFailure });

      function reportFailure(type, error) {
        setMessage("An error occured: " + error.message);
      }

      // Called when the HTTP request has completed.
      function populateLinkList(type, data, request) {
        setMessage("Request complete.");
        if (netscape.security.PrivilegeManager.enablePrivilege) {
          netscape.security.PrivilegeManager.enablePrivilege("UniversalBrowserRead");
        }

        posts = request.responseXML.getElementsByTagName("post");
      ...
```

The error-handling function is passed a dojo.io.Error object with members called number and message. You can ignore the first argument: it's always "error." You can also ignore the first argument to the *success*-handling function (it's always "load"). The second argument, called data above, is an interface to use Dojo's DOM manipulation interface. If you want to use the XMLHttpRequest interface instead, you can ignore that argument too.

Subverting the Browser Security Model

That's a provocative title but I stand by it. A web browser enforces a general rule that's supposed to prevent it from using code found on domain A to make an HTTP request to domain B. I think this rule is too strict, so I'm going to show you two ways around it: request proxying and JoD. I'm also going to show how these tricks put you at risk by making you, the Ajax programmer, accept responsibility for what some foreign server does. These tricks deserve to be regarded as cheats, because they subvert rather than fulfill the web browser's intentions. They often make the end user *less* secure than if his browser had simply allowed domain A's JavaScript to make an HTTP request to domain B.

There is a secure method of getting permission to make foreign web service calls in your JavaScript applications, which is to *ask* for the permission by calling:

```
netscape.security.PrivilegeManager.enablePrivilege("UniversalBrowserRead");
```

There's also an insecure method, which is to have your users use Internet Explorer with the security settings turned way down.

If your script is digitally signed, the client's browser shows your credentials to the end user. The end user makes a decision whether or not to trust you, and if he trusts you he gives you permission to make the web service calls you need to make. This is similar to the technique I mentioned in Chapter 8, where an untrusted web service client was trying to gain the end user's trust. The difference here is that the untrusted web service client is running *inside* the end user's trusted web browser.

There are two problems with the secure method. The first is that, as you might have guessed from the name `netscape.security.PrivilegeManager`, it only works in Mozilla, Firefox, and Netscape-like browsers. The second is that it's quite painful to actually get a signed script set up. Once you do get one set up, you find you've stored your HTML files in a signed Java archive file, and that your application is off the Web! Search engines won't pick up your HTML pages, and you'll only be able to address them through a weird `jar:` URI like `jar:http://www.example.com/ajax-app.jar!/index.html`.

And that's the *right* solution. As you can tell, this is an immature field. Until recently, web services weren't popular enough for people to seriously think about these problems. Though the hacks described below are potentially dangerous, their inventors meant no harm. They were motivated only by zeal for the enormous possibilities of in-browser web service clients. The challenge is to come up with ways of getting the same functionality without sacrificing security, adding too much complexity, or moving Ajax applications out of view of the Web. The W3C is working on this problem (see "Enabling Read Access for Web Resources" at *http://www.w3.org/TR/access-control/*.)

Although I'm focusing again on JavaScript applications, Java applets and Flash also run under security models that prevent them from sending data to foreign servers. The request proxying trick, described below, works for any kind of Ajax application, because it involves work on the server side. As its name implies, the JoD trick is JavaScript-specific.

Request Proxying

You're running a site, example.com, serving up Ajax applications that try to make XMLHttpRequest requests against yahoo.com. Naturally your clients' web browsers will complain. But what if they never made a request to yahoo.com? What if they made requests to example.com, which you handled by making your own, identical requests to yahoo.com without telling the client?

Welcome to the request proxy trick, well described in Yahoo's document "Use a Web Proxy for Cross-Domain XMLHttpRequest Calls" (*http://developer.yahoo.com/java script/howto-proxy.html*). In this trick, you set aside part of the URI space on your server to simulate the URI space on some other server. When you get a request to a URI in that space, you send it along without alteration to the foreign server, and then pipe the response right back to the client. From the client's point of view, it looks like you're providing someone else's web service. Really, you're just filing the domain names off their HTTP responses and replacing them with your own.

If you're using Apache and have mod_proxy installed, the simplest way to set up a proxy is in the Apache configuration. If you also have mod_ssl installed, you can enable SSLProxyEngine and proxy HTTPS requests. So long as you have mod_ssl installed, you can even proxy HTTPS requests from an HTTP server: perhaps *http://example.com/service/* is proxied to *https://service.com/*. Of course, this destroys the security of the connection. Data is secure between the proxy and your site, but not between your site and the end user. If you do this you'd better tell the end user what you're doing.

Let's say you want to make the del.icio.us Ajax application, given above, work from your site at example.com. You can set up a proxy so that all URIs beneath *https:// example.com/apis/delicious/v1/* are transparently forwarded to *https://api.del.icio.us/ v1/*. The simplest way to set up a proxy is with the ProxyPass directive, which maps part of your URI space onto a foreign site's URI space (see Example 11-10).

Example 11-10. Apache configuration with ProxyPass

```
SSLProxyEngine On
ProxyRequests Off # Don't act as an open proxy.
ProxyPass /apis/delicious/v1 https://api.del.icio.us/v1/
```

A more flexible solution is to use a rewrite rule with the [P] flag. This gives you the full power of regular expressions to map your URI-space onto the foreign site's. Example 11-11 shows a rewrite rule version of the del.icio.us API proxy:

Example 11-11. Apache configuration with rewrite rules

```
SSLProxyEngine On
ProxyRequests Off # Don't act as an open proxy.
RewriteEngine On RewriteRule ^apis/delicious/v1/(.*)$ https://api.del.icio.us/v1/$1 [P]
```

With a setup like one of those two, you can serve the Ajax application *delicious-ajax.html* from your own domain, without triggering browser security warnings. All you have to do is change this (from Example 11-4):

```
request.open("GET", "https://api.del.icio.us/v1/posts/recent",
             true, username, password);
```

to this:

```
request.open("GET", "https://example.com/apis/delicious/v1/posts/recent",
             true, username, password);
```

Most Apache installations don't have mod_proxy installed, because an open HTTP proxy is a favorite tool for spammers and other lowlife who want to hide their tracks online. If your web server doesn't have built-in proxy support, you can write a tiny web service that acts as a transparent proxy, and run it on your server. To proxy del.icio.us API requests, this web service might be rooted at `apis/delicious/v1`. It would pass any and all HTTP requests it received—HTTP headers and all—to the corresponding URI beneath *https://api.del.icio.us/v1/*. Yahoo! provides a sample proxy service, written in PHP, hardcoded to access the `yahoo.com` web services (*http://developer.yahoo.com/java script/howto-proxy.html*). You can model your own proxy service after that one.

Even when your proxy is properly configured, when it only proxies requests for a very small subset of the Web, there is danger for you and your end users. When you set up a proxy for Ajax clients, you're taking responsibility in your users' eyes for what the other web site does. The proxy trick sets you up as the fall guy for anything bad that happens on the other site. You're pretending what the other site is serving comes from you. If the web service crashes, cheats the end user, or misuses his personal data, guess what: it looks like *you* did those things. Remember, in an Ajax application the end user only sees your GUI interface. He doesn't necessarily know his browser is making HTTP requests in the background, and he certainly doesn't know that his requests to your domain are being proxied to another domain. If his web browser knew that was going on, it would step in and put a stop to it.

The proxy trick also sets you up as the fall guy for the requests your clients make. Your clients can make any web service request they like and it'll look like you're the cause. Depending on the nature of the web service this may cause you embarrassment or legal exposure. This is less of a problem for web services that require separate authorization.

JavaScript on Demand

It's rare for a human being to demand JavaScript, except in certain design meetings, but it's not uncommon among web browsers. The basis of this trick is that the HTML `script` tag doesn't have to contain hardcoded JavaScript code. It might just have a `src` attribute that references code at another URI. A web browser knows, when it encounters a `script` tag, to load the URI in the `src` attribute and run its contents as code.

We saw this in Example 11-6, the JSON example that does a Yahoo! image search for pictures of elephants.

The `src` attribute is traditionally used like C's `#include` or Ruby's `require`: to load in a JavaScript library from another URI. Example 11-12, reprinted from Chapter 2, shows this.

Example 11-12. Including a JavaScript file by reference

```
<!-- In a real application, you would save json.js locally
     instead of fetching it from json.org every time. -->
<script type="text/javascript" src="http://www.json.org/json.js"></script>
```

As you can see, the URI in the `src` attribute doesn't have to be on the same server as the original HTML file. The browser security model doesn't consider this insecure because... well, near as I can figure, because the `src` attribute was already in wide use before anyone started seriously thinking about the security implications.

Now cast your mind back to the elephant example in Example 11-6. It includes this line:

```
<script type="text/javascript"
src="http://api.search.yahoo.com/ImageSearchService/V1/imageSearch
?appid=restbook&query=baby+elephant&output=json&callback=formatImages" />
```

That big long URI doesn't resolve to a standalone JavaScript library, the way *http://www.json.org/json.js* does. If you visit it in your web browser you'll see that URI's representation is a *custom-generated* bit of JavaScript. In its developer documentation (*http://developer.yahoo.com/common/json.html*), Yahoo! promises that the representation of a resource like this one is a snippet of JavaScript code. Specifically, a snippet of JavaScript code that passes a data structure as the only argument into a callback function named in the URI (here, it's `formatImages`). The resulting JavaScript representation looks something like this:

```
formatImage({"ResultSet":{"totalResultsAvailable":"27170",...}})
```

When the client loads the HTML page, it fetches that URI and run its body as JavaScript, incidentally calling the `formatImage` method. Great for our application; not so great for the web browser. From a security perspective this is just like JavaScript code that uses `XMLHttpRequest` to get data from the Yahoo! web service, and then calls `formatImage` on the result. It bypasses the browser security model by making the HTTP request happen as a side effect of the browser's handling of an HTML tag.

JoD switches the traditional roles of a script embedded in an HTML page and a script included via `<script src="...">`. Your web browser requests a web service URI, thinking it's just a JavaScript library that application code in the HTML page will eventually call. But the library function is the one defined locally (it's `formatImage`), and the application code that calls that function is coming from a foreign site.

If you specify no callback in the URI when calling the Yahoo! web service, you get a "JavaScript" file containing nothing but a JSON data structure. Including this file in a `script` tag won't do anything, but you can fetch it with a programmable HTTP client (like `XMLHttpRequest`, or the Ruby client from way back in Example 2-15) and parse it as data:

```
{"ResultSet":{"totalResultsAvailable":"27170",...}}
```

Dynamically writing the script tag

The only example of JoD I've given so far has a hardcoded `script` tag. The URI to the web service resource is fixed in stone, and if the end user wants to see baby penguins instead of baby elephants he's just out of luck.

But one of the things you can do with JavaScript is add brand new tags to the DOM object representing the current HTML page. And `script` is just another HTML tag. You can use JavaScript to write a customized `script` tag into the document, and get the browser to load the URI mentioned in its `src` attribute as a side effect of the `script` processing. The browser allows this even if the `src` URI points to a foreign domain. That means you can use JavaScript to make requests to any URI that serves more JavaScript, and run it.

This works, but it's a hack on top of a hack, and a security problem on top of a security problem. In fact, from a security perspective this is *worse* than using `XMLHttpRequest` to get data from a foreign site. The worst `XMLHttpRequest` will do is make an HTTP request and parse some XML into a tree-like data structure. With JoD you make an HTTP request and run previously unseen JavaScript code as though it was part of your original program.

You and your end user are completely at the mercy of the service you're calling. Instead of JavaScript that does what you want, a malicious web service might decide to serve JavaScript that steals whatever cookies your domain set for this user. It might serve code that runs code as promised but also creates pop-up windows full of obnoxious ads. It might do anything at all. And since Ajax hides the HTTP request-response cycle from the end user, it looks like *your* site is responsible!

Now, maybe you trust a brand-name site like Yahoo! (unless it gets cracked), but you probably don't trust Mallory's House of Web Services. And that in itself is a problem. One of the nice things about the Web is that you can safely link to Mallory even if you don't trust her, don't have her permission, and think she's wrong about everything. A normal web service client can make calls to Mallory's web service, and examine the representation before acting on it in case she tries any trickery. But when the client is serving executable code, and the web service requested it through a hack that runs the code automatically, you're reduced to operating on blind trust.

JoD is not only sketchy from a security standpoint, it's a lousy tactic from a REST standpoint, because it forces you to use a crippled client. `XMLHttpRequest` supports all the features of HTTP, but with JoD you can only make GET requests. You can't send request headers, see the response code or headers, or handle representation formats other than JavaScript code. Any representation you receive is immediately executed as JavaScript.

The underlying technique, of referencing a new object in a `src` attribute, is safer when you use it to grab resources other than custom-generated JavaScript. `script` isn't the only HTML tag that makes the browser load a representation. Other useful tags include `img` and `frame`. Google Maps uses `img` tags rather than `XMLHttpRequest` calls to fetch its map tile images. Google's JavaScript code doesn't make the HTTP requests. It just creates the `img` tags and lets the browser make requests for the images as a side effect.

Library support

Jason Levitt has written a JavaScript class called `JSONscriptRequest` that makes JoD easy (*http://www.xml.com/pub/a/2005/12/21/json-dynamic-script-tag.html*). This class works sort of like `XMLHttpRequest`, except it supports fewer of HTTP's features, and instead of expecting the server to send an XML representation, it expects a snippet of JavaScript.

Example 11-13 shows a dynamic implementation of the image search Ajax application. The first part should be familiar if you've looked at the other Ajax applications in this chapter.

Example 11-13. Dynamic Yahoo! image search Ajax application

```
<!DOCTYPE HTML PUBLIC "-//W3C//DTD HTML 4.0 Transitional//EN"
"http://www.w3.org/TR/REC-html40/transitional.dtd">
<!--yahoo-ajax-dynamic.html-->
<!--An Ajax application that uses dynamic SCRIPT tags to interactively
    fetch data from Yahoo! Web Services and call predefined functions
    on that data.-->

<html>
<head><title>Javascript Yahoo! JSON - Dynamic</title></head>
<body>
<h1>Javascript Yahoo! JSON example with dynamic SCRIPT tags</h1>

<form onsubmit="callYahoo(); return false;">
 What would you like to see? <input id="query" type="text" /><br />
 <input type="submit" value="Fetch pictures from Yahoo! Image Search"/>
</form>

<div id="images">
</div>

<script type="text/javascript">
function formatImages(result)
{
  // First clear out any old images.
  var images = document.getElementById("images");
  while (images.firstChild)
  {
    images.removeChild(images.firstChild);
  }
```

```
    items = result["ResultSet"]["Result"];
    for (var i = 0; i < items.length; i++)
    {
        image = items[i];

        // Create a link
        var link = document.createElement("a");
        link.setAttribute("href", image["ClickUrl"]);

        // Put a thumbnail image in the link.
        var img = document.createElement("img");
        var thumbnail = image["Thumbnail"];
        img.setAttribute("src", thumbnail["Url"]);
        img.setAttribute("width", thumbnail["Width"]);
        img.setAttribute("height", thumbnail["Height"]);
        img.setAttribute("title", image["Height"]);
        link.appendChild(img);
        images.appendChild(link);
    }
}
</script>
```

Here's where this application diverges from others. I include Jason Levitt's
jsr_class.js file, and then define the `callYahoo` function to use it (see Example 11-14).
This is the function triggered when the end user clicks the submit button in the HTML
form above.

Example 11-14. Dynamic Yahoo! image search Ajax application continued

```
<script type="text/javascript" src="jsr_class.js"></script>

<script type="text/javascript">
function callYahoo()
{
    var query = document.getElementById("query").value;
    var uri = "http://api.search.yahoo.com/ImageSearchService/V1/imageSearch" +
              "?query=" + escape(query) +
          "&appid=restbook&output=json&callback=formatImages";
    alert(uri);
    var request = new JSONscriptRequest(uri);
    request.buildScriptTag();
    request.addScriptTag();
}
</script>

</body>
</html>
```

To make a web service request I pass the URI of a resource into a `JSONscriptRequest`
object. The `addScriptTag` method sticks a new `script` tag into the DOM. When the
browser processes its new tag, it makes a GET request to the foreign URI, and runs the
JavaScript that's served as a representation. I specified "callback=formatImages" in the
URI's query string, so Yahoo! serves some JavaScript that calls my `formatImages` func-

tion on a complex data structure. You can serve this Ajax application from anywhere, and use it to search for anything on Yahoo!'s image search, without triggering any browser warnings.

The Dojo library makes the `script` trick easy by providing a `dojo.io.SrcScript` transport class that uses it. It also provides a `dojo.io.IframeIO` class which uses a similar trick involving the `iframe` tag. This trick also requires cooperation from the server, but it does have the advantage that it doesn't automatically execute the response document as code.

## CHAPTER 12

Frameworks for RESTful Services

As the REST design philosophy becomes more popular, new frameworks are springing up to make RESTful design easy. Existing frameworks are acquiring RESTful modes and features. This, in turn, drives additional interest in REST. In this chapter, I and a few knowledgeable contributors show you how to write resource-oriented services in three popular frameworks: Ruby on Rails, Restlet (for Java), and Django (for Python).

Back in Chapter 1 I said that REST isn't an architecture, but a way of judging architectures. The Resource-Oriented Architecture is an architecture: it imposes constraints on your thinking that make it easy for you to break a problem down into RESTful resources. But these resources still only exist on an abstract level. They aren't real until you expose them through specific web services.

If you're writing a service from scratch (say, as a CGI script), you can translate your resources into code however you like. But most services aren't written from scratch: they're written using a web framework. A REST-aware web framework imposes constraints on your programming that make it easy for you to implement RESTful resources in a specific programming language. In this chapter I'll show you how to integrate the lessons of this book with real frameworks.

Ruby on Rails

The simplifying assumption is the main driver of the success of Ruby on Rails. Rather than give you a large number of tools for accomplishing any task you can think of, Rails gives you one way to accomplish a wide variety of common tasks. You can create a Rails application very quickly *if* you're trying to expose data from a relational database, *if* your database tables have certain names and structure, *if* you care to work with a Model-View-Controller architecture, and so on. Because so many problems in the web application domain fit these assumptions, the effect is rarely onerous and often liberating.

Earlier versions of Rails exposed a textbook REST-RPC hybrid architecture, but Rails 1.2 focuses on a more RESTful design. Perhaps this was inevitable: HTTP's uniform interface is just another simplifying assumption. I've already shown in Chapter 7 how Rails can be used to make sophisticated RESTful services in very little code. In this section, I take a step back and describe the RESTful architecture of Rails in more general terms.

Routing

When an HTTP request comes in, Rails analyzes the requested URI and routes the request to the appropriate controller class. As shown in Example 12-1, the file *config/routes.rb* tells Rails how to handle certain requests.

Example 12-1. A simple routes.rb file

```
# routes.rb
ActionController::Routing::Routes.draw do |map|
  map.resources :weblogs do |weblog|
    weblog.resources :entries
  end
end
```

A *config/routes.rb* file can get fairly sophisticated. The one in Chapter 7 is relatively complex: I had a lot of resources, and I had to fight the simplifying assumptions a little bit to get the URI structure I wanted. Example 12-1 shows a simpler *routes.rb* file that buys into the simplifying assumptions.

That file declares the existence of two controller classes (`WeblogsController` and `EntriesController`), and tells Rails how to route incoming requests to those classes. `WeblogsController` handles requests for the URI **/weblogs**, and for all URIs of the form **/weblogs/{id}**. When present, the path variable **{id}** is made available as `params[:id]`.

`EntriesController` handles requests for the URI **/weblogs/{weblog_id}/entries**, and all URIs of the form **/weblogs/{weblog_id}/entries/{id}**. The path variable **{weblog_id}** is made available as `params[:weblog_id]`, and **{id}**, if present, is made available as `params[:id]`.

Variables like **{id}** and **{weblog_id}** are typically used to associate a resource with a particular object in the system. They often correspond to database IDs, and get plugged into the ActiveRecord `find` method. In my del.icio.us clone I tried to give them descriptive names like **{username}**, and used them as identifying names rather than IDs.

Resources, Controllers, and Views

As I showed in Chapter 7, every Rails controller might expose two kinds of resources. You can have a single "list" or "factory" resource, which responds to GET and/or POST requests, and you can have a large number of "object" resources, which respond to GET, POST, and/or DELETE. The list resource often corresponds to a database table, and the object resources to the rows in the table.

Each controller is a Ruby class, so "sending" an HTTP request to a class means calling some particular method. Rails defines six standard methods per controller, as well as exposing two special view templates through HTTP GET. For illustration's sake, here are the seven HTTP requests made possible by my call to `map.resources :weblogs` back in Example 12-1:

- `GET /weblogs`: A list of the weblogs. Rails calls the `WeblogsController#index` method.

- `GET /weblogs/new`: The form for creating a new weblog. Rails renders the view in *app/view/welogs/new.rhtml*. This view is a hypermedia file describing what sort of HTTP request the client must make to create a new weblog.

  In other words, this is an HTML form (though it could also be a small WADL file). The form says that to create a new weblog, the client should send a POST request to `/weblogs` (see below). It also tells the client how to format its representation of the new weblog, so that the server can understand it.

- `POST /weblogs`: Create a new weblog. Rails calls the `WeblogsController#create` method.

- `GET /weblogs/{id}`: A weblog. Rails calls `WeblogsController#show`.

- `GET /weblogs/{id};edit`: The form for editing a weblog's state. Rails renders the view in *app/view/welogs/edit.rhtml*. This view is a hypermedia file describing what sort of HTTP request the client must make if it wants to edit a weblog's state.

  In practice, this means the view is an HTML form, or short WADL file. The hypermedia file tells the client how to send or simulate a `PUT` request to `/weblogs/{id}`.

- `PUT /weblogs/{id}`: Change a weblog's state. Rails calls `WeblogsController#update`. The "state" here is the state associated with this particular resource: things like the weblog's name and the author's contact information. Individual entries are exposed as separate resources.

- `PUT /weblogs/{id}`: Delete a weblog. Rails calls `WeblogsController#delete`.

You probably won't expose all seven access points in every controller you create. In particular, you probably won't use the special views unless you're running your web service as a web site. This is no problem: just don't implement the methods or view files you don't intend to expose.

Outgoing Representations

Rails makes it easy to send different representations of a resource based on the client's request. Example 12-2 shows some hypothetical Ruby code that renders three different representations of a weblog. Which representation is sent depends on the URI the client accessed, or on the value it provided in the `Accept` header. A client will get the HTML rendition if it accesses `/weblogs/1.html`, but if the client accesses `/weblogs/1.png` instead, the service will send a graphical PNG rendition. The `respond_to` function takes care of interpreting the client's capabilities and desires. All you have to do is implement the supported options, in order of precedence.

Example 12-2. Serving one of several representations

```
respond_to do |format|
  format.html { render :template => 'weblogs/show' }
  format.xml  { render :xml => weblog.to_xml }
  format.png  { render :text => weblog.generate_image,
                       :content_type => "image/png" }
end
```

Two especially common representation formats are HTML and the ActiveResource XML serialization format. HTML representations are expressed using Rails views, as they would be in a human-oriented web application. To expose an ActiveRecord object as an XML document, you can just call `to_xml` on an object or a list of objects.

Rails plugins make it easy to expose data in other representation formats. In Chapter 7, I installed the `atom-tools` Ruby gem so that I could render lists of bookmarks as Atom feeds. In Example 7-8 I have a `respond_to` code block, containing clauses which distinguish between requests for Atom and generic XML representations.

Incoming Representations

Rails sees its job as turning an incoming representation into a bunch of key-value pairs, and making those key-value pairs available through the `params` hash. By default, it knows how to parse form-encoded documents of the sort sent by web browsers, and simple XML documents like the ones generated by `to_xml`.

If you want to get this kind of action for your own incoming representations, you can add a new `Proc` object to `ActionController::Base.param_parsers` hash. The `Proc` object is a block of code whose job is to process an incoming representation of a certain media type. For details, see the Rails documentation for the `param_parsers` hash.

Web Applications as Web Services

Rails 1.2 does an excellent job of merging the human web and the programmable web. As I showed in Chapter 3, Rails comes with a code generator called `scaffold_resource` which exposes a database table as a set of resources. You can access the resources with a web browser, or with a web service client like ActiveResource.

If you use a web browser to access a `scaffold_resource` service, you're served HTML representations of the database objects, and HTML forms for manipulating them (generated by the *new.rhtml* and *edit.rhtml* I mentioned earlier). You can create, modify, and delete the resources by sending new representations in form-encoded format. PUT and DELETE requests are simulated through overloaded POST.

If you use a web service client to access a `scaffold_resource` service, you're served XML representations of the database objects. You manipulate objects by modifying the XML documents and sending then back with PUT. Non-overloaded POST and DELETE work like you'd expect.

There's no more compelling example of the human web's basic similarity to the programmable web. In Chapter 7 I largely ignored this aspect of Rails for space reasons, but it makes a compelling argument for using Rails if you're designing a web site and a web service to do the same thing. Rails makes it easy to expose them both as aspects of the same underlying code.

The Rails/ROA Design Procedure

The following list is a modified version of the generic design procedure from Chapter 6. It's what I used, unofficially, to design the service in Chapter 7. The main difference is that you divide the dataset into controllers and the controllers into resources, rather than dividing the dataset into resources. This reduces the chance that you'll end up with resources that don't fit Rails's controller system.

1. Figure out the dataset.
2. Assign the dataset to controllers.

   For each controller:

   a. Does this controller expose a list or factory resource?

   b. Does this controller expose a set of object resources?

   c. Does this controller expose a creation form or editing form resource?

   For the list and object resources:

   - Design the representation(s) accepted from the client, if different from the Rails standard.
   - Design the representation(s) served to the client.
   - Connect this resource to existing resources.
   - Consider the typical course of events: what's supposed to happen? The database-backed control flow from Chapter 9 should help here.
   - Consider error conditions: what might go wrong? Again, you can often use the database-backed control flow.

Restlet

by Jerome Louvel and Dave Pawson

The Restlet project (*http://www.restlet.org*) provides a lightweight but comprehensive framework for mapping REST concepts to Java classes. It can be used to implement any kind of RESTful system, not just RESTful web services, and it's proven a reliable piece of software since its inception in 2005.

The Restlet project was influenced by the other major Java technologies for developing Web applications: the Servlet API, Java Server Pages, `HttpURLConnection`, and Struts. The primary goal of the project is to provide the same level of functionality while sticking closer to the goals of REST as expounded in the Fielding thesis. Another key goal is to present a unified view of the Web, suitable for use in both client- and server-side applications.

The Restlet philosophy is that the distinction between HTTP client and HTTP server is architecturally unimportant. A single piece of software should be able to act as a web client, then as a web server, without using two completely different APIs.[*]

An early development was the split of the software into the Restlet API and Noelios Restlet Engine (NRE), a reference implementation. This separation allows other implementations to be compatible with the same API. The NRE includes several HTTP server connectors based on popular HTTP open source Java projects: Mortbay's Jetty, Codehaus's AsyncWeb, and the Simple framework. There's even an adapter that lets you deploy a Restlet application inside standard Servlet containers like Apache Tomcat.

Restlet also provides two HTTP client connectors, one based on the official `HttpURL Connection` class and the other on Apache's popular HTTP client library. Another connector allows you to easily manipulate a JDBC source via XML documents in a RESTful way, while an SMTP connector, based on the JavaMail API, lets you send email with an XML document.

The Restlet API includes classes that can build representations based on strings, files, streams, channels, and XML documents: it supports SAX and DOM for parsing, and XSLT for transformation. It's easy to build JSP-style template-based representations, using the FreeMarker or Apache Velocity template engines. You can even serve static files and directories, like an ordinary web server, using a `Directory` class, which supports content negotiation.

Throughout the framework, the design principles are simplicity and flexibility. The API aims to abstract the concepts of HTTP, URIs, and REST into a consistent set of classes, without fully hiding low-level information such as the raw HTTP headers.

Basic Concepts

The Restlet terminology matches the terminology of REST as described in the Fielding thesis: resource, representation, connector, component, media type, language, and so

---

[*] Here Restlet follows Benjamin Carlyle's sound advice (*http://soundadvice.id.au/blog/2005/11/12/#httpAPI*). Carlyle points out a flaw in the standard Java API: that "the `HttpURLConnection` class itself looks nothing like a servlet."

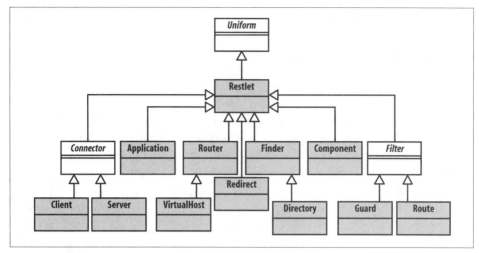

Figure 12-1. The Restlet class hierarchy

on. A lot of this terminology should be familiar to you from elsewhere in the book. Restlet adds some specialized classes like `Application`, `Filter`, `Finder`, `Router`, and `Route`, to make it easier to combine restlets with each other, and to map incoming requests to the resources that ought to handle them.

The central concept of Restlet is the abstract `Uniform` class, and its concrete subclass `Restlet`. As the name implies, `Uniform` exposes a uniform interface as defined by REST. This interface is inspired by HTTP's uniform interface but can be used with other protocols like FTP and SMTP.

The main method is `handle`, which takes two arguments: `Request` and `Response`. As you can see from Figure 12-1, every call handler that is exposed over the network (whether as client or server) is a subclass of `Restlet`—is a restlet—and respects this uniform interface. Because of this uniform interface, restlets can be combined in very sophisticated ways.

Every protocol that Restlet supports is exposed through the `handle` method. This means HTTP (server and client), HTTPS, and SMTP, as well as JDBC, the file system, and even the class loaders all go through `handle`. This reduces the number of APIs the developer must learn.

Filtering, security, data transformation, and routing are handled by chaining together subclasses of `Restlet`. `Filter`s can provide processing before or after the handling of a call by the next restlet. `Filter` instances work like Rails filters, but they respond to the same `handle` method as the other Restlet classes, not to a filter-specific API.

A `Router` restlet has a number of `Restlet` objects attached to it, and routes each incoming protocol call to the appropriate `Restlet` handler. Routing is typically done on some aspect of the target URI, as in Rails. Unlike Rails, Restlet imposes no URI conventions on your resource hierarchies. You can set up your URIs however you want, so long as you program your Routers appropriately.

Routers can stretch beyond this common usage. You can use a Router to proxy calls with dynamic load balancing between several remote machines! Even a setup as complex as this still responds to Restlet's uniform interface, and can be used as a component in a larger routing system. The VirtualHost class (a subclass of Router) makes it possible to host several applications under several domain names on the same physical machine. Traditionally, to get this kind of feature you've had to bring in a front-end web server like Apache's httpd. With Restlet, it's just another Router that responds to the uniform interface.

An Application object can manage a portable set of restlets and provide common services. A "service" might be the transparent decoding of compressed requests, or tunnelling methods like PUT and DELETE over overloaded POST using the method query parameter. Finally, Component objects can contain and orchestrate a set of Connectors, VirtualHosts, and Applications that can be run as a standalone Java application, or embedded in a larger system such as a J2EE environment.

In Chapter 6 you saw a sequence of steps for breaking a problem down into a set of resources that respond to HTTP's uniform interface. This procedure was modified in Chapter 7 to deal with the simplifying assumptions imposed by Ruby on Rails. There's no need to modify the procedure when working with Restlet, because Restlet makes no simplifying assumptions. It can implement any RESTful system. If you happen to be implementing a RESTful resource-oriented web service, you can arrange and implement the resources however you like. Restlet does provide some classes that make it easy to create resource-oriented applications. Most notably, there's a Resource class that can be used as the basis for all of your application resources.

Throughout this book, URI Templates are used as shorthand to designate whole classes of URIs (see Chapter 9"). Restlet uses URI Templates to map URIs onto resources. A Restlet implementation of the Chapter 7 social bookmarking application might specify the path to a particular bookmark like so:

```
/users/{username}/bookmarks/{URI}
```

You can use this exact syntax when attaching a Resource subclass to a Router. If it sounds too good to be true, just wait for the next section where I actually implement part of the bookmarking service covered in Chapter 7.

Writing Restlet Clients

In Example 2-1 you saw a Ruby client that retrieved XML search results from Yahoo!'s web search service. The code in Example 12-3 is a Java implementation of the same client, written against version 1.0 of Restlet. In order to compile and run the upcoming examples, you'll need to make sure that the following JARs are in your classpath:

- *org.restlet.jar* (Restlet API)

- *com.noelios.restlet.jar* (Noelios Restlet Engine core)
- *com.noelios.restlet.ext.net.jar* (HTTP client connector based on JDK's `HttpURLConnection`)

All these are available in the *lib* directory of the Restlet distribution. Make sure that your Java environment supports Java SE version 5.0 or higher. If you really need to, you can easily backport the Restlet code to Java SE version 4.0 with Retrotranslator (*http://retrotranslator.sourceforge.net/*).

Example 12-3. A Restlet client for Yahoo!'s search service

```
// YahooSearch.java
import org.restlet.Client;
import org.restlet.data.Protocol;
import org.restlet.data.Reference;
import org.restlet.data.Response;
import org.restlet.resource.DomRepresentation;
import org.w3c.dom.Node;

/**
 * Searching the web with Yahoo!'s web service using XML.
 */
public class YahooSearch {
    static final String BASE_URI =
    "http://api.search.yahoo.com/WebSearchService/V1/webSearch";

    public static void main(String[] args) throws Exception {
        if (args.length != 1) {
            System.err.println("You need to pass a term to search");
        } else {
            // Fetch a resource: an XML document full of search results
            String term = Reference.encode(args[0]);
            String uri = BASE_URI + "?appid=restbook&query=" + term;
            Response response = new Client(Protocol.HTTP).get(uri);
            DomRepresentation document = response.getEntityAsDom();

            // Use XPath to find the interesting parts of the data structure
            String expr = "/ResultSet/Result/Title";
            for (Node node : document.getNodes(expr)) {
                System.out.println(node.getTextContent());
            }
        }
    }
}
```

You can run this class by passing a search term as a command-line argument, just like with the Ruby example in Example 2-1. Here's a sample run:

```
$ java YahooSearch xslt
    XSL Transformations (XSLT)
    The Extensible Stylesheet Language Family (XSL)
    XSLT Tutorial
        ...
```

This example demonstrates how easy it is with Restlet to retrieve XML data from a web service and process it with standard tools. The URI to the Yahoo! resource is built from a constant and the user-provided search term. A client connector is instantiated using the HTTP protocol. The XML document is retrieved with a method (**get**) whose name mirrors the method of HTTP's uniform interface. When the call returns, the program has the response entity as a DOM representation. As in the Ruby example, XPath is the simplest way to search the XML I retrieved.

Also as in the earlier Ruby example, this program ignores the XML namespaces used in the result document. Yahoo! puts the entire document into the namespace `urn:yahoo:srch`, but I access the tags as, say, `ResultSet` instead of `urn:yahoo:srch:ResultSet`. The Ruby example ignores namespaces because Ruby's default XML parsers aren't namespace-aware. Java's XML parsers are namespace-aware, and the Restlet API makes it easy to deal with namespaces correctly. It doesn't make much difference in a simple case like this, but you can avoid some subtle problems by handling documents in a namespace-aware way.

Of course, saying `urn:yahoo.srch:ResultSet` all the time would get old pretty fast. The Restlet API makes it easy to associate a short prefix with a namespace, and then use the prefix in an XPath expression instead of the full name. Example 12-4 shows a variant of the document-handling code from the end of Example 12-3. This version uses namespace-aware XPath, so that Yahoo's `ResultSet` tag will never be confused with the `ResultSet` tag from some other namespace.

Example 12-4. Namespace-aware version of the document handling code from Example 12-3

```
DomRepresentation document = response.getEntityAsDom();

// Associate the namespace with the prefix 'y'
document.setNamespaceAware(true);
document.putNamespace("y", "urn:yahoo:srch");

// Use XPath to find the interesting parts of the data structure
String expr = "/y:ResultSet/y:Result/y:Title/text()";
for (Node node : document.getNodes(expr)) {
    System.out.println(node.getTextContent());
}
```

Example 2-15 showed a second Ruby client for Yahoo!'s search service. That one requested a JSON representation of the search data, instead of an XML representation. Example 12-5 is the equivalent program for Restlet. It gets its JSON support from two additional JAR files, both included with Restlet:

- *org.restlet.ext.json_2.0.jar* (Restlet extension for JSON)
- *org.json_2.0/org.json.jar* (JSON official library)

Example 12-5. A Restlet client for Yahoo!'s JSON search service

```
// YahooSearchJSON.java
import org.json.JSONArray;
import org.json.JSONObject;
import org.restlet.Client;
import org.restlet.data.Protocol;
import org.restlet.data.Reference;
import org.restlet.data.Response;
import org.restlet.ext.json.JsonRepresentation;

/**
 * Searching the web with Yahoo!'s web service using JSON.
 */
public class YahooSearchJSON {
    static final String BASE_URI =
    "http://api.search.yahoo.com/WebSearchService/V1/webSearch";

    public static void main(String[] args) throws Exception {
        if (args.length != 1) {
            System.err.println("You need to pass a term to search");
        } else {
            // Fetch a resource: a JSON document full of search results
            String term = Reference.encode(args[0]);
            String uri = BASE_URI + "?appid=restbook&output=json&query=" + term;
            Response response = new Client(Protocol.HTTP).get(uri);
            JSONObject json = new JsonRepresentation(response.getEntity())
                    .toJsonObject();

            // Navigate within the JSON document to display the titles
            JSONObject resultSet = json.getJSONObject("ResultSet");
            JSONArray results = resultSet.getJSONArray("Result");
            for (int i = 0; i < results.length(); i++) {
                System.out.println(results.getJSONObject(i).getString("Title"));
            }
        }
    }
}
```

When you write a client against Yahoo!'s service, you can choose the representation. Restlet supports both XML in the core API and JSON with an extension. As you'd expect, the only difference between the two programs is in processing the response. The JsonRepresentation class allows you to convert the response entity-body into an instance of JSONObject (contrast with Ruby's JSON library, which converted the JSON data structure into a native data structure). The data structure is navigated manually, since there's not yet any XPath-like query language for JSON.

Writing Restlet Services

The next set of examples is a little more complex. I'll show you how to design and implement a server-side application. I've implemented a subset of the bookmark management application originally implemented with Ruby on Rails in Chapter 7. To keep things relatively simple, the only features this application supports are the secure manipulation of users and their bookmarks.

The Java package structure looks like this:

```
org
  restlet
    example
      book
        rest
          ch7
              -Application
              -ApplicationTest
              -Bookmark
              -BookmarkResource
               -BookmarksResource
               -User
               -UserResource
```

That is, the class `Bookmark` is in the package `org.restlet.example.book.rest.ch7`, and so on.

Rather than include all the code here, I'd like you to download it from the archive (*http://www.oreilly.com/catalog/9780596529260*), which contains all examples from this book. It's also available on restlet.org (*http://www.restlet.org*). If you've already downloaded Restlet, you don't have to do anything, since the examples for this section are shipped with Restlet, see *src/org.restlet.example/org/restlet/example/book/rest*.

I'll start you off with some simple code in Example 12-6: the `Application.main`, which sets up the web server and starts serving requests.

Example 12-6. The Application.main method: setting up the application

```java
public static void main(String... args) throws Exception {
    // Create a component with an HTTP server connector
    Component comp = new Component();
    comp.getServers().add(Protocol.HTTP, 3000);

    // Attach the application to the default host and start it
    comp.getDefaultHost().attach("/v1", new Application());
    comp.start();
}
```

Resource and URI design

Since Restlets impose no restrictions on resource design, the resource classes and the URIs they expose flow naturally from considerations of ROA design. There's no need to design around the Restlet architecture, the way the resources in Chapter 7 were designed around Rails's controller-based architecture. Figure 12-2 shows how incoming URIs are mapped to resources with a `Router`, and how resources are mapped onto the underlying restlet classes.

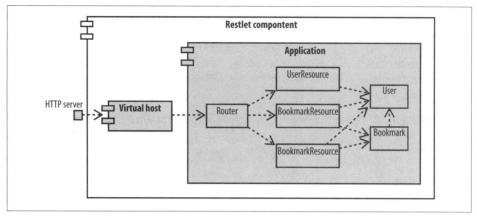

Figure 12-2. Restlet architecture of the social bookmarking application

To understand how these mappings are coded in Java, let's take a look at the `Application` class and its `createRoot` method (see Example 12-7). This is the equivalent of the Rails *routes.rb* file shown in Example 7-3.

Example 12-7. The Application.createRoot method: mapping URI Templates to restlets

```
public Restlet createRoot() {
    Router router = new Router(getContext());

    // Add a route for user resources
    router.attach("/users/{username}", UserResource.class);

    // Add a route for user's bookmarks resources
    router.attach("/users/{username}/bookmarks", BookmarksResource.class);

    // Add a route for bookmark resources
    Route uriRoute = router.attach("/users/{username}/bookmarks/{URI}",
                             BookmarkResource.class);
    uriRoute.getTemplate().getVariables()
      .put("URI", new Variable(Variable.TYPE_URI_ALL));
}
```

This code runs when I create an `Application` object, as I do back in Example 12-6. It creates a clean and intuitive relationship between the resource class `UserResource` and the URI Template `"/users/{username}"`. The `Router` matches incoming URIs against the templates, and forwards each request to a new instance of the appropriate resource class. The value of the template variables are stored in the request's attributes map (similar to the `params` map in the Rails example), for easy usage in the `Resource` code. This is both powerful and simple to understand, which is very helpful when you haven't seen the code for a few months!

Request handling and representations

Suppose a client makes a GET request for the URI `http://localhost:3000/v1/users/jerome`. I've got a `Component` listening on port 3000 of `localhost`, and an `Application` object attached to /v1. The Application has a Router and a bunch of Route objects waiting for requests that match various URI Templates. The URI path fragment "/users/jerome" matches the template "/users/{username}", and that template's Route is associated with the UserResource class: a rough equivalent to the Rails UsersController class.

Restlet handles the request by instantiating a new UserResource object and calling its handleGet method. The UserResource constructor is reproduced in Example 12-8.

Example 12-8. The UserResource constructor

```
/**
 * Constructor.
 *
 * @param context
 *              The parent context.
 * @param request
 *              The request to handle.
 * @param response
 *              The response to return.
 */
public UserResource(Context context, Request request, Response response) {
    super(context, request, response);
    this.userName = (String) request.getAttributes().get("username");
    ChallengeResponse cr = request.getChallengeResponse();
    this.login = (cr != null) ? cr.getIdentifier() : null;
    this.password = (cr != null) ? cr.getSecret() : null;
    this.user = findUser();

    if (user != null) {
        getVariants().add(new Variant(MediaType.TEXT_PLAIN));
    }
}
```

By this time, the framework has set up a Request object, which contains all the information I need about the request. The username attribute comes from the URI, and the authentication credentials from the request's Authorization header. I also call findUser to look up a user in the database based on the authentication credentials (to save space, I won't show the findUser method here). These are the jobs done by Rails filters in Chapter 7.

After the framework instantiates a UserResource, it invokes the appropriate handle method on the resource object. There's one handle method for every method of HTTP's uniform interface. In this case, the last act of the Restlet framework is to call UserResource.handleGet.

I don't actually define UserResource.handleGet, so the inherited behavior (defined in Restlet's Resource.handleGet) takes over. The default behavior of handleGet is to find the representation of the resource that best fits the client's needs. The client expresses its needs through content-negotiation. Restlet looks at the values of the Accept headers and figures out which "variant" representation is the most appropriate. In this case, there's only one representation format, so it doesn't matter what the client asks for. This is handled by the getVariants and getRepresentation methods. Back in the constructor, I defined text/plain as the only supported representation format, so my implementation of the getRepresentation method is pretty simple (see Example 12-9).

Example 12-9. UserResource.getRepresentation: building a representation of a user

```
@Override
public Representation getRepresentation(Variant variant) {
    Representation result = null;

    if (variant.getMediaType().equals(MediaType.TEXT_PLAIN)) {
        // Creates a text representation
        StringBuilder sb = new StringBuilder();
        sb.append("------------\n");
    sb.append("User details\n");
    sb.append("------------\n\n");
    sb.append("Name:  ").append(this.user.getFullName()).append('\n');
    sb.append("Email: ").append(this.user.getEmail()).append('\n');
    result = new StringRepresentation(sb);
    }

    return result;
}
```

That's just one method of one resource, but the other resources, and the other HTTP methods of UserResource, work the same way. A PUT request for a user gets routed to UserResource.handlePut, and so on. As I mentioned earlier, this code is part of a complete bookmarking application, so there's much more example code available if you're interested in learning more.

You should now understand how the Restlet framework routes incoming HTTP requests to specific Resource classes, and to specific methods on those classes. You should also see how representations are built up from resource state. You'll probably only have to worry about the Application and the Router code once, since a single router can work for all of your resources.

Compiling, running, and testing

The Application class implements the HTTP server that runs the social bookmarking service. It requires a classpath that contains the following JAR files:

- *org.restlet.jar*
- *com.noelios.restlet.jar*
- *com.noelios.restlet.ext.net.jar*
- *org.simpleframework_3.1/org.simpleframework.jar*
- *com.noelios.restlet.ext.simple_3.1.jar*
- *com.db4o_6.1/com.db4o.jar*

All of these JAR files are included with the Restlet distribution, and we've listed them relative to the *lib* directory in your Restlet installation. Two things to notice: the actual web server work is handled by a very compact HTTP server connector based on the Simple Framework. Second, instead of making you set up a relational database, we persist our domain objects (users and bookmarks) with the powerful db4o object database. Once all the example files have been compiled, run `org.restlet.example.book.rest.ch7.Application`, which acts as the server endpoint.

The `ApplicationTest` class provides a client interface to the service. It uses the Restlet client classes described in the previous section to add and delete users and bookmarks. It does this through HTTP's uniform interface: users and bookmarks are created with PUT and deleted with DELETE.

Run `ApplicationTest.class` from the command line and you'll get a message like this:

```
Usage depends on the number of arguments:
- Deletes a user      : userName, password
- Deletes a bookmark : userName, password, URI
- Adds a new user     : userName, password, "full name", email
- Adds a new bookmark: userName, password, URI, shortDescription,
                       longDescription, restrict[true / false]
```

You can use this program to add some users and give them bookmarks. Then you can view an HTML representation of the users' bookmarks by visiting the appropriate URIs in a standard web browser, such as *http://localhost:3000/v1/users/jerome* and so on.

Conclusion

The Restlet project delivered its final 1.0 version in early 2007. It took just more than 12 months to develop, and the project now has a thriving development and user community. The mailing list is friendly and welcoming to both new and experienced developers. Noelios Consulting, the founder and main developing force behind the project, offers professional support plans and training.

As of the time of writing, the 1.0 release is under maintenance, and a new 1.1 branch has been started. Future plans include submission of the Restlet API to the Java Community Process (JCP) for standardization. There's also a higher-level API for RESTful web services in development, submitted by Sun Microsystems to the JCP and known as JSR 311. This higher-level API should make it easy to expose Java domain objects as RESTful resources. This will nicely complement the Restlet API, especially its `Resource` class. Noelios Consulting is part of the initial expert group and will directly support the future annotations in its Restlet engine.

Django

by Jacob Kaplan-Moss

Django (*http://www.djangoproject.com/*) is a framework that makes it easy to develop web applications and web services in Python. Its design is very similar to Rails, though it makes fewer simplifying assumptions. You can apply the generic ROA design procedure to turn a dataset into a set of RESTful resources and implement those resources directly in Django.

I'll show you how I implemented a social bookmarking service in Django, along the lines of the Rails implementation in Chapter 7. Since this book isn't intended to be a Django tutorial, I'm leaving out most of the intermediary steps of Django development so I can focus on the parts that specifically apply to RESTful web services. If you're interested in learning more about Django, you should check out the free online *Django Book* (*http://www.djangobook.com/*) and the official Django documentation (*http://www.djangoproject.com/documentation/*).

Create the Data Model

Most Django developers start by designing the data model. This corresponds to the first step of the generic ROA procedure, "Figure out the data set." The model is usually stored in a relational database using Django's object-relational mapping (ORM) tools. It's certainly possible to write RESTful services that don't use a database, but for the social bookmarking application a database makes the most sense. It's fairly straightforward to translate the Rails migration from Example 7-1 into a Django model, as seen in Example 12-10.

Example 12-10. The Django model (models.py)

```
from datetime import datetime
from django.db import models
from django.contrib.auth.models import User

class Tag(models.Model):
    name = models.SlugField(maxlength=100, primary_key=True)

class Bookmark(models.Model):
    user              = models.ForeignKey(User)
    url               = models.URLField(db_index=True)
    short_description = models.CharField(maxlength=255)
    long_description  = models.TextField(blank=True)
    timestamp         = models.DateTimeField(default=datetime.now)
    public            = models.BooleanField()
    tags              = models.ManyToManyField(Tag)
```

There's a few subtleties and a lot of power squeezed into these few lines of code:

- I chose to use the built-in Django User model, rather than create my own users table as the Rails example does. This has a few advantages, the biggest being that the built-in User model will handle much of the authentication and authorization. For more information on this, see Chapter 12 of the Django Book (*http://www.djangobook.com/en/beta/chapter12/*).

- Django has no direct analog to the Rails `acts_as_taggable` plugin, so in the last line of the `Bookmark` definition I just define a many-to-many relation between `Bookmark` and `Tag`.

- I'm defining the tag's `name` as a `SlugField` rather than a string. This is a Django class that automatically restricts tag names to those that can show up in a URI. This makes it easy to prohibit tags that contain spaces or other non-alphanumeric characters.

- Most of the database indexes created explicitly in the Rails schema are automatically added by Django. In particular, slug fields and foreign keys automatically are given indexes. Notice, however, that I've had to explicitly specify `db_index=True` on the `url` field. That field won't get an index by default, but I want to search it.

Define Resources and Give Them URIs

The Rails implementation of the social bookmarking application exposes 11 resources. To keep the size of this section down, I'm only going to implement 4 of the 11:

- A single bookmark
- The list of a user's bookmarks
- The list of bookmarks a user has tagged with a particular tag
- The list of tags a user has used

In particular, notice that I'm not exposing user accounts as resources. To use this service you'll need to pre-create some sample user accounts in the database.

Ruby on Rails imposes simplifying assumptions that affect your URI design. Instead of defining resources, you define Rails controllers that expose resources at certain URIs. Django makes you design your URIs from scratch. Django's philosophy is that the URI is an important part of a web application's user interface, and should not be automatically generated. This fits in with the ROA philosophy, since a resource's *only* interface elements are its URI and the uniform interface of HTTP.

Since Django forces you to design URLs explicitly, there's no "path of least resistance" as there is in Rails, so I'm able to make my Django URIs a little more compact and readable than the Rails URIs were. I'll modify the URI structure given for the Rails application in three ways:

- The Django "house style" (as it were) is to always end URIs with a trailing slash. It's possible to go either way, of course, but to fit more with what Django developers expect I'll make all URIs include the trailing slash. That is, I'll use URLs like `/users/{username}/` instead of `/users/{username}`.

- Rails's controller-based architecture make it convenient to expose bookmarks as `/users/{username}/bookmarks/{URL}/`. In Django it's just as convenient to use the more compact `/users/{username}/{URL}/`, so that's what I'll use.

- Since I'm not exposing user accounts as resources, I can use URIs of the form /users/{username}/ for a different purpose. I'm going to expose my "bookmark list" resources there.

- The Rails implementation uses POST to create a new bookmark as a subordinate resource of a bookmark list. I'll create new bookmarks using the other technique: by sending a PUT to /users/{username}/{URI}/, bypassing the bookmark list altogether. Rails had a problem with embedding a URI in another URI, so back then I exposed URIs like /users/{username}/bookmarks/{URI-MD5}. Here I can use the actual URIs themselves.

I can easily use a Django URI configuration file to map these URIs to resources (Example 12-11). This is the equivalent of the routes.rb file in Example 7-3. It's a lot simpler, though, because Django doesn't try to make decisions about URI format for me.

Example 12-11. A Django URI configuration: urls.py

```
from django.conf.urls.defaults import *
from bookmarks.views import *

urlpatterns = patterns('',
    (r'^users/([\w-]+)/$',              bookmark_list),
    (r'^users/([\w-]+)/tags/$',         tag_list),
    (r'^users/([\w-]+)/tags/([\w-]+)/', tag_detail),
    (r'^users/([\w-]+)/(.*)',           BookmarkDetail()),
)
```

The *urls.py* file is a small Python module that maps incoming URIs (represented as regular expressions) to the functions that handle the requests. Any groups in the regular expression are passed as arguments to the function. So if a request comes in for users/jacobian/tags/python, Django will match it against the third regular expression, and call the tag_detail function with two arguments: "jacob" and "python".

Since Django evaluates the URI patterns in order, I have to put the tag URIs *before* the bookmark URLs: otherwise, Django would interpret /users/jacobian/tags/ as a request for a bookmark of the (invalid) URI tags.

Of course, now I'm committed to writing four functions in a module called bookmarks.views. I won't leave you hanging, so let's move onto those functions.

Implement Resources as Django Views

Django interprets the Model-View-Controller pattern differently than Rails does. In Rails, to implement a resource's behavior under the uniform interface, you put code in a controller class. In Django, that code goes into the view. The Django FAQ (*http://www.djangoproject.com/documentation/faq/*) has more on this distinction, but I'll show you the implementation of two views: the read-only view function for the "bookmark list" resource and the read/write view class for the "bookmark" resource.

The bookmark list view

The bookmark list view function is a nice simple one to start with, because the "bookmark list" resource only responds to GET (see Example 12-12). Remember, I'm exposing bookmark creation through PUT, not through POST on the bookmark list the way the Rails implementation does.

Example 12-12. First try at the bookmark list view

```
from bookmarks.models import Bookmark
from django.contrib.auth.models import User
from django.core import serializers
from django.http import HttpResponse
from django.shortcuts import get_object_or_404

def bookmark_list(request, username):
    u = get_object_or_404(User, username=username)
    marks = Bookmark.objects.filter(user=u, public=True)
    json = serializers.serialize("json", marks)
    return HttpResponse(json, mimetype="application/json")
```

The first step is to turn the argument `username` into a Django `User` object. The `user name` variable comes from the capture group in the regular expression from Example 12-11. It's everything between the parentheses in `^users/([\w-]+)/$`. Since a request for a non-existent user's bookmarks should return an HTTP response code of 404 ("Not Found"), I look up a user with Django's `get_object_or_404()` shortcut function. This will automatically raise a `Http404` exception if the user doesn't exist, which Django will turn into an HTTP response code of 404. This serves the same purpose as the `if_found` method defined in the Rails application, way back in Example 7-9.

In Chapter 7 I kept the implementation short by using ActiveRecord's `to_xml` function to convert objects from the database (such as user accounts) into XML representations. I've used a similar trick here. Rather than represent lists of bookmarks as Atom feeds, I use Django's serialization API to turn database rows into JSON data structures (see *http://www.djangoproject.com/documentation/serialization/*).

Django can also serialize database rows into a JSON data structure or an ActiveRecord-like XML representation: switching to the XML representation would be as easy as changing the serializer type in the third line of the view, and the `mimetype` in the last line. Django's default JSON output is relatively straightforward. Example 12-13 shows what it does to a row from my `bookmarks` table.

Example 12-13. A JSON representation of a bookmark

```
[{
    "pk": "1",
    "model": "bookmarks.bookmark",
    "fields": {
        "tags": ["example"],
        "url": "http:\/\/example.com\/",
        "timestamp": "2007-01-30 21:35:23",
        "long_description": "",
```

```
        "user": 1,
        "short_description": "Example",
        "public": true
    }
}]
```

The bookmark_list implementation from Example 12-12 will work, but it's a bit naive. It returns *all* of a user's bookmarks every time it's called, and that will chew up both database resources and bandwidth. Example 12-14 shows an implementation that adds support for conditional GET (see "Conditional GET" in Chapter 7). Adding handling for Last-Modified and If-Modified-Since does make this view more complex, but the bandwidth savings will make it worth the effort.

Example 12-14. Second try at the bookmark list view

```
import datetime
from bookmarks.models import Bookmark
from django.contrib.auth.models import User
from django.core import serializers
from django.http import *
from django.shortcuts import get_object_or_404

# Use the excellent python-dateutil module to simplify date handling.
# See http://labix.org/python-dateutil
import dateutil.parser
from dateutil.tz import tzlocal, tzutc

def bookmark_list(request, username):
    u = get_object_or_404(User, username=username)

    # If the If-Modified-Since header was provided,
    # build a lookup table that filters out bookmarks
    # modified before the date in If-Modified-Since.
    lookup = dict(user=u, public=True)
    lm = request.META.get("HTTP_IF_MODIFIED_SINCE", None)
    if lm:
        try:
            lm = dateutil.parser.parse(lm)
        except ValueError:
            lm = None # Ignore invalid dates
        else:
            lookup['timestamp__gt'] = lm.astimezone(tzlocal())

    # Apply the filter to the list of bookmarks.
    marks = Bookmark.objects.filter(**lookup)

    # If we got If-Modified-Since but there aren't any bookmarks,
    # return a 304 ("Not Modified") response.
    if lm and marks.count() == 0:
        return HttpResponseNotModified()

    # Otherwise return the serialized data...
    json = serializers.serialize("json", marks)
    response = HttpResponse(json, mimetype="application/json")
```

```
# ... with the appropriate Last-Modified header.
now = datetime.datetime.now(tzutc())
response["Last-Modified"] = now.strftime("%a, %d %b %Y %H:%M:%S GMT")
return response
```

There's a number of other improvements that could be made here—most notably the ability to show private bookmarks to authenticated users—but you've already seen these features in Chapter 7. I'll leave porting them to Django as exercises, and forge ahead.

The bookmark detail view

The second view I'll show you has more moving parts. A "bookmark list" resource only responds to GET, but a "bookmark" resource must handle three HTTP methods. GET on a bookmark retrieves a representation of the bookmark, PUT creates or updates a bookmark, and DELETE removes a bookmark. Since we don't want users modifying each others' bookmarks, the bookmark resource needs to take authentication into account.

The most obvious way to sketch out the `bookmark_detail` view is with a series of `if` clauses:

```
def bookmark_detail(request, username, bookmark_url):
    if request.method == "GET":
        # Handle GET
    elif request.method == "POST":
        # Handle POST
    elif request.method == "PUT":
        # Handle PUT
    elif request.method == "DELETE":
        # Handle DELETE
```

However, this is unelegant and will quickly lead to an unwieldy view. Instead, I'll take advantage of Python's "duck typing" and implement the bookmark detail view as a callable object. In Python, functions are first-class objects, and the syntax of a function call (`object(argument)`) is transformed into a method call on the object (`object.__call__(argument)`). This means that *any* object can be called like a function, if it defines the __call__ method. I'm going to take advantage of this trick by implementing the bookmark detail as a class with a __call__ method.

This is why the last line of Example 12-11 looks different from the other three. The first three tie regular expressions to Python function objects: `bookmark_list` and the like. The last one ties a regular expression to a custom object that happens to implement __call__. The __call__ implementation will do some preliminary work, check the HTTP method of the incoming request, and dispatch to an appropriate action function (see Example 12-15).

Example 12-15. The bookmark detail view, part 1: dispatch code

```
class BookmarkDetail:

    def __call__(self, request, username, bookmark_url):
        self.request = request
        self.bookmark_url = bookmark_url

        # Look up the user and throw a 404 if it doesn't exist
        self.user = get_object_or_404(User, username=username)

        # Try to locate a handler method.
        try:
            callback = getattr(self, "do_%s" % request.method)
        except AttributeError:
            # This class doesn't implement this HTTP method, so return
            # a 405 ("Method Not Allowed") response and list the
#allowed methods.
            allowed_methods = [m.lstrip("do_") for m in dir(self)
                                            if m.startswith("do_")]
            return HttpResponseNotAllowed(allowed_methods)

        # Check and store HTTP basic authentication, even for methods that
        # don't require authorization.
        self.authenticate()

        # Call the looked-up method
        return callback()
```

The `BookmarkDetail.__call__` method checks the HTTP method of the incoming requests, and dispatches each one to an appropriate method of the form `do_<METHOD>`. For instance, a GET request is dispatched to `do_GET`. Rails does something similar behind the scenes, turning a `GET` request into a call to `MyController#show`.

The `BookmarkDetail` class also needs to handle HTTP basic authentication, so let's take a look at that now. In a real application, these functions would go into a superclass to be used by every view that required authentication. Think back to Chapter 7, and the way I put the `must_authenticate` Rails filter into the base `ApplicationController` class (see Example 12-16).

Example 12-16. The bookmark detail view, part 2: authentication code

```
from django.contrib.auth import authenticate

class BookmarkDetail:

    # ...

    def authenticate(self):
        # Pull the auth info out of the Authorization header
        auth_info = self.request.META.get("HTTP_AUTHORIZATION", None)
        if auth_info and auth_info.startswith("Basic "):
            basic_info = auth_info.lstrip("Basic ")
            u, p = auth_info.decode("base64").split(":")
```

```
        # Authenticate against the User database. This will set
        # authenticated_user to None if authentication fails.
        self.authenticated_user = authenticate(username=u, password=p)
    else:
        self.authenticated_user = None

def forbidden(self):
    response = HttpResponseForbidden()
    response["WWW-Authenticate"] = 'Basic realm="Bookmarks"'
    return response
```

Now we can check `self.authenticated_user` within the individual `do_{METHOD}` methods. I've also written a `forbidden()` helper that sends an HTTP 401 (Forbidden) response with the correct `WWW-Authenticate` header.

Now I'll implement the "bookmark" resource's response to each HTTP method it exposes. GET is the simplest, so let's start there. Example 12-17 shows the implementation of `do_GET`. It illustrates the same concepts as the bookmark list's response to GET, back in Example 12-14. The only major difference is that we enforce the privacy of private bookmarks.

Example 12-17. The bookmark detail view, part 3: GET
```
def do_GET(self):
    # Look up the bookmark (possibly throwing a 404)
    bookmark = get_object_or_404(Bookmark,
        user=self.user,
        url=self.bookmark_url
    )

    # Check privacy
    if bookmark.public == False and self.user != self.authenticated_user:
        return self.forbidden()

    json = serializers.serialize("json", [bookmark])
    return HttpResponse(json, mimetype="application/json")
```

Next up is PUT (see Example 12-18). This method needs to take an incoming representation of a bookmark's state, and use it to either create a new bookmark or update an existing one. The incoming representation is available as `self.request.raw_post_data`, and I use the Django serialization library to turn it from a JSON data structure to a Django database object.

Example 12-18. The bookmark detail view, part 4: PUT
```
def do_PUT(self):
    # Check that the user whose bookmark it is matches the authorization
    if self.user != self.authenticated_user:
        return self.forbidden()

    # Deserialize the representation from the request. Serializers
    # work the lists, but we're only expecting one here. Any errors
    # and we send 400 ("Bad Request").
    try:
```

```
    deserialized = serializers.deserialize("json",
                                    self.request.raw_post_data)
    put_bookmark = list(deserialized)[0].object
except (ValueError, TypeError, IndexError):
    response = HttpResponse()
    response.status_code = 400
    return response

# Look up or create a bookmark, then update it
bookmark, created = Bookmark.objects.get_or_create(
    user = self.user,
    url = self.bookmark_url,
)
for field in ["short_description", "long_description",
              "public", "timestamp"]:
    new_val = getattr(put_bookmark, field, None)
    if new_val:
        setattr(bookmark, field, new_val)
bookmark.save()

# Return the serialized object, with either a 200 ("OK") or a 201
# ("Created") status code.
json = serializers.serialize("json", [bookmark])
response = HttpResponse(json, mimetype="application/json")
if created:
    response.status_code = 201
    response["Location"] = "/users/%s/%s" % \
                        (self.user.username, bookmark.url)
return response
```

After all that, DELETE (Example 12-19) looks very simple.

Example 12-19. The bookmark detail view, part 5: DELETE

```
def do_DELETE(self):
    # Check authorization
    if self.user != self.authenticated_user:
        return self.forbidden()

    # Look up the bookmark...
    bookmark = get_object_or_404(Bookmark,
        user=self.user,
        url=self.bookmark_url
    )

    # ... and delete it.
    bookmark.delete()

    # Return a 200 ("OK")
    response = HttpResponse()
    response.status_code = 200
    return response
```

Further directions

The tag views (and all the other interesting features like bundles, etc.) will follow a similar pattern. In fact, with a little work, this `BookmarkDetail` class could be refactored into a more general purpose resource class for handling many different types of objects.

Conclusion

Django isn't just a framework for handling HTTP requests. Like Rails, it contains a lot of sub-libraries that handle common problems in web application and web service design. You've seen the object-relational mapper that works like Rails's ActiveRecord, the built-in `User` model, and the serialization of model objects into JSON representations. Django has many other libraries, including a comment model and a tool for generating syndication feeds. Though it's mostly used for web applications, Django makes an excellent base for Python implementations of RESTful web services.

Some Resources for REST and Some RESTful Resources

The World Wide Web is the largest distributed application ever created, consisting of billions of resources. I've spent this book showing you how to seamlessly integrate a few resources of your own into this global application. Now I'm going to create a few links of my own. This appendix is a bit of hypermedia that connects this book to other discussions of REST, and to real live web services.

Standards and Guides

These are just a few of the sites that have helped me make sense of the programmable web.

HTTP and URI

- The HTTP standard (RFC 2616) (*http://www.w3.org/Protocols/rfc2616/rfc2616.html*).
- The URI standard (RFC 3986) (*http://www.ietf.org/rfc/rfc3986.txt*).
- The WEBDAV standard (RFC 2518) (*http://www.webdav.org/specs/rfc2518.html*), if you're interested in extensions to HTTP's uniform interface.
- The Architecture of the World Wide Web introduces concepts like resources, representations, and the idea of naming resources with URIs (*http://www.w3.org/2001/tag/webarch/*).
- Universal Resource Identifiers—Axioms of Web Architecture (*http://www.w3.org/DesignIssues/Axioms*).

RESTful Architectures

- The Fielding dissertation: *Architectural Styles and the Design of Network-Based Software Architectures* (*http://www.ics.uci.edu/~fielding/pubs/dissertation/top.htm*).

- The very active rest-discuss mailing list (*http://tech.groups.yahoo.com/group/rest-discuss/*).

- The RESTwiki (*http://rest.blueoxen.net/*).

- Joe Gregorio's "REST and WS (*http://bitworking.org/news/125/REST-and-WS*)" compares the technologies of REST to those of the WS-* stack while showing how to create a RESTful web service interface; if you don't care about the comparison part, try "How to create a REST Protocol (*http://bitworking.org/news/How_to_create_a_REST_Protocol*)" by the same author.

- Joe Gregorio has also written a series of articles on REST for XML.com (*http://www.xml.com/pub/au/225*).

- Duncan Cragg's The REST Dialogues (*http://duncan-cragg.org/blog/post/getting-data-rest-dialogues/*): This series of weblog entries is a thought experiment that re-envisions an RPC-style application as a web of interconnected resources (though it doesn't use those terms).

- Paul Prescod's *Common REST Mistakes* (*http://www.prescod.net/rest/mistakes/*).

Hypermedia Formats

- The XHTML standard (*http://www.w3.org/TR/xhtml1/*), which is just a set of small changes on top of the HTML standard (*http://www.w3.org/TR/html4*).

- The microformats web site (*http://microformats.org/*) and wiki (*http://microformats.org/wiki/*).

- The URI Templates draft (*http://bitworking.org/projects/URI-Templates/*).

- The Web Applications 1.0 standard (*http://www.whatwg.org/specs/web-apps/current-work/*), which forms the basis of the forthcoming HTML 5. I think the most interesting part of the standard is Web Forms 2.0 (*http://www.whatwg.org/specs/web-forms/current-work/*), which greatly improves HTML's hypermedia capabilities.

- The WADL standard, maintained at the development site for the Java WADL client (*http://wadl.dev.java.net/*).

Frameworks for RESTful Development

- As I showed in Chapter 7, Ruby on Rails (*http://rubyonrails.org/*) makes it easy to expose RESTful resources. The second edition of *Agile Web Development with Rails* by Dave Thomas et al. (Pragmatic Programmers) is the canonical reference for Rails.

- David Heinemeier Hansson's keynote at Railsconf 2006 (*http://www.scribemedia.org/2006/07/09/dhh/*) shows how Rails moved from a REST-RPC philosophy to one based on RESTful resources.
- The Restlet framework for Java (*http://www.restlet.org/*) can model any RESTful architecture, not just the resource-oriented web services covered in this book. As I write this, a Java standard for RESTful web services has just begun development as JSR 311 (*http://jcp.org/en/jsr/detail?id=311*).
- Django for Python (*http://www.djangoproject.com/*): As of the time of writing, a free Django book (*http://www.djangobook.com/*) was in development.

Weblogs on REST

The REST community is full of eloquent practitioners who argue for and explain RESTful architectures on their weblogs. I'll give out links to just a few. You can find more, in true REST fashion, by following links.

- Mark Baker (*http://www.markbaker.ca/blog/*)
- Benjamin Carlyle (*http://www.soundadvice.id.au/blog/*)
- Joe Gregorio (*http://bitworking.org/news/*)
- Pete Lacey (*http://wanderingbarque.com/nonintersecting/*)
- Mark Nottingham (*http://www.mnot.net/blog/*)
- *RESTful Web Services* co-author Sam Ruby (*http://www.intertwingly.net/blog/*)

Services You Can Use

The web is full of RESTful resources, but some are more technically interesting than others. Behind every RSS and Atom feed, behind every weblog and podcast, is a RESTful resource: an addressable, stateless "target of a hypertext link" that's full of links to other resources. You might think it's cheating to count these as RESTful web services. It's not. The world is full of Big Web Services that could be, or have been, replaced with a set of syndication feeds.

But you're probably not looking in this appendix for a list of interesting syndication feeds. You're probably interested in services that have more architectural meat to them. In this section I focus on RESTful web services that let the client create and modify resources. Read-only resource-oriented services are very common and fairly well understood. So are read/write REST-RPC hybrids. Read/write RESTful services are relatively rare, and those are the ones I want to showcase.

Service Directories

If you're trying to write a client, and you want to see whether there's a web service that does what you need, I refer you to one of these directories. You might find a RESTful resource-oriented service that works for you, or you might find an RPC-style or REST-RPC service you can use.

- ProgrammableWeb (*http://programmableweb.com/*) is the most popular web service directory. It tracks both the APIs that make up the programmable web, and the mashups that combine them. Its terminology isn't as exact as I'd like (it tends to classify REST-RPC hybrids as "REST" services), but you can't beat it for variety.

- By contrast, servicereg.com (*http://www.servicereg.com/*) hardly has any services registered with it. But I think it's got promise, because it's not just a web service directory: it's also a web service. The list of web services is exposed as a "collection" resource that speaks the Atom Publishing Protocol.

- MicroApps (*http://microapps.org/*) focuses on RESTful applications which are designed to be used as components in other applications, like Amazon S3.

Read-Only Services

As I said earlier, read-only RESTful services are very common and not very interesting architecturally. I'll just give three examples of read-only services that do especially interesting things. You can find many more examples on ProgrammableWeb.

- irrepressible.info (*http://irrepressible.info/api*) exposes a set of syndication feeds that help disseminate material censored by various governments.

- Audioscrobbler (*http://www.audioscrobbler.net/data/webservices/*) exposes a large dataset about music and people who listen to it.

- The Coral Content Distribution Network (*http://www.coralcdn.org/*) offers a simple interface to a distributed cache of web resources. It would also have been RESTful to have implemented this service with the interface of an HTTP proxy cache, but resource-oriented designs are more popular.

Read/Write Services

The Atom Publishing Protocol (covered in Chapter 9) is the most popular model for read/write RESTful services. There's a partial list of APP service and client implementations at *http://www.intertwingly.net/wiki/pie/Implementations*, which includes existing services and software that expose services when you install them. I'd like to call out some APP services explicitly so you can see the variety.

- Many of Google's web sites expose an APP extension called GData (*http://code.google.com/apis/gdata/*). Blogger, Google Calendar, Google Notebook, and other web applications also expose resources that conform to the GData protocol.

- The applications hosted on Ning (*http://www.ning.com/*) expose the APP. See *http://documentation.ning.com/sections/rest.php* for details.

- 43 Things (*http://www.43things.com/about/view/web_service_methods_atom*) exposes a list of life goals as an APP collection. (It also exposes a REST-RPC hybrid service.)

- Blogmarks (*http://dev.blogmarks.net/wiki/DeveloperDocs*) is a del.icio.us-like social bookmarking service that exposes lists of bookmarks as APP collections.

- Lotus Connections and Lotus Quick expose resources that respond to the APP.

There are also many public read/write services that don't use the APP. Rather, they expose some custom set of RESTful resources through a uniform interface.

- Amazon S3 (*http://aws.amazon.com/s3*), which I covered in detail in Chapter 3, lets you store data on Amazon's server and have it serve it via HTTP or BitTorrent. Amazon charges you for storage space and bandwidth. S3 probably has the most robust business model of any web service out there: companies are using it, saving money, and making money for Amazon.

- Amazon does it again with another low-level service. Simple Queue Service lets you decouple two parts of a system by having one part put messages in a queue, and the other part read messages from the queue (*http://www.amazon.com/Simple-Queue-Service-home-page/b? ie=UTF8&node=13584001&me=A36L942TSJ2AJA*). You get to choose the message formats.

- The BlinkSale API (*http://www.blinksale.com/api*) exposes a set of RESTful resources for managing invoices.

- The Stikkit API (*http://stikkit.com/api*) exposes read/write resources for short notes to yourself.

- CouchDb (*http://www.couchdb.com/*) is a "document database" that you access through a RESTful web service.

- The Object HTTP Mapper (*http://pythonpaste.org/ohm/*) is a client and a server for exposing Python objects as RESTful resources.

- The Beast forum package (*http://beast.caboo.se/*) is a Rails application that exposes an ActiveResource-compatible web service. An enhanced version of Beast, geared toward project collaboration, is called Dev'il (*http://rubini.us/*).

- linkaGoGo (*http://www.linkagogo.com/rest_api.html*) is another social bookmarking site. Its resources are nested folders that contain bookmarks.

- OpenStreetMap (*http://openstreetmap.org/*) is a project to build a freely available set of map data, and it provides a RESTful interface (*http://wiki.openstreetmap.org/index.php/REST*) to a road map of Earth. Its resources aren't images or places: they're the raw points and vectors that make up a map. If the fantasy map service from Chapter 5 piqued your interest, you might also be interested in this real-world service and the project behind it.

- The Numbler web service (*http://numbler.com/apidoc*) exposes resources for spreadsheets, the cells inside them, and cell ranges. Its use of PUT could be a *little* more resource-oriented, but that's just me being picky.

- The NEEScentral Web Services API (*http://it.nees.org/library/data/neescentral-web-services-api.php*) is a rather ominous-sounding web service for earthquake engineers, hosted by the Network for Earthquake Engineering Simulation. It exposes resources for Experiments, Trials, SensorPools, SimilitudeLawGroups, and so on. I don't know anything about earthquake engineering and I have no idea what those resources correspond to in the real world, but I understand the interface.

- Fozzy (*http://microapps.sourceforge.net/fozzy/*) is an installable application that exposes a RESTful interface to full-text search. You can set up a Fozzy installation and then integrate search into any other application or service.

- Tasty (*http://microapps.sourceforge.net/tasty/*) does something similar for tagging.

- The MusicBrainz web service (*http://wiki.musicbrainz.org/XMLWebService*) maintains metadata about albums of music, such as artist and track names. Unlike the other services in this section, it doesn't use HTTP's full uniform interface. It substitutes overloaded POST for PUT. It's still resource-oriented, though. A client changes the state of a MusicBrainz resource by POSTing to the same URI it uses when GETting the state—not to some unrelated URI that designates an RPC-style operation.

- Many modern version control systems like Subversion and Arch operate through a resource-oriented HTTP interface. They go in the other direction from services like MusicBrainz, adopting extensions to the standard HTTP methods, defined by standards like WebDAV and DeltaV. These services have a richer uniform interface: up to 26 methods per resource (including COPY and CHECKOUT), as opposed to HTTP's standard 8. The downside is that they're on a different Web from the rest of us, because they don't use the same methods. Note, though, that Arch can work using just the standard HTTP methods.

The HTTP Response Code Top 42

Many web services use HTTP status codes incorrectly. The human web hardly uses them at all. Human beings discover what a document means by reading it, not by looking at an attached numeric code. You'll see "404" in an HTML page that talks about a missing document, but your attention is on the phrase "missing document," not on the number. And even the "404" you see is part of the HTML page, put there for human convenience: your browser doesn't show you the underlying 404 response code.

So when there's an error condition on the human web, most applications send a response code of 200 ("OK"), even though everything's not OK. The error condition is described in an HTML entity-body, and a human being is supposed to figure out what to do about the error. The human never sees the response code in the first place, and the browser treats most response codes the same way, so why should the server bother picking the "right" code for a given situation?

On the programmable web, there are no human beings guiding the behavior of clients. A computer program can't reliably figure out what a document means just by looking at it. The same document might be an error message in one context, and the legitimate fulfillment of a GET request in another. We need some way of signalling which way of looking at the response is correct. This information can't go into the entity-body document, because then getting it out would require an understanding of the document. So on the programmable web, HTTP response codes become very important. They tell a client how to deal with the document in the entity-body, or what to do if they can't understand the document. A client—or an intermediary between server and client, like a firewall—can figure out how an HTTP request went, just by looking at the first three bytes of the response.

The problem is that there are 41 official response codes, and standards like WebDAV add even more. Many of the codes are rarely used, two of them are *never* used, and some are only distinguishable from one another by careful hairsplitting. To someone used to the human web (that's all of us), the variety of response codes can be bewildering.

In this appendix I give a brief explanation of every standard status code, with tips on when to use each one in your RESTful services, and my personal opinion as to how important each one is in the context of this book. If a client has to do something specific to get a certain response code, I explain what that is. I also list which HTTP response headers, and what kind of entity-body, the server ought to send along with a response code. This is an appendix for the web service author, but it's also for the client author, who's received a strange response code and doesn't know what it means.

I cover all 41 codes from the HTTP standard, even though some of them (mainly the ones to do with proxies) are a little beyond the scope of this book. I also cover 207 ("Multi-Status"), a response code from the WebDAV extension which I mentioned back in Chapter 8. WebDAV defines five response codes besides 207, and some web servers define the nonstandard code 509 ("Bandwidth Limit Exceeded"). Though not part of HTTP, these status codes are fairly well established, and you can use them if you like. I don't cover them because they're more explicit versions of standard response codes. You can always send 503 ("Service Not Available") instead of the 509 response code, and 409 ("Conflict") instead of WebDAV's 423 ("Locked"). I cover 207 ("Multi-Status"), because no standard status code does anything similar.

Three to Seven Status Codes: The Bare Minimum

If you don't like the proliferation of status codes, you can serve just three and still convey the basic information a client needs to know to handle the response.

200 ("OK")
> Everything's fine. The document in the entity-body, if any, is a representation of some resource.

400 ("Bad Request")
> There's a problem on the client side. The document in the entity-body, if any, is an error message. Hopefully the client can understand the error message and use it to fix the problem.

500 ("Internal Server Error")
> There's a problem on the server side. The document in the entity-body, if any, is an error message. The error message probably won't do much good, since the client can't fix a server problem.

There are four more error codes that are especially common in web services:

301 ("Moved Permanently")
> Sent when the client triggers some action that causes the URI of a resource to change. Also sent if a client requests the old URI.

404 ("Not Found") and 410 ("Gone")
> Sent when the client requests a URI that doesn't map to any resource. 404 is used when the server has no clue what the client is asking for. 410 is used when the server knows there used to be a resource there, but there isn't anymore.

409 ("Conflict")
> Sent when the client tries to perform an operation that would leave one or more resources in an inconsistent state.

SOAP web services use only the status codes 200 ("OK") and 500 ("Internal Server Error"). The 500 status code happens whether there's a problem with the data you sent the SOAP server, a problem with processing the data, or an internal problem with the SOAP server itself. There's no way to tell without looking at the body of the SOAP document, which contains a descriptive "fault." To know what happened with the request you can't just look at the first three bytes of the response: you have to parse an XML file and understand what it says. This is another example of how Big Web Services reimplement existing features of HTTP in opaque ways.

1xx: Meta

The 1xx series of response codes are used only in negotiations with the HTTP server.

100 ("Continue")

Importance: Medium, but (as of time of writing) rarely used.

This is one of the possible responses to an HTTP look-before-you-leap (LBYL) request, described in Chapter 8. This status code indicates that the client should resend its initial request, including the (possibly large or sensitive) representation that was omitted the first time. The client doesn't need to worry about sending a representation only to have it rejected. The other possible response to a look-before-you-leap request is 417 ("Expectation Failed").

Request headers: To make a LBYL request, the client must set the `Expect` header to the literal value "100-continue." The client must also set any other headers the server will need when determining whether to respond with 100 or 417.

101 ("Switching Protocols")

Importance: Very low.

A client will only get this response code when its request uses the `Upgrade` header to inform the server that the client would prefer to use some protocol other than HTTP. A response of 101 means "All right, now I'm speaking another protocol." Ordinarily, an HTTP client would close the TCP connection once it read the response from the server. But a response code of 101 means it's time for the client to stop being an HTTP client and start being some other kind of client.

The Upgrade header is hardly ever used, though it could be used to trade up from HTTP to HTTPS, or from HTTP 1.1 to a future version. It could also be used to switch from HTTP to a totally different protocol like IRC, but that would require the web server also to be an IRC server and the web client to also be an IRC client, because the server starts speaking the new protocol immediately, over the same TCP connection.

Request headers: The client sets Upgrade to a list of protocols it'd rather be using than HTTP.

Response headers: If the server wants to upgrade, it sends back an Upgrade header saying which protocol it's switching to, and then a blank line. Instead of closing the TCP connection, the server begins speaking the new protocol, and continues speaking the new protocol until the connection is closed.

2xx: Success

The 2xx error codes indicate that an operation was successful.

200 ("OK")

Importance: Very high.

In most cases, this is the code the client hopes to see. It indicates that the server successfully carried out whatever action the client requested, and that no more specific code in the 2xx series is appropriate. My bookmarking service sends this code, along with a representation, when the client requests a list of bookmarks.

Entity-body: For GET requests, a representation of the resource the client requested. For other requests, a representation of the current state of the selected resource, or a description of the action just performed.

201 ("Created")

Importance: High.

The server sends this status code when it creates a new resource at the client's request. My bookmarking service sends this code in response to a POST request that creates a new user account or bookmark.

Response headers: The Location header should contain the canonical URI to the new resource.

Entity-body: Should describe and link to the newly created resource. A representation of that resource is acceptable, if you use the Location header to tell the client where the resource actually lives.

202 ("Accepted")

Importance: Medium.

The client's request can't or won't be handled in real time. It will be processed later. The request looks valid, but it might turn out to have problems when it's finally processed.

This is an appropriate response when a request triggers an asynchronous action, an action in the real world, or an action that would take so long that there's no point making the web client wait around. It's an important part of the RESTful system for asynchronous operations that I described in Chapter 8.

Response headers: The pending request should be exposed as a resource so the client can check up on it later. The `Location` header can contain the URI to this resource.

Entity-body: If there's no way for the client to check up on the request later, at least give an estimate of when the request will be processed.

203 ("Non-Authoritative Information")

Importance: Very low.

This status code is the same as 200 ("OK"), but the server wants the client to know that some of the response headers do not come from the server. They may be mirrored from a previous request of the client's, or obtained from a third party.

Response Headers: The client should know that some headers may not be accurate, and others may be passed along without the server knowing what they mean.

204 ("No Content")

Importance: High.

This status code is usually sent out in response to a PUT, POST, or DELETE request, when the server declines to send back any status message or representation. The server may also send 204 in conjunction with a GET request: the resource requested exists, but has an empty representation. Compare 304 ("Not Modified").

204 is often used in Ajax applications. It lets the server tell the client that its input was accepted, but that the client shouldn't change any UI elements.

Entity-body: Not allowed.

205 ("Reset Content")

Importance: Low.

This is just like 204 ("No Content"), but it implies that the client should reset the view or data structure that was the source of the data. If you submit an HTML form in your web browser and the response is 204 ("No Content"), your data stays in the form and you can change it. If you get a 205, the form fields reset to their original values. In data entry terms: 204 is good for making a series of edits to a single record; 205 is good for entering a series of records in succession.

Entity-body: Not allowed.

206 ("Partial Content")

Importance: Very high for services that support partial GET, low otherwise.

This is just like 200 ("OK"), but it designates a response to a partial GET request: that is, one that uses the Content-Range request header. A client usually makes a partial GET request to resume an interrupted download of a large binary representation. I cover partial GET in Chapter 8.

Request headers: The client sends a value for the Content-Range header.

Response headers: The Date header is required. The ETag and Content-Location headers should be set to the same values that would have been sent along with the representation as a whole.

If the entity-body is a single byte range from the representation, the response as a whole must have a Content-Range header explaining which bytes of the representation are being served. If the body is a multipart entity (that is, multiple byte ranges of the representation are being served), each part must have its own Content-Range header.

Entity-body: Will not contain a full representation: just one or more sequences of bytes from the representation.

207 ("Multi-Status")

Importance: Low to medium.

This is a WebDAV extension to the HTTP standard which is useful in the response to a batch request. I showed a RESTful way of exposing batch operations in Chapter 8, and I pointed out that when a request operates on more than one resource, some operations might succeed while others fail. A single response code won't suffice to convey the status of the request.

This response code tells the client to look in the entity-body for a *list* of HTTP status codes: one for each operation in the batch request. This violates the principle that the client should be able to figure out what happened to the request just by looking at the first three bytes, but when a single request carries out more than one operation, there's no alternative.

Entity-body: Should contain an XML document that uses the WebDAV vocabulary to describe a number of HTTP responses. The WebDAV standard (RFC 2518) defines this XML vocabulary and gives several examples.

3xx: Redirection

The 3xx status codes indicate that the client needs to do some extra work to get what it wants. They're most commonly used with GET requests, and they usually tell the client that it can only get the representation it wants by sending a second GET request to some other URI. This secondary URI is sent in the `Location` response header.

This is the trickiest set of response codes, because 301 ("Moved Permanently"), 302 ("Found"), 303 ("See Other"), and 307 ("Temporary Redirect") are all very similar. Many applications use these status codes indiscriminately as a way of bouncing the client around from URI to URI, with little regard for what this means in terms of the underlying resources. My main goal in this section is to clear up the confusion.

300 ("Multiple Choices")

Importance: Low.

The server can send this status code when it has multiple representations of a requested resource, and it doesn't know which representation the client wants. Either the client didn't use the `Accept-*` headers to specify a representation, or it asked for a representation that doesn't exist.

In this situation, the server can just pick its preferred representation, and send it along with a 200 ("OK") status code. But it may decide instead to send a 300 along with a list of possible URIs to different representations.

Response headers: If the server has a preferred representation, it can put the URI to that representation in `Location`. As with other 3xx status codes, the client may automatically follow the URI in `Location`.

Entity-body: A list of URIs to representations, annotated with any information necessary to let the user make a choice between them. An XHTML list of links is a good format for this.

301 ("Moved Permanently")

Importance: Medium.

The server knows which resource the client is trying to access, but it doesn't care for the URI it used to request the resource. It wants the client to take note of the new URI, and use it in future requests.

You can use this status code to keep old URIs from breaking when your URIs change.

Response headers: The server should put the canonical URI in `Location`.

Entity-body: The server should send a short XHTML file with a hyperlink to the new location, but it's not necessary.

302 ("Found")

Importance: Very important to *know about*, especially when writing clients. I don't recommend *using* it.

This status code is the ultimate source of most redirection-related confusion. It's *supposed* to be handled just like 307 ("Temporary Redirect"). In fact, in HTTP 1.0 its name was "Moved Temporarily." Unfortunately, in real life most clients handle 302 just like 303 ("See Other"). The difference hinges on what the client is supposed to do when it gets a 302 in response to a PUT, POST, or DELETE request. See the entry for 307 below if you're interested in the details.

To resolve this ambiguity, in HTTP 1.1 this response code was renamed to "Found," and response code 307 was created. This response code is still in wide use, but it's ambiguous, and I recommend that your services send 303 and 307 instead. The only exception is if you know you're dealing with an HTTP 1.0 client that doesn't understand 303 or 307.

Response headers: The `Location` header contains the URI to which the client should resubmit the request.

Entity-body: Should contain a hypertext document linking to the new URI, as with 301.

303 ("See Other")

Importance: High.

The request has been processed, but instead of the server sending a response document, it's sending the client the URI of a response document. This may be the URI to a static status message, or the URI to some more interesting resource. In the latter case, a 303 is a way for the server to send a representation of a resource without forcing the client to download all that data. The client is expected to send a GET request to the value of `Location`, but it doesn't have to.

The 303 status code is a good way to canonicalize your resources. You can make them available through many URIs, but only have one "real" URI per representation. All the other URIs use a 303 to point to the canonical URI for that representation. For instance, a 303 might redirect a request for *http://www.example.com/software/current.tar.gz* to the URI *http://www.example.com/software/1.0.2.tar.gz*.

Compare to 307 ("Temporary Redirect").

Response headers: The `Location` header contains the URI of the representation.

Entity-body: Should contain a hypertext document linking to the new URI, as with 301.

304 ("Not Modified")

Importance: High.

This status code is similar to 204 ("No Content") in that the response body must be empty. But 204 is used when there is no body data to send, and 304 is used when there is data but the client already has it. There's no point in sending it again.

This status code is used in conjunction with conditional HTTP requests. If the client sends an `If-Modified-Since` header with a date of Sunday, and the representation hasn't changed since Sunday, then a 304 is appropriate. A 200 ("OK") would also be appropriate, but sending the representation again would use bandwidth to no purpose. The client already has the representation.

Response headers: The `Date` header is required. The `ETag` and `Content-Location` headers should be set to the same values that would have been sent if the response code were 200 ("OK").

The caching headers `Expires`, `Cache-Control`, and `Vary` are required if they've changed from those sent previously.

There are complicated caching rules about this that I won't cover here, but the server can send updated headers without sending a new body. This is useful when a representation's metadata has changed, but the representation itself hasn't.

Entity-body: Not allowed.

305 ("Use Proxy")

Importance: Low.

This status code is used to tell the client that it should repeat its request, but go through an HTTP proxy instead of going to the server directly. This code is rarely used because it's very rare for a server to care that the client use a specific proxy.

This code would be used more frequently if there were proxy-based mirror sites. Today, a mirror site for `http://www.example.com/` provides the same content but at a different URI, say `http://www.example.com.mysite.com/`. The original site might use the 307 ("Temporary Redirect") status code to send clients to an appropriate mirror site.

If there were proxy-based mirror sites, then you would access the mirror with the same URI as the original (`http://www.example.com/`), but set `http://proxy.mysite.com/` as your proxy. Here, the original `example.com` might use the 305 status code to route clients to a mirror proxy that's geographically close to them.

Web browsers typically don't handle this status code correctly: another reason for its lack of popularity.

Response headers: The `Location` header contains the URI to the proxy.

306: Unused

Importance: None.

The 306 status code never made it into an HTTP standard. It was described in the Internet Draft "HTTP/1.1 305 and 306 Response Codes" as "Switch Proxy," a status code sent by a proxy server to get the client to start using a different proxy. Don't worry about it.

307 ("Temporary Redirect")

Importance: High.

The request has not been processed, because the requested resource is not home: it's located at some other URI. The client should resubmit the request to another URI.

For GET requests, where the only thing being requested is that the server send a representation, this status code is identical to 303 ("See Other"). A typical case where 307 is a good response to a GET is when the server wants to send a client to a mirror site. But for POST, PUT, and DELETE requests, where the server is expected to take some action in response to the request, this status code is significantly different from 303.

A 303 in response to a POST, PUT, or DELETE means that the operation has succeeded but that the response entity-body is not being sent along with this request. If the client wants the response entity-body, it needs to make a GET request to another URI.

A 307 in response to a POST, PUT, or DELETE means that the server has not even tried to perform the operation. The client needs to resubmit the entire request to the URI in the Location header.

An analogy may help. You go to a pharmacy with a prescription to be filled. A 303 is the pharmacist saying "We've filled your prescription. Go to the next window to pick up your medicine." A 307 is the pharmacist saying "We can't fill that prescription. Go to the pharmacy next door."

Response headers: The Location header contains the URI to which the client should resubmit the request.

Entity-body: Should contain a hypertext document linking to the new URI, as with 301.

4xx: Client-Side Error

These status codes indicate that something is wrong on the client side. There's a problem with authentication, with the format of the representation, or with the HTTP library itself. The client needs to fix something on its end.

400 ("Bad Request")

Importance: High.

This is the generic client-side error status, used when no other 4xx error code is appropriate. It's commonly used when the client submits a representation along with a PUT or POST request, and the representation is in the right format, but it doesn't make any sense.

Entity-body: May contain a document describing why the server thinks there's a client-side error.

401 ("Unauthorized")

Importance: High.

The client tried to operate on a protected resource without providing the proper authentication credentials. It may have provided the wrong credentials, or none at all. The credentials may be a username and password, an API key, or an authentication token—whatever the service in question is expecting. It's common for a client to make a request for a URI and accept a 401 just so it knows what kind of credentials to send and in what format. In fact, the HTTP Digest mode of authentication depends on this behavior.

If the server doesn't want to acknowledge the existence of the resource to unauthorized users, it may lie and send a 404 ("Not Found") instead of a 401. The downside of this is that clients need to know, in advance, what kind of authentication the server expects for that resource: things like HTTP Digest won't work.

Response headers: The `WWW-Authenticate` header describes what kind of authentication the server will accept.

Entity-body: A document describing the failure: why the credentials (if any were provided) were rejected, and what credentials would be accepted. If the end user can get credentials by signing up on a web site, or creating a "user account" resource, a link to the sign up URI is useful.

402 ("Payment Required")

Importance: None.

Apart from its name, this status code is not defined in the HTTP standard: it's "reserved for future use." This is because there's no micropayment system for HTTP. That said, if there ever *is* a micropayment system for HTTP, web services are among the first places that system will start showing up. If you want to charge your users by the web service request, and your relationship with them makes that possible, you might have a use for this status code. But note that Amazon S3 doesn't use this status code, and it charges by the request just fine.

403 ("Forbidden")

Importance: Medium.

The client's request is formed correctly, but the server doesn't want to carry it out. This is not merely a case of insufficient credentials: that would be 401 ("Unauthorized"). This is more like a resource that is only accessible at certain times, or from certain IP addresses.

A response of 403 implies that the client requested a resource that really exists. As with 401 ("Unauthorized"), if the server doesn't want to give out even this information, it can lie and send a 404 ("Not Found") instead.

If the client's request is well-formed, why is this status code in the 4xx series (client-side error) instead of the 5xx series (server-side error)? Because the server made its decision based on some aspect of the request other than its form: say, the time of day the request was made.

Entity-body: Optionally, a document describing why the request was denied.

404 ("Not Found")

Importance: High.

Probably the most famous HTTP status code. 404 indicates that the server can't map the client's URI to a resource. Compare 410 ("Gone"), which is slightly more helpful. A web service may use a 404 response as a signal to the client that the URI is "free"; the client can then create a new resource by sending a PUT request to that URI.

Remember that a 404 may be a lie to cover up a 403 or 401. It might be that the resource exists, but the server doesn't want to let the client know about it.

405 ("Method Not Allowed")

Importance: Medium.

The client tried to use an HTTP method that this resource doesn't support. For instance, a read-only resource may support only GET and HEAD. Another resource may allow GET and POST, but not PUT or DELETE.

Response headers: The `Allow` header lists the HTTP methods that this resource does support. The following is a sample header:

```
Allow: GET, POST
```

406 ("Not Acceptable")

Importance: Medium.

The server may send this response code when the client places so many restrictions on what it considers an acceptable representation (probably using the `Accept-*` request headers) that the server can't send any representation at all. The server may instead choose to ignore the client's pickiness, and simply send its preferred representation along with a response code of 200 ("OK"). This is usually what happens on the human web.

Entity-body: A list of links to acceptable representations, in a format similar to that described in 300 ("Multiple Choices").

407 ("Proxy Authentication Required")

Importance: Low.

You'll only see this status code from an HTTP proxy. It's just like 401 ("Unauthorized"), except the problem is not that you can't use the web service without credentials: it's that you can't use the *proxy* without credentials. As with 401, the problem may be that the client provided no credentials, or that the credentials provided are bad or insufficient.

Request headers: To send credentials to the proxy, the client uses the `Proxy-Authorization` header instead of the `Authorization` header. The format is identical to that of `Authorization`.

Response headers: Instead of the `Authenticate` header, the proxy fills the `Proxy-Authenticate` header with information about what kind of authentication it expects. The format is identical to that of `Authenticate`.

Note that both the proxy and the web service may require credentials, so the client may clear up a 407 only to be hit with a 401 ("Unauthorized").

408 ("Request Timeout")

Importance: Low.

If an HTTP client opens a connection to the server, but never sends a request (or never sends the blank line that signals the end of the request), the server should eventually send a 408 response code and close the connection.

409 ("Conflict")

Importance: High.

Getting this response code means that you tried to put the server's resources into an impossible or inconsistent state. Amazon S3 gives this response code when you try to delete a bucket that's not empty. My bookmarking service gives it when you try to change your username to a name that's already taken.

Response headers: If the conflict is caused by the existence of some other resource (such as when you try to change your username to a name that's taken), the `Location` header should point to the URI of that resource: that is, the source of the conflict.

Entity-body: Should contain a document that describes the conflicts, so that the client can resolve them if possible.

410 ("Gone")

Importance: Medium.

This response code is like 404 ("Not Found"), but it provides a little more information. It's used when the server knows that the requested URI used to refer to a resource, but no longer does. The server doesn't know any new URI for the resource; if it did, it would send a 301 ("Permanent Redirect").

Like the permanent redirect, a 410 response code has the implication that the client should remove the current URI from its vocabulary, and stop making requests for it. Unlike the permanent redirect, the 410 offers no replacement for the bad URI: It's just gone. RFC 2616 suggests using a 410 response code "for limited-time, promotional services and for resources belonging to individuals no longer working at the server's site."

You might be tempted to send this response code in response to a successful DELETE request, but that's a little too cute. The client wouldn't know whether it deleted the resource or whether it was gone before it made their request. The correct response to a successful DELETE request is 200 ("OK").

411 ("Length Required")

Importance: Low to medium.

An HTTP request that includes a representation should set the `Content-Length` request header to the length (in bytes) of the representation. Sometimes this is inconvenient for the client: for instance, when the representation is being streamed from some other source. So HTTP doesn't require a client to send the `Content-Length` header with each request. However, the HTTP server is within its rights to require it for any given request. The server is allowed to *interrupt* any request that starts sending a representation without having provided a `Content-Length`, and demand that the client resubmit the request with a `Content-Length` header. This is the response code that goes along with the interruption.

If the client lies about the length, or otherwise sends too large a representation, the server may interrupt it and close the connection, but in that case the response code is 414 ("Request Entity Too Large").

412 ("Precondition Failed")

Importance: Medium.

The client specified one or more preconditions in its request headers, effectively telling the server to carry out its request only if certain conditions were met. Those conditions were in fact not met, so instead of carrying out the request the server sends this status code.

A common precondition is `If-Unmodified-Since`. The client may PUT a request to modify a resource, but ask that the changes take effect only if no one else has modified the resource since the client last fetched it. Without the precondition, the client might overwrite someone else's changes without realizing it, or might cause a 409 ("Conflict").

Request headers: The client might get this response code by using any of the `If-Match`, `If-None-Match`, or `If-Unmodified-Since` headers.

`If-None-Match` is a bit special. If the client specifies `If-None-Match` when making a GET or HEAD request, and the precondition fails, then the response code is not 412 but 304 ("Not Modified"). This is the basis of conditional HTTP GET. If a PUT, POST, or DELETE request uses `If-None-Match`, and the precondition fails, then the response code is 412. The response code is also 412 when a precondition uses the `If-Match` or `If-Unmodified-Since` headers, no matter what the HTTP method is.

413 ("Request Entity Too Large")

Importance: Low to medium.

This is similar to 411 ("Length Required") in that the server can interrupt the client's request with this status code, and close the connection without waiting for the request to complete. The 411 status code was for requests that didn't specify the length of their representation. This status code is for requests that send a representation that's too large for the server to handle.

A look-before-you-leap request (see Chapter 8) is the best way for a client to avoid being interrupted with this error. If the LBYL request gets a response code of 100 ("Continue"), the client can go ahead and submit the full representation.

Response headers: The problem may be temporary and on the server side (a lack of resources) rather than on the client side (the representation is just too damn big). If so, the server may set the `Retry-After` header to a date or a number of seconds, and the client can retry its request later.

414 ("Request-URI Too Long")

Importance: Low.

The HTTP standard imposes no official limit on the length of a URI (and, in my opinion, there shouldn't be any). However, most existing web servers impose an upper limit on the length of a URI, and a web service may do the same. The most common cause is a client putting representation data in the URI, when it should be in the entity-body. Deeply-nested data structures can also cause very long URIs.

415 ("Unsupported Media Type")

Importance: Medium.

The server sends this status code when the client sends a representation in a media type it doesn't understand. The server might have been expecting XML and the client sent JSON.

If the client sends a document that's got the right media type but the wrong format (such as an XML document written in the wrong vocabulary), a better response is the more generic 400 ("Bad Request"). That's what I use throughout my bookmark service. If you really want to treat that case specially, you can send the WebDAV extended response code 422 ("Unprocessable Entity").

416 ("Requested Range Not Satisfiable")

Importance: Low.

The server sends this status code when the client asks for a series of byte-ranges from a representation, but the representation is actually too small for any of the byte-ranges to apply. In other words, if you ask for byte 100 of a 99-byte representation, you'll get this status code.

Request headers: This status code will only be sent when the original request included the Range header request field. It will not be sent if the original request included the If-Range header request field;

Response headers: The server should send a Content-Range field that tells the client the actual size of the representation.

417 ("Expectation Failed")

Importance: Medium, but (as of time of writing) rarely used.

This response code is the flip side of 100 ("Continue"). If you make a LBYL request to see whether the server will accept your representation, and the server decides it will, you get a response code 100 and you can go ahead. If the server decides it won't accept your representation, you get a response code 417, and you shouldn't bother sending your representation.

5xx: Server-Side Error

The 5xx series of status codes is for representing problems on the server side. In most cases, these codes mean the server is not in a state to run the client's request or even see whether it's correct, and that the client should retry its request later. Sometimes the server can estimate *how much* later the client should retry its request, and put that information into the `Retry-After` response header.

There are fewer 5xx status codes than 4xx status codes, not because fewer things might go wrong on the server, but because there's not much point in being specific: the client can't do anything to fix a problem on the server.

500 ("Internal Server Error")

Importance: High.

This is the generic server error response. Most web frameworks send this status code if they run request handler code that raises an exception.

501 ("Not Implemented")

Importance: Low.

The client tried to use a feature of HTTP (possibly an extended feature) which the server doesn't support.

The most common case is when a client tries to make a request that uses an extended HTTP method, like WebDAV's COPY, which a plain web server doesn't support. This is similar to the response code 405 ("Method Not Allowed"), but 405 implies that the client is using a recognized method on a resource that doesn't support it. A response code of 501 means that the server doesn't recognize the method at all.

502 ("Bad Gateway")

Importance: Low.

You'll only get this response code from an HTTP proxy. It indicates that there was a problem with the proxy, or between the proxy and the upstream server, rather than a problem on the upstream server.

If the proxy can't reach the upstream server at all, the response code will be 504 ("Gateway Timeout") instead.

503 ("Service Unavailable")

Importance: Medium to high.

This status code means that the HTTP server is up, but the underlying web service isn't working properly. The most likely cause is resource starvation: too many requests are coming in at once for the service to handle them all.

Since repeated client requests are probably what's causing the problem, the HTTP server always has the option of refusing to accept a client request, rather than accepting it only to send a 503 response code.

Response headers: The server may send a `Retry-After` header telling the client when they can try submitting their request again.

504 ("Gateway Timeout")

Importance: Low.

Like 502 ("Bad Gateway"), you'll only see this from an HTTP proxy. This status code signals that the proxy couldn't connect to the upstream server.

505 ("HTTP Version Not Supported")

Importance: Very low.

This status code is sent by a server that doesn't support the version of HTTP the client is trying to use. Since HTTP 1.1 is backward compatible with 0.9 and 1.0, you're not likely to see this status code anytime soon. There are still some HTTP 1.0 servers around, and you might see it if you try to use features of HTTP 1.1 on them. Any HTTP 1.1 implementation that's complete enough to support this status code is probably also complete enough to support HTTP 1.0 and 0.9.

Entity-body: Should contain a document describing which protocols the server does support.

The HTTP Header Top Infinity

There are already two excellent guides to the standard HTTP headers. One's in the HTTP standard itself (*http://www.w3.org/Protocols/rfc2616/rfc2616.html*), and the other's in print, in Appendix C of *HTTP: The Definitive Guide* by Brian Totty and David Gourley (O'Reilly). In this description I'm giving a somewhat perfunctory description of the standard HTTP headers. For each header, I'll say whether it's found in HTTP requests, responses, or both. I'll give my opinion as to how useful the header is when building resource-oriented web services, as opposed to other HTTP-based software like web applications and HTTP proxies. I'll give a short description of the header, which will get a little longer for tricky or especially important headers. I won't go into detail on what the header values should look like. I figure you're smart and you can look up more detailed information as needed.

In Chapter 1 I compared an HTTP request or response to an envelope that contains a document (an entity-body). I compared HTTP headers to informational stickers on the envelope. It's considered very bad form to come up with your own HTTP methods or response codes, but it's fine to come up with your own stickers. After covering the standard HTTP headers I'll mention a few custom headers that have become de facto parts of HTTP, like Cookie; or that are used in important technologies, like WSSE's X-WSSE and the Atom Publishing Protocol's Slug.

Custom headers are the most common way of extending HTTP. So long as client and server agree on what the headers mean, you can send any information you like along with a request or response. The guidelines are: don't reinvent an existing header, don't put things in headers that belong in the entity-body, and follow the naming convention. The names of custom headers should start with the string "X-," meaning "extension." The convention makes it clear that your headers are extension headers, and avoids any conflict with future official HTTP headers.

Amazon's S3, covered in Chapter 3, is a good example of a service that defines custom headers. Not only does it define headers like X-amz-acl and X-amz-date, it specifies that S3 clients can send any header whose name begins with "X-amz-meta-." The header name and value are associated with an object as a key-value pair, letting you store arbitrary metadata with your buckets and objects. This is a naming convention inside a naming convention.

Standard Headers

These are the 46 headers listed in the HTTP standard.

Accept

Type: Request header.

Importance: Medium.

The client sends an `Accept` header to tell the server what data formats it would prefer the server use in its representations. One client might want a JSON representation; another might want an RDF representation of the same data.

Hiding this information inside the HTTP headers is a good idea for web browsers, but it shouldn't be the only solution for web service clients. I recommend exposing different representations using different URIs. This doesn't mean you have to impose crude rules like appending *.html* to the URI for an HTML representation (though that's what Rails does). But I think the information should be in the URI somehow. If you want to support `Accept` on top of this, that's great (Rails does this too).

Accept-Charset

Type: Request header.

Importance: Low.

The client sends an `Accept-Charset` header to tell the server what character set it would like the server to use in its representations. One client might want the representation of a resource containing Japanese text to be encoded in UTF-8; another might want a Shift-JIS encoding of the same data.

As I said in Chapter 8, your headaches will be fewer if you pick a Unicode encoding (either UTF-8 or UTF-16) and stick with it. Any modern client should be able to handle these encodings.

Accept-Encoding

Type: Request header.

Importance: Medium to high.

The client sends an `Accept-Encoding` header to tell the server that it can save some bandwidth by compressing the response entity-body with a well-known algorithm like compress or gzip. Despite the name, this has nothing to do with character set encoding; that's `Accept-Charset`.

Technically, `Accept-Encoding` could be used to apply some other kind of transform to the entity-body: applying rot13 encryption to all of its text, maybe. In practice, it's only used to compress data.

Accept-Language

Type: Request header.

Importance: Low.

The client sends an `Accept-Charset` header to tell the server what human language it would like the server to use in its representations. For an example, see Chapter 4 and its discussion of a press release that's available in both English and Spanish.

As with media types, I think that a web service should expose different-language representations of a given resource with different URIs. Supporting `Accept-Language` on top of this is a bonus.

Accept-Ranges

Type: Response header.

Importance: Low to medium.

The server sends this header to indicate that it supports partial HTTP GET (see Chapter 8) for the requested URI. A client can make a HEAD request to a URI, parse the value of this response header, and then send a GET request to the same URI, providing an appropriate `Range` header.

Age

Type: Response header.

Importance: Low.

If the response entity-body does not come fresh from the server, the `Age` header is a measure of how long ago it left the server. This header is usually set by HTTP caches, so that the client knows it might be getting an old copy of a representation.

Allow

Type: Response header.

Importance: Potentially high, currently low.

I discuss this header in "HEAD and OPTIONS", in Chapter 4. It's sent in response to an OPTIONS request and tells the client which subset of the uniform interface a particular URI exposes. This header will become much more important if people ever start using OPTIONS.

Authorization

Type: Request header.

Importance: Very high.

This request header contains authorization credentials, such as a username and password, which the client has encoded according to some agreed-upon scheme. The server decodes the credentials and decides whether or not to carry out the request.

In theory, this is the only authorization header anyone should ever need (except for `Proxy-Authorization`, which works on a different level), because it's extensible. The most common schemes are HTTP Basic and HTTP Digest, but the scheme can be anything, so long as both client and server understand it. In practice, HTTP itself has been extended, with unofficial request headers like `X-WSSE` that work on top of `Authorization`. See the `X-WSSE` entry below for the reason why.

Cache-Control

Type: Request and response header.

Importance: Medium.

This header contains a directive to any caches between the client and the server (including any caches on the client or server themselves). It spells out the rules for how the data should be cached and when it should be dumped. I cover some simple caching rules and recipes in "Caching" in Chapter 8.

Connection

Type: Response header.

Importance: Low.

Most of an HTTP response is a communication from the server to the client. Intermediaries like proxies can look at the response, but nothing in there is aimed at them. But a server can insert extra headers that are aimed at a proxy, and one proxy can insert headers that are aimed at the next proxy in a chain. When this happens, the special headers are named in the `Connection` header. These headers apply to the TCP connection between one machine and another, not to the HTTP connection between server and client. Before passing on the response, the proxy is supposed to remove the special headers and the `Connection` header itself. Of course, it may add its own special communications, and a new `Connection` header, if it wants.

Here's a quick example, since this isn't terribly relevant to this book. The server might send these three HTTP headers in a response that goes through a proxy:

```
Content-Type: text/plain
X-Proxy-Directive: Deliver this as fast as you can!
Connection: X-Proxy-Directive
```

The proxy would remove X-Proxy-Directive and Connection, and send the one remaining header to the client:

```
Content-Type: text/html
```

If you're writing a client and not using proxies, the only value you're likely to see for Connection is "close." That just says that the server will close the TCP connection after completing this request, which is probably what you expected anyway.

Content-Encoding

Type: Response header.

Importance: Medium to high.

This response header is the counterpart to the request header Accept-Encoding. The request header asks the server to compress the entity-body using a certain algorithm. This header tells the client which algorithm, if any, the server actually used.

Content-Language

Type: Response header.

Importance: Medium.

This response header is the counterpart to the Accept-Language request header, or to a corresponding variable set in a resource's URI. It specifies the natural language a human must understand to get meaning out of the entity-body.

There may be multiple languages listed here. If the entity-body is a movie in Mandarin with Japanese subtitles, the value for Content-Language might be "zh-guoyu,jp." If one English phrase shows up in the movie, "en" would probably *not* show up in the Content-Language header.

Content-Length

Type: Response header.

Importance: High.

This response header gives the size of the entity-body in bytes. This is important for two reasons: first, a client can read this and prepare for a small entity-body or a large one. Second, a client can make a HEAD request to find out how large the entity-body is, without actually requesting it. The value of `Content-Length` might affect the client's decision to fetch the entire entity-body, fetch part of it with `Range`, or not fetch it at all.

Content-Location

Type: Response header.

Importance: Low.

This header tells the client the canonical URI of the resource it requested. Unlike with the value of the `Location` header, this is purely informative. The client is not expected to start using the new URI.

This is mainly useful for services that assign different URIs to different representations of the same resource. If the client wants to link to the generic version of the resource, independent of any particular representation, it can use the URI given in `Content-Location`. So if you request `/releases/104.html.en`, specifying a data format and a language, you might get back a response that includes `/releases/104` as the value for `Content-Location`.

Content-MD5

Type: Response header.

Importance: Low to medium.

This is a cryptographic checksum of the entity-body. The client can use this to check whether or not the entity-body was corrupted in transit. An attacker (such as a man-in-the-middle) can change the entity-body and change the `Content-MD5` header to match, so it's no good for security, just error detection.

Content-Range

Type: Response header.

Importance: Low to medium.

When the client makes a partial GET request with the `Range` request header, this response header says what part of the representation the client is getting.

Content-Type

Type: Response header.

Importance: Very high.

Definitely the most famous response header. This header tells the client what kind of thing the entity-body is. On the human web, a web browser uses this to decide if it can display the entity-body inline, and which external program it must run if not. On the programmable web, a web service client usually uses this to decide which parser to apply to the entity-body.

Date

Type: Request and response header.

Importance: High for request, *required* for response.

As a request header, this represents the time on the client at the time the request was sent. As a response header, it represents the time on the server at the time the request was fulfilled. As a response header, `Date` is used by caches.

ETag

Type: Response header.

Importance: Very high.

The value of `ETag` is an opaque string designating a specific version of a representation. Whenever the representation changes, the `ETag` should also change.

Whenever possible, this header ought to be sent in response to GET requests. Clients can use the value of `ETag` in future conditional GET requests, as the value of `If-None-Match`. If the representation hasn't changed, the ETag hasn't changed either, and the server can save time and bandwidth by not sending the representation again.

The main driver of conditional GET requests is the simpler `Last-Modified` response header, and its request counterpart `If-Modified-Since`. The main purpose of `ETag` is to provide a second line of defense. If a representation changes twice in one second, it will take on only one value for `Last-Modified-Since`, but two different values for `ETag`.

Expect

Type: Request header.

Importance: Medium, but rarely used (as of time of writing).

This header is used to signal a LBYL request (covered in Chapter 8). The server will send the response code 100 ("Continue") if the client should "leap" ahead and make the real request. It will send the response code 417 ("Expectation Failed") if the client should not "leap."

Expires

Type: Response header.

Importance: Medium.

This header tells the client, or a proxy between the server and client, that it may cache the response (not just the entity-body!) until a certain time. Even a conditional HTTP GET makes an HTTP connection and takes time and resources. By paying attention to `Expires`, a client can avoid the need to make any HTTP requests at all—at least for a while. I cover caching briefly in Chapter 8.

The client should take the value of `Expires` should as a rough guide, not as a promise that the entity-body won't change until that time.

From

Type: Request header.

Importance: Very low.

This header works just like the `From` header in an email message. It gives an email address associated with the person making the request. This is never used on the human web because of privacy concerns, and it's used even less on the programmable web, where the clients aren't under the control of human beings. You might want to use it as an extension to `User-Agent`.

Host

Type: Request header.

Importance: *Required.*

This header contains the domain name part of the URI. If a client makes a GET request for *http://www.example.com/page.html*, then the URI path is `/page.html` and the value of the `Host` header is "www.example.com" or "www.example.com:80."

From the client's point of view, this may seem like a strange header to require. It's required because an HTTP 1.1 server can host any number of domains on a single IP address. This feature is called "name-based virtual hosting," and it saves someone who owns multiple domain names from having to buy a separate computer and/or network card for each one. The problem is that an HTTP client sends requests to an IP address, not to a domain name. Without the `Host` header, the server has no idea which of its virtual hosts is the target of the client's request.

If-Match

Type: Request header.

Importance: Medium.

This header is best described in terms of other headers. It's used like `If-Unmodified-Since` (described next), to make HTTP actions other than GET conditional. But where `If-Unmodified-Since` takes a time as its value, this header takes an `ETag` as its value.

Tersely, this header is to `If-None-Match` and `ETag` as `If-Unmodified-Since` is to `If-Modified-Since` and `Last-Modified`.

If-Modified-Since

Type: Request header.

Importance: Very high.

This request header is the backbone of conditional HTTP GET. Its value is a previous value of the `Last-Modified` response header, obtained from a previous request to this URI. If the resource has changed since that last request, its new `Last-Modified` date is more recent than the one. That means that the condition `If-Modified-Since` is met, and the server sends the new entity-body. If the resource has not changed, the `Last-Modified` date is the same as it was, and the condition `If-Modified-Since` fails. The server sends a response code of 304 ("Not Modified") and no entity-body. That is, conditional HTTP GET succeeds if this condition fails.

Since `Last-Modified` is only accurate to within one second, conditional HTTP GET can occasionally give the wrong result if it relies only on `If-Modified-Since`. This is the main reason why we also use `ETag` and `If-None-Match`.

If-None-Match

Type: Request header.

Importance: Very high.

This header is also used in conditional HTTP GET. Its value is a previous value of the `ETag` response header, obtained from a previous request to this URI. If the ETag has changed since that last request, the condition `If-None-Match` succeeds and the server sends the new entity-body. If the ETag is the same as before, the condition fails, and the server sends a response code of 304 ("Not Modified") with no entity-body.

If-Range

Type: Request header.

Importance: Low.

This header is used to make a *conditional* partial GET request. The value of the header comes from the `ETag` or `Last-Modified` response header from a previous range request. The server sends the new range only if *that part* of the entity-body has changed. Otherwise the server sends a 304 ("Not Modified"), even if something changed elsewhere in the entity-body.

Conditional partial GET is not used very often, because it's very unlikely that a client will fetch a few bytes from a larger representation, and *then* try to fetch only those same bytes later.

If-Unmodified-Since

Type: Request header.

Importance: Medium.

Normally a client uses the value of the response header `Last-Modified` as the value of the request header `If-Modified-Since` to perform a conditional GET request. This header also takes the value of `Last-Modified`, but it's usually used for making HTTP actions other than GET into conditional actions.

Let's say you and many other people are interested in modifying a particular resource. You fetch a representation, modify it, and send it back with a PUT request. But someone else has modified it in the meantime, and you either get a response code of 409 ("Conflict"), or you put the resource into a state you didn't intend.

If you make your PUT request conditional on `If-Not-Modified`, then if someone else has changed the resource your request will always get a response code of 417 ("Precondition Failed"). You can refetch the representation and decide what to do with the new version that someone else modified.

This header can be used with GET, too; see the `Range` header for an example.

Last-Modified

Type: Response header.

Importance: Very high.

This header makes conditional HTTP GET possible. It tells the client the last time the representation changed. The client can keep track of this date and use it in the `If-Modified-Since` header of a future request.

In web applications, `Last-Modified` is usually the current time, which makes conditional HTTP GET useless. Web services should try to do a little better, since web service clients often besiege their servers with requests for the same URIs over and over again. See "Conditional GET" in Chapter 8 for ideas.

Location

Type: Response header.

Importance: Very high.

This is a versatile header with many related functions. It's heavily associated with the 3xx ("Redirection") response codes, and much of the confusion surrounding HTTP redirects has to do with how this header should be interpreted.

This header usually tells the client which URI it should be using to access a resource; presumably the client doesn't already know. This might be because the client's request created the resource—response code 201 ("Created")—or caused the resource to change URIs—301 ("Moved Permanently"). It may also be because the client used a URI that's not quite right, though not so wrong that the server didn't recognize it. In that case the response code might be 301 again, or 307 ("Temporary Redirect") or 302 ("Found").

Sometimes the value of Location is just a default URI: one of many possible resolutions to an ambiguous request, e.g., 300 ("Multiple Choices"). Sometimes the value of Location points not to the resource the client tried to access, but to some other resource that provides supplemental information, e.g., 303 ("See Other").

As you can see, this header can only be understood in the context of a particular HTTP response code. Refer to the appropriate section of Appendix B for more details.

Max-Forwards

Type: Request header.

Importance: Very low.

This header is mainly used with the TRACE method, which is used to track the proxies that handle a client's HTTP request. I don't cover TRACE in this book, but as part of a TRACE request, Max-Forwards is used to limit how many proxies the request can be sent through.

Pragma

Type: Request or response.

Importance: Very low.

The Pragma header is a spot for special directives between the client, server, and intermediaries such as proxies. The only official pragma is "no-cache," which is obsolete in HTTP 1.1: it's the same as sending a value of "no-cache" for the Cache-Control header. You may define your own HTTP pragmas, but it's better to define your own HTTP headers instead. See, for instance, the X-Proxy-Directive header I made up while explaining the Connection header.

Proxy-Authenticate

Type: Response header.

Importance: Low to medium.

Some clients (especially in corporate environments) can only get HTTP access through a proxy server. Some proxy servers require authentication. This header is a proxy's way of demanding authentication. It's sent along with a response code of 407 ("Proxy Authentication Required"), and it works just like WWW-Authenticate, except it tells the client how to authenticate with the proxy, not with the web server on the other end. While the response to a WWW-Authenticate challenge goes into Authorization, the response to a Proxy-Authenticate challenge goes into Proxy-Authorization (see below). A single request may need to include both Authorization and Proxy-Authorization headers: one to authenticate with the web service, the other to authenticate with the proxy.

Since most web services don't include proxies in their architecture, this header is not terribly relevant to the kinds of services covered in this book. But it may be relevant to a client, if there's a proxy between the client and the rest of the web.

Proxy-Authorization

Type: Request header.

Importance: Low to medium.

This header is an attempt to get a request through a proxy that demands authentication. It works similarly to Authorization. Its format depends on the scheme defined in Proxy-Authenticate, just as the format of Authorization depends on the scheme defined in WWW-Authenticate.

Range

Type: Request.

Importance: Medium.

This header signifies the client's attempt to request only part of a resource's representation (see "Partial GET" in Chapter 8). A client typically sends this header because it tried earlier to download a large representation and got cut off. Now it's back for the rest of the representation. Because of this, this header is usually coupled with Unless-Modified-Since. If the representation has changed since your last request, you probably need to GET it from the beginning.

Referer

Type: Request header.

Importance: Low.

When you click a link in your web browser, the browser sends an HTTP request in which the value of the `Referer` header is the URI of the page you were just on. That's the URI that "refered" your client to the URI you're now requesting. Yes, it's misspelled.

Though common on the human web, this header is rarely found on the programmable web. It can be used to convey a bit of application state (the client's recent path through the service) to the server.

Retry-After

Type: Response header.

Importance: Low to medium.

This header usually comes with a response code that denotes failure: either 413 ("Request Entity Too Large"), or one of the 5xx series ("Server-side error"). It tells the client that while the server couldn't fulfill the request right now, it might be able to fulfill the same request at a later time. The value of the header is the time when the client should try again, or the number of seconds it should wait.

If a server chooses every client's `Retry-After` value using the same rules, that just guarantees the same clients will make the same requests in the same order a little later, possibly causing the problem all over again. The server should use some randomization technique to vary `Retry-After`, similar to Ethernet's backoff period.

TE

Type: Request header.

Importance: Low.

This is another "Accept"-type header, one that lets the client specify which transfer encodings it will accept (see `Transfer-Encoding` below for an explanation of transfer encodings). *HTTP: The Definitive Guide* by Brian Totty and David Gourley (O'Reilly) points out that a better name would have been "Accept-Transfer-Encoding."

In practice, the value of TE only conveys whether or not the client understands chunked encoding and HTTP trailers, two topics I don't really cover in this book.

Trailer

Type: Response header.

Importance: Low.

When a server sends an entity-body using chunked transfer encoding, it may choose to put certain HTTP headers at the end of the entity-body rather than before it (see below for details). This turns them from headers into trailers. The server signals that it's going to send a header as a trailer by putting its name as the value of the header called `Trailer`. Here's one possible value for `Trailer`:

```
Trailer: Content-Length
```

The server will be providing a value for `Content-Length` once it's served the entity-body and it knows how many bytes it served.

Transfer-Encoding

Type: Response.

Importance: Low.

Sometimes a server needs to send an entity-body without knowing important facts like how large it is. Rather than omitting HTTP headers like `Content-Length` and `Content-MD5`, the server may decide to send the entity-body in chunks, and put `Content-Length` and the like at the *after* of the entity-body rather than before. The idea is that by the time all the chunks have been sent, the server knows the things it didn't know before, and it can send `Content-Length` and `Content-MD5` as "trailers" instead of "headers."

It's an HTTP 1.1 requirement that clients support chunked transfer-encoding, but I don't know of any programmable clients (as opposed to web browsers) that do.

Upgrade

Type: Request header.

Importance: Very low.

If you'd rather be using some protocol other than HTTP, you can tell the server that by sending a `Upgrade` header. If the server happens to speak the protocol you'd rather be using, it will send back a response code of 101 ("Switching Protocols") and immediately begin speaking the new protocol.

There is no standard format for this list, but the sample `Upgrade` header from RFC 2616 shows what the designers of HTTP had in mind:

```
Upgrade: HTTP/2.0, SHTTP/1.3, IRC/6.9, RTA/x11
```

User-Agent

Type: Request header.

Importance: High.

This header lets the server know what kind of software is making the HTTP request. On the human web this is a string that identifies the brand of web browser. On the programmable web it usually identifies the HTTP library or client library that was used to write the client. It may identify a specific client program instead.

Soon after the human web became popular, servers started sniffing User-Agent to determine what kind of browser was on the other end. They then sent different representations based on the value of User-Agent. Elsewhere in this book I've voiced my opinion that it's not a great idea to have request headers like Accept-Language be the only way a client can distinguish between different representations of the same resource. Sending different representations based on the value of User-Agent is an even worse idea. Not only has User-Agent sniffing perpetuated incompatibilities between web browsers, it's led to an arms race inside the User-Agent header itself.

Almost every browser these days pretends to be Mozilla, because that was the internal code-name of the first web browser to become popular (Netscape Navigator). A browser that doesn't pretend to be Mozilla may not get the representation it needs. Some pretend to be both Mozilla and MSIE, so they can trigger code for the current most popular web browser (Internet Explorer). A few browsers even allow the user to select the User-Agent for every request, to trick servers into sending the right representations.

Don't let this happen to the programmable web. A web service should only use User-Agent to gather statistics and to deny access to poorly-programmed clients. It should not use User-Agent to tailor its representations to specific clients.

Vary

Type: Response header.

Importance: Low to medium.

The Vary header tells the client which request headers it can vary to get different representations of a resource. Here's a sample value:

```
Vary: Accept Accept-Language
```

That value tells the client that it can ask for the representation in a different file format, by setting or changing the Accept header. It can ask for the representation in a different language, by setting or changing Accept-Language.

That value also tells a cache to cache (say) the Japanese representation of the resource separately from the English representation. The Japanese representation isn't a brand new byte stream that invalidates the cached English version. The two requests sent different values for a header that varies (Accept-Language), so the responses should be cached separately. If the value of Vary is "*", that means that the response should not be cached.

Via

Type: Request and response header.

Importance: Low.

When an HTTP request goes directly from the client to the server, or a response goes directly from server to client, there is no `Via` header. When there are intermediaries (like proxies) in the way, each one slaps on a `Via` header on the request or response message. The recipient of the message can look at the `Via` headers to see the path the HTTP message took through the intermediaries.

Warning

Type: Response header (can technically be used with requests).

Importance: Low.

The `Warning` header is a supplement to the HTTP response code. It's usually inserted by an intermediary like a caching proxy, to tell the user about possible problems that aren't obvious from looking at the response.

Like response codes, each HTTP warning has a three-digit numeric value: a "warn-code." Most warnings have to do with cache behavior. This `Warning` says that the caching proxy at `localhost:9090` sent a cached response even though it knew the response to be stale:

```
Warning: 110 localhost:9090 Response is stale
```

The warn-code 110 means "Response is stale" as surely as the HTTP response code 404 means "Not Found." The HTTP standard defines seven warn-codes, which I won't go into here.

WWW-Authenticate

Type: Response header.

Importance: Very high.

This header accompanies a response code of 401 ("Unauthorized"). It's the server's demand that the client send some authentication next time it requests the URI. It also tells the client what kind of authentication the server expects. This may be HTTP Basic auth, HTTP Digest auth, or something more exotic like WSSE.

Nonstandard Headers

Many, many new HTTP headers have been created over the years, most using the X- extension. These have not gone through the process to be made official parts of HTTP, but in many cases they have gone through other standardization processes. I'm going to present just a few of the nonstandard headers that are most important to web services.

Cookie

Type: Request header.

Importance: High on the human web, low on the programmable web.

This is probably the second-most-famous HTTP header, after `Content-Type`, but it's not in the HTTP standard; it's a Netscape extension.

A cookie is an agreement between the client and the server where the server gets to store some semipersistent state on the client side using the `Set-Cookie` header (see below). Once the client gets a cookie, it's expected to return it with every subsequent HTTP request to that server, by setting the `Cookie` header once for each of its cookies. Since the data is sent invisibly in the HTTP headers with every request, it looks like the client and server are sharing state.

Cookies have a bad reputation in REST circles for two reasons. First, the "state" they contain is often just a session ID: a short alphanumeric key that ties into a much larger data structure on the server. This destroys the principle of statelessness. More subtly, once a client accepts a cookie it's supposed to submit it with all subsequent requests for a certain time. The server is telling the client that it can no longer make the requests it made precookie. This also violates the principle of statelessness.

If you must use cookies, make sure you store *all* the state on the client side. Otherwise you'll lose a lot of the scalability benefits of REST.

POE

Type: Request header.

Importance: Medium.

The `POE` header is sent by a client who wants a URI they can use in a Post Once Exactly request. I covered POE in Chapter 9.

POE-Links

Type: Response header.

Importance: Medium.

The `POE-Links` header is sent in response to a request that included a `POE` header. It gives one or more URIs the client can POST to. Each listed URI will respond to POST exactly once.

Set-Cookie

Type: Response header.

Importance: High on the human web, low on the programmable web.

This is an attempt on the server's part to set some semipersistent state in a cookie on the client side. The client is supposed to send an appropriate Cookie header with all future requests, until the cookie's expiration date. The client may ignore this header (and on the human web, that's often a good idea), but there's no guarantee that future requests will get a good response unless they provide the Cookie header. This violates the principle of statelessness.

Slug

Type: Request header.

Importance: Fairly high, but only in APP applications.

The Slug header is defined by the Atom Publishing Protocol as a way for a client to specify a title for a binary document when it POSTs that document to a collection. See "Binary documents as APP members" in Chapter 9 for an example.

X-HTTP-Method-Override

Type: Request header.

Importance: Low to medium.

Some web services support this header as a way of making PUT, DELETE, and other requests using overloaded POST. The idea is to accommodate clients that don't support or can't use the real HTTP methods. Such a client would use POST and put the "real" HTTP method in this header. If you're designing a service and want to support this feature, I recommend putting the "real" HTTP method in the URI's query string. See "Faking PUT and DELETE" in Chapter 8 for more details.

X-WSSE

Type: Request header.

Importance: Medium.

This is a custom header defined by the WSSE Username Token standard I described in Chapter 8. It's sent in conjunction with the Authorization header, and it contains the actual WSSE credentials. Why did the WSSE designers create a separate header instead that goes along with Authorization, instead of just using Authorization? Because WSSE was designed to be processed by CGI programs rather than by web servers.

When a web server invokes a CGI program, it doesn't pass in the contents of the `Authorization` header. Web servers think they're in charge of HTTP authentication. They don't understand `Authorization: WSSE profile="UsernameToken"`, so they ignore it, and assume there's no authentication required. The `Authorization` header never makes it into the CGI program. But the CGI standard requires that web servers pass on the values of any `X-` headers. The `X-WSSE` header is a way of smuggling authentication credentials through a web server that doesn't understand what they mean.

Index

Symbols and Numbers

, (commas)
    scoping information, 118–121
    URI design and, 233
/ (forward slash)
    Django "house style" and, 356
    using XPath, using, 24
// XPath expressions, 9
; (semicolons) scoping information, 118–121
[ ] (square brackets), using XPath, 24
100 "Continue" response code, 373
101 "Switching Protocols" response code, 373
200 "OK" response code, 54, 137, 140, 374
    database-backed control flow, 274
    modifying resources, 186
201 "Created" response code, 374
    creating resources, 186
    database-backed control flow, 274
202 "Accepted" response code, 229, 375
203 "Non-Authoritative Information" response code, 375
204 "No Content" response code, 375
206 "Partial Content" response code, 376
207 "Multi-Status" response code, 376
300 "Multiple Choices" response code, 377
301 "Moved Permanently" response code, 274, 372, 377
302 "Found" response code, 378
303 "See Other" response code, 139, 378
304 "Not Modified" response code, 245, 379
305 "Use Proxy" response code, 379
306 "Unused" response code, 380
307 "Temporary Redirect" response code, 380
400 "Bad Request" response code, 140, 381

database-backed control flow, 273
restrictions and, 187
401 "Unauthorized" response code, 156, 187, 239, 381
402 "Payment Required" response code, 381
403 "Forbidden" response code, 382
404 "Not Found" response code, 54, 139, 187, 373, 382
    database-backed control flow, 274
405 "Method Not Allowed" response code, 283, 382
406 "Not Acceptable" response code, 383
407 "Proxy Authentication Required" response code, 383
408 "Request Timeout" response code, 383
409 "Conflict" response code, 156, 373, 383
    database-backed control flow, 274
    unauthorized access and, 187
410 "Gone" response code, 274, 373, 384
411 "Length Required" response code, 384
412 "Precondition Failed" response code, 385
413 "Request Entity Too Large" response code, 385
414 "Request-URI Too Long" response code, 386
415 "Unsupported Media Type" response code, 156, 188, 386
    database-backed control flow, 273
416 "Requested Range Not Satisfiable" response code, 386
417 "Expectation Failed" response code, 386
500 "Internal Server Error" response code, 54, 140, 157, 372, 387
501 "Not Implemented" response code, 387
502 "Bad Gateway" response code, 387

We'd like to hear your suggestions for improving our indexes. Send email to *index@oreilly.com*.

503 "Service Unavailable" response code, 140, 157, 388
504 "Gateway Timeout" response code, 388
505 "HTTP Version Not Supported" response code, 388
"Abusing Amazon Images" (Gertler, Nat), 107
"Universal Resource Identifiers-Axioms of Web Architecture" (Berners-Lee, Tim), 82

A

Accept request header, 390
Accept-Charset request header, 390
Accept-Encoding request header, 30, 390
    compression algorithms and, 243
Accept-Language request header, 93, 391
Accept-Ranges request header, 391
"Accepted" 202 response code, 229, 375
access control, 64–70
"Access Key ID" (Amazon), 56
access policies, 69
ActionScript, 38, 316
    XML parsers and, 44
ActiveRecord, 183
ActiveResource, 25
    clients, making transparent with, 71–77
acts_as_taggable plugin, 168, 205
ad hoc XHTML, 268
addressability of URIs, 84–86, 216, 221
Age request header, 391
Ajax, 86
    advantages/disadvantages, 320
    architecture, 316
    cross-browser issues and, 327
    request proxying, 332
    requests, 323
    responses, handling, 324
    REST clients, as, 315
AllegroServe web server library (Lisp), 38
Allow request header, 392
Amazon Web Services, 3, 50
    addressablity, 85
    S3, 13, 52
        client library, using, 70
    wrappers, 25
Apache Tomcat, 344
API keys, 144
APP (Atom Publishing Protocol), 13, 49, 275–281
    collections, describing, 295

application forms, 284
application state, 90, 218
application/atom+xml media types, 263
application/json media type, 266
application/x-www-form-urlencoded media type, 266
application/xhtml+xml media type, 259
application/xml media type, 268, 269
applications and web interfaces, 254–257
applicaton/xhtml+xml
    ad hoc XHTML, 268
Architecture of the World Wide Web, 81
Asynchronous JavaScript And XML (see Ajax)
asynchronous operations, 228
AsyncWeb, 344
Atom, 168, 185, 263–265
"Atom Authentication" (Pilgrim, Mark), 241
atom-tools Ruby gem, 168
"authenticated" messages, 154
authenticated-read access policy, 70
authentication (HTTP), 146
    authorization and, 238–243
authorization, 146–147
    authentication and, 238
    unauthorized access and, 187
Authorization request header, 30, 239, 392
    S3 and, 64
    unauthorized access and, 187
    WSSE HTTP authentication, 241
authorization token, 254
AWS::S3, 50, 55
Axioms of Web Architecture (Berners-Lee, Tim), 236

B

"Bad Gateway" 502 response code, 387
"Bad Request" 400 response code, 140, 381
    database-backed control flow, 273
    restrictions and, 187
base 64 encoding, 238
Basic HTTP authentication, 30, 146, 238
batch operations, 230
Beautiful Soup XML parser, 42
Berners-Lee, Tim, 82, 236
best practices for REST, 215–258
Big Web Services, 5, 299–314
binary documents, 279
bookmarks, 26
    controllers for, 175

management for, 180
BPEL (Business Process Execution Language), 313
browser issues, 327
buckets, 4
    access policies, 69
buckets (S3), 50
Builder::XmlMarkup (Ruby), 203
Bunardzic, Alex, 81
bundlers controller, 179
Business Process Execution Language (BPEL), 313

C

C programming language, 38
    XML parsers and, 44
C#, 36
    XML parsers and, 43
C++ programming language, 38
    XML parsers and, 44
Cache-Control header, 248, 392
caching, 247–249
calendar controller, 178
__call__ method, 360
category documents (APP), 278
character encoding, 270
class HTML attribute, 260
client-side errors, 380–386
clients, 23–48
    ActiveResource, making transparent with, 71–77
    Python, using for, 76
    representations, 150–152, 159–161
    S3, 55–64
        library, using, 70
    writing, 30, 346–349
CLR (Common Language Runtime), 36, 43
collections (APP), 275
commas (,)
    scoping information, 118–121
    URI design and, 233
Common Language Runtime (CLR), 36, 43
Common Lisp, 38
    XML parsers, 44
compression, 243
conditional GET, 138, 189, 244–247
    caching and, 247
"Conflict" 409 response code, 156, 373, 383
    database-backed control flow, 274

unauthorized access and, 187
connectedness, 94–96, 218, 223
    service versioning, 235
Connection request header, 392
content negotiation, 92
Content-Encoding header, 243, 393
Content-Language request header, 393
Content-Length request header, 393
Content-Location header, 217, 249, 394
Content-MD5 request header, 394
Content-Range request header, 394
Content-Type header, 7, 394
    compression algorithms and, 243
    encodings and, 271
    HTTP response and, 137
    outgoing representations and, 234
    S3, 61
"Continue" 100 response code, 373
control flows (prepackaged), 272–284
controllers, 173, 175–179, 340
    code, 188–205
Cookie request header, 405
cookies, 89, 252
CPAN
    XML parsers and, 44
"Created" 201 response code, 374
    creating resources, 186
    database-backed control flow, 274
cross-browser issues, 327
Crypt:SSLeay module, 38
CSS, 39
curl, 37

D

data sets, 110–112, 148, 157, 168–171
    resources, splitting into, 157
databases, 169, 186
    ActiveRecord and, 183
    control flow and, 273–275
Date request header, 395
DCMI (Dublin Core Metadata Initiative), 267
dd tag (HTML), 131
Debian GNU/Linux, installing net/https library, 31
del.icio.us web service, 26–28
DELETE method, 8, 29, 97
    ActiveResource clients and, 75
    APP resources and, 281
    caching and, 249

faking, 251
S3, 52
S3::Bucket#delete method, 59
safety and idempotence, 102
uniform interface and, 219
user controllers and, 174
UsersController and, 196
web applications and web services and, 342
DELETE statement (SQL), 75
Digest HTTP authentication, 30, 146, 239–241
Django (Python), 167, 339, 355–364
implementing resources as views, 357–364
dl HTML tag, 260
document (entity-body), 6
document-based protocol, 5
Dojo, 45, 330
DOM parsers, 39
DOMIT! DOM parser (PHP), 43
Dublin Core Metadata Initiative (DCMI), 267

E

ECMAScript standards, 45
ElementTree (Python), 42
encoding issues, 270
Enterprise Service Bus (ESB), 313
entity-body, 6, 150
batch operations and, 230
form-encoding and, 151
HTTP libraries and, 29
Look-Before-You-Leap (LBYL) requests and, 249
PUT/DELETE, faking, 252
scoping informations and, 12
XML documents and, 28, 38
entries (Atom lists), 263
EntriesController class, 340
eRDF, 267
error (status codes)
client-side, 380–386
server-side, 387
ESB (Enterprise Service Bus), 313
ETag HTTP header, 30, 187, 395
conditional GET and, 189, 245
Expat XML parser, 44
Expect request header, 395
"Expectation Failed" 417 response code, 386
expiration dates, signing URIs, 69

Expires request header, 396
Extensible Open XHTML Outlines (XOXO), 262

F

federation, 311
feeds (Atom lists), 263
Firefox, 147
Flash, 38
Flickr
API, 8, 16
statelessness and, 90
user accounts and, 144
FOAF, 268
"Forbidden" 403 response code, 382
form-encoding, 183
key-value pairs, 38, 266
forms (HTML)
encoded representation of user accounts, 183
form-encoded key-value pairs and, 266
hypermedia and, 284
linking resources and, 135
user accounts and, 145
XHTML 4, 287
forward slash (/)
Django "house style" and, 356
XPath, using, 24
"Found" 302 response code, 378
4Suite, 42
Framework-specific serialization formats, 268
frameworks for RESTful services, 339–364
From request header, 396

G

"Gateway Timeout" 504 response code, 388
GData, 13, 281
gem program, 31
geo microformat specification, 263
Gertler, Nat, 107
GET method, 6, 29, 97
ActiveResource clients and, 75
APP resources and, 281
conditional HTTP, 138, 189
database-backed control flow and, 274
open-uri library and, 31
partial, 250
read-only resources and, 109

Ruby controllers and, 341
S3, 52, 59
safety and idempotence, 102
scoping information, 12
uniform interface and, 218
user controllers and, 174
Gmail, 86
Ajax and, 315, 326
"Gone" 410 response code, 274, 373, 384
Google, 10
Calendar, 254
GData, 281
links and connectedness, 94
maps, 127
representations and, 93
Resource-Oriented Architecture and, 86
SOAP and, 301
Web Accelerator and, 103
Gourley, David, 247
Gregorio, Joe, 33, 109
gs:doGoogleSearch remote procedure, 301
GUI elements, 317
gzip, 243

H

Hadley, Marc, 293
hAtom microformat specification, 263
hCalendar microformat specification, 261,
        268
hCard microformat specification, 261, 268
HEAD method, 29, 98
    caching and, 247
    read-only resources and, 109
    S3, 52, 62
    safety and idempotence, 102
    uniform interface and, 219
headers, 389–407
    nonstandard, 404–407
    standard, 390–404
hierarchy into path variables, 118–121
High REST, 21
Host request header, 396
How to create a REST Protocol (Gregorio, Joe),
        109
hpricot gem, 40
href attribute (link tag), 286
hResume microformat specification, 263
hReview microformat specification, 263
HTML, 4, 289

linking resources, 135
    XHTML and, 260
HTTP, 4, 5–7, 18
    authentication, 146, 238–243
    Basic authentication, 146, 238
    data sets and, 112
    Digest authentication, 146, 239–241
    encodings, 271
    libraries, 29
    methods, 97
    RPC-style architectures and, 14
    sessions, 89
    standard features of, 237–251
    WSSE authentication, 30, 146, 241
HTTP Basic authentication, 146
HTTP response codes (see response codes
        (HTTP))
"HTTP Version Not Supported" 505 response
        code, 388
HTTP+POX (HTTP plus Plain Old XML), 21
HTTP: The Definitive Guide (Totty, Gourley),
        247
HttpClient (Java), 34
httplib2 (Python), 33
HTTPS, 146
    certificates, 29
HttpURLConnection class, 344
HTTPWebRequest, 36
http_authentication Ruby plugin, 168
Hybrid architectures (RPC), 16
hypermedia, 95, 154, 161
    descriptions, 212
    natural-language description and, 210
    technologies, 284–298
        WADL and, 290–298
hypermedia as engine of application state (see
        connectedness)

I

iCalendar, 268
idempotence, 102–104
    uniform interface, 219
If-Match HTTP header, 396
If-Modified-Since HTTP header, 30, 138, 245,
        397
If-None-Match HTTP header, 138, 397
    conditional GET and, 245
If-Range HTTP header, 397
If-Unmodified-Since header, 398

image/svg+xml media type, 265
incoming representations, 234
INSERT statement (SQL), 75
"Internal Server Error" 500 response code, 54, 140, 157, 372, 387
ISO 8859-1 encoding, 270
itemsPerPage element (OpenSearch), 265

J

JAR files, 354
Java, 34, 316
    XML parsers and, 43
java.net.HttpURLConnection HTTP client, 34
java.net.URL object, 34
JavaScript, 37
    Ajax and, 316
    on Demand, 333
    XML parsers, 43–47
JavaScript Object Notation (see JSON)
javax.xml.* package, 43
javax.xml.stream package, 43
jbucket, 25
Jetty, 344
JSON (JavaScript Object Notation), 4, 44–47, 125, 266
    Ajax and, 325
    bookmarks, representing, 184
    encoding and, 272
json Ruby gem, 46

K

key-value pairs, 183, 266
keys (S3), 51

L

language (natural) description, 210
Last-Modified HTTP header, 30, 138, 187, 398
    conditional GET and, 189, 245
LBYL (Look-Before-You-Leap) requests, 249
"Length Required" 411 response code, 384
li HTML tag, 260
libcurl, 37
libgmail library, 315
libopenssl-ruby, 31
libraries
    HTTP, 29
    S3, using, 70

standard, 1
libwww-perl (LWP), 38
libxml2 library, 40
    PHP XML parsers and, 43
limit parameter, 190
link tag, 286
links, 58, 94–96
    hypermedia and, 284
    resources to existing resources, 154–155, 161–164
    S3 clients and, 224
    XHTML 4, 285
Linux, installing net/https library, 31
Lisp, 38
    XML parsers, 44
Location response header, 249, 377, 399
Look-Before-You-Leap (LBYL) requests, 249
Lovett, Chris, 43
Low REST, 21
LWP (libwww-perl), 38

M

Max-Forwards header, 399
media types, 7
members (APP), 275
metadata, 92
method information, 8
"Method Not Allowed" 405 response code, 382
methods, 8–11
    S3, 53
microformats with XHMTL, 261–263
model classes, 205–209
"Moved Permanently" 301 response code, 274, 372, 377
"Multi-Status" 207 response code, 376
"Multiple Choices" 300 response code, 377
MySQL, 169

N

names for resources, 117–123
natural-language description, 210
.NET Common Language Runtime (CLR), 36, 43
net/http library, 31
Net::HTTP class, 32, 39
NetworkCredential, 36
Nielsen, Jakob, 236

"No Content" 204 response code, 375
Noelios Restlet Engine (NRE), 344
"Non-Authoritative Information" 203 response
        code, 375
"Not Acceptable" 406 response code, 383
"Not Found" 404 response code, 54, 139, 187,
        373, 382
    database-backed control flow, 274
"Not Implemented" 501 response code, 387
"Not Modified" 304 response code, 245, 379
Nottingham, Mark, 283
NRE (Noelios Restlet Engine), 344

O

object (RDF assertion), 267
object-oriented design of S3, 50–51
object-relational mapping (ORM), 355
objects, 4
    S3, 50, 61–64
"OK" 200 response code, 54, 137, 140, 274,
        374
    modifying resources, 186
open-uri library, 30, 39
OpenSearch, 265
"Method Not Allowed" 405 response code,
        283
OPTIONS method, 29, 98
    uniform interface and, 219
org.w3c.dom.* package, 43
org.xml.sax.* package, 43
ORM (object-relational mapping), 355
outgoing representations, 234
overloaded POST, 101, 220
    PUT/DELETE, faking, 252
    safety and idempotence, 219
    URI design and, 233

P

params parameter, using list item resources
        and, 189
Park Place, 77
parsers (XML), 38
"Partial Content" 206 response code, 376
path variables
    designing URIs, 233
    encoding hierarchy into, 118–121
paths (URI), 6
"Payment Required" 402 response code, 381

Perl, 38
    XML parsers, 44
permanent URIs, 236
PHP, 37
    XML parsers, 43
Pilgrim, Mark, 241
places as resources, 114
PNG format, 126
POE (POST Once Exactly), 283
POE request header, 405
POE-Links header, 405
POST method, 8, 29, 99–102, 159
    ActiveResource clients and, 75
    APP resources and, 281
    caching and, 249
    objects, creating, 176
    Once Exactly (POE), 283–284
    overloading, 101, 219, 220, 233
    resources, creating/appending, 274
    Ruby controllers and, 341
    S3, 52
    subordinate resources, creating, 160
    uniform interface and, 219
    user controllers and, 174
    versus PUT, 220
    web applications and web services and,
        343
postNewAtomMember method (Atom), 296
Pragma header, 399
"Precondition Failed" 412 response code, 385
prepackaged control flows, 272–284
privacy (user accounts), 146–147
private access policy, 70
private keys (S3 requests), 65
programmable web, 1–21
    technologies on, 18–20
Prototype, 329
"Proxy Authentication Required" 407 response
        code, 383
proxy caches, 85
Proxy-Authenticate header, 400
Proxy-Authorization header, 400
ProxyPass, 332
public-read access policy, 70
public-write access policy, 70
pull parsers, 39
PUT method, 8, 97
    ActiveResource clients and, 75
    APP resources and, 281

caching and, 249
database-backed control flow and, 274
faking, 251
HTTP libraries and, 29
overloading
    PUT/DELETE, faking, 252
Ruby controllers and, 341
S3, 52, 63
S3::Bucket#put, 59
safety and idempotence, 102
uniform interface and, 219
user controllers and, 174
UsersController and, 196
versus POST, 99, 220
web applications and web services and,
    342
Python
    clients, 76
    httplib2, 33
    XML parsers, 42

Q

query strings, 183
query variables, 121–123
    URI design and, 233

R

Rails, 339–364
Range request header, 400
RDF (Resource Description Framework), 266
read-only resource-oriented services, 107–141
read-only web services, 17
read/write resource-oriented services, 143–
    166
readable URIs, 236
recent bookmark controller, 178
redirect loops, 30
redirection, 377–380
Referer request header, 401
regular expressions (Django), 358
rel attribute (link tag), 286
rel HTML attributes, 260
rel-license microformat specification, 261
rel-nofollow microformat specification, 262
rel-tag microformat specification, 262
reliable messaging, 311
Remote Procedure Calls (RPC), 19
repetition model (XHTML), 136

representations, 91–94, 216
    addressability and, 217
    designing, 123–134, 152, 183–185
    entity-body, 6
    formats, 259–272
    incoming, 342
    outgoing, 341
    outgoing/incoming, 234
    S3, 57
"Request Entity Too Large" 413 response code,
    385
request headers, 6
request signing, 64–70
"Request Timeout" 408 response code, 383
"Request-URI Too Long" 414 response code,
    386
"Requested Range Not Satisfiable" 416
    response code, 386
resource
    design, 108
    forms, 284
    state, 90, 124, 217
Resource Description Framework (RDF), 266
Resource-Oriented Architecture (ROA), 13,
    79–105, 215–258
    addressability, 84–86
    basics, 215
    procedure, 216
    read/write, designing, 143–166
    representations and, 91
    URIs, 81–84
    versus Big Web Services, 299–314
resources, 52, 143–166, 215, 340
    connecting, 185
    data sets, splitting into, 157
    design, 171–183, 227–233
    Django, implementing views, 357–364
    relationships between, 228
    URIs, naming resources with, 158
    user accounts, 144–157
resources, defining, 356
response codes (HTTP), 7, 54, 137–141, 324,
    371
    database-backed control flow, 274
responseXML parser (JavaScript), 43
REST (Representational State Transfer),
    sending representations and, 218
rest-open-uri library, 31
rest-open-uri, installing, 31

Restlet (Java), 167, 339, 343–354
    services, writing, 349–354
Retry-After response header, 401
rev attribute (link tag), 286
rev HTML attributes, 260
REXML, 40–42
REXML::document parser, 31
ROA (see Resource-Oriented Architecture)
routing (Rails), 340
RPC (Remote Procedure Calls), 19
RPC-style architectures, 14
Ruby
    Amazon Web Services and, 3
    HTTP client libraries, 31
    on Rails, 339–343
    XML parsers and, 40–42

S

S3 (Simple Storage Service), 4, 49–77
    addressability, 85
    client, 55–64
        library, using, 70
    connectedness and, 223
    request signing and access control, 64–70
S3::Bucket#delete method, 58
S3::Bucket#put method, 58
s3sh (command shell for Ruby), 4, 25
safety (HTTP methods), 102–104
SAX parsers, 39
scoping information, 11
    encoding hierarchy into path variables and,
        118–121
script tag, 335
search results, representing lists of, 133–134
"Secret Access Key" (Amazon), 56
Secure Socket Layer (see SSL)
security, 310
"See Other" 303 response code, 139, 378
SELECT statement (SQL), 75
semicolons (;) scoping information, 118–121
server-side errors, 387
service documents (APP), 276
"Service Unavailable" 503 response code, 140,
        157, 388
service versioning, 235
Service-Oriented Architecture (see SOA)
Service-Trampled REST (STREST), 21
services, 259–298
    Restlet, writing, 349–354

session affinity, 91
session replication, 91
sessions (HTTP), 89
Set-Cookie response header, 406
signatures, 310
Simple Storage Service (S3), 4, 49–77
    addressability, 85
    client, 55–64
        library, using, 70
    connectedness and, 223
    request signing and access control, 64–70
simple-http (Common Lisp), 38
Slug request header, 406
Snell, James, 81
SOA (Service-Oriented Architecture), 20, 314
SOAP, 10, 19, 300–303
    POST method, overloading, 220
    REST as a competitor to, 20
    S3 and, 53
    security and, 310
SQL databases, 75, 273
square brackets ([ ]), using XPath, 24
SSL (Secure Sockets Layer), 311
    certificates, 29
standard libraries, 1
standardization, 212
startindex element (OpenSearch), 265
state (see statelessness)
statelessness, 217, 222
    application state versus resource state, 90
    ROA, 86–91
STREST (Service-Trampled REST), 21
subject (RDF assertion), 267
subordinate resources, 158
    creating, 99
    HTTP POST requests, creating with, 160
Sun Web Services Developer Pack, 43
SVG format, 126, 265
"Switching Protocols" 101 response code, 373

T

table HTML tag, 260
tags, 26
    management for, 181
TagSoup XML parser, 43
TCP/IP sockets, 28
TE request header, 401
"Temporary Redirect" 307 response code, 380
terminology of web services, 4

text/html media, 259
text/xml media, 272
TLS (Transport Layer Security), 311
totalResults element (OpenSearch), 265
Totty, Brian, 247
to_xml (Rails), 184
    connecting resources and, 185
    Framework-specific serialization formats,
        268
TRACE method, 29
Trailer response header, 402
transactions, 231, 312
Transfer-Encoding header, 402
Transport Layer Security (TLS), 311
tree-style parsers, 39
triple (RDF assertion), 267
trust (user accounts), 146–147

U

UDDI, 309
ul HTML tag, 260
"Unauthorized" 401 response code, 239
"Unauthorized" 401 response code, 156, 187,
        381
unauthorized access, 187
Unicode, 270
    parsing XML and, 42
Uniform class (Restlet), 345
uniform interface, 79, 104, 218–221, 222
    exposing subsets of, 149, 158
Universal Encoding Detector, 271
Universal Product Codes (UPCs), 14
Universal Resource Identifier (see URIs)
"Unsupported Media Type" 415 response code,
        156, 188, 386
    database-backed control flow, 273
"Unused" 306 response code, 380
UPCs (Universal Product Codes), 14
UPDATE statement (SQL), 75
Upgrade request header, 402
URI Templating, 155
URIs (Universal Resource Identifier), 1, 15, 18,
        123
    addressability and, 216
    bookmarks and, 26–28, 176
    controller, 178
    design, 233
    Django and, 356
    permanent versus readable, 236

resources, naming, 149, 158
    ROAs and, 81–84
    signing, 68
    templates, 285
    using maximum length workarounds, 220
    web clients, writing, 24
"URL as UI" (Nielsen, Jakob), 236
urllib2 HTTP client, 33
URLs (see URIs)
US-ASCII encoding, 270
"Use Proxy" 305 response code, 379
user accounts, 144–157, 180
    linking resources, 154–155
user controllers, 174
user tags controller, 177
User-Agent request header, 403
UsersController, 196–199
UsersController#create Rails method, 174
UsersController#destroy Rails method, 174
UsersController#index Rails method, 174
UsersController#show Rails method, 174
UsersController#update Rails method, 174
UTF-8 encoding, 270

V

values (S3), 51
Vary response header, 403
VBScript, 316
vCard, 268
Via header, 404
views, 340
    Django, implementing resources as, 357–
        364
VirturalHost class (Restlet), 346
VoteLinks, 262

W

W-* technologies, 19
W3C's HTML validator, 176
WADL (Web Application Description
        Language), 20, 25, 47, 71, 308
    hypermedia technologies and, 285, 290–
        298
Warning response header, 404
Web Accelerator, 103
Web Application Description Language (see
        WADL)

Web Hypertext Application Technology
Working Group (WHATWG), 290
web interfaces and applications, 254–257
web service clients (see clients)
Web Service Description Language (see WSDL)
Web Services Developer Pack (Sun), 43
WebDAV, 104
WeblogsController class, 340
WHATWG (Web Hypertext Application
Technology Working Group), 290
Windows-1252 encoding, 270
wrapper libraries, 23
wrappers, 25
WS-Addressing standard, 5
WS-ReliableMessaging, 311
WS-Security Extension (see WSSE HTTP
authentication)
WSDL (Web Service Description Language),
10, 20, 304
POST method, overloading, 220
WSSE HTTP authentication, 30, 146, 241–
243
WWW-Authenticate header, 156, 404
Basic authentication and, 238
Digest authentication and, 239
WSSE HTTP authentication and, 241

X

x-amz-acl header, 69
X-HTTP-Method-Override request header,
406
X-WSSE request header, 406
Xerces, 43
XFN (XHTML Friends Network), 262
xFolk microformat specification, 263
XHTML, 125, 259–261, 289
ad hoc, 268
microformats, 261–263
XHTML 4, 285–289
XMDP (XHTML Meta Data Profiles), 262
XML, 4
ActiveRecord and, 184
ad hoc vocabularies, 269
encodings and, 271
parsers, 38
representation of user accounts, 183
SOAP, using, 300–303
XHTML and, 260
XML-RPC requests and, 15

XML for <SCRIPT>, 44
XML-RPC, 14, 19
POST method, overloading, 220
xml.sax module (Python), 42
XML::LibXML::Reader module (Perl), 44
XML::SAX::PurePerl module (Perl), 44
XML::Simple module (Perl), 44
XML::XPath modules (Perl), 44
XMLHttpRequest (JavaScript), 37, 43, 315,
323
cross-browser issues and, 327
XMLPull, 43
xml_parser_create function (PHP), 43
XOXO (Extensible Open XHTML Outlines),
262
XPath, 9, 28, 39, 348
exposition, 24
S3 and, 57

Y

YAGNI (You Aren't Gonna Need It), 314
Yahoo! web services, 13
searching the Web with, 23
user accounts and, 144

About the Authors

Leonard Richardson (*http://www.crummy.com/*) is the author of the *Ruby Cookbook* (O'Reilly) and of several open source libraries, including Beautiful Soup. A California native, he currently lives in New York.

Sam Ruby is a prominent software developer who has made significant contributions to many Apache Software Foundation open source projects, and to the standardization of web feeds via his involvement with the Atom web feed standard and the popular Feed Validator web service. He currently holds a Senior Technical Staff Member position in the Emerging Technologies Group of IBM. He resides in Raleigh, North Carolina.

Colophon

Our look is the result of reader comments, our own experimentation, and feedback from distribution channels. Distinctive covers complement our distinctive approach to technical topics, breathing personality and life into potentially dry subjects.

The animal on the cover of *RESTful Web Services* is a vulpine phalanger (*P. vulpina*). Phalanger is the general term given to animals of the Phalangeridae family, which includes possums and cuscuses. (One should not confuse the Australian possum with the American opossum; they are both marsupials, but very different.) The term phalanger is derived from the Greek word phalanges, which means finger or toe bone. The omnivorous phalanger uses its claw-fingered paws (with opposable thumbs) to climb, hunt, and live in trees. Phalangers are found in the forests of Australia, New Zealand, Tasmania, and some Indonesian islands. Like the most famous marsupial, the kangaroo, female phalangers carry their young around in a front pouch after birth.

Phalanger is also the name of a PHP complier project for the .NET framework.

The cover image is from *Wood's Natural History*. The cover font is Adobe ITC Garamond. The text font is Linotype Birka; the heading font is Adobe Myriad Condensed; and the code font is LucasFont's TheSans Mono Condensed.

Better than e-books

Buy *RESTful Web Services* and access the
digital edition FREE on Safari for 45 days.

Go to www.oreilly.com/go/safarienabled
and type in coupon code STOVJGA

Search
thousands of
top tech books

Download
whole chapters

Cut and Paste
code examples

Find
answers fast

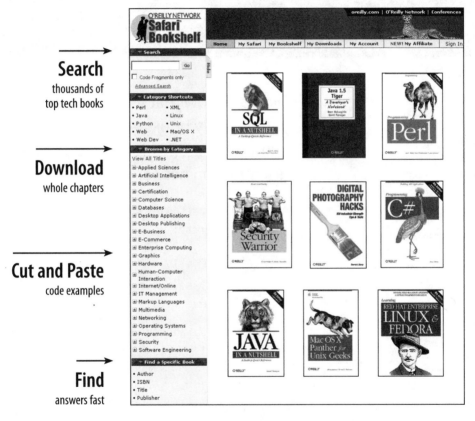

Search Safari! The premier electronic reference
library for programmers and IT professionals.

The O'Reilly Advantage

Stay Current and Save Money